A Laboratory Manual and Study Guide for

ANATOMY AND PHYSIOLOGY

Fourth Edition

Kenneth G. Neal
Barbara H. Kalbus
Long Beach City College
Long Beach, California

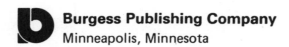

Burgess Publishing Company
Minneapolis, Minnesota

Editorial: Jeff Holtmeier, Janilyn Richardson, Elizabeth Weinstein
Production: Pat Barnes, Melinda Berndt, Morris Lundin, Judy Vicars
Copy Editor: Leslie Reindl
Cover: Judy Vicars

Burgess Publishing Company
7108 Ohms Lane
Minneapolis, Minnesota 55435

J   I   H   G   F   E

Contents

Preface

This manual is designed to be used in an introductory course in anatomy and physiology. It will serve the needs of students seeking careers in health-related professions, physical education, and home economics. It will serve any student who seeks an understanding of the structure and function of human body systems.

By using this manual, students will develop laboratory skills, become familiar with the methods of science, and learn the important concepts of anatomy and physiology. The manual provides students with an opportunity to apply what they have learned in textbooks and lectures in an interesting and informative way.

The fetal pig is the principal dissection specimen used in this text. Fetal pig structures are highly applicable to the understanding of human body systems, and the pig is a relatively inexpensive specimen. In addition, detailed instructions for dissecting several organs of sheep are given in the manual, and these may readily be adapted to beef or other mammalian structures.

The manual is easy for students to understand and use, and it does not require lengthy or elaborate interpretation by an instructor. The format is represented by four major elements.

1. Each exercise or experiment includes a precisely stated purpose (objective), the materials needed, a discussion (when appropriate), and a procedure with detailed instructions. The numerous illustrations, diagrams, and tables clarify the directions. As a general rule, little or no additional orientation is required. This saves time in preparing and performing laboratory activities for both student and instructor.

2. The Results and Questions section of each exercise (located at the end of the manual) is designed to be removed from the manual for recording data during an experiment, for answering questions, and for submitting material for evaluation.

3. Experiments of a physiological nature are supported (and balanced) with anatomical studies involving dissection of the fetal pig, sheep heart, sheep brain, sheep eye, and sheep kidney. Original drawings are included with instructions for dissection, which greatly facilitate identification of structures in the specimen.

4. Each major unit includes a relatively comprehensive self-test that covers lecture, laboratory, and practical applications. Keys to these self-tests are at the end of the manual. Most of the illustrations can also serve as self-tests.

The manual is flexible. It allows for the demonstration of key concepts with or without assorted pieces of apparatus. For example, living frog experiments may be conducted for the purpose of demonstrating the principles of nerve, muscle, and circulatory physiology without use of any elaborate equipment. However, experiments involving the use of physiological apparatus are also included; even if these are not performed, they provide a reference which may improve understanding of the nature of the experiments described in lecture and in the text.

Dissection may be done in the first few laboratories and then attention concentrated on physiological experiments or, as suggested by the location of exercises in the manual, dissection may be performed throughout the course. We recommend the latter method, wherein a portion of several laboratory periods is used for dissection. In many cases, this portion may amount to just 15 or 20 minutes. Furthermore, we suggest that students be allowed to continue dissection outside the regular laboratory time.

This new edition includes several additional illustrations. Many of the physiology experiments involving the physiograph have been rewritten to improve clarity; directions for the older model physiograph (the DMP-4A) have been eliminated.

The experiments and exercises in this manual are reliable and instructive. They have been thoroughly class-tested over many years of use in a variety of laboratory settings throughout the country and through our local use. The exercises teach effectively, and the experiments work.

Acknowledgments

We would like to acknowledge our appreciation to Robert Bush, who prepared most of the illustrations in this manual; to Judith Ramos, Ph.D., for her preparation of the illustrations and write-up for the dissection of the muscular system of the fetal pig; to Linda Neal, for the time she spent in preparing label lines, correcting illustrations, and proofreading much of the manuscript.

We wish to thank Burgess Publishing Co. for permission to use figures 1-3, 1-5, 1-6, 4-2, 6-1, 6-2, 6-3, 6-4, 6-5, 6-6, 6-7, 6-8, 6-9, 6-10, 6-11, 6-12, 6-13, 6-14, 8-1, 9-2, 9-7, 9-8, 9-9, 11-4, 11-5, 11-10, 12-1, 12-2, 12-3, 13-1, 13-2, 13-3, 13-4, 13-5, 13-6, 13-8, 13-9, 14-1, 16-1, 16-2, 17-4, 17-9, 17-10, 18-1, 18-5, 19-1, 20-5, 20-12.

All other illustrations in this manual are the copyrighted property of ELOT Publishing Co., Inc. (P.O. Box 8294, Long Beach CA 90808). Our thanks to ELOT for granting us permission to use these illustrations in this publication.

Kenneth G. Neal
Barbara H. Kalbus

Orientation and Suggestions for Students

A. INTRODUCTION

The laboratory provides an opportunity to study at close range materials related to the topics covered in lecture.

The laboratory experience can be the most rewarding part of the entire course if a student approaches it with the appropriate attitude—namely, with the desire for knowledge, an interest in the development of skills and techniques, and a willingness to accept the discipline of the laboratory. The latter is especially important in the development of habits essential to good scientific work. Discipline is required in virtually all branches of science and may be life-saving in many areas. The development of a scientific attitude is the result of thinking and acting in a scientific manner—carelessness, sloppiness, tardiness, preconceived ideas, and inefficiency may be accepted in some areas of human endeavor, but not in science.

During a laboratory, one of the most significant questions a student can ask is: "What is the purpose of this activity or experiment?" When using this manual, where the purpose (objective) of each experiment (or activity) is indicated, you should let the stated objectives permeate your thinking as you engage in the activities prescribed.

Critically observe all specimens or materials you are asked to study. Your own observations should provide answers to most of the questions that arise during the laboratory. *Learn to think independently*. The instructor will offer helpful suggestions but should not be expected to be a source of ready answers to each of your questions. No one can learn for you.

Do not interfere with the work of others. Work is to be done on an individual basis unless you are instructed otherwise. It is often necessary to do experiments with a laboratory partner. This is a cooperative effort, and the work should be shared equally. Furthermore, both partners should understand the experiment and share the results. However, the *write-up should be the result of individual effort*. Ordinarily there is no objection to the discussion of laboratory work with other students.

B. LABORATORY SUPPLIES

In the spaces provided, check the supplies your instructor indicates are to be provided by you.

1. _____ 3H pencil
2. _____ 4H pencil
3. _____ red pencil
4. _____ blue pencil
5. _____ box of colored pencils
6. _____ manila folder
7. _____ 6 microscope slides
8. _____ 6 cover glasses
9. _____ lens paper
10. _____ dissecting kit
11. _____ biology filler paper
12. _____ grease (wax) pencil
13. _____ black, felt-tip pen
14. _____ 6-inch ruler
15. _____ eraser (pink pearl)
16. _____ tape (Magic transparent)
17. _____

C. ASSIGNMENTS

All or most of the assignments will be given in advance of the laboratory. You are expected to read the introduction and objective and to preview procedures *before* the date of the assigned laboratory. In addition, a brief orientation will be given at the beginning of the laboratory.

D. GENERAL LABORATORY RULES

There are reasons for every rule imposed. If these are not readily apparent to you, *ask your instructor for an interpretation.* Since the laboratory environment and situation vary somewhat from school to school, and since methods employed may also vary from instructor to instructor, some of the following rules may not apply. On the other hand, your instructor may invoke still additional rules.

1. *Be on time.* Instructions are given at the beginning of laboratory. It is your responsibility to be present to receive them.
2. Bring your textbook, laboratory manual, and laboratory supplies to the laboratory.
3. Handle all equipment loaned to you with care. Damaged equipment will be charged against the liable student or students.
4. Check with your instructor concerning the policy for laboratory "breaks."
5. Do not leave the laboratory early without permission of the instructor.
6. Visitors are not allowed except by special permission.
7. Arrange all work to be handed in in sequence and place it in a manila folder. Write your name, class, day and hour class meets, and (if one is assigned) your section number on the index portion of the manila folder.
8. Before leaving, check to see if you have done the following:
   a. Cleaned the deck area.
   b. Turned out the desk lamp.
   c. Locked up the microscope and/or other supplies.
   d. Cleaned, dried, and returned all equipment consigned to your care.
   e. Returned microscope slides to their proper location.
9. Keep the sinks in your area clean. Do not put solid matter, such as dissectable materials, in the sinks. Wastebaskets are for solids, sinks for liquids.
10. Do not waste time at the beginning of the laboratory period. Whenever possible, begin work as soon as you enter the room.
11. Always keep in mind the meaning of the work you are doing.
12. Acknowledge the fact that extra time on laboratory work is often necessary.
13. Do not hesitate to consult your instructor if you have any problems with the course.

E. CARE OF PRESERVED SPECIMENS

Fetal Pig

The fetal pig is packaged in a plastic bag containing a liquid preservative. The tip of the bag should be cut open with scissors and the fluid poured into the sink. At the conclusion of any laboratory involving dissection of the pig, two or three thicknesses of paper towels moistened with tap water should be used to completely cover the specimen. The pig should then be replaced in the plastic bag, the opening secured with a rubber band, and the bag placed in the storage cabinet. Following this procedure ordinarily will keep the specimen in good condition throughout the course.

Organs (e.g., Sheep Eye, Heart, Kidney, Brain, etc.)

Each specimen should be wrapped in a double thickness of moistened paper towels and placed in the plastic bag with the fetal pig or in an individual plastic bag.

An alternative method is to place the organs in a 5% solution of formaldehyde. This solution is sufficiently concentrated to preserve the organs for the period of time they are being used.

F. WRITTEN WORK

At the end of this manual is a section containing results and questions for each chapter. To facilitate the recording of data during performance of an experiment or exercise, remove the appropriate Results and Questions section from the manual. Data and answers to questions should be written neatly and legibly and all kymograph or physiograph records should be pasted or taped in the appropriate spaces. Use either a number 2 pencil or ink (blue or black only) in recording your data and writing answers to the questions. When finished, write your name on each sheet and place the assignment in a labeled manila folder (see D. 7). Do not clip or staple the pages together.

G. LABORATORY TESTS

As one aspect of evaluation of work done in the laboratory, your instructor may give tests. The frequency of such tests will be announced by the instructor. The following types of tests are often employed in the laboratory:

Practical

This type of test may include actual specimens (e.g., bones), microscope slides, drawings, and questions. There are several ways in which such a test may be given. One method commonly used involves the establishment of thirty to forty test stations. One (or more) specimen, a microscope with a slide in focus, a diagram or drawing with structures to be identified, or a card containing written questions is located at each station. The student is provided with an answer sheet and stands at a specified station. At the signal to begin, the student answers the questions (usually three to five) asked at that station. The time allotted for answering varies from 45 seconds to 1½ minutes. When time is called, the student moves to the next station, and so forth until the test is completed.

Orals

In this type of test, the student is asked to bring a specimen he or she has dissected to the instructor, who then asks the student to identify selected structures. The student may also be asked to give functions of the structures identified. In some cases, models may be used for giving oral tests.

Written Tests

These may take a variety of forms (short answer, problem solving, identification, essay, etc.). Written tests are designed to determine the student's understanding of the experiments and exercises performed in the laboratory.

H. VOCABULARY

Your ability to communicate, to comprehend, and to reason and interpret depends on the acquisition of a functional vocabulary. This is especially true of any science course, wherein the vocabulary practically constitutes a "foreign language." It is therefore important for you to develop an understanding of all unfamiliar words with which you come in contact in the process of your reading and investigations. Define all new words in terms *you* understand. Make a conscious effort to use the new words until, by constant reinforcement, they are firmly entrenched in your mind.

I. RULES GOVERNING CHEMICALS

1. Treat all chemicals with respect.
2. Avoid contaminating chemicals within their containers. Do not insert your pipettes or medicine droppers into the stock solution. Use only pipettes (or medicine droppers) already in the stock solutions.
3. Keep all containers of chemicals clean and dry. Pour chemicals from bottles on the side away from the label (to avoid damaging the label).
4. When preparing dilute solutions of acid, always add acid to water rather than water to acid.
5. Avoid placing reagent bottles containing caustic agents directly on the tops of the laboratory decks.
6. Return all containers of chemicals to the appropriate location. Do not remove the chemicals from the area unless otherwise directed.

J. ILLUSTRATIONS AS SELF-TESTS

Many of the drawings in this manual are designed so that they may be used as self-tests. *Prestudy* of similar illustrations in the textbook, references, and wall charts as well as prestudy of models and specimens is one way to prepare yourself for the self-tests. You may then try to identify the parts indicated on a drawing, writing the answers on a separate piece of paper. Check your answers with the keys found in the chapter.

K. SELF-TESTS

At the end of each chapter is a true-false self-test. Each test item includes a key word, words, or phrase in **boldface** type. If the test item is false, the boldface portion should be corrected to make the statement true. In general, the self-tests cover material found in texts, covered in lecture, and applied in the laboratory. Keys are located at the end of the manual.

Suggestions for Using the Self-Tests

1. Take them as a **pretest** before studying the material covered.
   a. Write your answers on a separate sheet of paper but do not correct them at this time.
   b. This procedure will provide you with clues as to what to look for in your reading of the text, what to listen for in lecture, and what to watch for in the laboratory.
2. After you have had an opportunity to study the material covered, take the self-test again (**post-test**).
   a. Correct your pretest and post-test by using the key at the end of the manual.
   b. Compare the results of the post-test with those on the pretest to determine how much you actually learned.
3. Other suggestions:
   a. Always try to determine the reason why a given statement is or is not true. Merely knowing the answer to the statement may provide very little depth.
   b. Define from a suitable reference any words in a statement that are not understood.
   c. Try to correlate the concepts indicated in the statements with the material presented in lectures, discussions, the text, and the laboratory.

Limitations of Self-Tests

1. They may be a useful tool, but they are not comprehensive.
2. Courses vary in their emphasis on certain concepts, and this must be taken into consideration when the self-tests are used.
3. Tests usually sample bits of a student's knowledge—never the whole. Study-type tests, such as the self-tests in this manual, merely provide a basis for learning subject matter and showing trends in achievement.
4. Analysis of questions missed on a self-test may often imply that the student needs to study the entire block of knowledge from which the question was derived.
5. If self-tests are not used as suggested (e.g., as a supplement to other learning devices), the student may fail to attain the depth and insights essential for this course.

1

Introduction to Anatomy

EXERCISE 1-A
ORGANIZATION OF THE BODY AS A WHOLE

Objectives

To locate and identify the cavities and anatomic regions of the body; to identify the organs within the cavities and those underlying the regions.

Materials

Dissectable torso; anatomic charts; reference books.

Discussion

The human body is made up of **cells**. Cells that have similar specializations and are united in the performance of a particular function form a **tissue**. Tissues, in turn, make up an **organ**, which may be defined as several tissues grouped into a structural unit having a special function. A set or series of organs united in a common function is referred to as a **system**. While it is possible to distinguish individual parts (e.g., a cell, a tissue, or an organ) in the human organism, these parts function as an integrated whole.

In doing the following exercises, and throughout your study of anatomy and physiology, keep the following question constantly before you: how does this part of the body fit in with the concept of the body as an integrated whole?

PART 1. CAVITIES OF THE BODY

Procedure

1. Using your text and reference books for orientation, locate the following body cavities on the dissectable torso:
   a. Cranial   e. Abdominal
   b. Nasal   f. Pelvic
   c. Buccal (oral)   g. Ventral
   d. Thoracic   h. Dorsal
2. Under each label on Figure 1-1, indicate the major structures found in the cranial, vertebral, thoracic, abdominal, and pelvic cavities. Use anatomic charts, your text, and references to aid you.

PART 2. REGIONS OF THE BODY

Procedure

1. Locate the following regions of the body on the dissectable torso and on your own body: epigastric, umbilical, hypogastric (pubic), right and left hypochondriac, right and left lumbar (lateral), and right and left inguinal (iliac). Use your text and other references for orientation.
2. Use Figure 1-2 as a self-test for the nine body regions. See Illustrations as Self-Tests on page xiii for a suggested approach.
3. Compare Figure 1-3 with Figure 1-2. Using Figure 1-3 and your text, answer the questions in the Results and Questions section.

Figure 1-1.　Body cavities.

KEY TO FIGURE 1-2

1. right hypochondriac
2. right lumbar (lateral)
3. right inguinal (iliac)
4. left hypochondriac
5. epigastric
6. umbilical
7. left lumbar (lateral)
8. left inguinal (iliac)
9. hypogastric (pubic)

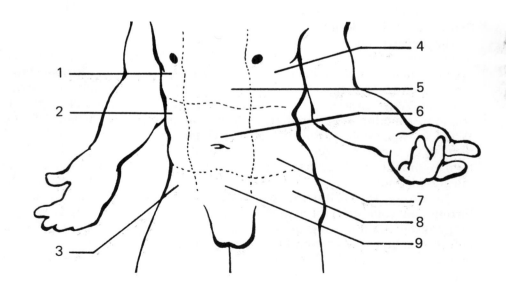

Figure 1-2.　Abdominopelvic regions of the body.

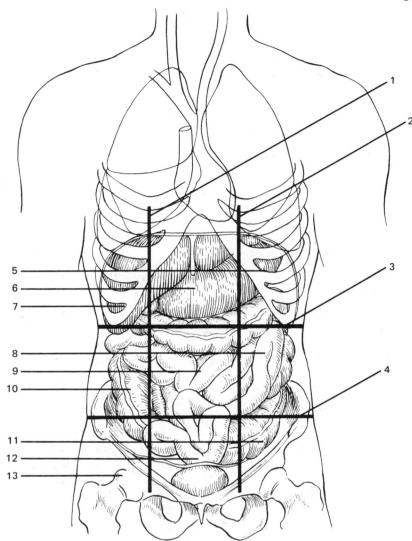

KEY TO FIGURE 1-3

1. right lateral line
2. left lateral line
3. transpyloric line
4. transtubercular line
5. left hypochondriac
6. epigastric
7. right hypochondriac
8. left lumbar (lateral)
9. umbilical
10. right lumbar (lateral)
11. left inguinal
12. hypogastric (pubic)
13. right inguinal

Figure 1-3. Abdominopelvic regions of the body and underlying organs.

EXERCISE 1-B
ANATOMIC TERMINOLOGY

Objective

To develop a functional knowledge of anatomic terminology.

Materials

Dissectable torso; anatomic charts; reference books.

Discussion

Terms for locating the various structures of the human body are vital to any precision in the study of anatomy and physiology. Directional terms and terms for the planes of the body are essential tools that will be used repeatedly throughout the course. Build a firm foundation by learning their meanings; then reinforce your understanding by applying them whenever possible.

In lower animals the **ventral** surface (belly) faces downward while the **dorsal** surface (back) faces upward. Since man assumes an upright position, the ventral surface is forward, and the term ventral is, in humans, synonymous with the word **anterior**. Futhermore, dorsal is synonymous with **posterior** in humans. In an animal, such as a dog, the head is anterior, while in humans the head is **superior (cephalic)**.

4

The tail of the dog is posterior, while the tailbone (coccygeal vertebrae) in humans is **inferior** (or caudal). The term **"caudad"** (or **caudal**) may be used to describe either the tail portion of the dog or the lower part of a human. The term **"cephalad"** (or **cephalic**) may be used to describe the cranial (or head) portion of either the dog or human.

PART 1. USING DIRECTIONAL TERMS

Procedure

Self-test: Without referring to the key below, use directional terms to fill in the blank spaces.

1. The head is _____ to the neck.
2. The foot is _____ to the ankle.
3. The umbilicus is _____ to the lumbar vertebrae.
4. The fibula is _____ to the tibia.
5. The vertebral column is _____ to the digestive tract.
6. The ulna is on the _____ side of the forearm.
7. The elbow (olecranon process) is _____ to the shoulder.
8. The kneecap (patella) is _____ to the ankle.
9. The layer of the peritoneum lining the abdominal cavity is called the _____ layer.
10. The layer of the peritoneum covering the internal organs is called the _____ layer.

KEY TO SELF-TEST

1. superior (cranial, cephalic)
2. inferior (distal)
3. anterior (ventral)
4. lateral
5. posterior (dorsal)
6. medial
7. distal
8. proximal (superior)
9. parietal
10. visceral

PART 2. PLANES OF THE BODY

Procedure

1. Examine Figure 1-4 showing the planes of the body.
2. Identify the planes of the body on yourself and on your laboratory partner.

PART 3. ANATOMIC POSITION

Procedure

1. Study Figures 1-5 and 1-6 showing anterior and posterior views of the body in anatomic position.
2. Answer the questions relating to anatomic position in the Results and Questions section.

EXERCISE 1-C
EXTERNAL CHARACTERISTICS OF THE FETAL PIG

Objective

To become familiar with the external characteristics of the fetal pig.

Materials

Fetal pig; dissecting board or tray: string.

Discussion

Since farmers find it profitable to breed any female they plan to sell, pig fetuses are by-products of slaughterhouses. The period of gestation is 112 to 115 days, and there are, on the average, seven to eight offspring in a litter. At birth, pigs vary from 12 to 14 inches in length. The approximate age of the fetus thus can be determined by measuring the length of the body from the tip of the snout to the rump (not including the tail). The following are approximate body length-to-age relationships:

Body length, mm (in.)	Approximate age, days
11 (0.44)	21
17 (0.68)	35
28 (1.12)	49
40 (1.6)	56
220 (8.8)	100
300 (12.0)	112-115 (full term)

As a laboratory animal the fetal pig has a number of advantages. Since it is small, it does not require much storage space. Being a mammal, its structures are similar to those of humans. In addition to having relatively mature organs, it also has fetal structures that are directly comparable with those of human

5

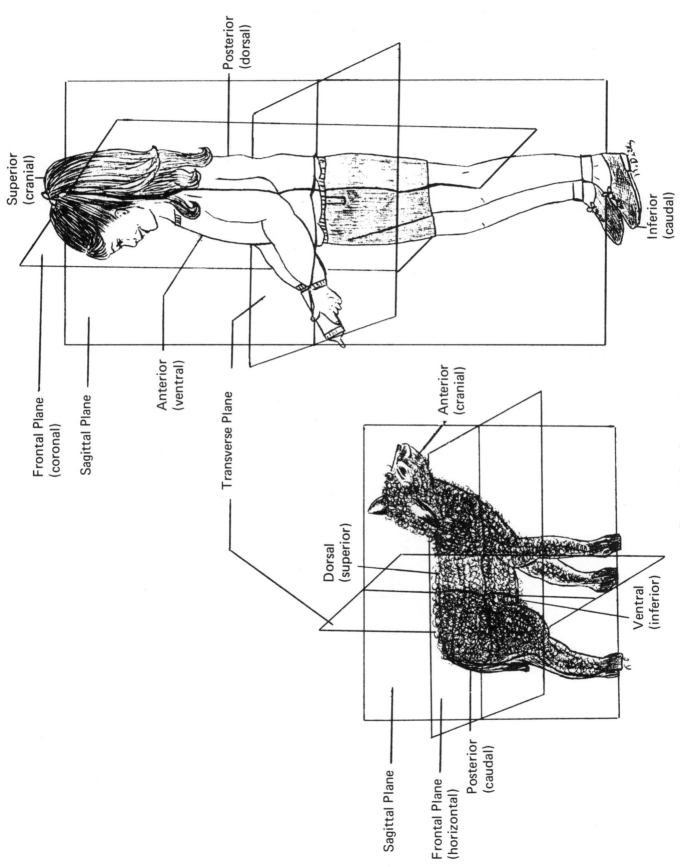

5

Superior (cranial)

Posterior (dorsal)

Inferior (caudal)

Frontal Plane (coronal)

Sagittal Plane

Anterior (ventral)

Transverse Plane

Anterior (cranial)

Dorsal (superior)

Ventral (inferior)

Sagittal Plane

Frontal Plane (horizontal)

Posterior (caudal)

Figure 1-4. Planes of the body.

6

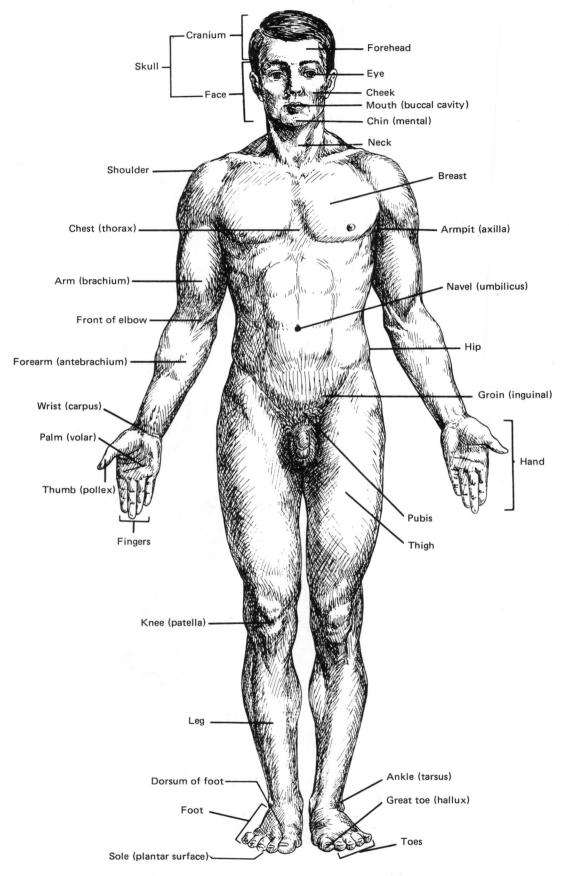

Figure 1-5. Anatomic position (anterior view).

7

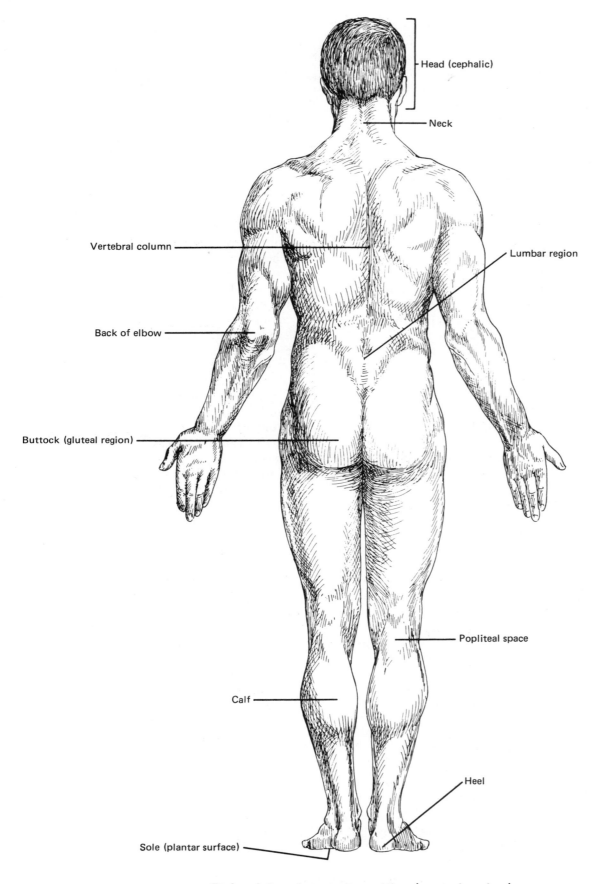

- Head (cephalic)
- Neck
- Vertebral column
- Lumbar region
- Back of elbow
- Buttock (gluteal region)
- Popliteal space
- Calf
- Heel
- Sole (plantar surface)

Figure 1-6.   Anatomic position (posterior view).

beings. These include the umbilical cord and the circulatory structures specialized for fetal circulation.

As the fetal pig is dissected and studied throughout the course, the structures identified should be compared with those of the human.

Dissection is not merely "cutting" the animal, but a systematic technique of bringing into view structures which, in their normal position, cannot readily be seen. Follow instructions exactly. Do not cut or remove any structure unless directed to do so. Always separate structures *carefully*, by dissecting away connective tissue.

You may find that the substances used to preserve the specimens irritate your skin. If so, apply Pro-tek (or some similar substance) to your hands before dissecting or wear thin rubber or plastic gloves. Remove as much of the preservative from your specimen as possible by frequent washings with tap water. Keep your fingers away from your eyes during dissection.

At the conclusion of each laboratory period, clean up the working area thoroughly. Wrap the pig in wet paper towels and replace in the plastic bag provided. Do not leave any solid material in the sink. Clean and dry the laboratory table.

The terms "**right**" and "**left**" always refer to the pig's right and left. In a quadruped, **anterior** or **cranial** refers to the head end, **posterior** or **caudal** to the tail end, **dorsal** or **superior** to the back, **ventral** or **inferior** to the belly. **Lateral** refers to the side, **medial** to a position nearer the midline of the body. (See Figure 1-4.)

Procedure

1. Examine the pig for body hair, although this is usually not conspicuous at this early age.
2. Note the **epitrichium**, which is a layer of embryonic skin that is visibly peeling. This skin is lost as the hair develops. It may be removed by rinsing the pig in tap water. It will plug the sink, and care should be taken to prevent this.
3. On the head locate the following structures:
    a. The **mouth**, bounded by upper and lower **jaws** and soft lips, is sometimes partially open, revealing a soft **tongue**. The front end of the head is prolonged into a **snout**. The snout is used for rooting around in the soil for roots, insects, and other materials used for food.
    b. Observe the two **nostrils (external nares)** at the end of the snout.
    c. The **eyes** (usually closed) are covered by upper and lower **eyelids** fringed with **eyelashes**. Make an incision extending forward from the medial corner of the eye and pull the upper eyelids apart. The **nictitating membrane** should be visible in the medial corner of the eye. This membrane can move across the eyeball to help keep it clean. Is this structure present in the human eye?
    d. The opening into the ear is called the **external acoustic (auditory) meatus** and the flattened flap of skin is called the **pinna**. The pinna and the external acoustic meatus make up the **external ear** in the pig as well as in the human.
4. Note that the short **neck** joins the thorax in front of the first pair of legs. There is usually an incision in the right lateral part of the neck where blood is withdrawn and colored latex injected.
5. The **trunk** can be divided into two general regions, an anterior **thorax** and a posterior **abdomen**.
    a. Note that the front limbs are attached to the thorax. The ribs making up the thorax are soft at this stage of development because they are cartilage.
    b. Locate the nipples, which are present in both sexes. These form a double row of small **teats** or **mammary papillae** on the ventral surface of the abdomen. The number and location of mammary glands vary in different species, but mammary glands are characteristic of all mammals.
    c. Observe the **umbilical cord** near the center of the ventral surface of the abdomen. Make a fresh cut across the end of the cord. Three large openings should now be visible. The largest is the **umbilical vein**, which carries blood from the placenta to the fetal pig. This vessel may contain blue latex. The other two, smaller and with thick walls, are the **umbilical arteries**, which may contain red latex. These vessels carry blood from the fetus to the placenta. Between or near the umbilical arteries a small, hard core

of tissue, the **allantoic stalk**, can be felt. All the structures present in the cord are embedded in a gelatinous connective tissue.

  d. Locate the **anus** just ventral to the tail. This is the posterior opening of the digestive tract.

  e. Determine the sex of your specimen. In the female, the external **urogenital opening** (with a small **genital papilla** projecting from it) is ventral to the anus. This is the common orifice of the urinary and reproductive tracts. In the male, the external **urogenital** opening is a very small hole just posterior to the umbilical cord at the tip of the **penis**. If your specimen is a male, note the two **scrotal sacs** below and ventral to the anus. The penis lies under the skin, passing from the urogenital opening posteriorly between the hind legs. Feel the penis through the skin. Later this will be dissected out. Each student is expected to identify the sexual organs in both sexes. Compare your fetal pig with a pig of the opposite sex.

6. Note that there are only four toes or **digits** on each limb, as compared with five in humans.

7. Examine the legs and note that they have the same general structure as those of humans and other animals, although they are somewhat modified.

  a. Examine the posterior surface of one of the hind legs and note the large protuberance about 2 inches above the toes. This is comparable to the human heel, and the region from it to the toes corresponds to the human foot. Since the pig walks on the tips of the toes, the ankle and most of the foot are elevated above the ground.

  b. Locate the **wrist** and **elbow** of the forelimb and the **knee** and **ankle** of the hindlimb.

8. Tie a 12- to 18-inch length of cord around each ankle. These will be used to tie the pig to either a dissecting board or pan and should be left permanently attached to the pig.

9. Tie a label to the tail of the animal with a piece of string long enough to allow the label to project out of the plastic bag. The label should have printed on it, with pencil (ink runs), your name, your partner's name, and the course, section number, and time of meeting.

SELF-TEST—INTRODUCTION TO ANATOMY

Directions

The following statements are either true or false. If a test item is false, alter the portion in boldface type to make the statement true. It is suggested that you write your answers on a separate sheet of paper. This simplifies using the test for review, when it is usually undesirable to have the answers exposed. Check your answers by referring to the key at the end of the manual. For more extensive suggestions concerning the use of self-tests, their functions, and their limitations, see K. Self-Tests under Orientation and Suggestions for Students, page xiv.

1. The **midsagittal** plane divides the body into a top and bottom half.

2. **Sagittal and coronal** planes divide the body into upper and lower parts.

3. The knee is **proximal** to the foot.

4. The part of the nervous system found within the **dorsal cavity** is called the central nervous system.

5. In relation to the mandible, the maxilla is **inferior**.

6. **Proximal** is a term meaning the part farthest from the trunk.

7. **Visceral** is applied to organs located within the body cavities.

8. A cut through the body or body structures dividing it (or them) into front and back portions is called a **transverse cut**.

9. The hands are the **proximal** portion of the upper extremities.

10. The spinal cord and brain are found within the **ventral** cavity.

11. When an individual stands in anatomic position the radius is **mesial** in position.

12. A part of the body located toward the outside of the body is said to be **peripheral**.

13. In the anatomic position, the arms are at the side with the palms of the hands **supinated**.

14. With reference to the esophagus, the stomach is **inferior**.

15. Two terms that apply to the back part of humans are **posterior and ventral**.

16. The large intestine is located within the **abdominal and pelvic cavities**.

17. **Homeostasis** is a term meaning relative uniformity of cellular environment.

18. The spleen is found within the **mediastinum**.

19. The lungs are located in the **thoracic cavity**.

20. The liver is in the **abdominal cavity**.

21. The type of mirror-image symmetry that is shown by a human being is known as **radial** symmetry.

22. The surface of a pig's body that forms its back is known as the **ventral** surface.

23. In man, the back of the body may be called **either the dorsal or the posterior** surface.

24. The **anterior** end of a pig's body is the one to which the head is attached.

25. When you lie on your ventral surface you are said to be in a **supine** position.

26. Fingerprints are made by pressing the **palmar** surfaces of the fingers against an object.

27. Any part of the body that is away from the midline is said to be **mesial** in location.

28. The **abdomen** may be divided into four sections called quadrants.

29. The part of an appendage that lies farthest from the midline of the body is the **caudal** portion.

30. The crest of the hip bone is **dorsal** to the vertebrae.

31. The pain of appendicitis is frequently felt in the **lower left** quadrant of the abdomen.

32. The female gonads are located within the **vertebral cavity**.

33. The **buccal cavity** opens into the oropharynx.

2

Basic Microscopy

EXERCISE 2-A
STRUCTURE OF THE MICROSCOPE

Objectives

To learn the functions of the parts of the microscope and the focusing procedure.

Materials

Microscope; microscope lamp.

Procedure

1. Examine the drawing of the microscope (Fig. 2-1). Compare this drawing with your microscope and learn the names and functions of all parts indicated by your instructor.
2. Use of the microscope:
   a. When it is necessary to lift the microscope, hold the **arm** of the microscope with one hand and add support at the **base** with the other hand.
   b. Place the microscope on the deck with the arm facing you.
   c. Since tilting results in poor light regulation and unwanted movement in fresh preparations, do not tilt this instrument unless instructed to do so.
   d. Always begin by cleaning the **ocular** (eyepiece), **objectives, slide,** and **mirror** (when present) with **lens paper.**
   e. To avoid eyestrain and subsequent headache, it is best to look through the microscope with both eyes open. Practice makes this a simple procedure.

f. Focusing procedure:
   (1) Turn the **revolving nosepiece** until the **low power objective** (10X) clicks into position over the hole in the **stage** of the microscope. Always begin with the low power objective.
   (2) Open the **iris diaphragm** approximately halfway or turn the disc diaphragm to the III setting.
   (3) If your microscope is equipped with a mirror, arrange the microscope lamp and concave side of the mirror so that a maximum amount of light will be reflected into the condenser. This adjustment is made while you are looking through the eyepiece (ocular). To regulate light intensity, adjust the iris or disc diaphragm (not the mirror) when the slide is in focus. If your microscope is equipped with an in-base illuminator, turn on the illuminator.
   (4) Use the coarse adjustment knob to raise the nosepiece for easier access of the stage and then place a slide on the stage of the microscope. Position the specimen to be observed directly above the center of the condenser.
   (5) Usually a stop is present on the microscope that will prevent the

Optical and Mechanical Features of
THE MICROSCOPE

Virtual Image Distance 250mm

Inclined Reversible Monocular Body Tube

Virtual Image

Focusable (Spring Loaded) Nosepiece

Disc Aperture Diaphragm

In-Stage Condenser

In-Base Illuminator

Light Switch

Retinal Image

Eyepoint

Eyepiece

Field Diaphragm and Pointer

Arm

Infinity Corrected Objective

Object

Slide Clip

Stage

Fine Adjustment Knob

Coarse Adjustment Knob

Base

Optical and Mechanical Features of Series SIXTY Microscope

Cross section of scanning objective, 4X.

Cross section of low power objective, 10X.

Cross section of "high dry" objective, 43X.

Cross section of oil immersion objective,100X.

Figure 2-1.   The microscope. (Courtesy of American Optical Corporation, Scientific Instrument Division, Buffalo, N.Y. 14215.)

low power objective from striking the slide. Determine if this is true of your instrument by lowering the 10X objective as close to the slide as possible without touching it, or until the tube can be lowered no farther.

(6) If the microscope is equipped with an autofocus, when the low power objective is as close to the slide as possible the specimen can be brought into sharp focus by slowly rotating the **fine adjustment knob** either down or up. If the microscope is not equipped with an auto-focus, look through the eyepiece and turn the coarse adjustment to *slowly raise* the objective from the slide until the specimen comes into focus. The image should then be brought into sharp focus with the fine adjustment knob. This knob should also be used for observing depth in a specimen.

(7) Adjust the amount of light to the optimum when the slide is in focus. If there is too much light, so that the specimen cannot be seen clearly against the glare, rotate the disc diaphragm to a smaller opening. If a condenser with an iris diaphragm is being used, close down the diaphragm. When using a mirror, if the field of view is not uniformly illuminated, adjust the mirror or the position of the illuminator so that the specimen field is evenly illuminated.

(8) Move the slide to find the specific area you desire to view in more detail. Since the quality of slides and individual portions of slides may vary, always select a slide (or area of the slide) that seems typical.

(9) Once the object is in sharp focus and centered with the 10X objective, rotate the revolving nosepiece to the **high power objective** without changing the position of the coarse adjustment knob. (The microscope

should be **parfocal.** This means that when the high power objective is brought into position in place of the low power objective, the object will be in focus, or almost in focus, provided you make certain that the material to be viewed is centered and in sharp focus before turning from low power.)

(10) Adjust the fine adjustment knob to bring the specimen into sharp focus with the high power objective. *Never focus downward with the coarse adjustment knob when using high power.* Each time a different objective is used, the disc or iris diaphragm setting must be changed.

(11) Unless otherwise directed, drawings should be made using the high power objective.

(12) Always return the slide to the correct position in the slide box after use.

EXERCISE 2-B
MICROSCOPE DRAWINGS

Objective

To learn basic microscope technique and the procedure to be used in making drawings.

Materials

Plain white paper (or Biology Filler paper); 3H pencil; practice slides.

Discussion

Drawings are a valuable means of recording and checking the results of your observations. A drawing should indicate the accuracy and detail of all observations made. Properly completed drawings provide a basis for reviewing material you have observed under the microscope. They also provide evidence to the instructor that you have seen the significant structures.

The practice slides used in this exercise may consist of assorted tissues on damaged slides. It is not the purpose of this exercise to identify the various tissues; the student should, however, use these slides to learn how to use the microscope and how to make a drawing.

Procedure

1. Select one or more of the practice slides and, using the procedure indicated in Exercise 2-A, practice focusing (on both low and high power) until you are thoroughly familiar with the technique.

2. On one of the practice slides, locate two or three cells and draw them in accordance with the following specifications. (This is the procedure to be used for any drawings requested, unless instructions to the contrary are given.)

   a. Make all drawings on Biology Filler (or plain white) paper.

   b. In the upper right-hand corner of the page, print your name. Under your name, print the title of the course and the section number of your laboratory.

   c. In the upper left-hand corner, print the exercise number and, under this, the date the work was done.

   d. Centered at the top of the page, print the title of the exercise.

   e. As a general rule, do not include drawings of more than one exercise on a page. Use only one side of a page.

   f. Drawings must be large and neat, with the size of the cells in correct proportion to the drawing as a whole. When making the drawing, use firm continuous lines—not several indistinct, discontinuous lines. Individual drawings should not be boxed off in squares, rectangles, or circles.

   g. The drawing should be approximately centered on the page (or slightly to the left) with the labels to the right, except where excessive crowding makes this impractical.

   h. Draw only what is actually observed, but always look for a typical view of the structure being observed.

   i. An appropriate subtitle, which identifies the specific drawing, should be placed under each drawing. The subtitle should include the following: magnification and type of section, such as cross section (x.s. or c.s.), longitudinal section (l.s.), tangential section (t.s.), whole mount, fresh mount, or smear.

   j. Print all labels on lines *drawn with a*

ruler parallel to the top and bottom margins of the page. None of the label lines should cross each other. The label line should be touching the edge or should be within the structure indicated. Arrows should not be used.

   k. Use brackets to enclose related labels. For example, the parts of the nucleus should be labeled separately, and then bracketed with the general title "Nucleus."

   l. Be accurate in your spelling (look up the word if you are in doubt).

EXERCISE 2-C
ORIENTATION OF IMAGES VIEWED THROUGH THE COMPOUND MICROSCOPE

Objective

To determine orientation of images viewed through the compound microscope.

Materials

Microscope; letter "e" slide; newspaper slide.

PART 1. LETTER "e" SLIDE
Procedure

1. Obtain a prepared slide containing the printed letter "e" under the cover glass. Note that you can read the letter with the naked eye.

2. Place the slide on the stage of your microscope and observe with the low power objective.

3. Draw the letter "e" as you observed it with the naked eye (Drawing A) and as seen through the microscope (Drawing B).

_____   _____
(Drawing A)   (Drawing B)

4. Move the slide so that the letter appears in the upper left corner of the field. Now, center the letter while looking through the microscope. In which directions did you move the slide? _____

PART 2. NEWSPAPER SLIDE

Procedure

1. Obtain a newspaper slide (approximately 1-inch x 3-inch piece with printing on its surface).
2. Draw an asymmetrical letter as it normally appears on the paper slide (Drawing A).
3. Orient the slide under the low power objective of the microscope so that the asymmetrical letter is in the same relative position as when observed in step 2.
4. Draw the letter as it appears under the microscope (Drawing B).

_____   _____

(Drawing A)   (Drawing B)

5. Move the slide so that the letter appears in the upper left corner of the field. Now, center the letter while looking through the microscope. In which directions did you move the slide? _____

EXERCISE 2-D
THREAD SLIDE

Objective

To develop technique in determining depth in microscopic specimens.

Materials

Microscope; thread slide.

Discussion

This exercise requires careful technique. It demonstrates the fact that objects viewed through a microscope are three-dimensional, and that detail exists at varying levels that can only be observed by careful manipulation of the fine adjustment knob.

Procedure

1. Obtain a prepared slide containing three colored, crossed threads.
2. Begin with the slide slightly out of focus _below_ the three threads.
3. Using the fine adjustment knob, turn the body of the microscope upward until the bottom thread comes into focus, then the middle thread, then the upper thread. Repeat this procedure until you have determined the correct sequence of the threads. (Use the low power objective, then check the results with the high power objective.)
4. Record your observations in the spaces provided below.
   Slide Letter. _____
   Color of thread on bottom. _____
   Color of thread in middle. _____
   Color of thread on top. _____
5. Have the instructor check your results.
   Approved_____

SELF-TEST—MICROSCOPY

Directions

See Chapter 1, Self-Test, page 9.

1. The **nosepiece** of the microscope is a device for holding two or more readily interchangeable objectives.
2. **Parfocal** refers to objectives or lenses on a nosepiece that focus at the same position.
3. The **iris diaphragm** controls the amount of light passing through the object.
4. A ~~larger~~ _smaller_ portion of a specimen is seen with a high power objective than with a low power objective.
5. More detail of the specimen can be observed using a **high power objective** than a **low power objective.**
6. The ability of a lens to distinguish the fine detail in the structure of a specimen is known as its ~~magnification~~ _(resolving)_ power.

7. A microscope that includes both objective and eyepiece lenses is called a **compound** microscope.

8. If an object is observed with a microscope having a 5X eyepiece and a 20X objective, it is magnified ~~50~~ *100* times.

9. When using the high power objective, the ~~coarse~~ *fine* **adjustment knob** is used for focusing.

10. A micron is **1000 times** smaller than a millimeter.

11. A cell is 100 microns long. It would require approximately ~~1000~~ *250* such cells to stretch an inch when the cells are placed end to end.

12. The ~~higher~~ *lower* the power of the objective, the easier it is to locate the specimen to be observed.

13. Light rays passing from the atmosphere into water bend. This phenomenon is known as **refraction.**

14. By using a lens of the proper shape, light rays can be made to converge to a point known as the **focus,** from which point they go on to form an image beyond.

15. An electron microscope converges ~~light rays~~ *electron beams* to a focus by means of electromagnets or an electrostatic field.

16. A possible abbreviation for a longitudinal section is ~~l.s.~~ *L. S.*

17. Selective regulation of light intensity **is essential** to good microscopy.

18. The diameter of an erythrocyte is about 8 microns. Therefore, ~~100~~ *50* erythrocytes would be visible if lined up across a microscope field 400 microns wide.

3

Cells, Mitosis, Tissues, and Skin

EXERCISE 3-A
STRUCTURES AND FUNCTIONS OF CELLS

Objectives

To learn selected structures and functions of cells; to compare the characteristics of an ameba with those of human cells.

Materials

Living amebae (*Ameba proteus* or *Chaos chaos*); slides (plain and depression); cover glasses.

PART 1. STRUCTURES OF A CELL OBSERVED WITH A LIGHT MICROSCOPE COMPARED WITH THOSE OF A CELL OBSERVED WITH AN ELECTRON MICROSCOPE

Discussion

Cells are highly diversified, both structurally and functionally, but all living cells have certain things in common. This part of the exercise provides an introduction to structures and functions that almost all cells have in common.

Procedure

1. Except for the nucleus, few of the structures of a cell are visible with the light microscope. Figure 3-1 illustrates cellular structures visible in a specially prepared and stained slide. Most of these structures may also be observed in the cells making up tissues. Figure 3-1 may be used as a self-test (see section J, page xiii for a suggested approach).
2. Figure 3-2 illustrates the structure of a generalized cell as viewed with an electron microscope. Figure 3-2 may be used as a self-test.
3. Using your text and/or other references, determine the functions of the structures indicated in Figures 3-1 and 3-2 and

KEY TO FIGURE 3-1

1. plasma membrane
2. centriole
3. centrosphere
4. cytoplasm
5. mitochondrion
6. nuclear membrane
7. chromatin
8. nucleolus
9. nucleoplasm
10. nucleus

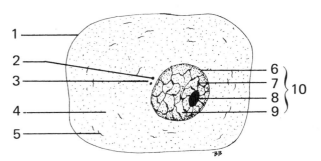

Figure 3-1. **Structure of cell (observed with the light microscope).**

18

KEY TO FIGURE 3-2

1. Golgi apparatus
2. mitochondria
3. lipid droplets
4. plasma membrane
5. lysosome
6. centrosphere
7. centrioles
8. nuclear membrane
9. vacuole
10. nucleus (nucleoplasm)
11. endoplasmic reticulum
12. nucleoli
13. ribosomes
14. glycogen inclusions
15. pinocytic vesicle
16. cytoplasm

Figure 3-2.   Generalized animal cell (as viewed with an electron microscope).

record them in the places provided under Results and Questions.

PART 2. OBSERVATION OF AN AMEBA

Discussion

Amebae are unicellular animals. There are many similarities between these organisms and white blood cells (leukocytes) in humans. Since they move quite slowly, amebae are ideal for observing the properties of protoplasm and the structures of a living cell.

Procedure

1. Prepare a clean depression (well) slide and cover glass. If a depression slide is not

available use a plain slide. Be certain that the slides and cover glasses used have not had formaldehyde or other preservatives on them at any time, since amebae are very sensitive to such chemicals and it is almost impossible to remove these contaminants by merely washing the slides.

2. Obtain a drop of culture containing amebae from your instructor.

3. If a depression slide is not used, be very cautious in placing the cover glass over the culture drop. If you drop the cover glass, the amebae may be crushed. The best procedure is to touch an edge of the cover glass to the drop and then allow the other edge to descend gradually, while

supporting it with the tip of a pencil or probe.

4. If a depression slide is available, the culture drop may be placed directly into the well (depression) and the cover glass applied, or the hanging-drop method may be used. If the latter method is used, ring the depression on the slide with petroleum jelly; then place a drop of culture on the cover glass and invert this over the depression.

5. Avoid continued exposure of the amebae to the heat emitted by the microscope lamp, as this will induce cyst formation (the organisms "ball up"). Encystment may be avoided by using only room lights.

6. Make your initial observations with the naked eye while holding the slide over a dark background. The amebae can be seen as tiny irregular masses of transparent material. They tend to glisten as light passes through them.

7. Next, examine the cell under low power. The amebae are difficult to find, since they are nearly transparent. Therefore, it is necessary to reduce the light source considerably by reducing the size of the opening of the iris diaphragm. In the dim light they can be readily observed due to the motion of the internal granules. There should be from three to ten amebae on your slide.

8. Do not ask for more material until you have searched the slide for at least 5 minutes. If you are then convinced your slide contains no organisms, call the instructor.

9. In Figure 3-3 some of the structures of an ameba are identified. See how many of these you can locate on the living specimen.

10. Observe the method of locomotion employed by the ameba. The fingerlike structures that seem to flow out of the cell are pseudopods (false feet). Movement by the formation of pseudopodia is called ameboid movement.

EXERCISE 3-B
MITOSIS

Objectives

To identify the major phases of mitosis; to understand the significance of mitosis.

Materials

Microscope; prepared slides of whitefish blastula; charts; references.

Discussion

Mitosis is a systematic sequence of events resulting in the production of two daughter cells from a single initiating or mother cell. Each of the two daughter cells contains identical sets of chromosomes and genes. Genes provide the basis for inheritance. They are the "recipes" that determine what an organism will become (both structurally and functionally). These determinations take place within the cells as a result of many biochemical reactions initiated either directly or indirectly by the substance of the genes—deoxyribonucleic acid (DNA).

Through mitosis the number of somatic cells is increased during the growth of the body. Mitosis is also the means by which worn-out cells of the body are replaced.

The blastula, which is an early stage of embryological development, shows all of the

KEY TO FIGURE 3-3

1. contractile vacuole
2. nucleus
3. food vacuole
4. pseudopod
5. plasma membrane
6. endoplasm

Figure 3-3.   Ameba proteus.

various phases of animal mitosis. In this exercise, the whitefish blastula is used because slides of it are readily available and the phases of mitosis that occur are the same as those that occur in humans.

Procedure

1. Select a prepared slide of the whitefish blastula and focus under the low power objective.
2. Now, using the high power objective, explore the slide and locate the following stages of mitosis: interphase, prophase, metaphase, anaphase, telophase, and daughter cells.
3. As each stage of mitosis is located, compare it with the same stage in Figure 3-4. Note the characteristics that identify each stage of mitosis.
4. Figure 3-4 may be used as a self-test.

EXERCISE 3-C
EPITHELIAL TISSUE

Objective

To learn the unique characteristics of selected epithelial tissues.

Materials

Microscope; prepared slides of simple columnar, simple cuboidal, and stratified squamous epithelial tissues; 3H pencil; drawing paper; 1% methylene blue; toothpicks.

Discussion

Epithelial tissues are specialized to protect, absorb, and secrete. They cover and line various surfaces. Secretory epithelium usually exists in the form of glands, which are groups of epithelial cells that have grown down into the underlying tissue from a surface epithelial membrane.

Preliminary study should precede examination of tissues under the microscope. The drawings of epithelial tissues (Figs. 3-5, -6, -7, -8, and -9) have been made from prepared slides similar to the ones used in the laboratory. Use these and other reference material as a guide. In studying tissues, think in terms of the characteristic appearance of the cells making up the tissues as well as of the locations and functions of each tissue.

PART 1. SIMPLE SQUAMOUS EPITHELIAL TISSUE (CHEEK CELL SMEAR)

Discussion

The following procedure involves use of the surface cells of stratified squamous epithelial tissue that lines the mouth. Such cells are comparable to simple squamous epithelial tissue.

Procedure

1. With the broad end of a toothpick, scrape the lining of your cheek two or three times to collect some of the cells from the mucous membrane.
2. Move the toothpick across a clean glass slide to leave a thin layer of the collected material on it.
3. Allow the preparation to air dry.
4. Cover the smear with 2 to 3 drops of 1% methylene blue stain.
5. After *1 minute*, gently rinse the slide in cold tap water to remove excess dye. Do this by holding the slide under a slow-running tap or by flooding it two or three times by means of a medicine dropper. Gently blot (do not rub) the slide dry with a paper towel.
6. Examine the slide under both low and high power objectives of your microscope.
7. Draw from three to six cells just as they appear under your microscope and label all the parts you can identify. The epithelial cells should be drawn at least 1 inch in diameter. You may also observe the presence of bacteria (usually bacilli) on the slide. Include these (if present) in your drawing.

Alternate Procedure— Amphibian (Frog) Skin

1. Select a prepared slide of frog skin. The frog skin is two cells thick and the structure of the cells can be readily seen.
2. Locate an area on the slide where the cells appear to be one cell thick. Draw from three to six squamous epithelial cells as seen under high power and label the parts. The cells have only one nucleus per cell. If another nucleus is visible, it belongs to the second layer of cells. Do not include it in your drawing.

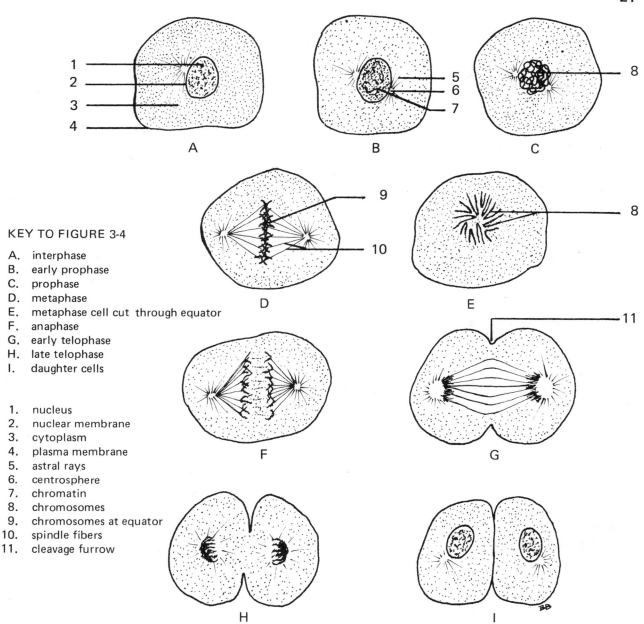

KEY TO FIGURE 3-4

A. interphase
B. early prophase
C. prophase
D. metaphase
E. metaphase cell cut through equator
F. anaphase
G. early telophase
H. late telophase
I. daughter cells

1. nucleus
2. nuclear membrane
3. cytoplasm
4. plasma membrane
5. astral rays
6. centrosphere
7. chromatin
8. chromosomes
9. chromosomes at equator
10. spindle fibers
11. cleavage furrow

Figure 3-4.   Mitosis (as observed in whitefish blastula).

PART 2. SIMPLE COLUMNAR EPITHELIAL TISSUE

Discussion

Simple columnar epithelium makes up the outer layer of the villi in the wall of the small intestine. The villi, in cross-sectional view, have the appearance of fingerlike projections. **Ciliated columnar epithelium** is a modified type of epithelial tissue which contains cilia on the surface of each cell. **Goblet cells** are unicellular glands which secrete mucus; these are found in both simple and ciliated columnar epithelium.

Procedure

1. Obtain a slide entitled "Simple columnar epithelium, intestine."
2. Locate the villi on low power and select an area where individual columnar cells may be seen clearly. Then turn to high power and observe the details of the cells.

Figure 3-5. Simple squamous epithelium (surface view).

Figure 3-6. Simple columnar epithelium (cross section).

Figure 3-7. Ciliated columnar epithelium (cross section).

Figure 3-8. Simple cuboidal epithelium (cross section).

Figure 3-9. Stratified squamous epithelium (cross section).

3. Draw from three to six cells (at least 1/2 inch wide) and label all the parts you can identify. Include a goblet cell, a unicellular gland which secretes mucus.
4. Your drawing should show clearly the shape, size, and location of the nucleus, the parts of the nucleus, the brush border, and any additional structures you can identify.

PART 3. SIMPLE CUBOIDAL EPITHELIAL TISSUE

Discussion

The cells of this tissue are almost cube shaped. This tissue is found in many glands.

Procedure

1. Select a prepared slide and locate the cuboidal epithelial tissue under the microscope.
2. Draw from three to six cuboidal cells as observed under the high power objective and label the parts.

PART 4. STRATIFIED SQUAMOUS EPITHELIAL TISSUE

Discussion

As the name implies, this tissue is layered (in strata). The deepest cells are almost cube

shaped, but they become more and more flattened as the surface is approached. At the surface the cells are completely flat (similar to simple squamous epithelium). The tissue varies in thickness from a few to many cell layers, depending on its location.

Procedure

1. Select a prepared slide and locate the tissue with the low power objective; then move the slide until a relatively thin area is found. Select an area that shows details of individual cells.
2. Using the high power objective, draw a section, at least four cells wide, from the deepest layer of the tissue to the surface.

EXERCISE 3-D CONNECTIVE TISSUE

Objective

To learn the characteristics of selected connective tissues.

Materials

Microscope; prepared slides of areolar connective tissue, adipose tissue, hyaline cartilage, bone, and blood; 3H pencil; drawing paper.

Discussion

Connective tissues are specialized for providing support and holding other tissues together. They are characterized by a much larger content of intercellular substances (the matrix) than that of other tissues.

PART 1. AREOLAR (LOOSE) CONNECTIVE TISSUE

Discussion

This tissue is distributed quite extensively throughout the body. It consists of white **collagenous** fibers, yellow **elastic** fibers, assorted tissue cells, and a semifluid to fluid ground substance. The fibers and the fluid (tissue fluid) constitute the matrix. Before viewing a slide of areolar tissue, examine Figure 3-10 and other reference material for orientation.

Procedure

1. Obtain a slide of areolar connective tissue.
2. Locate the tissue with the low power objective; then turn to high power to distinguish the different types of fibers and cells.
3. To distinguish between the two kinds of fibers, look for differences in thickness. The white collagenous fibers occur in parallel bundles and thus resemble slightly wider bands. The yellow elastic fibers are single, thin strands which may branch.
4. **Fibroblasts** will be found among the fibers in the matrix. The cytoplasm in these cells

is difficult to see without careful light regulation, although the nuclei are relatively easy to observe. The elongated or star-shaped bodies of the fibroblasts send out sharp processes. **Histiocytes** or **macrophages** are usually elongated, spindle-shaped cells.

5. Draw a section of the slide including the following: matrix, collagenous fibers, elastic fibers, and connective tissue cells. Label all structures drawn.

PART 2. ADIPOSE TISSUE

Discussion

Fat cells are scattered singly or in groups in areolar tissue. A mature fat cell contains one large drop of fat. The cytoplasm is reduced to a thin membrane surrounding the drop of fat. When fat cells form in large numbers and crowd out other cells, areolar tissue is transformed into adipose tissue.

Examine Figure 3-11 and other reference material before viewing a prepared slide of adipose tissue.

Procedure

1. Obtain a slide containing adipose tissue.
2. Locate the tissue with the low power objective, then examine it under the high power objective. (If the tissue has been stained, the cells will appear black if osmic acid was used, or orange if Sudan III was used.)
3. Draw from three to six cells and label all of the parts.

Figure 3-10.   Areolar connective tissue.

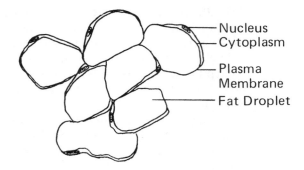

Figure 3-11.   Adipose tissue.

PART 3. HYALINE CARTILAGES

Discussion

a) Hyaline cartilage forms the tracheal rings, part of the larynx, the covering of articular surfaces of bones, etc. Each **chondrocyte** (cartilage cell) is enclosed within a **lacuna.** The chondrocyte completely fills this depression during life. There may be as many as four cells in a lacuna in mature cartilage. The cells are nourished by the **perichondrium,** a fibrous membrane covering the cartilage.

b) **Fibrous cartilage** (white fibrocartilage) differs from hyaline cartilage in that it has collagenous (white) fibers within the matrix. This cartilage forms the symphysis pubis and the intervertebral discs.

c) **Elastic cartilage** (yellow fibrocartilage) differs from hyaline cartilage in that it has elastic fibers in the matrix. This tissue may also have a limited amount of collagenous fibers within the matrix. It is found in the external ear, the eustachian tube, parts of the larynx, etc.

Examine Figure 3-12 before viewing the prepared slide of hyaline cartilage under the microscope.

Figure 3-12.   Hyaline cartilage.

Procedure

1.   Obtain a slide of hyaline cartilage.
2.   Locate the tissue first with the low power objective, then observe it with the high power objective.
3.   On the basis of your observations, draw and label a segment of tissue which includes the matrix, lacunae, and chondrocytes. You should be able to observe nuclei and other structures in the cells.
4.   Which tissues can be observed on either side of the strip of cartilage?
5.   Demonstrations:
    a.   Examine a fibrous cartilage slide under the microscope, noting the characteristics indicated in the preceding discussion.
    b.   Examine an elastic cartilage slide under the microscope. Note the characteristics indicated in the preceding discussion.

PART 4. OSSEOUS (BONY) TISSUE

Discussion

The shaft (diaphysis) of a typical long bone consists of a cortex of **compact** (dense) osseous tissue and an inner lining of **cancellous** (spongy) bony tissue. Spongy bone consists of plates (trabeculae) and bars forming a network that is well adapted for providing mechanical support. It lacks haversian canals and related structures that are found in compact bone.

Compact bone is made up of layers (**lamellae**) of calcified interstitial substance (or bone **matrix**). The lamellae are concentric circles of matrix and lacunae. The **lacunae** (cavities) in living bone are completely filled with **osteocytes** (bone cells). Minute canals called **canaliculi** arise from very fine apertures in the walls of the lacunae and penetrate the matrix in all directions, branching profusely to form a network in which frequent anastomoses occur.

Within the compact bone of the diaphysis of any long bone are numerous **haversian canals.** These are cylindrical, vertically branching and anastomosing canals which may contain one or more blood vessels (usually two capillaries). They communicate with the external surface of the bone and the bone marrow cavity by means of the horizontal **Volkmann's canals.**

Before viewing the slide of ground, compact bone, examine the following three figures showing relationships between gross bone and haversian systems. Figure 3-13 shows a small portion of the diaphysis of a bone and its marrow. It has been magnified to demonstrate both longitudinal and cross-sectional aspects of haversian systems. Figure 3-14 provides a microscopic view of a longitudinal section of haversian canals. Figure 3-15 shows a cross section of two haversian systems as viewed under the microscope.

Procedure

1. Obtain a slide entitled "Ground bone" or "Bone, human."
2. Locate the tissue on low power, then draw it while observing it under high power. Since the tissue is quite thick, with the cover glass raised, use caution on high power to avoid breaking the slide.
3. Diagram one complete haversian system. Include a wedge from the center to the edge of the system, drawn in detail. Include the following structures:
   a. **Haversian canal,** the large opening in the center. This may appear empty,

may contain remnants of blood vessels, or may appear dark due to the grinding process.
   b. **Lacunae,** small depressions arranged more or less symmetrically around the haversian canal. Osteocytes are not present in these lacunae due to the grinding process. Observe the position and shape of the lacunae.
   c. **Canaliculi,** tiny canals that lead to and from the lacunae and haversian canal. Observe the position, shape, and length of the canaliculi. The canaliculi in the outer ring loop back into the haversian system.
   d. **Matrix,** the ground substance between the lacunae and canaliculi.
   e. **Lamellae,** the circular layers of bone laid down by the osteocytes. Each lamella consists of a ring of lacunae and matrix.

PART 5. BLOOD
Discussion

The slide to be examined consists of a thin smear of blood stained with either Wright's

KEY TO FIGURE 3-13

1. periosteum
2. periosteal vein
3. periosteal artery
4. haversian system
5. haversian canal
6. Volkmann's canal
7. medullary artery
8. marrow cavity

Figure 3-13. Cross section of diaphysis (magnified).

KEY TO FIGURE 3-14

1. haversian canal
2. Volkmann's canal
3. lacuna

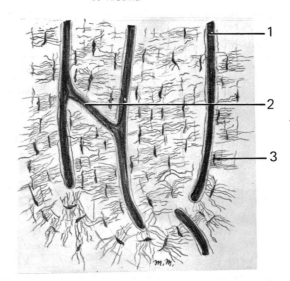

Figure 3-14. Longitudinal section through compact bone (430X).

Figure 3-15.   Cross section through two haversian systems.

stain or Giemsa's stain. With these dyes, granules in the cytoplasm of various kinds of leukocytes are differentially stained. The nuclei of the leukocytes are stained blue and the erythrocytes are stained a pale red.

The following outline provides some of the identifying characteristics of the cells that may be observed on the prepared slide:

A. **Erythrocytes** (red blood cells): The great majority of the cells you will observe will be of this type. They are small, **biconcave** disks. Many vertebrates have nucleated red cells (e.g., amphibians such as frogs and salamanders); however, the erythrocytes of mammals are **anucleate.**

B. **Leukocytes** (white blood cells):

1. **Lymphocytes** (20% to 25% of all leukocytes). These are found in large numbers in lymph nodes and lymph as well as in the circulating blood. They have a large, single nucleus approximately spherical in shape and a narrow band of cytoplasm.

2. **Monocytes** (3% to 8% of all leukocytes). These cells consist of a single nonlobed nucleus. The nucleus is frequently curved in the form of a crescent. The cytoplasm is granular and more abundant than in lymphocytes (i.e., microlymphocytes).

3. **Granulocytes.** The cytoplasm of these cells contains numerous granules, which may vary in density and coarseness depending on the type. They are distinguished on the basis of the color

they stain with various dyes. These differentiating stains are included in Wright's stain.

a. **Neutrophils** (65% to 75% of all leukocytes). They are also called polymorphonuclear leukocytes because their nuclei consist of several (usually three to five) lobes. Upon careful observation (high power) it will be noted that the lobes are interconnected. The granules in the cytoplasm are relatively fine grained, stain with a neutral dye, and appear faint red.

b. **Eosinophils** (2% to 5% of all leukocytes). The dense granules of these cells, seen in the cytoplasm, are stained red by the eosin in Wright's stain. The nucleus is usually bilobed, but this may be difficult to observe due to the dense granular cytoplasm.

c. **Basophils** (0.5% to 1% of all leukocytes). These cells contain such coarse granules that they all but blot out the nucleus. The granules take a basic dye and appear to be blue or purple.

d. **Thrombocytes (platelets).** The platelets are about half the size of an erythrocyte. They are derived from the fragmentation of giant (up to 100 microns (μ) in diameter) megakaryocytes found in the marrow.

Procedure

1. Obtain a slide of a human blood smear.
2. For orientation, refer to the drawings of blood cells (Fig. 3-16) and other references.
3. Note that the great majority of cells on the slide are erythrocytes. Draw two or three of the cells as they appear in different positions.
4. Identify and draw a lymphocyte.
5. Identify and draw a neutrophil.
6. Optional: If time permits, identify and draw an eosinophil, a basophil, a monocyte, and a group of thrombocytes.

EXERCISE 3-E
MUSCLE TISSUE

Objective

To distinguish the characteristics of the three kinds of muscle tissue.

Materials

Microscope; slides of skeletal, smooth, and cardiac muscle; drawing paper; 3H pencil.

PART 1. SKELETAL (STRIATED) MUSCLE

Discussion

Each skeletal muscle fiber is a multinucleate, unbranched fiber containing many bands called striations. The longest striated muscle fibers are estimated to be about 40,000 μ.

Procedure

1. Obtain a slide showing teased skeletal muscle tissue.
2. Compare a fiber, as seen under high power, with Figure 3-17.
3. Draw one muscle fiber as seen in longitudinal section.
4. Label sarcolemma, sarcoplasm, and striations. Include nuclei if they are visible. Note their size (relative to the striations) and their position.

KEY TO FIGURE 3-16

A.   erythrocytes (red blood cells)

B-1. macrolymphocyte
B-2. microlymphocyte

C.   monocytes

D.   neutrophils

E.   eosinophil   granulocytes

F.   basophil

leukocytes

G.   thrombocytes (platelets)

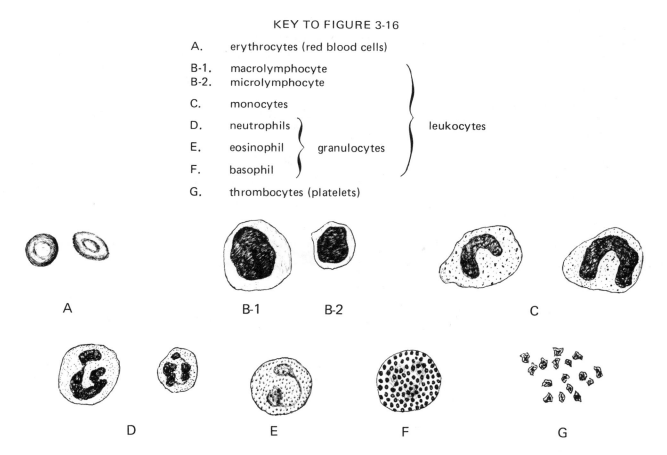

Figure 3-16.   Human blood cells.

Nucleus
Striation
Sarcolemma
Sarcoplasm

Figure 3-17.   Skeletal muscle fiber (l.s.).

PART 2. VISCERAL (SMOOTH) MUSCLE

Discussion

The cells of this tissue are up to 500 μ in length; each spindle-shaped cell has tapered ends. The cells are uninucleate and unbranched.

Procedure

1.   Obtain a slide of teased smooth (visceral) muscle tissue.
2.   Compare the cells observed with those shown in Figure 3-18.
3.   Draw one representative cell and label all parts identified.

PART 3. CARDIAC MUSCLE

Discussion

Somewhat fainter striations are observed in this tissue than in skeletal muscle tissue. Also, this tissue contains unique dark bands called **intercalated discs.** The electron microscope has revealed that these discs are places where two cell membranes abut at the ends of adjacent cardiac fibers. The cardiac fibers form a continuum by repeatedly branching.

Procedure

1.   Obtain a slide of cardiac muscle tissue.
2.   Compare this tissue, as observed under high power, with Figure 3-19.
3.   Draw and label three or four fibers showing the branching nature of the tissue, striations, and intercalated discs.

EXERCISE 3-F
NERVE TISSUE

Objectives

To observe the characteristics of a motor neuron and a myelinated nerve fiber.

Materials

Microscope; slides of motor neurons and myelinated nerve fibers; drawing paper; 3H pencil.

PART 1. MOTOR NEURONS

Discussion

The slide to be examined was prepared by smearing and staining the ventral horn of the spinal cord. The cell bodies (**cytons**) of motor neurons in a spinal cord smear are among the largest in the cord. In the process of preparing the slide, the axon and dendrites of these large cells were broken. On this slide, neuroglia cells are visible between the separated neurons.

Procedure

1.   Obtain a slide entitled "Nerve cells, ox spinal cord."

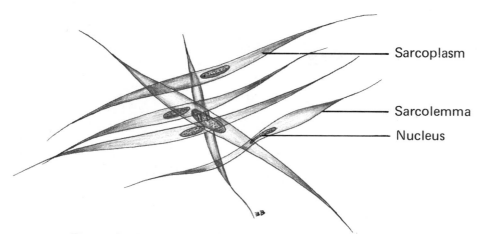

Sarcoplasm

Sarcolemma

Nucleus

Figure 3-18.   Smooth (visceral) muscle fibers (teased).

Figure 3-19.   Cardiac muscle tissue (l.s.).

2. Locate one neuron and compare it with the motor neuron illustrated in Figure 3-20.
3. Draw the neuron under low power. Include in your drawing (and label) the cyton, axon, dendrites, and nucleus with nucleolus and any other parts visible.

PART 2. MYELINATED (MEDULLATED) NERVE FIBER

Discussion

Myelinated nerve fibers are located in the central nervous system and in peripheral nerves. The name is derived from the fact that such fibers are surrounded by a pearly white, lipid substance called the myelin sheath. In the central nervous system the myelin sheath is formed by glial cells, and fibers containing it make up the white matter. (Gray matter is composed mainly of cell bodies and fibers that lack myelin; hence, it is gray in color.) In the peripheral nerves, axons of motor neurons are surrounded by sheaths of myelin which are formed by neurilemmal cells. All myelin sheaths are interrupted at regular intervals at points referred to as nodes of Ranvier. All nerve fibers outside the central nervous system have the thin membrane called the neurilemma, whether they are myelinated or not. The flat cells forming the neurilemma are called cells of Schwann. There is usually only one of these cells between two successive nodes of Ranvier.

Procedure

1. Obtain a slide containing teased myelinated nerve fibers.
2. Locate a fiber that appears to be typical and compare it with Figure 3-21.
3. Using the high power objective, draw a segment of the fiber which includes two nodes of Ranvier, neurilemma, nucleus of Schwann cell, myelin sheath, and axis cylinder.

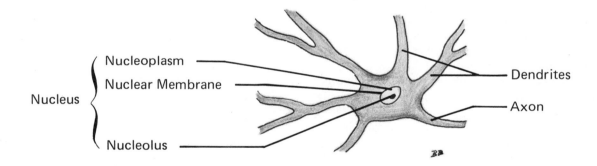

Figure 3-20.   Motor neuron (smear).

Figure 3-21.   Myelinated nerve fiber (l.s.).

EXERCISE 3-G
SKIN

Objective

To identify the structures present in the skin.

Materials

Microscope; slide of human skin; model of skin; references; anatomic charts.

Discussion

Skin consists of two principal layers: the **epidermis** (cuticle), and the **dermis** (corium or true skin). The epidermis contains an outer layer of stratified squamous cells which are keratinized (protoplasm replaced by nonliving protein called keratin). These cells are flattened and scalelike and are constantly being lost by the body. This layer of cells is known as the **stratum corneum,** or horny layer; the cells are replaced as a result of mitotic divisions of the inner layer of the epidermis, which is known as the **stratum germinativum.**

The dermis (corium), like the epidermis, varies in thickness in different parts of the body. For example, it is especially thick over the palms of the hands and the soles of the feet. This portion of the skin is composed of matted masses of connective tissue and elastic fibers. Numerous blood vessels, nerves, and lymphatics pass through the dermis.

Appendages of the skin include hair, nails, **sudoriferous** (sweat) glands, and **sebaceous** (oil) glands.

The subdermal tissue (subcutaneous layer) contains fat cells, connective tissue, blood ves-sels, lymphatics, and nerves. These tissues provide a connection between the skin and deeper tissues. Where the connecting fibers are loose (as in the neck), the skin can be moved quite easily. Where the skin is attached more firmly (as in the palms and soles), only limited movement is possible.

The specialized receptors located within the skin (for receiving such stimuli as cold, heat, touch, pain, etc.) are discussed under the Introduction in Chapter 17.

Procedure

1. Using Figure 3-22 as a guide, examine the structures on the model of human skin.
2. Obtain a slide of human skin. Using references, anatomic charts, the skin model, and Figure 3-22, explore the slide for the following structures (check off each structure identified).
   a. _____ Adipose tissue
   b. _____ Arrector pili muscle
   c. _____ Blood vessel
   d. _____ Bulb of hair
   e. _____ Dermis
   f. _____ Duct of sweat gland
   g. _____ Epidermis
   h. _____ Hair shaft
   i. _____ Nerve fiber
   j. _____ Pore of sweat gland
   k. _____ Sebaceous gland
   l. _____ Stratified squamous epithelium
   m. _____ Stratum germinativum
   n. _____ Stratum corneum
   o. _____ Subdermis (subcutaneous layer)
   p. _____ Sudoriferous gland

SELF-TEST—CELLS, MITOSIS, TISSUES, AND SKIN

Directions

See Chapter 1, Self-Test, page 9.

1. A group of cells of similar structure constitutes **an organ.**
2. Epithelial tissue **covers and lines.**
3. Nervous tissue **supports and binds.**
4. Epithelial tissue can be distinguished from connective tissue by the **sparseness of intercellular materials.**
5. Goblet cells are unicellular glands found in **certain connective tissues.**

KEY TO FIGURE 3-22

A. epidermis (stratified squamous epithelium)
B. dermis (true skin)
C. subdermis (subcutaneous tissue)
1. pore of sweat gland
2. stratum corneum (horny layer)
3. stratum germinativum
4. duct of sweat gland

5. hair shaft
6. sebaceous (oil) gland
7. arrector pili muscle
8. hair follicle
9. sudoriferous (sweat) gland
10. bulb of hair (with papilla)
11. adipose tissue

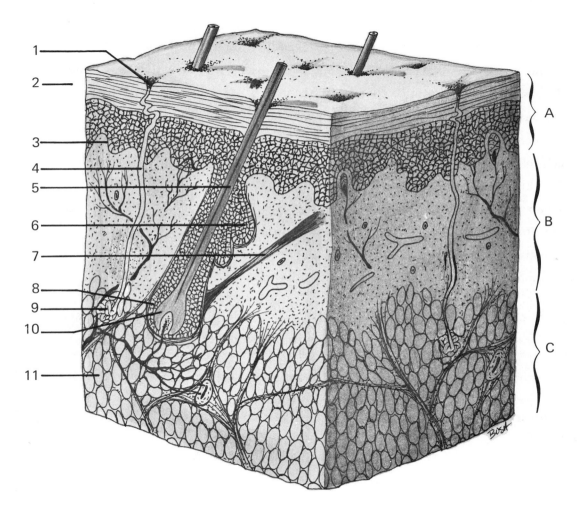

Figure 3-22.   The skin (cross section).

6. Cartilage is a variety of connective tissue which contains **osteocytes** in lacunae.

7. One location of **elastic cartilage** is within the external ear.

8. Histiocytes, also known as fixed macrophages, become **phagocytic** in case of infection.

9. Skin is **a tissue**.

10. The single layer of flat cells that lines the blood vessels is classified as **mesothelium**.

11. **Simple columnar epithelium** lines the stomach and intestines.

12. Stratified squamous epithelium is found, primarily, **covering the outside of the body**.

13. **Pseudostratified ciliated columnar epithelium** is found lining much of the respiratory tract.

14. Cilia are found on the surface of **all epithelial cells**.

15. Goblet cells produce **mucus**.

16. **Mucous membranes** line the alimentary, respiratory, and genitourinary tract.

17. **Serous membranes** line body cavities and cover organs that lie within the cavities.

18. **Haversian canals** are minute channels in the matrix of bone tissue extending to lacunae.

19. The haversian system is a nutritive arrangement of cells in **cancellous** bone.

20. The periosteum is a **fibrous membrane** covering bone.

21. The cell is both the **structural and functional** unit of the body.

22. The skin contains **striated** muscle fibers.

23. A hair is a product of **epidermal** cells.

24. The upper surface of the epidermis is the **stratum granulosum**.

25. Sensitivity of the skin is determined by sense organs lying in the **epidermis**.

26. The most important means of protection by the skin is due to its **unbroken surface which prevents entrance of bacteria**.

27. **Hemoglobin** is the dark brown pigment that gives color to hair, eyes, and the skin.

28. A suntan "fades" in winter, because **normally pigmented cells in the deep skin layers** are pushed upward to replace the highly pigmented cells on the surface as they are worn away.

29. Some injections with hypodermic needles hurt more than others because **pain receptors** may be hit.

30. **Contractions of arrector pili muscles** push hair up and pull the skin down, causing "goose-pimples."

31. The **epidermis** layer of the skin is the only layer lacking a direct blood supply.

32. As an excretory structure the skin eliminates **protein metabolites**.

33. Acne is an inflammation of **sudoriferous** glands.

34. The **epidermis** is the thickest layer of skin.

35. **Sebaceous glands** lubricate the skin and keep it from cracking.

36. **Melanoblasts** are specialized cells in the lower part of the epidermis which produce melanin.

37. The phase of mitosis when chromosomes line up in the center of the spindle is called **anaphase**.

38. The nuclear membrane disappears during the **metaphase** of mitosis.

39. The chromosomes consist of a pair of chromatids held together by a centromere in the **prophase** of mitosis.

40. During metaphase, the centromeres **divide** and the chromatids start to **separate from each other**.

41. During mitosis, chromosomes appear to be short rods due to **the spiral arrangement of each chromosome**.

42. In the **anaphase** of mitosis there are individual chromosomes, each with a single centromere.

43. The **nucleus** of a cell contains the Golgi apparatus.

44. Mitochondria are found in **both the cytoplasm and the nucleus of a cell**.

45. Energy is released as the result of enzymatic reactions occurring in **ribosomes**.

46. The Golgi apparatus is apparently concerned with **secretion**.

47. **Vacuoles** may serve as a storage place for foods.

48. Deoxyribonucleic acid is found primarily in **cytoplasm**.

49. Secretion in the body **always** involves some form of epithelial tissue.

50. **Mucous membranes** line passageways which open to the outside, whereas **serous membranes** line closed cavities.

51. **Osteoblasts** form the hard intercellular matrix of bone.

4

The Skeletal System

EXERCISE 4-A
COMPOSITION AND STRUCTURE OF BONE

Objectives

To study the composition and structure of a typical long bone.

Materials

Sectioned femur; bone soaked in dilute acetic acid; baked bone.

Discussion

The skeletal system includes the bones and the joints. The study of the bones is termed osteology; that of the joints arthrology. The functions of the skeletal system include the following: protection of internal organs such as the heart and lungs, support of the body, attachment for muscles, storage of calcium and phosphorus, and manufacture of blood cells (hemopoiesis).

The dried bones used in the laboratory have been cleansed of all membranes and muscle tissue. In a fresh bone, a membrane called the **periosteum** surrounds the **diaphysis** (shaft) of a long bone. The periosteum serves for growth in circumference, for repair, and for nutrition of the bone. The periosteal blood vessels penetrate into the bone by way of Volkmann's canals, carrying blood rich in food and oxygen. A similar membrane, called the **endosteum**, lines the marrow cavity (medullary cavity). In children this membrane contains cells called **osteoclasts** which destroy bone, enlarging the marrow cavity. The **articular cartilage**, composed of hyaline cartilage, covers the **epiphyses** (ends) of the long bones. It serves to prevent friction at joints. In a sectioned bone of an adult, an **epiphyseal line** can be seen at each end of the bone at the junction between the epiphysis and the diaphysis. This is the remnant of the epiphyseal cartilage, which serves for growth in length of the bone.

In a fresh bone, the shaft of the bone is filled with yellow bone marrow, composed primarily of adipose tissue. The ends of some of the long bones, the flat bones, the bodies of vertebrae, the cranial bones, the sternum, and the ribs contain red bone marrow. This type of marrow manufactures erythrocytes, granulocytes (leukocytes containing granules), and thrombocytes.

Procedure

1. Examine the sectioned femur. Locate the following structures on this bone using Figure 4-1.
    a. Compact bone. Note the thick layer in the shaft and the thin layer covering the epiphyses.
    b. Cancellous (spongy) bone. This type is contained in the epiphyses; a thin layer also lines the marrow cavity.
    c. Marrow cavity.
    d. Epiphyseal line.
2. Examine the bone that has been soaked in dilute acetic acid for several days. The acid dissolves the minerals in the bone, leaving only organic materials. Examine the consistency of the bone. Try to bend the bone.

3. Examine the bone that has been baked at high temperature for 8 hours. The heat removes the organic materials in the bone, leaving the minerals. Note the color of the bone. Gently press on the bone. Determine whether this bone can be bent.

EXERCISE 4-B
THE SKELETON

Objectives

To identify the bones of the skeleton and the major processes on these bones.

Materials

Articulated and disarticulated skeletons; disarticulated skull; sectioned skull; text; references.

Discussion

The skeleton in a typical adult contains 206 bones, although this number can vary. The skeleton is divided into two parts, the appendicular skeleton and the axial skeleton. The appendicular skeleton, composed of 126 bones, includes bones of the appendages and the girdles (shoulder and pelvic), which connect the appendages to the axial skeleton.

The axial skeleton, composed of 80 bones, includes the bones of the skull, vertebral column, and thorax.

Procedure

1. Locate each of the bones illustrated in Figures 4-3 through 4-44 on an articulated skeleton. (Use Figure 4-2 as a guide.)
2. Compare the parts of the bone indicated in each figure with those in your text and other references and with those of the bones of a disarticulated skeleton. Determine the function of each part by using references.
3. Practice identifying the bones of the disarticulated skull until you can distinguish each of the separate bones. Verify your identification of the facial bones with the instructor.
4. Determine the characteristics of the vertebrae in each region of the vertebral column.

KEY TO FIGURE 4-1

1. periosteum
2. endosteum
3. compact bone
4. cancellous (spongy) bone
5. epiphyseal line
6. yellow bone marrow
7. marrow cavity
8. epiphysis
9. diaphysis

Figure 4-1.   Longitudinal section through femur.

36

KEY TO FIGURE 4-2

1. hyoid bone
2. clavicle
3. scapula
4. sternum
5. humerus
6. ulna
7. radius
8. carpals
9. phalanges
10. metacarpals
11. femur
12. patella
13. tibia
14. fibula
15. tarsals
16. metatarsals
17. phalanges
18. ilium of os coxae
19. lumbar vertebra

Figure 4-2.   Anterior view of entire skeleton.

KEY TO FIGURE 4-3

1. acromial extremity (lateral end)

omit ~~2. conoid tubercle~~

3. sternal extremity (medial end)

Figure 4-3.   Right clavicle (cranial aspect), superior surface.

KEY TO FIGURE 4-4

omit ~~1.~~ medial (superior) angle

2. superior border

3. supraspinous fossa

omit ~~4.~~ scapular notch

5. spine

6. infraspinous fossa

7. vertebral (medial) border

8. coracoid process

9. acromion process

10. glenoid cavity

omit ~~11.~~ lateral angle

12. axillary (lateral) border

omit ~~13.~~ inferior angle

Figure 4-4.   Right scapula (posterior view).

38

Figure 4-5.
Right humerous
(anterior view).

Figure 4-6.
Right humerous
(posterior view).

KEY TO FIGURE 4-7

1. head
2. neck
3. radial tuberosity
4. styloid process
5. ulnar notch

KEY TO FIGURE 4-8

1. olecranon process
2. semilunar notch (*or trochlear notch*)
3. coronoid process
4. radial notch
omit 5. head
6. styloid process

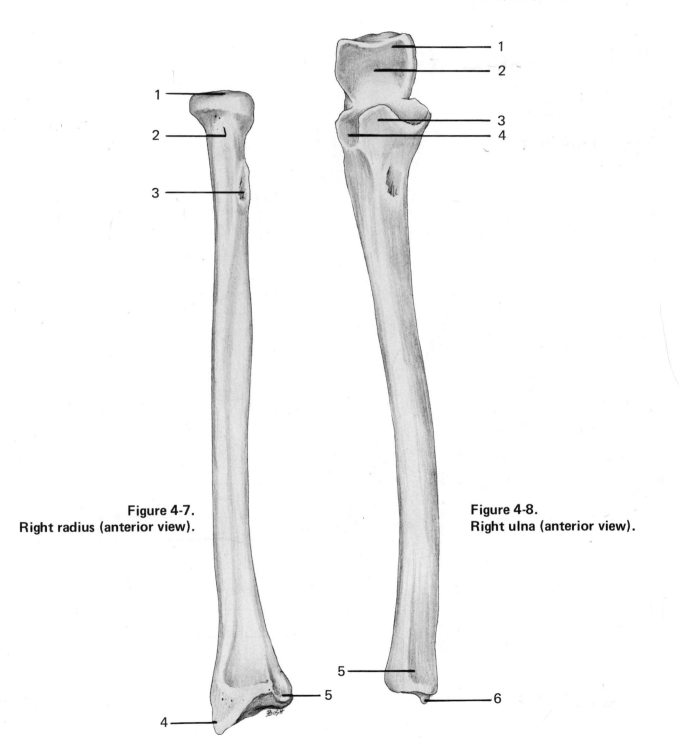

Figure 4-7.
Right radius (anterior view).

Figure 4-8.
Right ulna (anterior view).

KEY TO FIGURE 4-9

1. ~~third~~ phalanx *distal*
2. ~~second~~ phalanx *middle*
3. ~~first~~ phalanx *proximal*
4. phalanges
5. fifth metacarpal
omit 6. ~~capitate~~
7. hamate
omit 8. ~~triangular~~ (triquetrum)
9. pisiform
omit 10. ~~lunate~~ (semilunar)
11. navicular (scaphoid)
omit 12. ~~lesser multangular~~ (trapezoid)
omit 13. ~~greater multangular~~ (trapezium)
14. eight carpals = carpus
15. five metacarpals = metacarpus

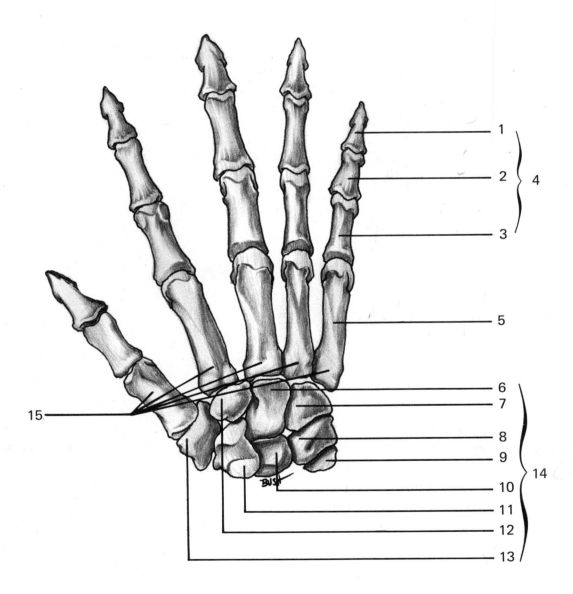

Figure 4-9.   Right hand, dorsal surface.

41

KEY TO FIGURE 4-10

1. ~~area of~~ ilium
2. posterior superior iliac spine
omit 3. posterior inferior iliac spine
4. greater sciatic notch
5. ischial spine
omit 6. lesser sciatic notch
7. ischium
8. ischial tuberosity
9. iliac crest
10. anterior superior iliac spine
omit 11. anterior inferior iliac spine
12. acetabulum
13. crest of pubis
14. pubis
15. obturator foramen

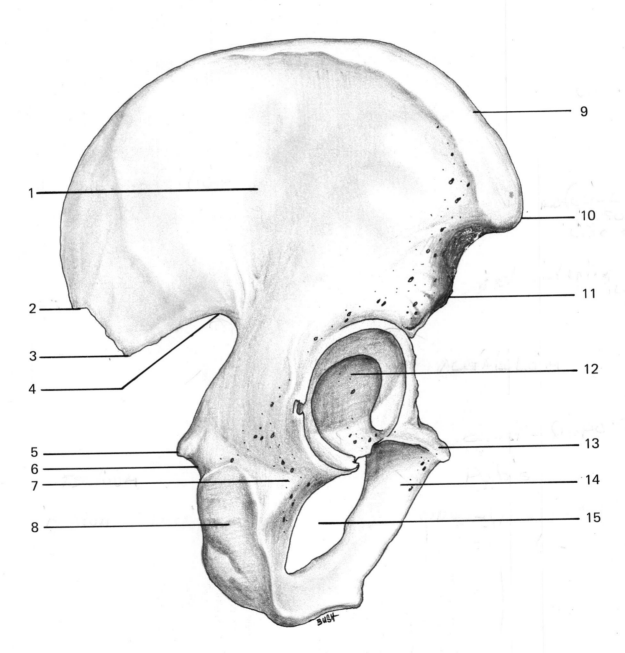

Figure 4-10.   Right os coxae (lateral view).
≅ 1, 7 ; 14

42

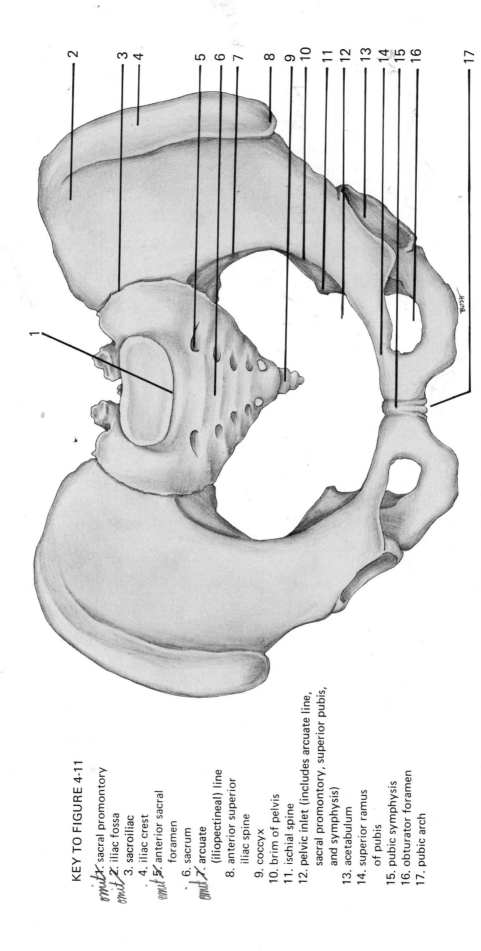

Figure 4-11. Female pelvis.

KEY TO FIGURE 4-11

omit 1. sacral promontory
omit 2. iliac fossa
3. sacroiliac
omit 5. iliac crest
     anterior sacral
     foramen
6. sacrum
7. arcuate
   (iliopectineal) line
8. anterior superior
   iliac spine
9. coccyx
10. brim of pelvis
11. ischial spine
12. pelvic inlet (includes arcuate line,
    sacral promontory, superior pubis,
    and symphysis)
13. acetabulum
14. superior ramus
    of pubis
15. pubic symphysis
16. obturator foramen
17. pubic arch

KEY TO FIGURE 4-12

1. greater trochanter
2. lesser trochanter
3. lateral epicondyle
4. patellar surface
5. head
6. neck
7. medial epicondyle

KEY TO FIGURE 4-13

1. head
2. greater trochanter
3. neck
4. lesser trochanter
5. linea aspera
6. intercondyloid fossa
7. lateral condyle
8. medial condyle

Figure 4-12. Right femur (anterior view).

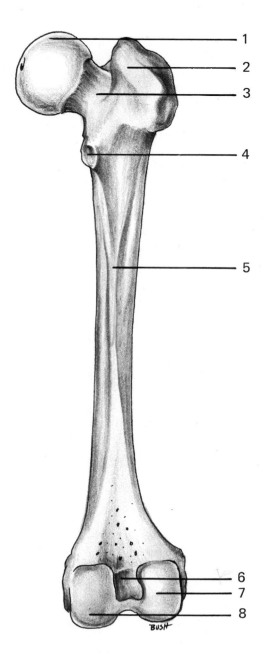

Figure 4-13. Right femur (posterior view).

44

Patella
(anterior view)

**Figure 4-14. Right fibula
(anterior view).**

**Figure 4-15. Right tibia
(anterior view).**

45

KEY TO FIGURE 4-16

1. ~~third~~ phalanx (distal)
2. ~~second~~ phalanx (middle)
3. ~~first~~ phalanx (proximal)
4. phalanges
5. first metatarsal

6. first (medial) cuneiform
7. navicular
8. talus
9. calcaneus

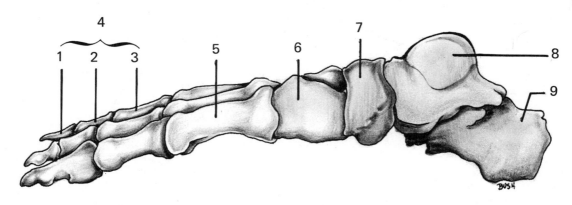

Figure 4-16.   Bones of the right foot (medial view).

KEY TO FIGURE 4-17

1. ~~third~~ phalanx D
2. ~~second~~ phalanx M
3. ~~first~~ phalanx P
4. phalanges
5. fifth metatarsal
6. five metatarsals = metatarsus
7. third (lateral) cuneiform
8. second (intermediate) cuneiform

9. first (medial) cuneiform
10. cuboid
11. navicular
12. talus
13. calcaneus
14. seven tarsals = tarsus

Figure 4-17.   Bones of the right foot, dorsal surface.

141-143 in text

46

KEY TO FIGURE 4-18

1. parietal bone
2. lambdoidal suture
3. squamosal suture
4. temporal bone
5. wormian bones
6. occipital bone
7. mastoid process (Temporal)

8. styloid process (Temporal)
9. coronal suture
10. frontal bone
11. sphenoid bone Gw
12. nasal bone
13. lacrimal bone
14. ethmoid bone

15. zygomatic bone
16. maxilla
17. zygomatic arch of Temporal bone
18. external acoustic (auditory)
    meatus (Temporal bone)
19. mandible

lamina papyracea

Figure 4-18.   The skull (lateral view).

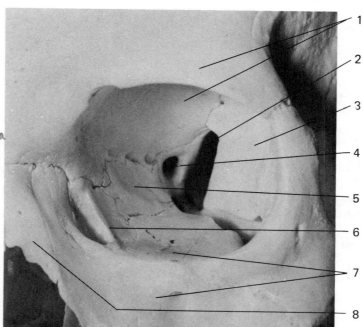

KEY TO FIGURE 4-19
(pg 142 text)

1. frontal bone
omit 2. superior orbital fissure
3. zygomatic bone
4. optic foramen Sphenoid bone
5. ethmoid bone lamina papyracea
6. lacrimal bone
7. maxillary bone
8. nasal bone

Figure 4-19.   Left orbital
cavity.

47

KEY TO FIGURE 4-20

1. sagittal suture
2. supraorbital notch(foramen)
3. greater wing of sphenoid
4. temporal bone
5. optic foramen (Sphenoid)
6. superior orbital fissure
7. sphenoid (orbital surface)
8. inferior orbital fissure
9. middle nasal concha
10. infraorbital foramen
11. inferior nasal concha
12. vomer
13. mandible
14. coronal suture
15. parietal bone
16. frontal bone
17. superciliary arch
18. glabella
19. supraorbital margin
20. nasal bone
21. ethmoid (L P)
22. lacrimal bone
23. zygomatic bone
24. perpendicular plate of ethmoid
25. maxilla
26. mental foramen
27. alveolar process of mandible

Figure 4-20.   The skull (anterior view).

48

KEY TO FIGURE 4-21

1. frontal bone
2. sella turcica → sphenoid
3. optic foramen → sphenoid
4. frontal sinus
5. nasal bone
6. perpendicular plate
   of ethmoid
7. sphenoidal sinus
8. vomer
9. hard palate
10. alveolar process (of maxilla)
11. pterygoid process (of sphenoid)
12. parietal bone
13. internal acoustic
    meatus
14. temporal bone
15. jugular foramen
16. occipital bone
17. hypoglossal canal
18. occipital condyle
19. styloid process

Figure 4-21. Sagittal section of the skull (crista galli not shown in order to expose frontal sinus).

KEY TO FIGURE 4-22

1. perpendicular plate
2. crista galli
3. cribriform plate
4. ethmoidal air cells
5. lamina papyracea
   (lateral masses)

6. *Superior Nasal Concha*
   Middle Nasal Concha
7. *Inferior Nasal Concha (really a seperate bone)*

Figure 4-22.   The ethmoid (superior view).

KEY TO FIGURE 4-23

1. optic foramen
2. sphenoid sinus
3. body
4. sella turcica
5. lesser wing
6. inferior orbital
   fissure

7. greater wing
8. foramen rotundum
9. lateral pterygoid
   process
10. medial pterygoid
    process

Figure 4-23.   The sphenoid (anterior view).

KEY TO FIGURE 4-24

maw ◯

1. greater wing
2. superior orbital fissure
3. anterior clinoid process

4. foramen rotundum
5. posterior clinoid process
6. foramen ovale
7. foramen spinosum

8. lesser wing
9. optic foramen
10. optic groove
11. sella turcica
12. dorsum sellae

Figure 4-24. The sphenoid (superior view).

KEY TO FIGURE 4-25

1. superior nuchal line
2. condyloid canal
3. occipital condyle
4. hypoglossal canal

5. external occipital protuberance
6. external occipital crest (median nuchal line)

7. inferior nuchal line
8. foramen magnum
9. jugular notch
10. basilar part

Figure 4-25. The occipital (inferior view).

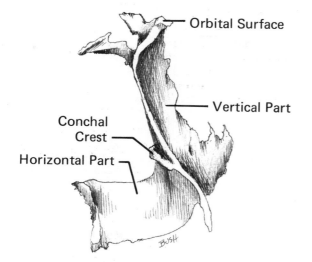

Orbital Surface

Vertical Part

Conchal Crest

Horizontal Part

Figure 4-26.   Left palatine.

Nasopalatine Groove

Ala

Figure 4-30.   Vomer.

Figure 4-31.   Right inferior nasal concha (lateral surface).

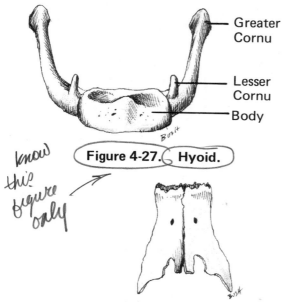

Greater Cornu

Lesser Cornu

Body

Figure 4-27.   Hyoid.

know this figure only

Figure 4-28.   Nasal bones (outer surface).

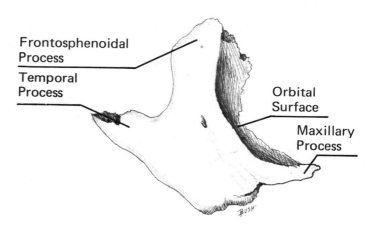

Frontosphenoidal Process

Temporal Process

Orbital Surface

Maxillary Process

Figure 4-32.   Zygomatic (malar).

Lacrimal Groove

Figure 4-29.   Lacrimal (lateral aspect).

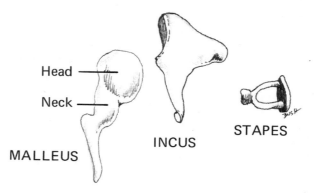

Head

Neck

MALLEUS

INCUS

STAPES

Figure 4-33.   Auditory ossicles.

52

KEY TO FIGURE 4-34

1. coronoid process   6. mandibular foramen
2. mandibular notch   7. alveolar process
3. condyloid process   8. mental foramen
4. ramus   9. mental protuberance
5. body

mau →

Figure 4-34.   The mandible.

KEY TO FIGURE 4-35

1. orbital surface
2. infraorbital groove
3. zygomatic process
4. frontal process
5. infraorbital foramen
6. anterior nasal spine
7. alveolar process

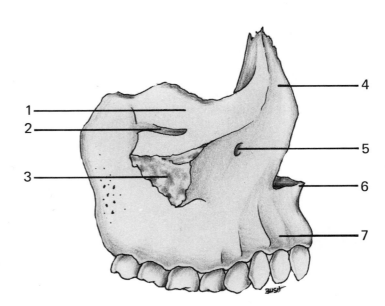

Figure 4-35.   The right maxilla (lateral view).

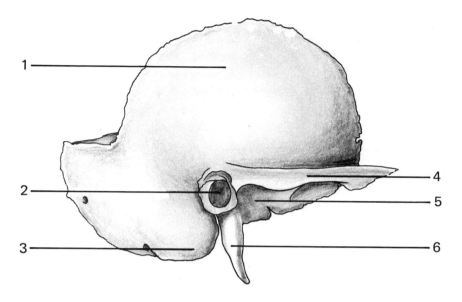

Figure 4-36. The right temporal (lateral aspect).

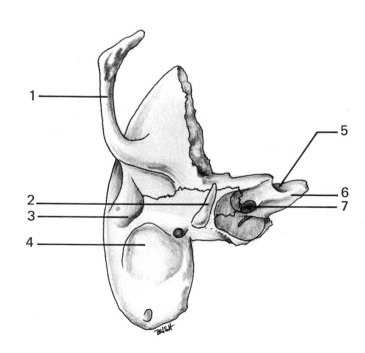

Figure 4-37. The right temporal (basal aspect).

KEY TO FIGURE 4-38

1. anterior arch
2. superior articular surface
3. transverse foramen
4. posterior arch
5. transverse process
6. ~~groove for vertebral artery~~

KEY TO FIGURE 4-39

1. body
2. dens (~~odontoid process~~)
3. superior articular surface
4. transverse foramen
5. transverse process
6. lamina
7. bifid spinous process

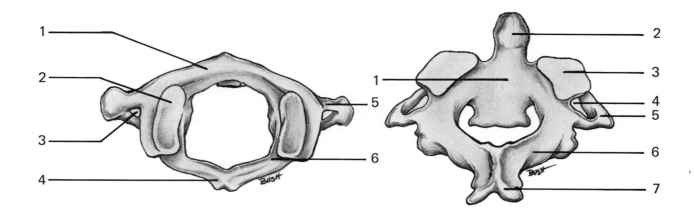

Figure 4-38.   The atlas (first cervical vertebra).

Figure 4-39.   The axis (second cervical vertebra).

KEY TO FIGURE 4-40

1. body
2. transverse foramen
3. pedicle
4. transverse process
5. lamina
6. spinous process
7. superior articular process
8. vertebral (spinal) foramen

Figure 4-40.   Seventh cervical vertebra.

55

KEY TO FIGURE 4-41

1. costal demifacet
2. body
3. vertebral notch
4. superior articular process
5. facet for rib
6. transverse process
7. inferior articular
   process
8. spinous process

KEY TO FIGURE 4-42

1. spinous process
2. vertebral (spinal)
   foramen
3. inferior articular process
4. lamina
5. transverse process
6. superior articular
   process
7. pedicle
8. body (centrum)

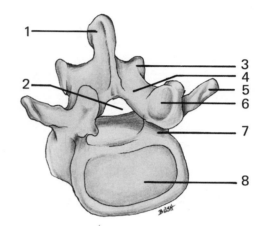

Figure 4-41.   Typical thoracic vertebra.   **Figure 4-42.   Typical lumbar vertebra.**

KEY TO FIGURE 4-43

1. ala
2. lateral mass
3. pelvic surface
4. articular process
5. articular surface
6. sacral promontory
7. anterior sacral foramen
8. body of 3rd sacral vertebra
9. coccyx

**Figure 4-43.   The sacrum and coccyx
(ventral aspect).**

KEY TO FIGURE 4-44

A-G. seven true ribs
H-L. five false ribs
K and L. two floating ribs
✳ ⎡5, 8, and 9. sternum⎤

1. clavicular notch
2. suprasternal notch
   (jugular notch)
3. sternal angle
4. costal notch

5. manubrium
6. costal cartilage
7. rib
8. body (gladiolus)
9. xiphoid (ensiform) process
10. intervertebral disc
11. 12th thoracic vertebra
12. floating rib

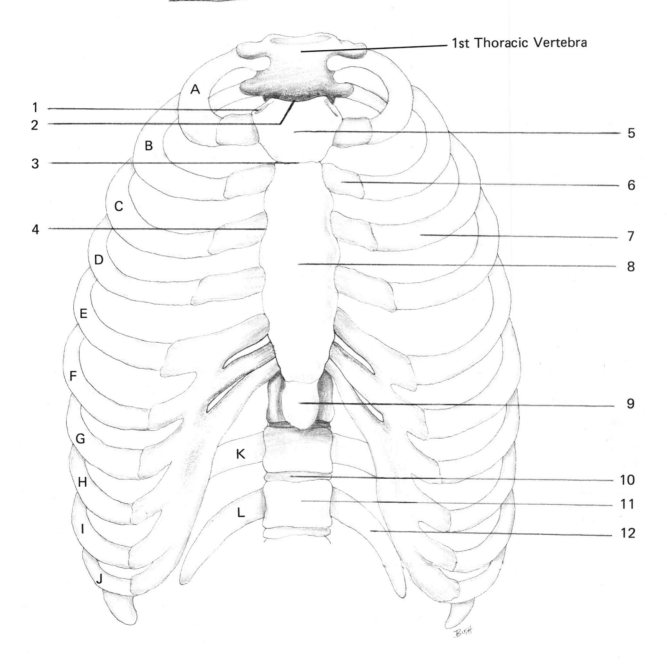

Figure 4-44.   The bony thorax.

EXERCISE 4-C
THE FETAL SKELETON

Objective

To compare the fetal skeleton with the adult skeleton.

Materials

Skeletons of an adult and a fetus.

Discussion

The number of separate bones in the fetus and child is greater than the 206 found in the typical adult skeleton. This is due to the fact that many bones in the adult are composed of several parts fused together; these parts are separate bones in the fetus and child. For example, in a child the three regions of the os coxae bone (the ilium, ischium, and pubis) form separate bones; in the adult these have united to make one hip bone.

Procedure

1. Use Figures 4-45 and 4-46, two views of the skull at birth, as self-tests.
2. Examine the fetal and adult skeletons and observe any differences in degree of ossification. Give special attention in the fetal skeleton to the structures listed below. Compare the bone or process with the corresponding structure in the adult. Record your observations in the chart under Results and Questions.
   a. Frontal bone.
   b. Sternum.
   c. Patella.
   d. Os coxae.
   e. Spinous processes of vertebrae.
   f. Carpals.

KEY TO FIGURE 4-45

1. frontal bone
2. frontal suture
3. anterior (frontal) fontanel
4. sagittal suture
5. parietal bone
6. posterior (occipital) fontanel
7. lambdoidal suture
8. occipital bone

KEY TO FIGURE 4-46

1. coronal suture
2. lambdoidal suture
3. anterolateral fontanel
4. squamosal suture
5. posterolateral fontanel

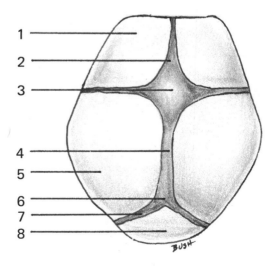

Figure 4-45. Fetal skull (superior surface).

Figure 4-46. Fetal skull (lateral view).

g. Proximal epiphysis of humerus.
3. Determine the sex of the fetal skeleton.

EXERCISE 4-D
JOINTS

Objective

To determine the structure of a typical joint.

Materials

Beef knee joint; x-ray viewing box; x-rays of bones and joints.

Discussion

A joint is the site of articulation between two bones. Joints may be divided into three classes, depending on the amount of movement between the articulating bones: synarthroses (immovable joints), amphiarthroses (slightly movable joints), and diarthroses (freely movable joints). Joints may also be divided into five classes, based on the structure of the joint (synostoses, syndesmoses, synchondroses, symphyses, and synovial joints). Most of the common joints in the body are freely movable synovial joints.

Procedure

1. The instructor will demonstrate a series of x-ray films. This will give you an opportunity to study the bones and joints as they are commonly seen in the hospital or doctor's office.
2. Study Figure 4-47 and your text. In what ways does the shoulder joint differ from the knee joint?
3. Study Figures 4-48 and 4-49; then locate the following structures on a prepared section through a beef knee joint.
   a. Synovial membrane.
   b. Articular cartilage.
   c. Synovial fluid (joint cavity).
   d. Ligaments.
   e. Tendons.
   f. Patella.

Figure 4-47.   Shoulder joint (anterior view).

Figure 4-48.   Knee joint (anterior view).

Figure 4-49.   Knee joint (lateral view, sagittal section).

SELF-TEST—SKELETAL SYSTEM

Directions

See Chapter 1, Self-Test, page 9.

1. The **malleus** is attached to the tympanic membrane.

2. Bones **lack** blood vessels.

3. The **periosteum** is the membrane responsible for nourishing the bone.

4. A **greenstick** fracture is one wherein the bone breaks the skin.

5. The **pelvic girdle** is actually several bones joined together for the protection of organs in the **pelvic** region.

6. The **floating** ribs provide protection for the heart.

7. The toes contain **a greater** number of bones than the fingers.

8. Ossification begins at the **epiphyses** and extends to the **diaphysis**.

9. Spongy bone is found in **flat bones** as well as in **long bones**.

10. The function of the **trochlea** is to articulate with the ulna.

11. Haversian systems are responsible for nutrition in **compact** bony tissue.

12. Haversian systems are characteristic of **spongy** bone.

13. Red bone marrow is found in the **medullary cavity** of some long bones of the adult.

14. The constricted portion of a long bone is called the **shaft**.

15. **Epiphyses** of bones tend to be **rounded** into condyles, trochanters, and heads.

16. The acetabulum is the socket in which the head of the **humerus** articulates.

17. During childhood, the long bones of the extremities continue to grow at the **epiphyseal cartilage**.

18. Hemopoiesis may occur in the adult in the **ribs and sternum**.

19. The lining of the medullary cavity is called the **periosteum**.

20. The primary curves of the vertebral column are the thoracic and **lumbar**.

21. Bending the elbow is an example of **flexion**.

22. Styloid processes are found upon the radius, ulna, and temporal, **but not** on the femur.

23. The fusion time of the anterior fontanel of the baby's skull is approximately **18 months**.

24. The **longitudinal arch** extends from the heel to the base of the toes.

25. Touching the little finger with the thumb is called **opposition**.

26. The iliopectineal line is found in the **skull**.

27. The **sella turcica** contains the pituitary gland.

28. The **male** pelvis has a circular pelvic inlet.

29. The **female** pelvis includes wide, flared ilia.

30. Spinal nerves are transmitted by way of **intervertebral foramina**.

31. The spinal cord is located in the **neural arches**.

32. The nasal septum is composed of the **ethmoid** and **vomer** bones, as well as hyaline cartilage.

33. The air sinuses which open directly into the nasal cavity **do not** include the mastoid sinus.

34. The **secondary curves** of the vertebral column are the cervical and lumbar.

35. Movement of the ankle to turn the sole outward is called **eversion**.

36. The condyles of the occipital bone and the depressions of the **atlas** allow for nodding movements of the head.

37. In turning the head from side to side the **atlas** rotates around a process of the axis called the **dens**.

38. A **foramen** is a tube-shaped passageway.

39. A hollow or depression is called a **cavity**.

40. A small, rounded projection is a **tuberosity**.

41. **Synchondroses** are freely movable joints with joint cavities.

42. **Circumduction** combines several types of joint movement.

43. **Both** prominent bursae and articular capsules may be present at ball and socket and hinge joints.

44. A **symphysis** joint occurs between bodies of vertebrae.

45. The elbow is an example of a **ball and socket** joint.

46. Swinging the arms around at the shoulder is an example of **circumduction**.

47. The position of the foot when standing on the toes is known as **plantar flexion**.

48. Nodding the head involves **both flexion and extension**.

49. Moving the arms straight out from the sides is called **adduction**.

50. Bending the trunk backward is an example of **extension**.

51. Moving the thigh forward, as in marching, is an example of **flexion**.

52. Spreading the fingers apart is an example of **adduction**.

53. Turning the palm of the hand up is an example of **pronation**.

54. Shaking the head is an example of **rotation**.

55. A major function of the bony rib cage is to protect the soft organs within the **abdomen**.

56. A **sulcus** is a groove or furrow.

57. Lateral curvature of the spine is called **kyphosis**.

58. A **sprain** is a joint injury with stretching or tearing of the ligaments.

59. Moving a bone backward is known as **retraction**.

60. A patient was diagnosed as having a greenstick fracture, left femur. The difference between this and an ordinary fracture is that this is **a clean break**.

61. Judging from the diagnosis the patient is a child, because children have more organic matter in their bones than adults so that their bones are more likely to **break clean**.

62. The x-rays showed obvious bands of cartilage near the epiphyses, which meant that this patient's bones **were still growing**.

63. The **periosteum** is important during healing of a fracture because it nourishes the bone and promotes growth and repair.

64. Milk products provide **calcium**, which is essential in building strong bones.

65. A **deviated nasal septum**, which means the partition between the nasal cavities is bent to one side, may obstruct breathing.

66. An increase in the thoracic curvature is called **lordosis or swayback**.

67. In a sternal puncture **yellow** marrow is obtained from the sternum.

68. A baby is born who has a spina bifida. This congenital defect is caused by a failure of the **vertebral laminae** to unite.

5

Physical Transport of Materials

Objectives

To compare filterable materials with non-filterable materials; to demonstrate the importance of pressure induced by the weight of a fluid column.

Materials

Funnel; filter paper; test tube; cylinder; Lugol's solution; a mixture of charcoal, copper sulfate, and 0.5% boiled starch in water.

Discussion

Filtration is concerned with the passage of substances in solution through a membrane. If filter paper, serving as the membrane, is placed in a funnel which is then filled with fluid, the fluid will be seen to drip through rapidly when the funnel is full, but as the height of the fluid decreases, the individual drops appear less frequently.

The rate of drop formation depends upon the surface area allowed for filtration and the hydrostatic pressure (i.e., the weight of the fluid column). In this experiment it is gravity that "pulls" the particles of the substance through the pores of the membrane (filter).

Additional force could be exerted by other means. If, for example, the upper part of the filter were contained in the tubular system that was closed and possessed a pump, an increase in pressure could be exerted upon the filter. In the circulatory system of the body, both gravity and pumping contribute to the hydrostatic pressure exerted at capillary membranes (the filter). A prime example of filtration in the human body occurs in the kidneys.

In the following experiment, copper sulfate is used as an example of a crystalloid, starch as a colloid, and charcoal as an example of particles forming a suspension.

Procedure

1. Fold a piece of filter paper in quarters and place in a funnel. Add a few drops of water to fix the paper in position.
2. Place the funnel in a cylinder, as illustrated in Figure 5-1.
3. Shake the mixture of powdered wood charcoal (black), copper sulfate (blue), starch (white), and water and pour into the funnel until it almost reaches the top edge of the filter paper.
4. To observe the difference in rate of filtration as the height of the solution in the funnel decreases, count the number of drops passing through the filter in the first 10 seconds. (Make an estimate if an exact count is not possible.) _____
5. When the fluid level is reduced by about one-third, count the number of drops passing through the filter for a period of 10 seconds. _____
6. Repeat this procedure when the level is reduced by about two-thirds. _____
7. Record these results under Results and Questions.
8. It is not necessary to continue filtration until the funnel is empty. Observe which substances passed through the filter paper by their color. Check the filter paper to

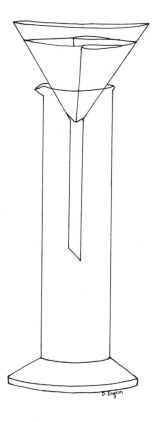

Figure 5-1. Setup for filtration experiment.

determine whether any colored particles were not filterable.

9. To determine whether starch passed through the filter paper, place approximately 2 ml of the filtrate in a test tube; add a few drops of Lugol's solution. A pale-blue to blue-black color indicates that starch is present.

EXERCISE 5-B
DIFFUSION

Objective

To become familiar with the process of diffusion.

Discussion

Diffusion is the dispersion of substances as a result of the movement of their ions or molecules. Under appropriate conditions, gas particles may diffuse into another gas, a liquid, or a solid; a liquid may diffuse into a gas, another liquid, or a solid; and a solid may diffuse into a gas, a liquid, or another solid. Diffusion of solute particles occurs from a region of higher concentration of the particles to a region of lower concentration of the particles. When equilibrium is reached, diffusion occurs equally in all directions. Since the living cells of organisms are not actively involved in the process, diffusion is considered a passive transport mechanism.

PART 1. DIFFUSION OF A LIQUID INTO A GAS
Objective

To demonstrate the diffusion rate of ether into the atmosphere.

Materials

Ethyl ether; a petri dish.

Procedure

1. Close all doors and windows in the classroom.
2. Ether will now be poured into a petri dish at the front of the room.
3. Obtain the following data and record them in Results and Questions:
   a. The exact time the ether was poured into the petri dish.
   b. The seconds required for the first student to detect the odor. (Students will raise their hands as soon as they detect the odor.)
   c. The seconds required for students in the first row to detect the odor.
   d. The seconds required for students in each subsequent row to detect the odor.
   e. The percentage of students detecting the odor at the conclusion of the experiment.
4. The experiment will be conducted for a minimum of 5 minutes.

PART 2. DIFFUSION OF A SOLID IN A LIQUID
Objective

To demonstrate the diffusion of potassium permanganate in water.

Materials

A crystal of potassium permanganate; a beaker of water.

Procedure

1. Drop a single crystal of potassium permanganate into a beaker of water.
2. Observe this preparation when made and then at intervals during the laboratory period. The container should not be touched or disturbed in any way. Record your observations under Results and Questions.

PART 3. DIFFUSION OF A SOLID IN AGAR

Objective

To demonstrate the relationship between molecular weight and speed of diffusion.

Materials

Petri dishes containing 2% agar; crystals (of equal size) of potassium permanganate and methyl orange.

Discussion

Agar molecules form a colloid when mixed with water. The molecules of the crystals used in this experiment diffuse through water channels in the agar.

The molecular weight of potassium permanganate is 158; that of methyl orange is 327.

Procedure

1. Place a single crystal of potassium permanganate and a single crystal of methyl orange about 2 inches apart on a film of agar in a petri dish.
2. After 1/2 hour observe the size of the colored ring around each crystal. Record your observations under Results and Questions.
3. At the completion of all observations, scrape the agar into a paper towel, wrap securely, and place in the wastepaper basket. Clean and dry the petri dish.

EXERCISE 5-C
DIALYSIS

Objective

To demonstrate the types of substances that are dialyzable.

Materials

Dialysis shell or tubing; prepared solution containing sodium chloride, glucose, albumin, and starch in distilled water; distilled water; Benedict's solution; concentrated nitric acid; Lugol's solution; 1% silver nitrate solution ($AgNO_3$); beaker; test tubes; bunsen burner; Clinistix; and Albustix.

Discussion

Since some qualitative tests are to be made in this experiment, it is important that certain precautions be taken to prevent contamination. Because of the presence of chlorides in tap water, only distilled water should be used throughout this exercise in preparing solutions and in washing test tubes or other glassware.

Procedure

1. Rinse all equipment (beaker, dialysis shell, and one test tube) with a small amount of distilled water.
2. Place a prepared solution containing starch, sodium chloride, glucose, and albumin in a dialysis shell. Be very careful not to spill any liquid down the outside of the membrane. Do not touch the membrane on the part that is to placed in the water (i.e., below the planned waterline) because of the salt contained in perspiration.
3. Place the dialysis shell in a beaker of distilled water.
4. After 1 hour perform the following tests on the water in the beaker to see which, if any, of the materials placed in the dialysis shell have diffused through it.
   a. Sodium chloride: Place about 2 ml of the beaker water into a clean test tube and add several drops of silver nitrate ($AgNO_3$). The formation of a white cloudy precipitate indicates the presence of sodium chloride.
   b. Starch: Place about 2 ml of the beaker water into a test tube. Add several drops of Lugol's solution. A blue or blue-black color is positive for starch.
   c. Glucose: Place about 5 ml of Benedict's solution into a test tube and add to it 5 ml of beaker water. Boil for 2 minutes. Formation of a green, yel-

low, orange, or red color or precipitate in the test tube is positive for glucose. If the test is negative, repeat with a larger amount of beaker water.

d. Clinistix test for glucose: Dip the test end of the strip briefly into the beaker water. Tap the edge of the strip against the side of the container. *Exactly 10 seconds* after removing the strip from the beaker water, compare the tip with the color chart. A positive test is indicated by a purple color in the test area. If the test is negative, the test area remains red. This test is specific for glucose.

e. Albumin: Place 2 ml of beaker water in a test tube. Tilt the test tube and carefully add several drops of concentrated nitric acid (HNO_3) so that it moves down the inner wall of the tube. The acid will cause a white coagulum to appear if the test is positive.

f. Abustix test for albumin: Dip the test area of the strip into the beaker water and remove it immediately. Tap the edge of the strip against the container. Immediately (up to 1 minute after dipping) compare the test area with the color chart.

EXERCISE 5-D
PLASMOLYSIS

Objective

To demonstrate osmotic relationships through the process of plasmolysis.

Materials

Elodea; slide; cover glass; 8% sodium chloride (NaCl) solution.

Discussion

Elodea is a water plant with numerous relatively small leaves which are only two cells thick. An entire leaf may thus be observed under the microscope and some of the characteristics of living cells can be studied. In contrast to animal cells, plant cells include (outside the plasma membrane) a permeable cell wall consisting primarily of cellulose (a polysaccharide) which provides them with a varying degree of rigidity. In green plants, such as *Elodea,* specialized structures called chloroplasts (absent in animal cells) may be observed. These are involved in the process of photosynthesis (manufacture of food using light as the source of energy). Plant cells also contain a large central vacuole which contains approximately 5% dissolved substances.

Procedure

1. Remove a healthy looking leaf from a sprig of *Elodea* found in the container at the front of the room and mount it on a clean slide. Add 1 or 2 drops of water to the leaf from the container and cover with a cover glass.

2. Locate a cell that is typical of the majority. The green bodies are chloroplasts. See Figure 5-2, which may be used as a self-test, to aid in identification of the structures in the cell. (Optional—draw a typical cell.)

3. With the cell in focus, remove the water from under the cover glass by holding a piece of paper towel or blotting paper at its edge. When most of the water has been removed, introduce an 8% solution of NaCl by holding a pipette (medicine dropper) at the edge of the cover glass and gently squeezing out the fluid (which will move under the cover glass). Continue this procedure until the leaf is completely surrounded by the solution.

4. Immediately observe the cell (or cells) you were looking at previously. Continue these observations until distinct changes occur.

5. Draw one or two cells in which a noticeable change has occurred.

6. Remove the leaf and soak it in distilled water for 5 minutes, then remount it. Examine the leaf to observe whether plasmolysis is reversible.

EXERCISE 5-E
OSMOSIS

Objective

To demonstrate the occurrence of osmosis by means of an osmometer.

KEY TO FIGURE 5-2

1. nucleolus
2. nuclear membrane
3. nucleoplasm
4. chromatin
5. nucleus
6. cell wall
7. plasma membrane
8. cytoplasm
9. vacuole
10. chloroplast

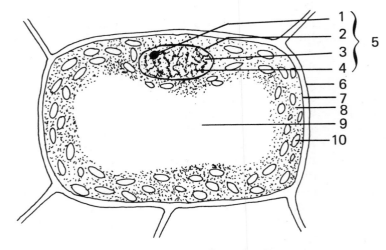

Figure 5-2.   Elodea cell.

Materials

Osmometer containing a 10% NaCl solution stained with methylene blue; a beaker of water.

Procedure

1. Examine the demonstration osmometer. Compare this setup with that illustrated in Figure 5-3.
2. Note the level of the fluid in the tube at the beginning of the laboratory period and again near the end of the period.

EXERCISE 5-F
HEMOLYSIS AND CRENATION

Objectives

To demonstrate hemolysis and crenation.

Materials

Test tubes; slides; cover glasses; 0.9% (or 0.15 M) NaCl; distilled water; 3% NaCl; blood (human or ox).

Discussion

The term "hemolysis" is used to indicate a special case of lysis in erythrocytes wherein the hemoglobin is lost from the cell. A 0.9% (or 0.15 M) solution of NaCl forms an isotonic solution for erythrocytes. Hemolysis may occur when such cells are placed in a sufficiently

Figure 5-3.   Apparatus for osmosis demonstration.

hypotonic solution, due to movement of water into the cells by osmosis. Hemolysis also occurs when the erythrocytes (RBCs) are placed in a solvent (e.g., ether) that destroys the plasma membrane, or when solute particles can penetrate the plasma membrane.

Blood becomes a transparent cherry red color (instead of a dull opaque color) when the hemoglobin becomes uniformly dissolved in the surrounding liquid. Thus, a change in blood from opacity to transparency may be regarded as an indication of the occurrence of hemolysis.

When cells are placed in hypertonic solutions they may become wrinkled in appearance. The shrinking is due to the loss of water from the cell owing to osmosis. This process is known as crenation.

Procedure

1. Add 3 to 5 drops of blood to a test tube containing 2 ml of 0.9% (or 0.15 M) NaCl solution.
2. Add the same amount of blood to a second test tube containing 2 ml of distilled water.
3. Add the same amount of blood to a third test tube containing 2 ml of 3% NaCl solution.
4. Compare the transparency of the three solutions by looking at a printed page through each tube. Record your observations under Results and Questions.
5. Mount 1 or 2 drops of the solution from each of the three test tubes on clean glass slides. Cover with a cover glass and observe with the microscope (on high power).
6. In the appropriate spaces below, draw three or four cells as observed from each test tube.

0.9% (or 0.15 M) NaCl	Distilled water	3% NaCl

SELF-TEST—PHYSICAL TRANSPORT OF MATERIALS

Directions

See Chapter 1, Self-Test, page 9.

1. In **active** transport, no energy is expended by the cell in the transfer of material.
2. Active transport involves movement of ions **against** a concentration gradient.
3. Hydrostatic pressure **increases** as the height of a column of fluid increases.
4. The rate of filtration through capillary walls is **the same** in all parts of the body.
5. Diffusion occurs as the result of **the constant motion of molecules.**
6. Osmotic pressure is **proportional to the number of particles** in the solution.
7. A **hypotonic** solution has a higher osmotic pressure than the blood.
8. The living cell is surrounded by a **permeable** membrane.
9. The principal **cation** in intracellular fluid is K⁺.
10. In active transport, solutes pass from the **more** concentrated to the **less** concentrated solution.
11. Hydrostatic pressure is **higher** in the glomerulus than in other capillaries; this is largely responsible for filtration of blood in the kidneys.
12. Hemolysis of erythrocytes occurs in a **hypertonic** solution.
13. Plasmolysis is the rounding up of plant cell protoplasm due to a loss of **salt.**
14. The concentration of sodium chloride in a physiological saline solution is **0.9%.**

15. A **hypertonic** solution is a solution more dilute than the solution of a cell.

16. **Filtration** is the passage of water and dissolved substances through a membrane due to a difference in hydrostatic pressure on the two sides of the membrane.

17. Diffusion is the movement of molecules of a substance from a region of **lower** concentration (of the substance) to one of **higher** concentration.

18. A cell containing 0.5% NaCl is placed in a solution of 7% NaCl. Water **leaves** the cell.

19. An **isometric** solution is one that has the same concentration of dissolved substances as the cell.

20. Crenation occurs in a **hypertonic** solution.

21. Speed of diffusion is **directly** proportional to molecular weight.

22. Iodine is used to test for the presence of **albumin.**

23. **Protein** passes through the wall of a dialysis shell.

24. Particles forming **a suspension** will pass through filter paper.

25. Colloidal suspensions of liquids within liquids are called **colloids.**

26. A colloidal suspension can be separated from a true solution by the process of **dialysis.**

27. Diffusion of water through a semipermeable membrane from a region of high water concentration to a region of low water concentration is called **osmosis.**

28. The direction of diffusion is determined primarily by the **size** of the diffusing particles.

29. The direction in which a substance moves through a membrane by osmosis depends mainly upon differences **in concentration of water molecules.**

30. A colloid solute particle is **larger** than a crystalloid solute particle.

31. Only the solvent moves through a membrance by osmosis, but both solute and solvent may move through a membrane by **diffusion or filtration.**

32. **Diffusion, osmosis, and filtration** are related to the concentrations of the solution on both sides of a membrane.

33. The size of red blood cells immersed in 0.9% glucose would be **greater** than those immersed in 0.9% sodium chloride.

34. Diffusion of one substance through another is slowed down **by heating.**

35. Glucose and fructose both have the empirical formula $C_6 H_{12} O_6$; thus they are **isotopes.**

6

The Muscular System

EXERCISE 6-A
GROSS ANATOMY OF THE MAJOR SUPERFICIAL HUMAN MUSCLES

Objectives

To become familiar with the location and action of selected major human muscles.

Materials

Text; reference books; anatomic charts; dissectable torso.

Discussion

The basic function of muscle is to produce movement of the body or part of the body. In addition, muscles serve to protect the internal organs, maintain posture, and produce a large amount of body heat.

The muscles studied in this exercise are skeletal muscles. See Chapter 3 for the histology of skeletal, smooth, and cardiac muscle. The student should learn in this exercise the names of the major superficial muscles of the body and their actions.

Procedure

1. Study Figures 6-1 through 6-14 showing human muscles.
2. Each of the preceding figures may be used as self-tests.
3. Following is a list of muscles that are especially significant in the field of nursing. (Your instructor may want to add to this list.) You should be able to locate most of these muscles on Figures 6-1 through 6-14.
4. Using your text and other references, locate and learn the origin, insertion, and action for each of the muscles in this list (or for those your instructor indicates).
5. To contract, a skeletal muscle must receive a message from a nerve (or nerve fiber) that has been stimulated. Using your text or other reference, identify the source of innervation for each of the muscles.

SELECTED MUSCLES

1. pectoralis major
2. pectoralis minor
3. serratus anterior
4. trapezius
5. latissimus dorsi
6. deltoid
7. biceps brachii
8. brachialis
9. triceps brachii
10. brachioradialis
11. gluteus maximus
12. gluteus medius
13. gluteus minimus
14. tensor fasciae latae
15. iliopsoas
16. sartorius
17. quadriceps femoris, which includes the:
    a. rectus femoris
    b. vastus lateralis
    c. vastus medialis
    d. vastus intermedius

list continued on page 78

KEY TO FIGURE 6-1

1. FRONTALIS
2. TEMPORALIS
3. ORBICULARIS OCULI
4. LEVATOR LABII SUPERIORIS
5. MASSETER
6. STERNOCLEIDOMASTOIDEUS
7. OMOHYOIDEUS
8. TRAPEZIUS
9. STERNOHYOIDEUS
10. PECTORALIS MAJOR
11. SERRATUS ANTERIOR
12. TRICEPS BRACHII
13. BRACHIALIS
14. BRACHIORADIALIS
15. EXTENSOR CARPI RADIALIS LONGUS
16. EXTENSOR CARPI RADIALIS BREVIS
17. FLEXOR DIGITORUM SUPERFICIALIS
18. GLUTEUS MEDIUS
19. FLEXOR POLLICIS LONGUS
20. FLEXOR CARPI ULNARIS
21. ABDUCTOR POLLICIS BREVIS
22. SHEATHS OF FLEXOR TENDONS
23. VASTUS LATERALIS
24. FASCIA LATA
25. SOLEUS
26. PERONEUS LONGUS
27. TIBIALIS ANTERIOR
28. EXTENSOR DIGITORUM LONGUS
29. PERONEUS BREVIS
30. EXTENSOR DIGITORUM BREVIS
31. PROCERUS
32. NASALIS
33. ZYGOMATICUS MINOR
34. ZYGOMATICUS MAJOR
35. ORBICULARIS ORIS
36. DEPRESSOR ANGULI ORIS
37. PLATYSMA
38. DELTOIDEUS
39. LATISSIMUS DORSI
40. BICEPS BRACHII
41. TRICEPS BRACHII
42. RECTUS ABDOMINIS
43. EXTERNAL ABDOMINAL OBLIQUE
44. FLEXOR CARPI RADIALIS
45. PALMARIS LONGUS
46. PSOAS MAJOR
47. TENSOR FASCIAE LATAE
48. PECTINEUS
49. SARTORIUS
50. GRACILIS
51. RECTUS FEMORIS
52. RICHER'S BAND
53. VASTUS MEDIALIS
54. PATELLA
55. TIBIA
56. GASTROCNEMIUS
57. SOLEUS
58. FLEXOR DIGITORUM LONGUS

Figure 6-1.   Anterior view of the muscles.

KEY TO FIGURE 6-2

1. TRAPEZIUS
2. TRICEPS BRACHII
3. OLECRANON PROCESS
4. EXTENSOR CARPI RADIALIS LONGUS
5. EXTENSOR DIGITORUM COMMUNIS
6. EXTENSOR CARPI ULNARIS
7. TENDON OF EXTENSOR INDICIS
8. GRACILIS
9. SEMITENDINOSUS
10. SOLEUS
11. CALCANEAL TENDON
12. TIBIALIS POSTERIOR
13. OCCIPITALIS
14. SPLENIUS CAPITIS
15. DELTOIDEUS
16. INFRASPINATUS
17. TERES MAJOR
18. TRICEPS BRACHII
19. LATISSIMUS DORSI

20. EXTERNAL OBLIQUE
21. TENDON OF LATISSIMUS DORSI
22. ABDUCTOR POLLICIS LONGUS
23. GLUTEUS MEDIUS
24. EXTENSOR POLLICIS BREVIS
25. GLUTEUS MAXIMUS
26. ADDUCTOR MAGNUS
27. FASCIAE LATAE
28. VASTUS LATERALIS
29. BICEPS FEMORIS
30. SEMIMEMBRANOSUS
31. SARTORIUS
32. SEMITENDINOSUS
33. PLANTARIS
34. GASTROCNEMIUS
35. PERONEUS LONGUS
36. PERONEUS BREVIS
37. FLEXOR HALLUCIS LONGUS
38. EXTENSOR DIGITORUM BREVIS

Figure 6-2.   Posterior view of the muscles.

KEY TO FIGURE 6-3

1. buccinator
2. depressor labii inferioris
3. mentalis
4. platysma
5. orbicularis oris
6. risorius
7. zygomaticus major
8. levator labii superioris
9. orbicularis oculi
10. frontalis

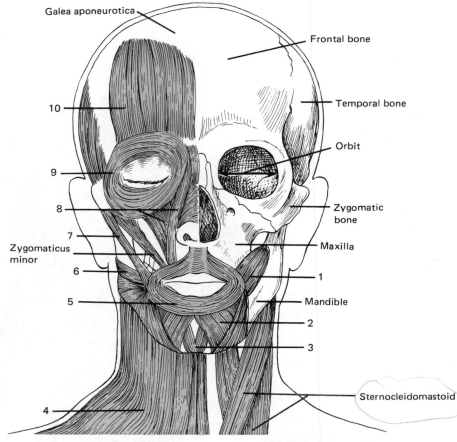

Figure 6-3. Muscles of facial expression.

a. **Anterior superficial view.**   b. **Anterior deep view.**

KEY TO FIGURE 6-4

1. frontalis
2. orbicularis oculi
3. levator labii superioris
4. zygomaticus major
5. buccinator
6. orbicularis oris
7. risorius
8. platysma
9. occipitalis

c. **Right lateral superficial view.**

Figure 6-4. Muscles of facial expression.

KEY TO FIGURE 6-5

1. temporalis
2. masseter
3. lateral pterygoid
4. medial pterygoid

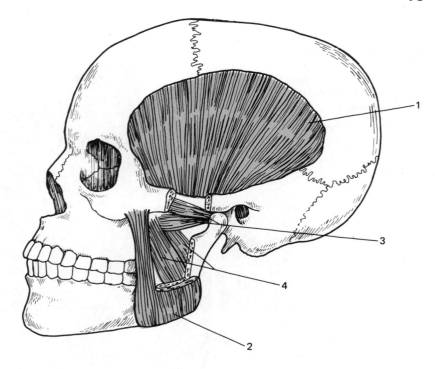

Figure 6-5.   Muscles that move the lower jaw.

KEY TO FIGURE 6-6

1. internal oblique
2. transversus abdominis
3. rectus abdominis
4. external oblique

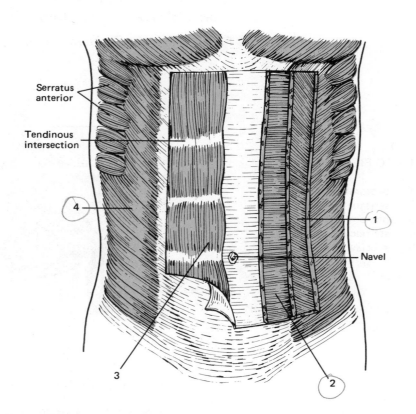

Figure 6-6.   Muscles of the anterior abdominal wall.

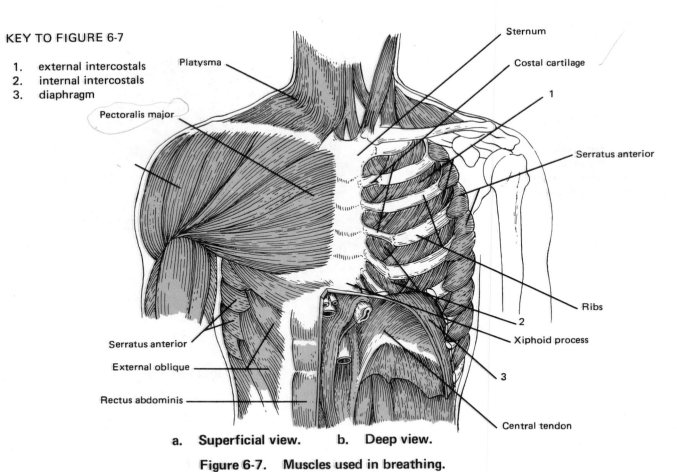

KEY TO FIGURE 6-7

1. external intercostals
2. internal intercostals
3. diaphragm

Platysma

Pectoralis major

Sternum

Costal cartilage

1

Serratus anterior

Ribs

2

Xiphoid process

3

Serratus anterior

External oblique

Rectus abdominis

Central tendon

a. **Superficial view.**   b. **Deep view.**

Figure 6-7.   Muscles used in breathing.

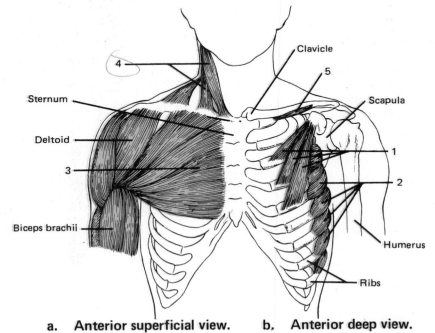

KEY TO FIGURE 6-8

1. pectoralis minor
2. serratus anterior
3. pectoralis major
4. sternocleidomastoid
5. subclavius

4

Sternum

Deltoid

3

Biceps brachii

Clavicle

5

Scapula

1

2

Humerus

Ribs

a. **Anterior superficial view.**   b. **Anterior deep view.**

Figure 6-8.   Muscles that move the shoulder girdle.

KEY TO FIGURE 6-9

1. supraspinatus
2. infraspinatus
3. teres minor
4. teres major
5. latissimus dorsi
6. deltoid

Figure 6-9. Muscles that move the arm.

a. **Posterior superficial view.**   b. **Posterior deep view.**

KEY TO FIGURE 6-10

1. triceps brachii
2. brachioradialis
3. brachialis
4. pronator teres
5. supinator
6. biceps brachii

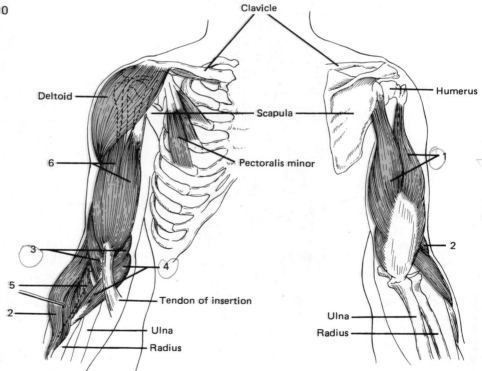

Figure 6-10. Muscles that move the forearm.

KEY TO FIGURE 6-11

1. extensor carpi radialis longus
2. extensor digitorum communis
3. extensor indicis proprius
4. extensor carpi ulnaris
5. flexor carpi radialis
6. flexor carpi ulnaris
7. flexor digitorum profundus
8. flexor digitorum superficialis

Figure 6-11. Muscles that move the wrist and fingers.

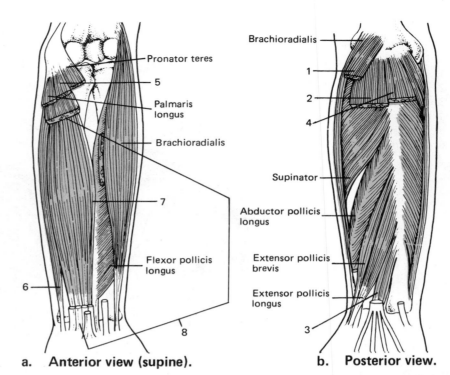

a. Anterior view (supine).

b. Posterior view.

KEY TO FIGURE 6-12

1. gluteus medius
2. gluteus maximus
3. gluteus minimus
4. piriformis
5. obturator internus
6. adductor magnus
7. adductor longus
8. adductor brevis
9. pectineus
10. tensor fasciae latae
11. iliacus
12. psoas major

Figure 6-12. Muscles that move the thigh.

a. Anterior view.

b. Posterior view.

KEY TO FIGURE 6-13

1. semitendinosus
2. biceps femoris
3. semimembranosus
4. gracilis
5. sartorius
6. vastus medialis
7. vastus lateralis
8. vastus intermedius
9. rectus femoris

Figure 6-13. Muscles that act on the leg.

a. **Anterior view.**   b. **Posterior view.**

KEY TO FIGURE 6-14

1. peroneus longus
2. extensor digitorum longus
3. tibialis anterior
4. peroneus brevis
5. gastrocnemius
6. soleus
7. flexor digitorum longus
8. tibialis posterior
9. flexor hallucis longus

Figure 6-14. Muscles that move the foot and toes.

a. **Anterior view.**   b. **Posterior view.**

18. gracilis
19. adductor muscles including the:
    a. adductor longus
    b. adductor brevis
    c. adductor magnus
20. biceps femoris
21. semitendinosus
22. semimembranosus
23. gastrocnemius
24. soleus
25. tibialis posterior
26. tibialis anterior
27. external oblique
28. internal oblique
29. transversus abdominis
30. rectus abdominis
31. quadratus lumborum
32. diaphragm
33. external intercostals
34. internal intercostals
35. sternocleidomastoid
36. sacrospinalis
37. muscles of perineum including the:
    a. levator ani
    b. coccygeus

EXERCISE 6-B
DISSECTION OF THE MUSCULAR SYSTEM OF THE FETAL PIG

Objectives

To identify selected muscles of the fetal pig and to compare them and their functions with corresponding human muscles.

Discussion

As you dissect the muscles of the pig, determine the major differences between them and those in man. As you locate the *origin* of the muscle (the site of attachment to a fixed bone) and the insertion (the attachment to a more freely movable bone), determine the function of the muscle. Remember that as a muscle contracts, it pulls the insertion toward the origin. Muscles are usually attached to bones by **tendons,** which are bands of dense white fibrous connective tissue. Some muscles insert by way of an aponeurosis.

In each of the following steps, attempt to locate each muscle before making any incisions. It will be necessary to clean the surface of each of the muscles, by gently pulling off or cutting away superficial fascia and fat, to see the direction of the muscle fibers. Usually all the fibers of a muscle run in one direction, while the fibers of an adjacent muscle run in a different direction.

Do not cut into the fibers of the muscles you are separating. The groups of fibers comprising a muscle are surrounded by deep fascia. This fascia should not be removed from the muscle. If the muscle fibers are visible, it means that the muscle has been cut into, rather than being separated from adjacent muscles.

To examine the deep muscles it is frequently necessary to sever a superficial muscle. Do not bisect a muscle unless directed to do so. To **bisect** means to cut into two parts. When bisecting a muscle, make an incision through it at right angles to the direction of the muscle fiber and halfway between the origin and the insertion. In order to see the underlying muscles, it is then necessary to *reflect* the superficial muscle (pull the ends back—one toward the origin and the other toward the insertion). If these directions are followed, the origin and insertion of the muscle will be retained.

Procedure

1. To remove the skin from your pig, make a small longitudinal incision through the skin in the middorsal neck region. Continue the incision down the midline of the back to the tail, pulling the cut edges as you proceed. Be careful not to cut through the underlying muscles.
2. Make additional incisions through the skin around the neck, down the lateral surface of each leg, and around the wrists and ankles.
3. Beginning on the back, gradually separate the skin from the underlying muscles. This can be done most easily by pulling the skin away from the body with one hand, using the dull end of your scalpel or your fingers to separate the skin from fascia and muscles. The skin should be left on the head, tail, feet, and genital region (including the scrotum and penis in the male).
4. Note the fine brownish muscle fibers that attach to the undersurface of the skin in the region posterior to the armpit. These are part of the **cutaneous maximus,** a

muscle that moves the skin of the pig but is not found in man.

5. Carefully remove the fat and connective tissue from the lateral surface of the left shoulder and neck.

6. Locate the **trapezius** muscle, a thin triangular muscle on the upper back (Fig. 6-15). Separate the anterior and posterior borders of this muscle from the underlying fascia. The trapezius moves the scapula dorsally and posteriorly.

7. The **brachiocephalic** is a thick, band-shaped muscle just anterior to the trapezius, extending from the back of the head behind the ear to the proximal humerus (Fig. 6-15). This muscle protracts the arm. Separate the muscle from the underlying fascia.

8. The **deltoid** extends from the spine of the scapula near the insertion of the trapezius to the proximal humerus next to the insertion of the brachiocephalic (Fig. 6-15). It is difficult to distinguish from adjacent muscles, but if the lateral shoulder region is carefully cleaned, the borders of the deltoid can be seen and freed from the underlying fascia. The deltoid flexes and abducts the arm.

9. The large triangular muscle on the back, posterior to the trapezius, is the **latissimus dorsi** (Fig. 6-15). Free both borders and separate the muscle from the underlying fascia. This muscle retracts the arm.

10. Place the pig on its back. Tie the arms out slightly, being careful not to tear the anterior chest muscles.

11. The **superficial pectoralis** extends from the sternum to the proximal humerus near the insertion of the brachiocephalic (Fig. 6-17). It adducts the arm. Bisect and reflect this muscle.

12. Deep to the superficial pectoralis is the **pectoralis profundus** (Fig. 6-17). It originates along the entire length of the sternum, the fibers extending anteriorly and laterally under the superficial pectoralis. This muscle may appear double, since the anterior band of fibers extends in front of the scapula and along its anterior border, while the posterior fibers insert ventrally on the proximal humerus. This muscle adducts and retracts the forelimb.

13. Remove the skin and fascia from the left side of the neck and face. Be careful not to remove the blood vessels, lymph nodes, and salivary glands in this region.

14. Examine the ventral surface of the neck. Locate the **sternomastoid**, the band-shaped muscle that extends from the sternum diagonally toward the mastoid region of the skull (Fig. 6-17). This muscle passes deep to the external jugular vein. The sternomastoid flexes the head. Free both borders of this muscle.

15. The **sternohyoids** are the narrow pair of muscles that lie along the midventral line of the neck (Fig. 6-17). These muscles extend from the sternum to the hyoid bone, and depress the hyoid. Free both borders of the left sternohyoid.

16. Locate the brachiocephalic muscle again. The thin band-shaped muscle just anterior to it is the **cleidomastoid** (Fig. 6-17). It is attached to the brachiocephalic near the point where the clavicle would be located if one were present, and extends diagonally toward the mastoid region of the skull. Free the cleidomastoid along both borders.

17. The **digastric** muscle is the superficial muscle extending along the inner surface of the mandible (Fig. 6-17). It runs from the base of the skull to the mandible, and opens the jaw.

18. The superficial muscle running transversely in the midline and passing deep to the digastric is the **mylohyoid** (Fig. 6-17). It is a thin sheetlike muscle that raises the floor of the mouth.

19. The large muscle mass located posterior to the angle of the jaw is the **masseter** muscle (Fig. 6-15). It extends from the zygomatic arch to the mandible, and closes the jaw.

20. Lay the pig back on its side. Bisect and reflect the trapezius muscle (Fig. 6-16).

21. Deep to the trapezius you will see three muscles that extend from the dorsal border of the scapula to the spines of the cervical and thoracic vertebrae. From anterior to posterior these are the **rhomboideus capitis**, a straplike muscle extending forward along the side of the neck, the **rhomboideus cervicis**, and the **rhomboideus thoracis** (Fig. 6-16). These muscles pull the scapula dorsally.

22. Deep to the rhomboideus capitis is a large muscle, the **splenius**, that covers most of

80

Figure 6-15. Lateral view of superficial muscles.

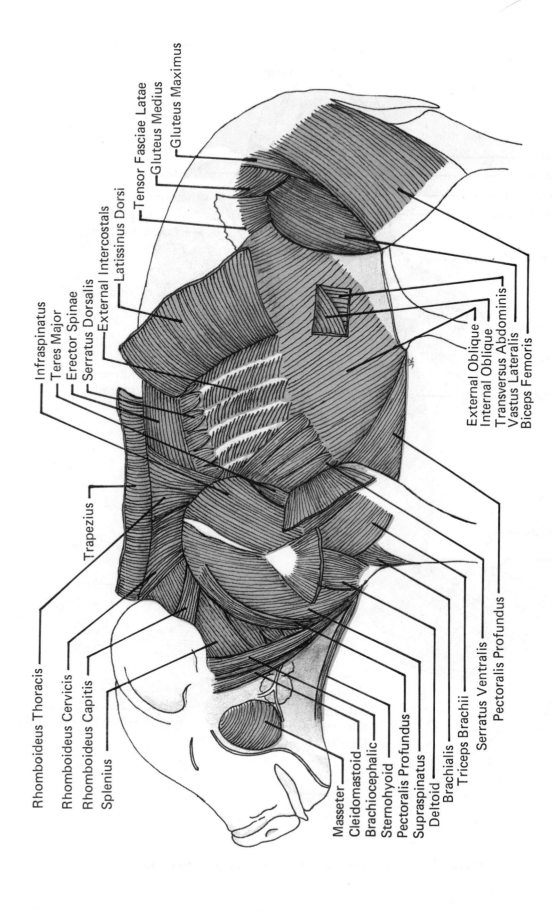

81

Infraspinatus
Teres Major
Erector Spinae
Serratus Dorsalis
External Intercostals
Latissinus Dorsi
Tensor Fasciae Latae
Gluteus Medius
Gluteus Maximus

External Oblique
Internal Oblique
Transversus Abdominis
Vastus Lateralis
Biceps Femoris

Trapezius

Rhomboideus Thoracis
Rhomboideus Cervicis
Rhomboideus Capitis
Splenius

Masseter
Cleidomastoid
Brachiocephalic
Sternohyoid
Pectoralis Profundus
Supraspinatus
Deltoid
Brachialis
Triceps Brachii
Serratus Ventralis
Pectoralis Profundus

Figure 6-16. Lateral view of deep muscles.

82

Digastric

Mylohyoid

Sternohyoid

Sternomastoid

Superficial Pectoralis

Pectoralis Profundus

Masseter

Cleidomastoid

Pectoralis Profundus

Coracobrachialis

Biceps Brachii

Triceps Brachii
(medial head)

Triceps Brachii
(long head)

Subscapularis

Serratus Ventralis

Sartorius

Gracilis

Psoas Major

Iliacus

Rectus Femoris

Vastus Medialis

Sartorius

Gracilis

Soleus

Gastrocnemius

Pectineus

Adductor

Semimembranosus

Semitendinosus

Figure 6-17.   Ventral view of superficial and deep muscles.

the dorsal and lateral surface of the neck (Fig. 6-16). Its function is to extend the head.

23. Locate the spine of the scapula on its lateral surface. The thick muscle anterior to the spine and passing deep to the anterior end of the pectoralis profundus is the **supraspinatus** (Fig. 6-16). Its fibers extend from the supraspinous fossa to the proximal humerus. The supraspinatus protracts the arm.

24. The muscle posterior to the scapular spine is the **infraspinatus** (Fig. 6-16). Only part of this muscle can be seen, since it passes deep to the deltoid. Lift the edge of the deltoid to more completely expose this muscle. The infraspinatus arises from the infraspinous fossa of the scapula and inserts on the proximal humerus; it rotates the arm laterally.

25. Bisect and reflect the latissimus dorsi. The small muscle along the posterior border of the scapula is the **teres major** (Fig. 6-16). It inserts on the proximal humerus with the latissimus dorsi.

26. Pull the arm and scapula laterally. The large fan-shaped muscle originating by separate slips from the ribs, passing deep to the scapula, and inserting on its dorsal border is the **serratus ventralis** (Fig. 6-16). This muscle is also visible on the lateral surface of the body anterior and posterior to the scapula (Fig. 6-15).

27. The subscapular fossa of the scapula is filled with the **subscapularis** muscle (Fig. 6-17), which inserts on the humerus and rotates it medially.

28. Carefully clean the fascia from the lateral and medial surfaces of the arm (be careful not to cut the blood vessels under the scapula). The large muscle on the posterior arm is the **triceps brachii**. This muscle consists of three heads, all of which insert on the proximal end of the ulna and extend the forearm. The **long head,** located on the posterior surface of the humerus, is the largest (Fig. 6-15). Free both borders of this muscle.

29. Locate the **lateral head** of the triceps just anterior to the long head on the lateral surface of the arm (Fig. 6-15). Free both borders.

30. The **medial head** of the triceps can be seen deep between the long and lateral heads, or on the medial surface of the arm deep to the large group of blood vessels and nerves (Fig. 6-17).

31. The **brachialis** is located on the ventrolateral surface of the humerus anterior to the lateral head of the triceps. It arises from the humerus and inserts on the proximal end of the ulna. The brachialis flexes the forearm (Fig. 6-16).

32. The **biceps brachii** lies on the ventromedial surface of the humerus. It can be seen by lifting the cut end of the superficial pectoralis (Fig. 6-17). The biceps brachii originates on the scapula and inserts on the radius; it flexes the forearm.

33. The small **coracobrachialis** can be seen just posterior to the proximal end of the biceps brachii (Fig. 6-17). It extends from the coracoid process of the scapula to the proximal humerus, and adducts the arm.

34. Clean off the ventral and lateral surfaces of the trunk. As in man, the lateral abdominal wall of the pig is composed of three layers of muscle. All three muscles help support and compress the abdomen.

35. The outermost of the lateral abdominal wall muscles is the **external oblique** (Fig. 6-16). Notice that the fibers of this muscle pass ventrally and posteriorly to insert along the **linea alba,** the midventral line of connective tissue formed by the union of the aponeuroses of the lateral abdominal wall muscles.

36. Make a shallow incision about 1½ inches long at right angles to the fibers of the external oblique on the lateral surface of the abdomen. Reflect back the cut edges of the external oblique to expose the **internal oblique** (Fig. 6-16). Notice that its fibers run ventral and anterior, or at right angles to those of the external oblique.

37. Make a shallow incision through the internal oblique at right angles to the fibers to reveal the **transversus abdominis** (Fig. 6-16).

38. To locate the **rectus abdominis,** the longitudinal band of muscle lying lateral to the linea alba, reflect the external oblique. The rectus abdominis extends from the pubis to the sternum and costal cartilages and helps support the abdominal wall.

39. To study the intercostal muscles, raise the posterior border of the origin of the serratus ventralis to expose the ribs. The

fibers of the **external intercostals** can be seen passing ventrally and posteriorly between the ribs (Fig. 6-16). The external intercostals lift the ribs in inspiration.

40. Bisect one external intercostal muscle to expose the **internal intercostals,** the fibers of which run at right angles to the external intercostals. The internal intercostals depress the ribs in forced expiration.

41. The thin muscle slips that arise from a middorsal aponeurosis and insert on the dorsal part of the ribs make up the **serratus dorsalis** (Fig. 6-16).

42. Reflect the serratus dorsalis by separating it from its origin to expose the **erector spinae** group of muscles (Fig. 6-16). The fibers of this muscle pass longitudinally on either side of the vertebral column and extend the spine.

43. Carefully remove the fat and fascia from the thigh and buttocks region.

44. A small triangular muscle, the **tensor fasciae latae,** can be seen on the anterolateral thigh (Fig. 6-15). It originates from the ilium and inserts on a layer of fascia (fascia lata) near the knee. The tensor fasciae latae tenses the fascia lata and extends the shank.

45. The broad muscle posterior to the tensor fasciae latae and covering most of the lateral surface of the thigh is the **biceps femoris** (Fig. 6-15). It originates on the sacrum and ischium and inserts on the tibia and fascia of the shank. It abducts and extends the thigh and flexes the shank. Free both borders of this muscle.

46. Locate the **gluteus maximus** between the biceps femoris and tensor fasciae latae (Fig. 6-15). Note that it may be partly fused to the biceps femoris.

47. Anterior to the gluteus maximus is the **gluteus medius,** whose fibers pass posteriorly and ventrally and go deep to those of the gluteus maximus (Fig. 6-15). It is a larger muscle than the gluteus maximus in the pig. The gluteus medius originates from the lateral ilium and inserts on the femur. It abducts and extends the thigh.

48. The straplike muscle arising from the ischial tuberosity and inserting on the tibia posterior and medial to the biceps femoris is the **semitendinosus** (Fig. 6-17). It extends the thigh and flexes the shank.

49. Carefully clean the fat and fascia from the medial surface of the thigh. The large,

wide, flat muscle covering the posterior half of the medial thigh is the **gracilis** (Fig. 6-17). Free both borders and then bisect and reflect this muscle. The gracilis originates on the pubis and inserts on the tibia and fascia of the shank. It adducts the thigh.

50. Anterior to the gracilis is the **sartorius,** a small band-shaped muscle (Fig. 6-17). Bisect and reflect the sartorius (this should expose the underlying femoral blood vessels). This muscle helps adduct the thigh.

51. The large muscle deep to the gracilis is the **semimembranosus** (Fig. 6-17). It originates on the ischium and inserts on the distal femur and proximal tibia. It extends and adducts the thigh. The semimembranosus, the semitendinosus, and the biceps femoris form the hamstring group of muscles.

52. The large triangular muscle just anterior to the semimembranosus is the **adductor** (Fig. 6-17). The origin of the adductor is on the ischium and pubis and it inserts on the femur; it adducts the thigh. The adductor muscle in the pig is not subdivided as it is in humans and some other mammals.

53. Locate the smaller **pectineus** muscle anterior to the adductor (Fig. 6-17). It also adducts the thigh.

54. Clean fascia from the region anterior and posterior to the proximal end of the femoral blood vessels. Two muscles can be seen passing deep to the blood vessels, the medial **psoas major** and the more lateral **iliacus** (Fig. 6-17). In man these two muscles fuse to form the iliopsoas. The psoas major arises from the lumbar vertebrae, and the iliacus from the ilium; together they insert on the proximal femur. These muscles rotate and flex the thigh.

55. To locate the **quadriceps femoris** group of muscles, bisect the fascia lata and reflect it and the tensor fasciae latae. The large muscle now exposed on the anterolateral surface of the thigh is the **vastus lateralis** (Fig. 6-16).

56. Medial to the vastus lateralis on the front of the thigh is the thick **rectus femoris** (Fig. 6-17).

57. The muscle on the ventral surface of the thigh medial to the rectus femoris is the **vastus medialis** (Fig. 6-17).

58. Carefully separate the vastus medialis from the rectus femoris. Bisect the rectus femoris. The fourth head of the quadriceps femoris, the **vastus intermedius,** can be seen deep to the rectus femoris. The three vastus muscles originate from the proximal femur, while the rectus femoris arises from the ilium; all four insert together by way of the patellar ligament on the anterior tibia. The entire complex extends the shank.
59. The large calf muscle, the **gastrocnemius,** is visible on the posterior leg (shank) (Fig. 6-17). It can be seen most easily by care-fully separating the distal ends of the semitendinosus and semimembranosus. The gastrocnemius originates from the distal femur and inserts by way of the thick **tendon of Achilles** on the calcaneus. The muscle plantar flexes the foot.
60. Examine the medial surface of the calf, ventral to the gastrocnemius, to locate the **soleus** (Fig. 6-17). It arises from the fibula and inserts by way of the tendon of Achilles (together with the gastrocnemius) on the calcaneus. It also plantar flexes the foot.

SELF-TEST—MUSCULAR SYSTEM

Directions

See Chapter 1, Self-Test, page 9.

1. **Striated** muscle contains branched fibers.
2. A skeletal muscle has its insertion on a relatively **immovable** part of the skeleton.
3. The "hamstring" muscles are found **in the shoulder.**
4. The muscle of the calf of the leg that is most prominent when taking a step is the **deltoid.**
5. The insertion of the biceps brachii is on the **ulna.**
6. Muscles of expression include the **orbicularis oculi and orbicularis oris.**
7. The principal muscle involved in flexion of the arm is the **pectoralis major.**
8. The pectoral muscles bring the arms **across the chest.**
9. Flexion of the trunk is brought about by the contraction of the **vastus lateralis** muscles.
10. In walking, the heel is elevated by the contraction of both the **gastrocnemius and soleus.**
11. The back muscles that extend the vertebral column are the **erector spinae** and the **semispinalis.**
12. The **triceps brachii** is a powerful extensor or antigravity muscle which aids in standing and in extending the leg in walking.
13. The pectoral muscles act in **adduction** of the arm.
14. Extension of the foot is bending the foot **upward.**
15. The membrane surrounding a single muscle cell is called the **sarcolemma.**
16. The cytoplasm of the skeletal muscle cell is called **myoplasm.**
17. An **aponeurosis** is a sheet of white fibrous tissue connecting a muscle to another muscle.
18. A **motor unit** consists of a ventral horn cell in the spinal cord, its axon, and all the muscle fibers it innervates.
19. Women cannot run as fast as men because the thigh bone is attached to the pelvis **at a more oblique angle.**
20. Muscular dystrophy is a **communicable** disease.
21. The broadest muscle of the back is the **trapezius.**

22. The **superior rectus** muscles turn the eyes toward the nose.

23. The deltoid muscle originates on the **occipital.**

24. The muscle filling the ventral surface of the scapula is the **serratus anterior.**

25. The quadriceps femoris **extends** the leg.

26. The **zygomaticus** produces the expression of smiling.

27. The biceps brachii **extends** the forearm.

28. The iliopsoas **extends** the thigh.

29. The biceps femoris, semimembranosus, and semitendinosus form the **quadriceps femoris** group of muscles.

30. The muscle covering the top of the skull is the **epicranius.**

31. The latissimus dorsi **flexes** the arm.

32. The external intercostals **elevate** the ribs.

33. The rhomboids **adduct** the scapulae.

34. The sternocleidomastoid **extends** the head.

7

Introduction to Stimulating and Recording Apparatus

EXERCISE 7-A
FARADIC CURRENT

Objective

To demonstrate the characteristics of faradic current as a stimulating agent.

Materials

Induction stimulator; wires.

Discussion

Although a muscle can be stimulated in different ways, direct electrical stimulation of the muscle or of the nerve supplying the muscle is used most frequently in physiology laboratories. This is because the procedure is simple; the stimulus can be accurately measured, is easily controlled as to strength and duration, closely resembles the physiological process of excitation, and leaves the tissue relatively unharmed; and the results are reproducible.

Faradic current is an induced current. Closure of the key in the primary circuit induces a current in the secondary circuit that flows only when there is a change in the magnetic field; therefore, current flows only when the circuit is made or broken. Moving the key or switch to close a circuit is referred to as the "make" ("making" the current); moving the key to open the circuit is known as the "break" ("breaking" the current). With faradic current, the break current is stronger than the make. Faradic current is used more frequently than galvanic current (direct current, a steadily flowing current) in physiology experiments.

The Model 330 Induction Stimulator contains a 1.5-volt battery, a key, a vibrating stepup transformer, and a voltage control system. Any of three voltage ranges—0 to 5, 0 to 50, and 0 to 500 volts—can be selected by a range multiplier switch. Each range is variable from zero to its maximum voltage by means of a potentiometer. The approximate voltage of the break stimulus is indicated by the voltage dial setting (0 through 50 volts) multiplied by the range selector position (X.1, X1, X10). The make stimulus voltage is approximately 1/10th that indicated by the voltage dial setting multiplied by the range selector position. The Model 330 Induction Stimulator is illustrated in Figure 7-1.

There are two pairs of terminals on the induction stimulator. A signal magnet may be connected to the two terminals marked MAG. The signal magnet circuit delivers a fixed 1.5 volts suitable for driving a signal magnet when the key is depressed. Insulated copper wires (with the ends scraped bare of insulation) or platinum electrodes may be connected to the other two terminals, marked STIM. The variable voltage obtained is suitable for stimulating muscle or nerve.

Procedure

1. Connect two wires to the two terminals of the induction stimulator marked STIM. (Loosen the screw tops of the terminals and insert the wires in the holes in the terminals; retighten the screw tops.) Place the other ends of the wires on the tongue. Both wires must touch the tongue but

Figure 7-1. Model 330 Induction Stimulator.

should not touch each other.

2. Turn the voltage range selector to X.1 and the voltage dial to 0.

3. At each position of the voltage dial, pull the switch or key to SINGLE. Any current felt with the switch in this position is the **make** current. With the electrodes still in position, release the key. Any current now felt is the **break shock.**

4. Make and break the circuit with the voltage dial on 0. Did you feel a shock on either make or break? Should you feel a shock at these settings?

5. Increase the voltage until a shock is felt on the break. (It may be necessary to move the range selector to X1 or even X10.) The first break shock felt is called the **liminal** or **threshold** stimulus. Record the voltage and in parentheses record the range used and the voltage dial reading under Results and Questions.

6. Continue increasing the voltage until a shock is also felt on the make. It may be necessary to remove the electrodes from the tongue before breaking the circuit to avoid sending a strong current through the tongue on the break. Record the vol-

tage necessary for the liminal make shock under Results and Questions.

7. Note whether a current is felt during the time the key is depressed (between make and break).

8. Remove the electrodes from the tongue. Leave the voltage controls set where strong make and break shocks were felt. Depress the key.

9. Replace the electrodes on the tongue for 5 seconds and note whether any shock is felt.

10. Remove the electrodes from the tongue, then break the circuit.

11. Was a make or break shock felt in steps 8 through 10?

12. In many experiments it is necessary to use constant strength current. Since the make and the break are not of the same intensity, it is necessary in such experiments to short-circuit one or the other to elicit a number of shocks of the same intensity in fairly rapid succession.

13. To short-circuit the make, set the voltage dial to a value that produced a good break and make shock. Place the electrodes on the tongue. Set the voltage dial at 0. Make

the circuit. Return the voltage dial to the
first setting. Break the circuit. If directions
have been followed, a break shock should
have been felt but not a make shock.

EXERCISE 7-B
TETANIZING STIMULATION

Objectives

To learn the characteristics of tetanizing
current as a stimulating agent; to compare the
threshold stimulus of tetanizing current with
that obtained with single induction shocks.

Materials

Induction stimulator; wires.

Discussion

Tetanizing stimulation is used when it is
desired to apply stimuli to a muscle in rapid
succession. The shocks obtained with the induction stimulator using the procedure in Exercise 7-A were single-induction shocks. If the
key is raised toward MULT (see Figure 7-1),
the circuit is made and broken automatically 50
times per second, thus producing a frequency of
stimulation of 50 per second.

Procedure

1. Using the same subject for this experiment
   as in the experiment with single shocks,
   determine the liminal stimulus for tetanizing current in the same manner as with
   single-induction shocks. A buzzing sound
   should be heard when the key is raised
   toward MULT.
2. Fill in the table under Results and
   Questions.

EXERCISE 7-C
USE OF THE KYMOGRAPH AND INK
RECORDING APPARATUS

Objective

To learn the use of the kymograph and ink
recording apparatus.

Materials

Kymograph; flat base stand; double clamp;
signal magnet with ink adapter; string; paper;
scissors; tape.

Discussion

The function of the kymograph is to record
motion and to make a permanent record of an
experiment. It consists of a drum, a mechanism
to move the drum, and a mechanism to change
the speed of movement of the drum. The
motion is transferred to a lever or stylus (pen),
one end of which rests against a surface (kymograph paper) moving at a known rate of speed.
The kymograph paper is wrapped around the
drum which, when in operation, continuously
rotates *away* from the point of contact with the
stylus (see Figure 7-2). The stylus is so con-
structed that motion transferred to it as a result
of an experiment (e.g., the contraction of a
muscle) causes it to move in directions perpendicular to the motion of the paper (see
Figure 7-2). The stylus must be so aligned that
it is in constant contact with the paper, otherwise a complete tracing of the process being
recorded will not be obtained. Anything less is
of limited value.

Figure 7-2 illustrates the direction in which
the kymograph drum revolves, as well as the
vertical motions made by the stylus (pen).

The kymograph described here is the electric
Model 600-000 (by Harvard Apparatus Co.),
which consists of a gear train designed to
transmit twelve separate rates of speed to the
drum (multispeed transmission). When actu-
ated by the **selector knob,** a selector gear comes
into contact with one of the other gears (which
are in constant motion while the kymograph is
being operated). Depending on the position
selected for the knob, the drum is either
speeded or slowed in its revolving action.

Among the twelve possible selections (selector knob positions 1-12), drum speed varies
from one revolution per second to one revolution per 5,000 seconds. Any rate of drum
rotation selected may be repeatedly (and accurately) reproduced.

Figure 7-2. Movement of the kymograph drum.

The speed of drum (seconds required to complete a revolution) and number of centimeters the drum moves per second in a given amount of time are given in Table 7-1.

The drum of the kymograph is 50 cm in circumference. When the knob is at position 1, the drum revolves once (a distance of 50 cm) per second. At knob position 6, the drum speed is reduced to a rate of only 1 cm/sec, and it takes 50 seconds for it to complete one revolution. Therefore, the lower the number of the knob position, the more rapid the rate of revolution of the drum. The fast drum speeds (1 or 2) may be used when timing single, short-term events, such as the muscle twitch. Slower speeds are used when a sequence of events, such as many muscle twitches, is to be recorded.

Procedure

1. Screw the long, steel, drum-supporting rod into the hole located near the back on the upper surface of the kymograph.
2. Place the drum and its hollow cylinder, with the screw or lever on top, over this rod and rotate it until the pin at the lower end of the hollow cylinder fits into the depression provided for it on the kymograph.
3. Practice raising and lowering the drum. To do this, loosen the screw holding the drum to the rod, move the drum to the desired position, and retighten the screw.
4. To change speeds of the kymograph, the selector knob must be pulled upward (disengaging the selector gear) and turned to the desired position and released. *Do not attempt to change speeds without first pulling out the selector knob.* While all the gears can be shifted when the motor is running, it is recommended that the motor be shut off when shifting to positions 1, 2, or 3.
5. Practice starting and stopping the kymograph and changing drum speeds.

6. To rotate the drum by hand, the motor may be left on but the selector knob must be at position N (neutral).
7. For each selector knob position, the number of cm/sec the drum moves is known (see Table 7-1). For example, at knob position 7, the drum moves 0.5 cm/sec. Therefore, a recorded event that occupies 10 cm on the drum (easily measured with a ruler) must have taken 20 seconds.

The following equation may be used to determine the duration of an event:

$$E = \frac{L}{S}$$

where
E = duration of the event in seconds,
L = length of the recorded events in centimeters, and
S = drum (paper) speed in centimeters per second.

8. *Always* record the position of the selector knob used, in case the drum speed is to be used in calculations.
9. The glazed side of the kymograph paper is used for ink writing. Lay a piece of kymograph paper on the table with the glazed surface facing downward.
10. Cut a piece of string approximately 1 foot long. Remove the drum and support cylinder and lay the drum in the center of the paper, *base toward the student.* Place the string on top of the drum so that the ends extend over both the upper and lower edges of the drum. (Do not let the drum roll onto the floor or allow anything to mar its surface. It is essential to have a true smooth surface.)
11. Wrap the paper tightly around the drum so that the junction of the ends of the paper is over the string. Tape the *left margin of the paper over the right.* This prevents the pen from dragging on the seam.

Table 7-1. Kymograph Drum Speeds

Knob Position	1	2	3	4	5	6	7	8	9	10	11	12
Sec/rev	1	2.5	5	10	20	50	100	200	500	1000	2000	5000
Cm/sec	50	20	10	5	2.5	1	.5	.25	.1	.05	.025	.010

12. Shake the drum slightly to make sure the paper does not slide. If it does move, remove the paper and reapply it firmly enough to prevent the sliding.

13. To remove the paper from the drum at the conclusion of the experiment, move the string carefully to one side of the seam. To avoid dropping the paper when the junction is torn, press the string and at least one edge of the paper firmly against the lower part of the drum with the left hand. Now, grasp the upper part of the string with the right hand and carefully tear the paper by pulling the string.

14. The ink writing system consists of a stainless steel pen, adapter, ink tube, bottle, and bottle clamp. The bottle is of soft polyethylene, which allows the ink to be forced to the pen tip when the bottle is squeezed and the cap is tight. The fine pen tip provides a thin line and, because of its small bore, ensures adequate capillary action.

15. To obtain good results with the kymograph, always observe the following precautions:

    a. Set up the equipment so the stand with its attached levers (recording apparatus) is to the right of the kymograph. This allows the drum to glide away from the pen point, not toward it.

    b. Make certain that the semicircular base (expanded portion) of the stand is toward the drum to prevent the stand from falling over when heavy equipment is used.

    c. The writing on the surface of the kymograph paper should always face the operator.

    d. The pen must always be horizontal and make a tangent with the recording surface (drum). This means it must touch the surface at right angles in the precise center of the front of the drum.

    e. The pen (or any other stylus used) must make a distinct mark over the entire surface covered by its vertical (up and down) movements. This means the pen must be in *constant* contact with the surface of the paper. This contact should not, however, be so firm that the vertical motion is restricted. To obtain these results, all levers must be exactly horizontal and at right angles (i.e., tangent) to the drum surface. *The ink adapter must also be in a vertical position.*

    f. Always begin each experiment (unless directed otherwise) with the *drum high* on its axis and the *recording equipment low*. Begin each tracing about 1 inch above the edge of the paper, then lower the drum when additional records are needed. The drum is lowered in preference to raising the position of the recording apparatus.

    g. Always begin the tracing about 1 inch to the right of the overlapping part of the paper. Any record on the overlapping portion will be lost when the paper is removed from the drum.

    h. Before removing the record from the drum, label it as fully as possible and show it to the instructor for approval. It is permissible to cut up the records so that each student has a copy. The unused portions can then be discarded. Therefore, label only good results, and place the student's name and experiment number on that part of the record.

    i. Paste the record in the appropriate position under Results and Questions. The record must always be discussed. If it is necessary for the entire group to use one tracing, indicate which student's results contain the tracing.

16. Mount the signal magnet on the flat base stand as directed in Exercise 7-D, making certain that the handle is on the *beveled* area in the double clamp and that it is oriented in accordance with the above instructions.

17. Connect the ink adapter with the shortest pen to the stylus of the signal magnet as directed in Exercise 7-D. If the ink bottle is less than half full, use a funnel to refill it.

18. Clamp the bottle in a vertical position on the handle of the signal magnet. The ink level in the bottle should be at approximately the same level as the pen tip. If the ink does not flow out with sufficient pressure, the level of the bottle should be raised.

19. To protect the surfaces of laboratory tables, always place a paper towel below the kymograph drum before starting the

ink flow. The towel may be removed during the experiment, but should be replaced when removing the ink from the pen.

20. To start the ink flow, screw down the bottle cap and gently squeeze the body of the bottle. The cap is then loosened while the bottle is under pressure. It may be necessary to squeeze the bottle occasionally to maintain the flow of ink.

21. At the end of an experiment, the ink should be withdrawn from the pen by reversing the procedure. With the bottle cap still slightly loosened, squeeze the bottle, tighten the cap, then release the pressure. The ink should flow back into the bottle. Next, detach the ink bottle and attach a second ink bottle filled with water. Force water through the tubes and pen until all the ink is removed. This procedure will prevent dried ink from clogging the pen.

22. Practice starting and reversing the flow of ink.

23. Position the pen so that it is at right angles to the recording surface. Use the least pressure on the tip consistent with a good recording.

24. Start the drum revolving and check the appearance of the line. Answer the questions under Results and Questions.

EXERCISE 7-D
THE SIGNAL MAGNET

Objectives

To demonstrate the advantages and disadvantages of the signal magnet as a timing device; to demonstrate the advantages and disadvantages of the signal magnet as a device to indicate the precise time of application of a stimulus.

Materials

Kymograph; signal magnet with ink adapter; induction stimulator; stand; double clamp; wire; stopwatch or watch with a second hand.

Discussion

The signal magnet is used to record the time of application of a stimulus, to record the opening and/or closing of a circuit, to record a change in experimental procedure, or as a timing device.

The signal magnet consists of an electromagnet (a coil of wire) and a vibrating, spring-loaded armature extended out to form a stylus (see Figure 7-3).

When current is applied ("make" = M), the stylus deflects, thus producing a permanent record of the event. When the circuit is broken ("break" = B), the stylus moves upward to its original position. Therefore, on a moving drum, the record appears as follows:

M B M B M B M B M B

If the signal magnet is used as an independent time base marker (independent of the induction stimulator), a 1.5-volt battery is required to operate it. Generally, however, the signal magnet is used with the induction stimulator to record the time of application of a stimulus to a heart or a skeletal muscle, because it writes at the same instant the current passes to the muscle. This provides information as to the exact time the structure received the stimulus.

Figure 7-3. The signal magnet.

The signal magnet has two Allen head set screws on the upper surface for making adjustments. The set screw near the vibrating point is used to adjust the excursion of the point. The other set screw is used to adjust the frequency response (the latter should be touching the armature gently). Both adjustments have been set at the factory for 1.5 volts and a frequency of 60 cycles per second. However, if the signal magnet stylus does not move, it may be necessary to adjust them. An Allen wrench is provided for making any necessary adjustments.

Procedure

1. Mount the signal magnet on the stand so the coil of wire faces the operator.
2. Connect two wires from the induction stimulator terminals marked MAG to the binding posts on each side of the handle. Run the wire through the opening and then tighten the screw.
3. Make and break the current to determine whether the signal magnet works properly. When the current is applied, the stylus should descend. When the current is withdrawn (broken), the stylus should return to its original position.
4. Now connect the ink adapter with the shortest pen to the stylus of the signal magnet by means of a small piece of colophonium cement softened by the heat of the fingers. Check again to make sure the pen falls and rises with the making and breaking of the current. The amount of wax may have to be adjusted so that the pen works properly.
5. Place the pen tangent to the drum and check it to be certain that it is writing correctly. It is important that the pen does not press too tightly against the drum, since this prevents rapid excursions of the pen.
6. Obtain an individual record for each student in the group for each part of the experiment.
7. At a drum speed of 6, hold the key down ("make") for 1 second, then release ("break") for 1 second. The intervals should be timed with a stopwatch and the sequence continued for at least 10 seconds. Label the record with the time in seconds.
8. Repeat the procedure, first at a drum speed of 11 (for at least 20 seconds), then at a drum speed of 2 (which will result in just one make and one break mark on the kymograph paper). At drum speed 2, start the drum, make the circuit, break the circuit one second later, then immediately rotate the semicircular stand away from the drum so that the pen is removed from the paper. This prevents overlapping of the recording. Label both records.
9. Answer all questions and place all records under Results and Questions.

EXERCISE 7-E
THE TUNING FORK

Objectives

To determine the advantages and disadvantages of the tuning fork as a timing device; to determine the advantages and disadvantages of the tuning fork as a device to indicate the time of application of a stimulus.

Materials

Flat base stand; tuning fork with ink adapter; tuning fork starter; double clamp; kymograph.

Discussion

The tuning fork is used to measure the duration of events that occupy a short period of time. It is most useful with short-lived, single events, such as a muscle twitch, heart beat, or a single breath.

The tuning fork vibrates 100 times per second. An ink pen is attached to record the vibrations. The time elapsed from the crest of one vibration to the crest of the next (a-b, in the following diagram) is 1/100th second. The number of vibrations (a-b) should be multiplied by 0.01 to obtain the total time for any event measured.

The setup for using a tuning fork is shown in Figure 7-4. Since the tuning fork is difficult to use, the known drum speed will ordinarily be used to calculate the duration of an event. The results obtained should be the same with both methods.

Figure 7-4. Diagram for tuning fork setup.

Procedure

1. Each student must obtain an individual record of the results in this experiment at drum speeds 6, 4, 2, and 1.
2. Attach the tuning fork to the semicircular stand by means of a double clamp (make sure the rod fits in the beveled portion of the clamp). Attach the pen to the back of the bottom prong of the tuning fork. The prongs of the tuning fork must be perfectly horizontal in relation to the drum, and the pen tangent to the kymograph.
3. Set the drum speed at 6 and start the flow of ink.
4. Near the end and on the very edge of the tuning fork place the tuning fork starter (the starter has a small handle attached to a U-shaped part which is used to compress the prongs of the tuning fork). A quick, sideways blow will knock the tuning fork starter off the tuning fork, causing it to vibrate. Practice this procedure several times, with the pen away from the drum. Do not allow the starter to hit the tuning fork after it is deflected.
5. Begin the writing operation 1 inch to the right of the taped portion of the paper. Start the drum and make certain that the pen is writing on the drum.

6. After the pen writes a baseline approximately 1 inch long, deflect the tuning fork starter. Stop the drum after the tuning fork has ceased vibrating. Repeat at drum speed 4.
7. The drum moves so rapidly at the faster speeds (2 and 1) that it may be necessary to have the tuning fork vibrating before starting the drum. To prevent the record from overlapping at speeds of 2 and 1, be sure to stop the drum after one revolution. This can be done most easily, at fast speeds, by rotating the base of the semicircular stand away from the drum and thus disengaging the pen.
8. Label each of the four tracings with the drum speed. Label each record in which individual vibrations are visible with the time in 1/100th seconds.
9. Answer the questions and put your record in the appropriate place under Results and Questions.

EXERCISE 7-F
USE OF THE PHYSIOGRAPH

Objectives

To learn how to operate the physiograph and the stimulator; to determine the characteristics of the current output from the stimulator; to calculate the duration of an event.

Materials

Physiograph with stimulator; photoelectric pulse pickup; pin electrodes; stimulator output extension cable; transducer coupler.

Discussion

The physiograph is an instrument used extensively for the measurement and recording of physiological data. It is essentially a group of independently operated recording channels mounted in a main frame assembly which provides power distribution, control and monitoring circuitry, and means for mounting accessory plug-in modules. It can be operated as a single-channel recorder for a single function or it can be used to record simultaneously a variety of functions, such as heart beat, respiration, and blood pressure.

A typical recording channel consists of a transducer, a transducer coupler, an amplifier, a pen motor, and a recording stylus.

Transducers are devices that convert one form of energy into another form of energy. For example, a loudspeaker is a transducer that converts electrical energy into sound. In the operation of the physiograph, the transducer converts the physiological event into a proportional electrical signal. Transducers are available to convert blood pressure, muscle pull, and heart beat into proportional electrical signals. Some transducers connect directly to the input connector on the channel amplifier. Others operate in connection with preamplifiers. Typical transducers are the myograph, the photoelectric pulse pickup, and the heart sounds microphone.

Preamplifiers are used in place of transducers or with transducers to measure physiological potentials. Biopotentials are very small; consequently a preamplifier must be used to amplify the transducer output signal to match the input requirements of the amplifier. Sometimes the transducer and preamplifier are combined into the same unit. Typical preamplifiers are the impedance pneumograph, the hi-gain preamplifier, and the electrosphygmograph.

A coupler is used to match the transducer or the signal from the subject to the channel amplifier. It is also used to vary the sensitivity and to calibrate the system.

Since transducers normally are designed to absorb as little energy as possible from the preparation measured, the output signal is small and must be amplified considerably to drive the pen motor. The function of the amplifier is to provide the required increase in signal strength while retaining the proportional relationship of the electric signal and the physiological activity which it represents. The output of the amplifier drives the pen motor. The pen is numbered to correspond to the amplifier channel.

The pen motor converts electrical energy into rotary motion. It receives the electrical signals from the amplifier and drives the recording stylus. The excursions of the stylus across the moving chart are proportional to the physiological activity and they provide a permanent record of the experiments.

The basic layout for the physiograph can be diagrammed as follows:

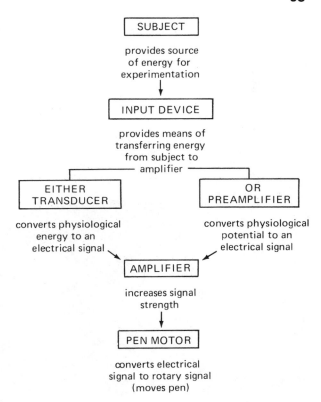

The directions described in this section are written for the Narco Bio-Systems Desk Model Physiograph DMP 4-B. This physiograph has four compartments for plug-in modules. Three recording channels can be used for recording events and one compartment for the stimulator. This model is illustrated in Figure 7-5. To perform all the experiments described in this manual, it is assumed that there are three recording channels on the physiograph, a stimulator, and a time and event marker.

Procedure

PART 1: USE OF A RECORDING CHANNEL AND THE PHOTOELECTRIC PULSE PICKUP

A recording of the pulse will be obtained to familiarize the student with the use of a recording channel and with one method of calculation of the duration of an event.

1. Press all power and record switches off. Install the plug-in modules to be used in the experiment, if they are not already installed. In this exercise, the stimulator, one channel amplifier, the photoelectric pulse pickup, and the transducer coupler

TIME MARKER SWITCH: selects interval between timing marks recorded on Time and Event Channel.

PAPER SPEED SWITCH: controls chart paper speed.

PAPER DRIVE TENSION WHEEL: if moved to the left, it moves the paper and lowers the pens; if moved to the right, it raises the pens and stops the paper.

PAPER GUIDES: paper must be under the guides to move.

RECORDER SWITCH: applies power to DMP-4B when placed in ON position.

COUPLER: matches signal from subject or transducer to the channel amplifier.

CHANNEL AMPLIFIER: amplifies signal from the subject.

GROUND TERMINAL: provides connection for grounding wire.

PLUG: connects to power cable.

RECORDER SWITCH INDICATOR LAMP: glows when power is on.

CHANNEL MONITOR: provides connections to external monitoring devices for each recording channel.

INKWELL ASSEMBLY: upward increases the ink flow; downward reduces ink flow.

EVENT MARKER: push-button for operating the event marker to correlate events (e.g., drug injections) with physiological responses.

EXTERNAL EVENT: connects external switch for remote operation of event marker.

Figure 7-5.   The Narco Bio-Systems desk model physiograph DMP-4B.

will be used. If the transducer coupler is not already installed in channel 3, remove the coupler in that position by unscrewing the large screw on the lower center of the top panel of the coupler. Then lift the coupler straight up, insert the transducer coupler, and tighten the large screw.

2. Connect the power cable to the power connector on the side of the physiograph and to a 115-volt power source. If a three-prong cable is not used, attach a grounding wire from the control panel ground terminal on the main frame to a water pipe, gas outlet, etc.

3. Check the paper supply to verify that there is sufficient paper in the physiograph for the experiment. The paper is packed (500 sheets to a box in a continuous folded chart) printed side up, but is fed into the physiograph printed side down. The paper box should be pushed all the way against the back of the paper compartment, with the bottom of the box against the left inner wall. Disengage the paper tension wheel (by pressing it to the right) and insert the paper into the paper feed guide (see Figure 7-6). When the paper emerges onto the upper surface of the physiograph, make certain that each edge of the paper is under the paper guides.

4. If the pens are not installed, insert the stylus of the pen horizontally under the retaining spring. The support pins should fit firmly into the stirrup cradle (see Figure 7-7).

5. The inking assembly may be one of the two types illustrated in Figure 7-8. The flow of ink to the stylus is a function of the height of the inkwell, since this is a gravity feed system. To adjust the ink flow to the recording paper, move the inkwell up or down in the grommet hole. Start the flow of ink in the pen connected to the channel with the transducer coupler and to the pen connected to the time and event marker.

   a. If your assembly is of the type on the left in Figure 7-8, it consists of a plastic inkwell (refillable), a mounting rod, and tubing. Place the finger over the hole in the inkwell and squeeze lightly on the inkwell. Wait for a drop of ink to appear on the tip of the

Figure 7-6. Paper loading for the DMB-4B.

Figure 7-7.   Pen assembly.

Figure 7-8. Inking assemblies.

stylus. When the drop appears, release the pressure on the inkwell and remove the finger from the hole.

b. If using the super ink cartridge (illustrated on the right in Figure 7-8), start the ink flow by placing the finger over the hole on the rubber bulb and squeezing lightly on the bulb. When a drop of ink appears on the tip of the stylus, release the pressure.

c. Check the level of ink in the ink bottles before the start of each experiment. The type on the left in Figure 7-8 may be refilled from the refill bottle available in the laboratory. If it is necessary to replace the super ink cartridge, puncture the center of the recessed area of the ink cartridge with a probe. Then install the pierce and prime unit from the empty cartridge (see Figure 7-9). Rotate the unit to bring the horizontal surface of the pierce and prime unit flush with the top surface of the ink cartridge.

6. Study the function of each part of the channel amplifier and the transducer coupler as listed on Figures 7-10 and 7-11.

7. Attach the detecting head of the photoelectric pulse transducer to the ventral surface of the finger so that the light source and the photocell are in contact with the finger (see Figure 7-11). Fit the foam rubber black band over the pulse pickup and wrap the band snugly around the finger. The pulse pickup is light sensitive and must be shielded with the black band. Connect the photoelectric pulse transducer into the 7-pin INPUT connector of the transducer coupler.

8. Press the RECORDER switch on the main frame ON.

a. Practice varying the paper control to become familiar with this operation. The paper moves at twelve fixed speeds from 0.0025 to 10 cm/sec. Set the paper speed to 0.5 cm/sec.

b. The paper control unit provides time signals every 1, 5, 30, or 60 seconds, which are recorded as momentary downward deflections of the time and event channel pen. One time mark is omitted each minute in the 1-second position to indicate 1-minute intervals. Set the time marker to 1.

9. Set the channel amplifier controls as follows:

a. Press the POWER switch ON.

b. Press the RECORD switch OFF (if it is on). This switch must be off before

Pierce and Prime Unit

Recess
Ink Cartridge

Cartridge Holder

Figure 7-9.   Replacement of super ink cartridge.

any connections are made to the physiograph. It should be on only during actual recording.

c. Set the POLARITY to positive (+). All channels should routinely be set to positive at this time and left in that position.

d. Set the VARIABLE control (the upper knob of the double knob in the center) to its maximum clockwise position. All channels should be routinely set to this position at this time and left in this position.

e. Set the FILTER switch to 10K.

f. Set the mV/CM switch to 20.

g. Set the recording pen to the center dark-green line, using the POSITION control.

10. Move the paper drive lever to the left. This starts the movement of the paper and lowers the recording pens onto the chart paper.

11. Press the RECORD switch ON. Adjust the transducer coupler BALANCE con-

trol to restore the recording pen to the previously established baseline. After the pen stabilizes in position, turn the mV/CM switch until the recording is of the desired amplitude (the lower the number, the higher the amplitude). An amplitude of no more than 1 inch is desirable in most experiments. If the recording does not resemble Figure 7-12, press the RECORD switch OFF and reposition the pulse pickup on the finger. A poor record is produced if the black band is too tight.

12. Record the pulse for at least 70 seconds at paper speed 0.5 cm/sec. This will be approximately 1¼ pages.

13. Increase the paper speed to 5 cm/sec and record the pulse for one entire piece of chart paper.

14. Press the RECORD switch on the channel amplifier OFF. Press the POWER switch on the channel amplifier OFF.

15. Move the paper drive lever to the right to stop the paper and raise the recording pens.

100

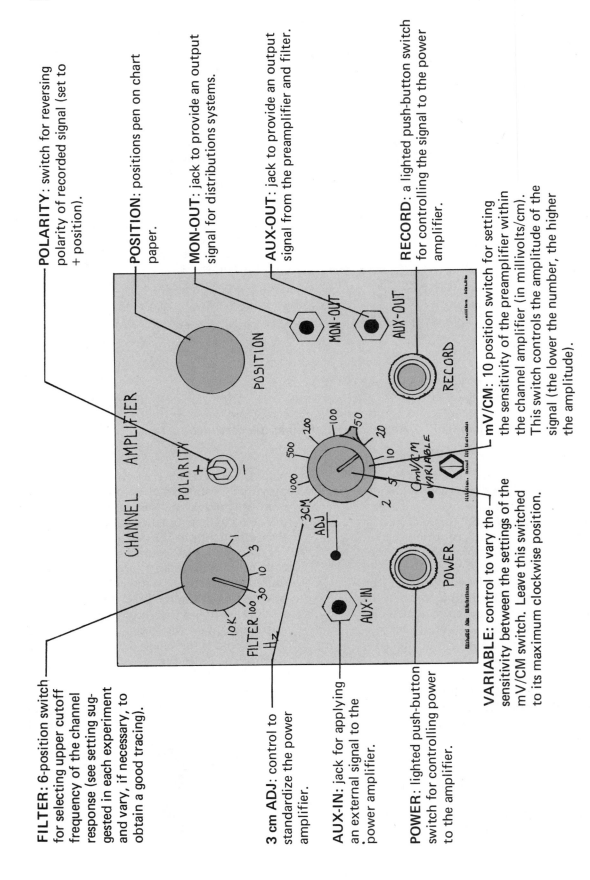

FILTER: 6-position switch for selecting upper cutoff frequency of the channel response (see setting suggested in each experiment and vary, if necessary, to obtain a good tracing).

POLARITY: switch for reversing polarity of recorded signal (set to + position).

POSITION: positions pen on chart paper.

MON-OUT: jack to provide an output signal for distributions systems.

AUX-OUT: jack to provide an output signal from the preamplifier and filter.

RECORD: a lighted push-button switch for controlling the signal to the power amplifier.

mV/CM: 10 position switch for setting the sensitivity of the preamplifier within the channel amplifier (in millivolts/cm). This switch controls the amplitude of the signal (the lower the number, the higher the amplitude).

3 cm ADJ: control to standardize the power amplifier.

AUX-IN: jack for applying an external signal to the power amplifier.

POWER: lighted push-button switch for controlling power to the amplifier.

VARIABLE: control to vary the sensitivity between the settings of the mV/CM switch. Leave this switched to its maximum clockwise position.

Figure 7-10. Channel amplifier on the DMP-4B.

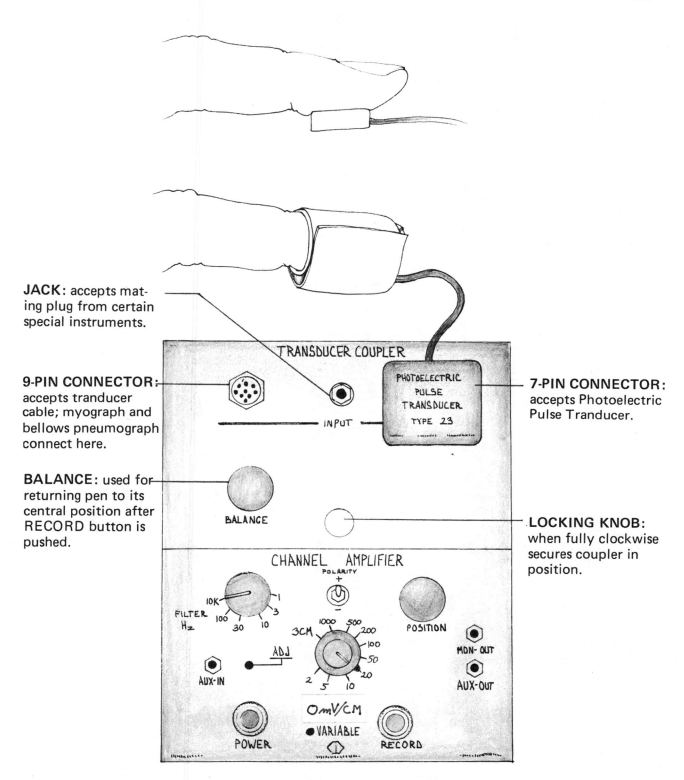

JACK: accepts mating plug from certain special instruments.

9-PIN CONNECTOR: accepts tranducer cable; myograph and bellows pneumograph connect here.

BALANCE: used for returning pen to its central position after RECORD button is pushed.

7-PIN CONNECTOR: accepts Photoelectric Pulse Tranducer.

LOCKING KNOB: when fully clockwise secures coupler in position.

TRANSDUCER COUPLER

PHOTOELECTRIC PULSE TRANSDUCER TYPE 23

INPUT

BALANCE

CHANNEL AMPLIFIER

POLARITY
+
−

FILTER Hz
10K 1
100 3
30 10

ADJ
AUX-IN

3CM
1000 500 200
100
50
2 20
5 10

POSITION

MON-OUT
AUX-OUT

O mV/CM
● VARIABLE

POWER

RECORD

Figure 7-11.   Photoelectric pulse pickup with the DMP-4B.

Figure 7-12.   Recording of pulse.

PART 2: USE OF THE PHYSIOGRAPH STIMULATOR

1. The pen for the time and event marker is the only pen needed in this part of the experiment.
2. The stimulator can deliver either a single pulse or continuous pulses. It is possible to adjust the voltage of the stimulus from 0 to 120 volts, the frequency from 0.2 to 250 impulses per second, and the duration from 0.1 to 120 milliseconds (see Figure 7-13). At this time the CONT-OFF-SINGLE switch should be in the OFF position. Turn the ON-OFF switch to ON. The pilot lamp will glow.
3. Place the MONOPHASIC-BIPHASIC switch to MONOPHASIC.
4. Turn the paper speed to 0.5 cm/sec. Set the seconds on the paper control unit to 1.
5. The following three steps of the procedure should occupy approximately 1½ sheets of chart paper. Repeat the procedure for each member of the group.
   a. Start the paper by moving the paper drive lever to the left and observe the time marks. Note that the marker omits one mark every 60 seconds. Depress the red event marker button next to the time and event pen. The pen should deflect upward when activated by the event marker pushbutton.
   b. Place the CONT-OFF-SINGLE switch in the SINGLE position. The neon indicator should flash once. The event marker pen will indicate the pulse with a single momentary upward deflection.
   c. Place the switch in the CONT position for 3 seconds. Repeated pulses are delivered in this position; the event marker pen will deflect upward and hold for the duration of the pulses.
   d. Now place the switch in the OFF position. Turn off the paper. Label the record according to the directions under Results and Questions.
6. Loosen the red and black binding posts on the stimulator, exposing an opening in each one. Connect one end of the stimulator output extension cable to this RF-isolated output on the stimulator (see Figure 7-14) and tighten the red and black binding posts. Connect the other end of the stimulator output extension cable to a pair of pin electrodes (loosen the screws on the stimulator output extension cable, insert the pin of the pin electrodes through the openings, and tighten the screws).
7. To determine the characteristics of the output current from the stimulator, set the duration at 7 milliseconds (multiplier at X1), volts at 0 (multiplier on X1), frequency at 5 (multiplier at X10), and monophasic. Do not have the paper moving in this part of the experiment.
8. Place the sterile pin electrodes on the tongue of the subject ½ inch apart. Gradually increase the volts from 0, placing the switch in the SINGLE position for a single shock each time, until the initial shock is felt. Record the threshold voltage, the voltage at which the first shock is felt. _____
9. Decrease the duration to 2 milliseconds (multiplier on X1) and determine again the volts needed for the threshold stimulus (reset the volts at 0 and gradually increase the voltage). _____
10. Repeat steps 8 and 9 several times until the subject is certain that he or she feels a difference.
11. Reset the volts at 0. Return the duration to 7 milliseconds. With the frequency at 50 per second (frequency at 5, multiplier at X10), place the switch in the CONT position for repeated pulses. Determine the volts for the threshold stimulus.
   _____
12. Turn off the stimulator.

PART 3: SHUTDOWN (Go through these steps at the conclusion of experiments with the physiograph)

1. At the conclusion of any experiment, move the paper drive lever to the right to stop the paper movement and raise the pens.
2. Press all channel amplifier RECORD switches OFF, press all channel amplifier POWER switches OFF. Press the main frame RECORDER switch OFF.
3. Push the inkwell assemblies down to the lowest level.
   a. If using the ink assembly shown on the left in Figure 7-8, put the tips of the pens into the ink bottles if they are

104

RF ISOLATED OUTPUT: (to be used with output extension cable; connects stimulator with subject electrodes).

FREQUENCY CONTROL: (regulates number of impulses per second when using continuous stimulations; range .2/sec to 250/sec).

MULTIPLIER SWITCH: (to be used with frequency control).

DURATION CONTROL: (controls duration of each stimulus; range .1 to 120 msec).

MONO: direct coupling.
BI: capacitator coupling.
MULTIPLIER SWITCH: (to be used with duration control).

TRIG IN: (to use an external trigger).

ON-OFF SWITCH:

VOLT REGULATOR: (regulates number of volts applied to subject; range .05 to 120 volts).

MULTIPLIER SWITCH: (used with volt regulator; multiplies volts x switch setting).

STIMULATION CONTROL: (regulates type of stimulus, whether single or continuous).

TRIG OUT: (used for attachment of accessory equipment as oscilloscope, etc.).

PILOT LAMP: (glows when stimulator is on).

LOCK: (locks stimulator to physiograph cabinet.)

DURATION LAMP: (flashes when stimulus applied).

Figure 7-13. Stimulator.

Pin Electrodes ————

———— Stimulator Output Extension Cable

Figure 7-14.   Setup for stimulation of tongue.

to be used within a few hours. If not, withdraw ink from the styluses and tubes as follows:

(1) Squeeze the inkwell.
(2) Place the finger over the hole in the inkwell and release the squeezing pressure.
(3) Repeat as necessary to draw all the ink from the pen.

b. If using the super ink cartridges (right assembly in Figure 7-8):

(1) Squeeze the bulb.

(2) Place the finger over the hole in the bulb and release the squeezing pressure.
(3) Repeat as necessary to draw all the ink from the pen.

4. Disconnect input devices. Connect the ends of the transducer cables (if used in the experiment) for protection of the prongs. Do not touch the ends with the fingers.

5. Disconnect the power cable and ground.

6. Replace the protective dust cover.

8

Muscle Physiology

EXERCISE 8-A
STRENGTH OF STIMULUS AND HEIGHT OF CONTRACTION

Objectives

To demonstrate the characteristics of faradic current as a stimulating agent for muscle; to show the effect of the strength of the stimulus on the height of contraction; to determine whether skeletal muscle, as a whole, follows the all-or-none law.

Materials

Beaker; frog Ringer's solution; frog; dissecting set; watch glass; medicine dropper; *either* wires, moist chamber, light muscle lever, induction stimulator, kymograph, stand, 10-gram weight, three double clamps and signal magnet (optional) *or* physiograph, frog board, clips, stand, myograph B, pin electrodes, stimulator output extension cable, and transducer cable.

Discussion

The gastrocnemius muscle, the large calf muscle of the frog, will be used in these muscle experiments. This muscle is easily prepared and has been extensively studied. It originates on the femur just above and behind the knee joint and terminates in a long tendon, the tendon of Achilles, which, in the frog, is inserted under the foot rather than on the calcaneus as in man (see Figure 8-1).

The force of a muscle contraction depends, within limits, on the strength of the stimulus. If the stimulus is subliminal, no contraction results; however, as the strength of the stimulus is increased, the threshold of the most irritable muscle fibers is reached and a feeble contraction occurs. As the strength of the stimulus is increased further, more muscle fibers contract, and the height of the contraction increases to the point at which all the muscle fibers are contracting. A further increase in current will not produce an additional increase in the height of contraction, since all the fibers are contracting to their maximum.

Each of the following experiments is divided into two parts, one part for the use of the kymograph and one for the use of the physiograph. This procedure for the preparation of the frog and the setup of the equipment should be used in all experiments in this chapter unless directed otherwise.

Procedure using the Kymograph and Induction Stimulator

1. Pith (see Exercise 14-A for pithing procedure) a frog or decapitate it by placing the blade of the large shears in its mouth as far back as possible (see Figure 8-2). With one cut (behind the eyes) remove the upper portion of the head with the brain. (If this is done rapidly the animal will not be caused unnecessary pain.) Place the frog on a paper towel.
2. Cut completely across the trunk of the frog at the midabdominal region, discarding the upper half of the trunk.
3. Separate the two legs by cutting through the midline. Give one leg to another group of students.

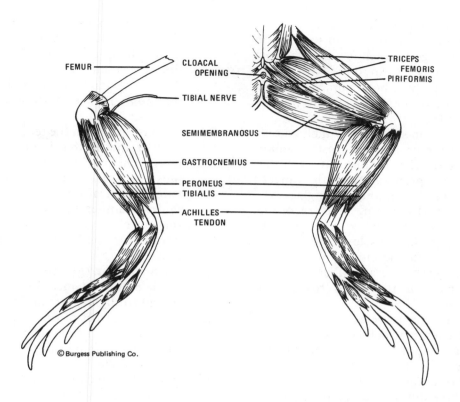

FEMUR

CLOACAL OPENING

TIBIAL NERVE

SEMIMEMBRANOSUS

GASTROCNEMIUS

PERONEUS

TIBIALIS

ACHILLES TENDON

TRICEPS FEMORIS

PIRIFORMIS

© Burgess Publishing Co.

Figure 8-1.   Muscles of hind limb of frog.

Figure 8-2.   Decapitation of the frog.

4. The skin of the frog is loosely attached and can be removed by peeling. Cut around the skin at the ankle (cutting only through the skin). Now grasp the leg with one hand and peel back the skin with the other.

5. Lay this preparation on a watch glass. Do not touch the exposed tissues with the fingers unless absolutely necessary. Keep the preparation moist with Ringer's solution.

6. To facilitate placing the femur in the femur clamp, clean away the muscles from the bone. However, be careful at the knee joint not to remove the origin of the gastrocnemius muscle from the distal femur.

7. Slip the head of the femur out of the socket at the hip and discard the remainder (trunk portion) of the preparation.

8. Loosen the tendon of Achilles beneath the heel by inserting the blade of the scissors

under it. Sever the tendon, keeping it as long as possible. Now lift up the tendon and free the gastrocnemius muscle from underlying muscles, up to the knee joint.

9. Cut the tibio-fibula bone immediately below the knee joint and discard this portion of the frog leg.

10. The preparation should now include only the entire femur and the gastrocnemius muscle with the tendon of Achilles. Moisten the preparation with Ringer's solution and place in the watch glass.

11. Set up the stimulating and recording apparatus as described in Exercise 7-C. Always have the muscle preparation to the right of the kymograph, with the writing facing the operator. Place the semicircular base of the stand toward the kymograph.

12. For recording a muscle contraction, use the muscle lever, which consists of a yoke supporting an axle to which a tapered metal tube with a double S hook is attached (see Figure 8-3).

13. Attach three double clamps to the stand. Attach the moist chamber to the upper clamp, the light muscle lever to the middle clamp, and the signal magnet to the lowest clamp (see Figure 8-4).

14. The muscle lever should be placed in the double clamp so that the after-loading screw (or "afterloader") is in a superior position (see Figure 8-4). In this position the S hook should be vertical.

15. The after-loading screw should be raised so that it *does not touch the lever*. This ensures that the muscle is constantly held taut by the weight. A muscle thus prepared is called a free-loaded muscle.

16. Attach the intermediate (10 cm) length ink adapter and pen to the muscle lever. This length pen will magnify the height of muscle contraction. Attach the ink reservoir to the handle of the muscle lever.

17. Attach the shortest ink adapter to the stylus of the signal magnet with a small piece of colophonium cement.

18. Connect two insulated copper wires from the induction stimulator terminals, marked MAG, to the signal magnet. Connect two similar wires from the induction stimulator terminals marked STIM to two terminals (any two of the four) on the inferior surface of the moist chamber.

19. Moisten the muscle with Ringer's solution. Fasten the femur horizontally into the femur clamp on the moist chamber. Position the femur so that the tendon of Achilles extends straight down through the hole on the bottom of the moist chamber.

20. Tie a thread from the tendon to the upper part of the double hook on the muscle lever. The resting position of the lever must be horizontal and the string must extend vertically through the hole in the moist chamber to the hook. Reposition the muscle lever in the double clamp to obtain this condition. The string must be taut.

21. Tie a 10-gram (g) weight to the lower end of the S hook by means of a short piece of thread to slightly stretch the muscle.

22. Take two pieces of fine, uninsulated, copper wire of sufficient length to reach from the upper terminals of the moist chamber to the muscle.

23. Using the same two terminals on the moist chamber as in step 18, run one piece of copper wire from a terminal on the moist chamber to the inferior end of the muscle belly. Wrap the wire around the muscle several times to make good contact. However, do not constrict the muscle with the wire. Extend the other wire from the second terminal to the upper end of the muscle and fasten similarly. The two wires must not touch each other.

24. Moisten a paper towel with water, fold it in thirds, and place it around the inner surface of the cover of the moist chamber, leaving a window in front.

25. Check the adjustment and alignment of all equipment as follows:

  a. Place the writing point of the signal magnet (which will indicate the point of introduction of the current into the muscle) immediately beneath the writing point of the muscle lever stylus.

  b. The muscle must be aligned vertically so that the tendon does not touch the sides of the hole in the base of the moist chamber.

  c. The S hook must be directly beneath the tendon so that the tendon is vertical.

  d. The position of the muscle lever must be adjusted so that there is no slack in

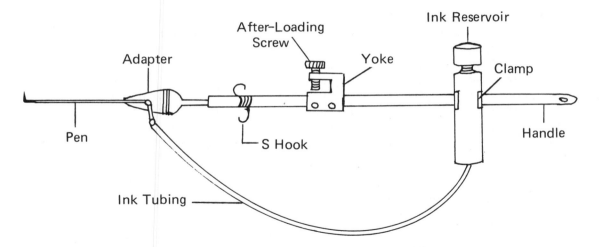

Figure 8-3.   Muscle lever with ink adapter.

Figure 8-4.   Faradic stimulation of muscle.

the thread or the muscle. This can be done most readily by adjusting the position of the muscle lever.

e.   The after-loading screw must not touch the muscle lever.

26.   Stimulate the muscle once, to make sure that the current passes to the muscle and the signal magnet and that the pen writes

during both the contraction and relaxation phases of the muscle twitch.

27.   Before making any kymograph recordings, determine both the break threshold (the least intensity of stimulus that will cause a response on break) and the make threshold (the least intensity of stimulus that will cause a response on make), by

gradually increasing the strength of the current. Record these values below and in Results and Questions.
Make Threshold. _____
Break Threshold. _____

28. Now increase the voltage and set the induction stimulator at a voltage that will produce a *submaximal make and break contraction*. (If the current is too strong, several twitches may result.)

29. Start the drum revolving slowly (speed 9). The speed must be such that the muscle contraction resembles a straight vertical line.

30. With the muscle at rest, let the pen write a short introductory baseline on the drum.

31. Make the circuit (hold down the key). The muscle should contract and relax in the same vertical line. (*Do not* release the key.)

32. Let the drum revolve approximately 1 cm. Now break the circuit (release the key). The muscle should again contract and relax.

33. Repeat this procedure three times for each member of the group.

34. Label the record completely, including title, M (make), and B (break). Include the record in your results under Results and Questions.

35. To demonstrate the effect of strength of stimulus upon height of contraction, it will be necessary to eliminate the make and to use a *constant strength break current*. (To do this, turn the voltage selector to zero, then make the circuit. While the key is depressed, reset the voltage to the desired value. Then break the circuit.)

36. Rotate the drum by hand (have drum speed selector on N), so that the contracting muscle writes a vertical line. After each stimulus, rotate the drum 1 cm.

37. Before starting this part of the experiment, determine which voltage will cause the muscle to barely contract on the break, then *reduce the voltage* below this value.

38. Stimulate the muscle with this reduced voltage. The muscle should not contract, as this is a **subliminal** or **subthreshold** stimulus. Record this voltage (and subsequent voltages) on the record.

39. Increase the voltage by increments of 5 volts or less until the muscle barely responds (height of contraction about 1 mm) to the break shock. This is the break **threshold** or **liminal** stimulus.

40. Steadily increase the voltage (recording each voltage used). The muscle should contract to a progressively greater extent with an increase in voltage. These contractions are called **submaximal** contractions. When using the range selector to change voltage ranges, note that the 50-volt setting and the 5-volt setting on the next higher range produce identical voltages. For example, range X.1 and 50 volts = 5 volts; range X1 and 5 volts = 5 volts. Therefore, start above the 5-volt position on the new (higher) range.

41. Continue stimulation until there is no further increase in the height of the muscle contraction with increasing voltage. This is the **maximal** stimulus.

42. Continue increasing the strength of the stimulus (**supramaximal** stimulus) about five more times to see if there is a resultant decrease in height of contraction with a very strong current. Too strong a current may decrease the efficiency of the muscle, as it may irritate it and increase fatigue.

Procedure Using the Physiograph and Myograph

1. Detailed directions for the use of the physiograph can be found in Exercise 7-F. The myograph is a photoelectric force transducer used primarily for quantitative measurements of smooth, cardiac, and skeletal muscle contractions. Three types of myographs (A, B, and C) with different sensitivities are available. Myograph B will be used in these experiments.

2. Connect the myograph to the laboratory stand with the mounting rod and clamp (see Figure 8-5). Attach the frog board to the stand. Attach the transducer cable to the myograph and to the 9-hole input connector on the transducer coupler.

3. Attach the stimulator output extension cable to the RF Isolated Output on the stimulator, red to red, black to black. Then, using the clip at the opposite end of the extension cable, attach the cable to the stand where the frog will be attached. Keep the clip near the bottom of the stand. This will minimize the effect of movement of the frog on the record.

Figure 8-5. Setup for frog muscle stimulation with DMP-4B.

4. Attach a set of pin electrodes (blue and yellow) to the clip electrodes attached to the stand. Color of attachment is not important. Make sure that the pin electrodes are fastened securely to the screw holders on the clip.

5. Double pith (see Exercise 12-G for procedure) or decapitate (see Exercise 8-A, step 1, for procedure) the frog. Then place the frog on its ventral surface on the frog board. Using large pins, fasten down the forelegs and one of the hindlegs.

6. Place the knee of the other hindleg of the frog into the small clip on the frog board. It may be necessary to twist the body of the frog. As soon as the knee is inserted securely, insert a straight pin through the holes in the clip through the joint at the knee. (You may be able to pass it through the bone at this point.)

7. Remove the skin around the ankle so the Achilles tendon is visible. Pass the scissors underneath the Achilles tendon and draw a piece of thread under the tendon. Tie the thread to the tendon. After the thread is attached, cut through the tendon distal to the knot, so that the foot will not contract when the muscle is stimulated. Free the gastrocnemius from the remaining muscles and fascia of the foot and leg by gently separating the belly from the fascia.

8. Tie the other end of the thread in a fixed loop and slip the loop over the myograph leaf spring hook. Adjust the vertical position of the myograph to maintain a constant tension on the thread connected to the muscle or use the tension adjustor to adjust the tension. The thread must be taut but not too tight. The muscles and tendon should be vertical and positioned directly below the hook on the myograph.

9. Insert the pin electrodes into the proximal and distal ends of the belly of the gastrocnemius muscle.

10. Set the physiograph controls as follows:
    a. Set the paper speed to 0.1 cm/sec.
    b. Set the time marker to 1 per second.
    c. Press the main frame RECORDER switch ON. Press the POWER switch ON.
    d. Press the RECORD switch OFF (if it is glowing).
    e. Set the filter to 10K.
    f. Set the mV/CM switch to 100. The amplitude may have to be readjusted later to produce a good height of contraction.
    g. Set the pen on the center dark-green line using the POSITION control.
    h. Start the ink flowing in the pen associated with the transducer coupler and the pen attached to the time event marker.

11. Turn on the stimulator. Set the duration to 7, multiplier on X1. Set the volts on 0, multiplier on X.1. It is not necessary to set the frequency control because single stimuli will be used in this experiment. The CONT-OFF-SINGLE switch should be in the OFF position.

12. Press the channel amplifier RECORD switch ON. Use the BALANCE control to reset the pen to the pen centerline.

13. Increase the voltage until the muscle barely contracts. Then reduce the voltage below this value.

14. Start the paper.

15. Stimulate the muscle once with this reduced voltage. The muscle should not contract, as this is a **subliminal** or **subthreshold** stimulus. Record this voltage (and subsequent voltages) on the record.

16. Gradually increase the voltage until the muscle barely responds (height of contraction about 1 mm). This is the **threshold** or **liminal** stimulus.

17. Steadily increase the voltage (recording each voltage used). The muscle should contract to a progressively greater extent with an increase in voltage. These contractions are called **submaximal** contractions. When using the multiplier to change voltage ranges, note that the 10-volt setting and the 1-volt setting on the next higher range produce identical voltages. For example, range X.1 and 10 volts = 1 volt. Range X1 and 1 volt = 1 volt. Therefore, start above the 1-volt position on the new (higher) range.

18. Continue stimulation until there is no further increase in the height of the muscle contraction with increasing voltage. This is the **maximal** stimulus.

19. Continue increasing the strength of the stimulus about five more times to see if there is a resultant decrease (**supramaximal** stimulus) in the height of contraction with a very strong current. Too

strong a current may decrease the efficiency of the muscle as it may irritate it and increase fatigue.

EXERCISE 8-B
GENESIS OF TETANUS

Objective

To demonstrate tetanus.

Materials

Beaker; frog Ringer's solution; frog; dissecting set; watch glass; medicine dropper; *either* wires, moist chamber, light muscle lever, kymograph, stand, 10-g weight, induction stimulator Model 330 or stimulator Model 340, and two double clamps *or* physiograph, frog board, clips, stand, myograph B, pin electrodes, stimulator output extension cable, and transducer cable.

Discussion

A tetanic contraction occurs when the muscle is stimulated 30 to 100 times per second (the frequency needed to produce complete tetanus depends upon the muscle). At this frequency, the muscle is stimulated so rapidly that there is no opportunity for relaxation between twitches; therefore, the twitches fuse together, producing a smooth curve. The height of the tetanic contraction is greater than the height of single twitches.

Procedure Using the Kymograph

1. Use the same muscle preparation as in the previous experiment. It is not necessary to use the signal magnet in this experiment.
2. Use drum speed 9. At this speed the muscle contraction will produce a vertical line on the drum, rather than a curve.
3. If the induction stimulator Model 330 is used, select a *maximal strength faradic stimulus*, so that the make and break stimulations produce the same height contraction.
4. Stimulate the muscle approximately five times at a rate of once per second. All muscle twitches should be distinct, but close together. Let the muscle rest for 1 minute. Label these contractions single twitches.

5. Increase the rate of stimulation to 2 per second, for a period of 4 seconds. At this frequency, the muscle may not have time to relax completely before the second stimulation is introduced. Allow the muscle to rest for 1 minute.
6. Continue to increase the rate of stimulation (maintaining the stimulation in each case for 3 to 4 seconds with a 1-minute rest period in between) to produce incomplete tetanus. The individual twitches should be visible, but the muscle lever should not return to the baseline between twitches.
7. Increase the rate of stimulation further to obtain complete tetanus. If possible, do this by making and breaking the circuit very rapidly.
8. If this is not possible, raise the key to the MULT. position. This produces a tetanic current, where the current is made and broken 50 times per second. This is of sufficient frequency to produce complete tetanus, but it results in rapid muscle fatigue. The record should show a complete fusion of twitches; individual contractions should not be visible.
9. Label single twitches, incomplete tetanus, and complete tetanus. Include the record under Results and Questions.
10. If the stimulator Model 340 (see Figure 8-6) is used, attach the wires from the

Figure 8-6. Stimulator model 340.

bottom of the moist chamber to the terminals on the stimulator marked STIM.

11. Plug in the stimulator and set the voltage controls to produce a contraction between 1 and 2 inches in height. Note that this stimulator has a frequency control. The numbers indicate the frequency of stimulation per second. Set the lever marked SINGLE and MULTIPLE to MULTIPLE and follow the above directions (steps 4 through 7), gradually increasing the frequency of stimulation from 1 per second until complete tetanus is obtained. The experiment can be performed on this instrument more easily and accurately than on the induction stimulator.

Procedure Using the Physiograph

1. Use the same muscle preparation and setup as in Exercise 8-A, Procedure Using the Physiograph and Myograph, steps 1 through 10.
2. Turn on the stimulator. Set the frequency control to 5 and the multiplier on X1. The CONT-OFF-SINGLE switch should be in the OFF position.
3. Press the RECORD button. Adjust the transducer BALANCE control to reposition the pen on the center dark-green line, if necessary.
4. Increase the voltage and adjust the mV/CM switch to produce a single contraction 1 to 2 inches in height with the CONT-OFF-SINGLE switch set on SINGLE.
5. Set the paper speed at .1 cm/sec and the time marker to 1 per second. Start the ink flowing. Allow the muscle to rest 15 seconds between each period of stimulation. With a frequency of once every 2 seconds (frequency at 5, multiplier at X1) move the CONT-OFF-SINGLE switch to CONT and stimulate the muscle four to six times. Increase the frequency to 1 per second (frequency on 10, multiplier at X1) and stimulate the muscle approximately six times. Then turn the multiplier to X1 and the frequency to 2 (frequency 2 per second) and stimulate the muscle approximately ten times. Gradually increase the frequency to a frequency adequate to obtain complete tetanus. Each period of stimulation should occupy about 2 cm of chart paper.

6. Label the record completely with the frequency of each period of stimulation. Label single twitches, incomplete tetanus, and complete tetanus.

EXERCISE 8-C
DURATION OF A SINGLE MUSCLE TWITCH

Objective

To measure the duration of a single muscle twitch.

Materials

Beaker; frog Ringer's solution; frog; dissecting set; watch glass; medicine dropper; *either* wires, moist chamber, light muscle lever, kymograph, stand, 10-g weight, induction stimulator, three double clamps, and signal magnet *or* physiograph, frog board, clips, stand, myograph B, pin electrodes, stimulator output extension cable, and transducer cable.

Discussion

A single contraction of a muscle is called a single muscle twitch. There are three phases of the muscle twitch: the latent period, the period of contraction, and the period of relaxation. The latent period is the time between the introduction of the stimulus and beginning of the contraction. This is usually 0.01 second or less. The contraction phase is the time during which the muscle shortens. This averages about 0.04 second in the gastrocnemius muscle of the frog. The relaxation period is the time during which the muscle regains its original length. This may be 0.05 second or longer. The entire muscle twitch lasts approximately 0.1 second or longer. These figures vary greatly as the temperature of the muscle and the load to which it is subjected vary.

Procedure Using the Kymograph

1. Use the same equipment setup and frog as in Exercise 8-A.
2. Place the writing point of the signal magnet (which will indicate the point of introduction of the current into the muscle) immediately beneath the writing point of the muscle lever stylus.
3. To measure the duration of a single muscle twitch, use a rapidly rotating drum

(speed 2). At this speed the drum moves 20 cm/sec.

4. Since only one contraction is desired, it is necessary to short-circuit the break. In order to use only the make, depress the key at the proper time during the experiment. *Do not release the key* until after the conclusion of the experiment.

5. Start the drum rotating, then make the circuit. Rotate the stand away from the drum after one contraction of the muscle and before one complete revolution of the drum to prevent doubling up on the tracing. Then break the circuit.

6. Replace the muscle pen in its original position. Let it write a baseline, as illustrated in Figure 8-7.

7. To obtain the proper time relationship, turn the stand slightly away from the drum. Place the top of the pen at point c (see Figure 8-7). Let the pen fall gently, describing an arc, to the baseline.

8. Construct an appropriate vertical line from the signal magnet tracing to the baseline, as indicated on Figure 8-7.

9. Label the curve as follows:
   a. Point of introduction of the current.
   b. Beginning of contraction of the muscle.
   c. End of contraction.
   d. End of relaxation.
   e. Where arc crosses the baseline.

10. Calculate the duration of each phase of the muscle twitch, as directed under Results and Questions. Include your kymograph record in Results.

Procedure Using the Physiograph

1. Use the same equipment setup and frog as in Exercise 8-A.

2. Set the physiograph controls as follows:
   a. Set the paper speed to 10 cm/sec.
   b. Set the time marker to 1 per second.
   c. Press the main frame RECORDER switch ON.
   d. Press POWER switch ON.
   e. Press the RECORD switch OFF (if it is glowing).
   f. Set the filter to 10K.
   g. Set the mV/CM switch to 100. The amplitude may have to be readjusted later to produce a good height of contraction.

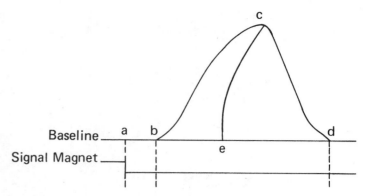

Figure 8-7. Duration of a muscle twitch as measured with the kymograph.

   h. Set the pen on the dark-green center line using the POSITION control.
   i. Start the ink flowing in the pen associated with the transducer coupler and the pen attached to the time-event marker.

3. Turn on the stimulator. Set the duration on 7 and the multiplier on X1. Set the volts on approximately 5 volts (voltage necessary to obtain an adequate height of contraction). The CONT-OFF-SINGLE switch should be in the OFF position.

4. Press the channel amplifier RECORD switch ON. Use the BALANCE control to reset the pen to the dark-green center line.

5. Adjust the voltage and the mV/CM switch to obtain a contraction 1 to 2 inches in height.

6. After starting the paper, stimulate the muscle once. The time-event pen should indicate the precise point of stimulation.

7. Using a ruler, draw a baseline across the bottom of the recording (see Figure 8-8). Draw vertical lines from the top of the curve to the baseline and from the point of introduction of the stimulus to the baseline.

8. Label your record as follows:
   a. Point of introduction of the current.
   b. Beginning of contraction of the muscle.
   c. End of contraction.
   d. End of relaxation.
   e. Where vertical line crosses the baseline.

9. Calculate the duration of each phase of the muscle twitch, as directed under Results and Questions.

Figure 8-8. Duration of a muscle twitch as measured with the physiograph.

EXERCISE 8-D
MUSCLE FATIGUE

Objectives

To demonstrate the factors causing muscle fatigue; to demonstrate the restorative effect of rest.

Materials

Beaker; frog Ringer's solution; frog; dissecting set; watch glass; medicine dropper; *either* wires, moist chamber, light muscle lever, kymograph, stand, 10-g weight, induction or electronic stimulator, and two double clamps *or* physiograph, frog board, clips, stand, myograph B, pin electrodes, stimulator output extension cable, and transducer cable.

Discussion

As a muscle continues to contract, it gradually becomes fatigued and loses its ability to contract. The time of appearance of fatigue depends upon the strength of the stimulus and the load. This experiment must be the last in any series with the frog muscle since the muscle will not recover from the fatigue to any extent.

Procedure Using the Kymograph

1. Set up the recording and stimulating apparatus as in Exercise 8-A.
2. Load the muscle with 10 g. Do not set the after-loading screw. Make certain that the resting position of the muscle lever is horizontal.
3. Use a slowly moving drum (speed 10) so that the muscle contraction produces a vertical line.
4. Either the Harvard Model 330 Induction Stimulator or the Harvard Model Electronic Stimulator can be used in this experiment. The electronic stimulator is easier to use, since it can be set to stimulate the muscle automatically at a preset frequency. To use the electronic stimulator, connect two wires from the two terminals marked STIM to the two terminals on the inferior surface of the moist chamber. Set the frequency at 1 per second. Set the voltage at a level sufficient to produce a muscle contraction 1 to 2 inches in height. Start the drum and set the switch to MULTIPLE.
5. If the Model 330 Induction Stimulator is used, stimulate the muscle once per second with a constant strength maximal break current. Short-circuit the make. Practice this procedure before beginning the experiment.
6. Continue stimulating the muscle once per second until the muscle no longer contracts. Disregard contractions less than 1 mm in height on the record.
7. Continue the stimulation (without a period of rest) for one more minute to see if there is any recovery. The muscle may not contract for 15 to 30 seconds, even though

it is stimulated, and then it may contract slightly several times.

8. Allow the muscle to rest for 5 minutes. Then, using the same strength and rate of stimulation, determine whether the muscle has recovered from fatigue.
9. Label the record completely and include it under Results and Questions.

Procedure Using the Physiograph

1. Set up the physiograph as described in Exercise 8-A. Set the time event marker to 1 per second. Use a paper speed of 0.05 cm/sec. Set the frequency of stimulation at 1 per second (frequency at 10. multiplier at X.1) and the duration at 7, multiplier at X1. Set the voltage of stimulation at a level sufficient to produce a muscle contraction 1 to 2 inches in height. (The muscle will fatigue faster at a higher voltage.) Start the paper and set the switch to CONT for continuous stimulation.
2. Continue stimulating the muscle once per second until the muscle no longer contracts. Disregard contractions less than 1 mm in height on the record.
3. Continue the stimulation (without a period of rest) for one more minute to see if there is any recovery. The muscle may not contract for 15 to 30 seconds, even though it is stimulated, and then it may contract slightly several times.
4. Allow the muscle to rest for 5 minutes. Then, using the same strength and rate of stimulation, determine whether the muscle has recovered from fatigue.
5. Label the record completely and include it under Results and Questions.

EXERCISE 8-E
PHYSIOLOGY OF HUMAN MUSCLE

Objectives

To demonstrate the change in size of skeletal muscle during contraction; to demonstrate human muscle fatigue.

Materials

Kymograph; ergograph; pen (intermediate length ink stylus, ball-point pen, or pencil); sphygmomanometer; tape measure.

Discussion

When a muscle contracts, it shortens, pulling the insertion toward the origin. The belly of the muscle becomes shorter and thicker. This change in size of a muscle will be measured in this exercise.

The ergograph is a device for measuring the amount of work performed in muscular action. It consists of an adjustable tension spring with a writing point and trigger, fastened in a support mounted for stability on a heavy board.

Repeated contraction of a muscle produces fatigue. Fatigue is caused by an accumulation of waste products, such as lactic acid, or by a deficiency in oxygen, glucose, and other raw materials. The compression of the brachial artery caused by the use of a sphygmomanometer in this experiment results in interference with the blood supply to the muscles of the fingers. The muscles thus should fatigue faster than usual.

Procedure

1. Measure the circumference of your partner's arm with the forearm extended and flexed. Be certain to apply the tape measure to exactly the same place on the arm each time. Record your measurements under Results and Questions.
2. Set up the kymograph and ergograph as in Figure 8-9, with the ergograph to the right of the kymograph.
3. Use the bottom perforation on the spring housing, so that the tension is at its highest level.
4. Adjust the ink supply so that the ink does not flow out too freely. A ball-point pen or lead pencil can be taped to the arm of the ergograph and used instead of the ink stylus.
5. Adjust the height of the kymograph so that the first tracings are approximately 2 inches from the bottom of the paper.
6. Use drum speed 9 throughout the experiment.
7. The subject should be seated comfortably and should grasp the trigger of the ergograph with the index finger of the dominant hand. It is important to keep the index finger in constant contact with the trigger.
8. Start the kymograph. Have the subject rhythmically squeeze the trigger at a rate

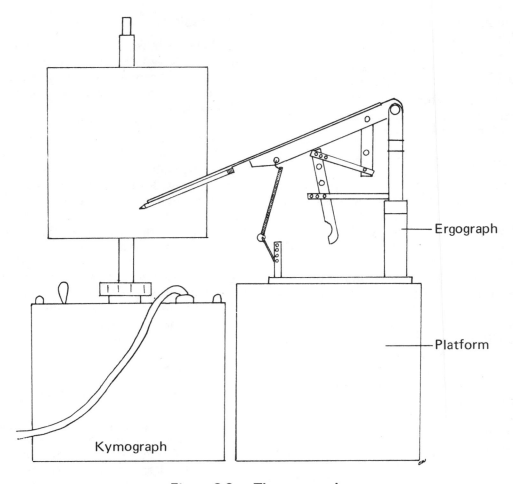

Figure 8-9.   The ergograph.

of about two times per second until complete fatigue develops.

9. Allow the subject to rest exactly 30 seconds and then repeat the above procedure.

10. Allow the subject to rest 5 minutes. Place a sphygmomanometer cuff on the subject's arm immediately above the elbow. Inflate this to a pressure of 140 mm Hg and repeat the above procedure.

11. Calculate the length of time necessary to fatigue the muscle initially, after 30 seconds' rest, and with use of the sphygmomanometer. Compare the initial force of contractions with that after 30 seconds' rest and with that produced with the use of the sphygmomanometer.

12. Compare the length of time necessary to produce fatigue on your record with that of your partner. Record your observations and answer the questions under Results and Questions.

Alternate Procedure

1. It is possible to perform approximately the same experiment without the ergograph. Lay your left forearm on the deck, palm up.

2. Flex and extend the fingers rapidly at the metacarpal-phalangeal joint until they are fatigued. Record the time needed to cause fatigue.

3. Rest your fingers for 5 minutes.

4. Apply the blood pressure cuff immediately above the elbow. Inflate the sphygmomanometer to 140 mm Hg. Repeat step 2, recording the time necessary to cause fatigue.

SELF-TEST—MUSCLE PHYSIOLOGY

Directions

See Chapter 1, Self-Test, page 9. Also see the Self-Test at the end of Chapter 6.

1. A muscle fiber uses oxygen during the **contraction** period.

2. Myasthenia gravis involves an overproduction of **acetylcholine.**

3. Products formed during the contraction of a muscle include **ADP, creatine, and lactic acid.**

4. One result of muscular contractions is a change in the chemical composition of **the urine.**

5. Reciprocal innervation involves **both** stimulating and relaxing impulses.

6. A **tonic** spasm is a continued muscular contraction, whereas a **clonic** spasm consists of a series of alternate contractions and relaxations.

7. **Fibrillation** is an ineffective quivering of muscle fibers.

8. **Flaccid paralysis** involves complete paralysis, abolishment of muscle tone, and "limp" extremities.

9. Muscle **spasm** is a steady, partial contraction present at all times in healthy muscles.

10. Visceral muscle reacts to stimuli **more** rapidly than does skeletal muscle.

11. Such drugs as Anectine, Intocostrin, and other curare-like compounds are used in the operating room to **prevent** muscular relaxation by blocking nerve impulses.

12. **Choline acetylase** is a chemical needed to stimulate muscle fibers to action.

13. **Cholinesterase** inactivates acetylcholine, thus preventing continued action of the muscle fibers.

14. An individual poisoned by curare may die as a result of paralysis of the **diaphragm.**

15. Each skeletal muscle cell has **many** nuclei.

16. The advantage of recording muscular contractions on a moving surface such as the kymograph or oscillograph is that **the time element is amplified** so that the separate events are spread out and can be studied in detail.

17. The chemical and physical processes in a single muscle twitch of a muscle from a cold-blooded vertebrate will be carried out in **less time** than would be required for those in a mammalian muscle.

18. The endings of axons of an **afferent** nerve fiber on the muscle fibers they innervate are called motor end plates or myoneural junctions.

19. The number of muscle fibers in a motor unit is **unrelated** to the degree of precision with which a muscle is capable of acting.

20. Work **is** performed by isometric contraction.

21. Muscles **can** contract in the absence of oxygen.

22. In the chemical reactions associated with muscular contraction, the resynthesis of glycogen **can** take place anaerobically.

23. **Hemoglobin** is the name of the iron-containing protein in muscle.

24. Posture is maintained primarily by **isometric contraction** of muscles.

25. The slight muscular tonus or tension which continues, even under resting conditions, depends on **asynchronous contraction** of different muscle units.

26. Contraction of a muscle without shortening is called **isometric** contraction.

27. The warming up process in an isolated muscle that shows successive increases in the degree of shortening of the muscle in response to stimuli of constant strength is called **treppe.**

28. The time interval between application of a stimulus and the beginning of a response is called the **latent period.**

29. Work may be calculated by multiplying the **height** a load is lifted by the **weight** load.

30. When a muscle contracts, the blood within it becomes **slightly acid.**

9

The Digestive System

EXERCISE 9-A
ANATOMY OF THE HUMAN DIGESTIVE SYSTEM

Objectives

To become familiar with the location and functions of the true and accessory human digestive organs.

Materials

Dissectable torso; anatomic charts; reference books.

Discussion

The digestive system is concerned with receiving, transporting, digesting, and absorbing food. The alimentary canal or digestive tract, a tube approximately 30 feet long, is subdivided into the following regions: mouth, pharynx, esophagus, stomach, small intestine, and large intestine, all of which are considered true digestive organs. In addition, other organs are connected to the alimentary canal and are considered part of the digestive system. These accessory digestive organs include the tongue, teeth, salivary glands, liver, gall bladder, and pancreas.

For food to be absorbed into the bloodstream, it must first be broken down into small, diffusable substances. This is accomplished by digestive enzymes, which break down complex foods into simple compounds that are readily absorbed from the digestive tract. This type of chemical reaction, which involves the addition of water, is called hydrolysis. The end products of digestion are absorbed into the bloodstream, primarily through the walls of the small intestine, by the processes of dialysis and active absorption.

Procedure

1. Locate the structures listed in the key to Figure 9-1 on the dissectable torso and determine at least one important function of each.
2. Figure 9-2 shows the right salivary glands. As you dissect the fetal pig, compare the locations of these glands.
3. Learn the parts of a typical tooth and the various types of teeth by studying Figures 9-3, 9-4, and 9-5.
4. Figure 9-6 may be used as a self-test. It shows the interrelationships of various ducts, blood vessels, and accessory organs of digestion.
5. Study Figure 9-7, which shows the gross anatomy of the stomach.
6. In Figure 9-8, note the taenia coli. This is one of the three longitudinal bands of muscle fiber in the large intestine. These bands of muscle tissue are responsible for the scalloped appearance of the large intestine (the resulting bulges are called haustra). Note also the epiploic appendages, which are accumulations of fat between the wall of the colon and the serosal covering. Study the other structures illustrated.
7. Study Figure 9-9, which shows the structure of the rectum and the anus.

122

KEY TO FIGURE 9-1

1. nasal chamber	9. ileum	17. stomach
2. oral cavity	10. cecum	18. spleen
3. pharynx	11. vermiform appendix	19. pancreas
4. right lung	12. larynx	20. transverse colon
5. liver	13. trachea	21. jejunum
6. gall bladder	14. left bronchus	22. descending colon
7. duodenum	15. esophagus	23. sigmoid colon
8. ascending colon	16. diaphragm	24. rectum

Figure 9-1.   Digestive organs.

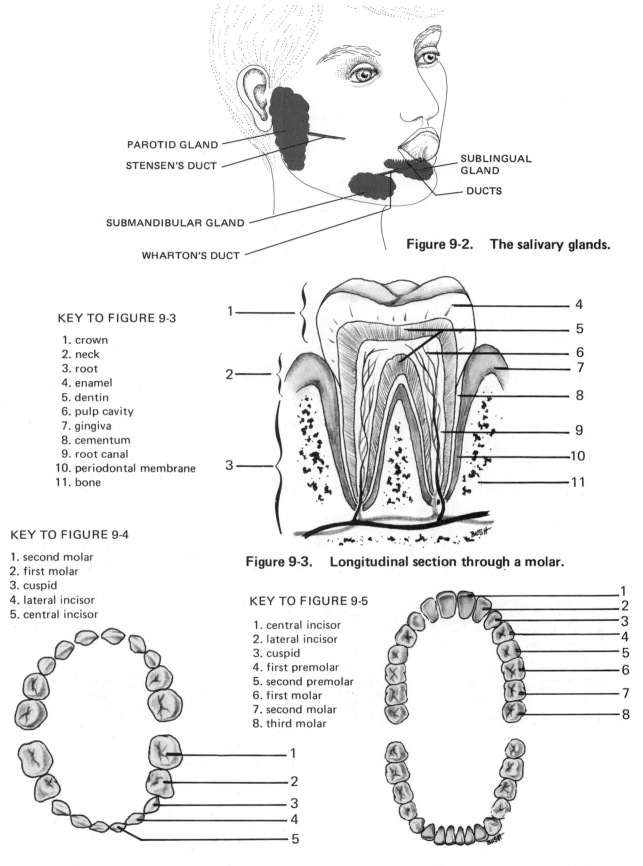

Figure 9-2. The salivary glands.

PAROTID GLAND

STENSEN'S DUCT

SUBLINGUAL GLAND

DUCTS

SUBMANDIBULAR GLAND

WHARTON'S DUCT

KEY TO FIGURE 9-3

1. crown
2. neck
3. root
4. enamel
5. dentin
6. pulp cavity
7. gingiva
8. cementum
9. root canal
10. periodontal membrane
11. bone

Figure 9-3. Longitudinal section through a molar.

KEY TO FIGURE 9-4

1. second molar
2. first molar
3. cuspid
4. lateral incisor
5. central incisor

KEY TO FIGURE 9-5

1. central incisor
2. lateral incisor
3. cuspid
4. first premolar
5. second premolar
6. first molar
7. second molar
8. third molar

Figure 9-4. The deciduous teeth.

Figure 9-5. The permanent teeth.

124

KEY TO FIGURE 9-6

1. liver
2. gall bladder
3. hepatic duct
4. cystic duct
5. hepatic artery
6. portal vein
7. duodenum
8. common bile duct

9. accessory pan-
    creatic duct
10. pancreatic duct
11. duodenal papilla
12. sup. mesenteric V.
13. R. hepatic duct
14. L. hepatic duct
15. gastric artery

16. celiac artery
17. adrenal gland
18. left kidney
19. splenic artery
20. spleen
21. aorta
22. pancreas
23. sup. mesenteric A.
24. ampulla of Vater

Figure 9-6.   Human abdominal blood vessels and ducts.

125

Figure 9-7.   The stomach.

Figure 9-8.   The colon.

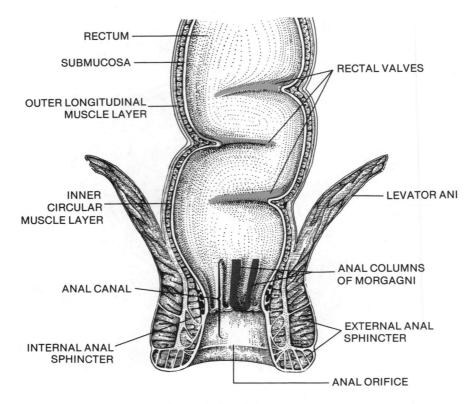

RECTUM

SUBMUCOSA

OUTER LONGITUDINAL MUSCLE LAYER

RECTAL VALVES

INNER CIRCULAR MUSCLE LAYER

LEVATOR ANI

ANAL CANAL

ANAL COLUMNS OF MORGAGNI

INTERNAL ANAL SPHINCTER

EXTERNAL ANAL SPHINCTER

ANAL ORIFICE

Figure 9-9.   The rectum.

EXERCISE 9-B
DISSECTION OF THE DIGESTIVE SYSTEM OF THE FETAL PIG

Objectives

To identify the digestive organs of the fetal pig and to compare them with the corresponding human structures.

Materials

Fetal pig; dissecting board or tray; dissecting set.

Discussion

The digestive organs of the fetal pig are very similar to those of the human. Observe carefully the differences between the two organisms, such as the arrangement of the colon and the absence of both the vermiform appendix and the uvula in the pig. Be prepared to trace the path of food through the digestive tract.

Procedure

1. Lay the pig, ventral surface up, on the dissecting board. To spread the legs of the specimen, tie a length of cord from each ankle to the nails on the sides of the board, or loop the cord underneath the board and tie it.

2. Use Figure 9-10 as a guide for the following dissection:
    a. Make an incision with the scalpel through the skin from the small, hairy **papilla** on the upper part of the throat down the midline to a point just anterior (cranial) to the umbilical cord.
    b. Continue to deepen the incision very carefully, cutting through the cartilaginous sternum, until the body cavity is reached. Be careful not to cut the large veins and arteries.
    c. Cut around the cord (as illustrated) and continue the incision laterally on each side to the head of the femur in the ventral thigh region. If the directions are followed, a flap will be produced which includes the umbilical cord and some urogenital organs.
    d. If the body cavity is filled with a dark fluid, flush it out with water; be careful not to damage any organs or tear the umbilical vein.

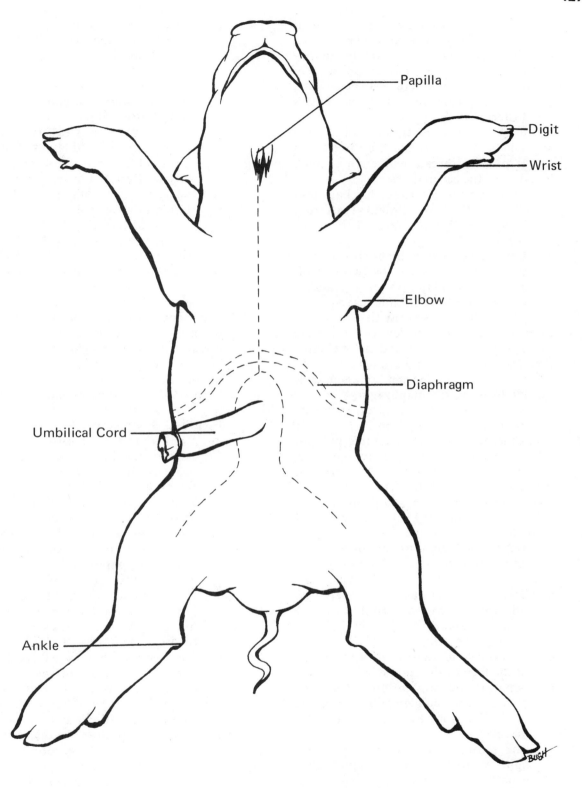

Figure 9-10. Diagram showing initial incisions for fetal pig dissection.

3. Pull the flap that contains the umbilical vessels back carefully and observe the **umbilical vein,** which runs from the umbilical cord to the liver. The umbilical vein continues on as the **ductus venosus,** which passes through the liver and then enters the posterior vena cava.

4. Tie a thread around the umbilical vein and cut the vein between the thread and the flap. The thread will enable quick location of the severed vessel.

   a. Pull the ventral flap further back and observe the two **umbilical arteries,** injected with red latex, on the inner surface.

   b. Locate the **urinary bladder,** the large sac situated between the two umbilical arteries, at the posterior (caudal) portion of the abdominal cavity.

5. To enlarge the exposed cavities, make the following incisions, which will facilitate subsequent dissections and at the same time leave the diaphragm intact:

   a. Cut laterally, on each side, immediately above the **diaphragm.**

   b. Make a second incision on each side directly below the diaphragm.

6. As in the human, there are three pairs of salivary glands in the pig, in the same general location. However, their size and shape are variable in the fetal pig, making dissection and accurate identification difficult. Using Figure 9-11 as a guide, limit your dissection to the location of the parotid and submandibular glands. Use the following instructions for this dissection:

   a. Starting at the base of the **left** ear, inferior to the external auditory meatus, make a shallow incision **through the skin.**

   b. Continue the incision down the side of the face to the shoulder.

   c. Separate the skin carefully from the musculature and glands on either side of the incision. Locate the masseter muscle.

   d. The **parotid gland** is a large, thin, light colored, triangular gland that usually extends from the base of the ear to the shoulder. It is underdeveloped in the fetal pig.

   e. **Stensen's duct,** the thin, white duct of the parotid gland, is located on the anteroventral border of the masseter muscle, the large muscle anterior to the parotid gland covering the angle of the lower jaw. The duct opens into the oral cavity by the fourth upper premolar.

   f. The **submandibular gland** lies deep to the parotid gland. To locate this gland, make a shallow incision through the parotid gland at the level of the inferior border of the masseter muscle. Reflect the lower portion of the parotid. The submandibular gland should now be visible.

   g. The **sublingual gland** is located anterior to the inferior border of the submandibular gland. A small **lymph node** may be located by separating the dorsal anterior border of the parotid from the masseter.

7. Cut through the angle of each jaw (corner of mouth), toward the ears, until it is possible to see the **epiglottis** and the opening into the throat (pharynx). The interior of the mouth can now be examined (see Figure 9-12). Compare your dissection to a model of the human larynx and to Figure 11-3 in Chapter 11.

   a. Locate the **vestibule,** the space between the lips and the teeth, and the **oral cavity,** the principal cavity inside the mouth.

   b. The **tongue** is attached ventrally throughout most of its length by a membrane called the **lingual fenulum.**

   c. The surface of the tongue contains numerous **papillae.** Taste buds are associated with the papillae.

   d. If the **teeth** are not visible, cut into the jaw and expose them. The dental formula for the deciduous set of teeth in the pig is 3 1 4 0.

   e. Observe the bony ridged **hard palate** and the muscular **soft palate,** posterior to the hard palate. The pig lacks the uvula, which is the posterior extension of the soft palate in humans.

   f. Identify the **fauces,** the opening of the oral cavity into the **oropharynx.**

   g. The pharynx is divided into three regions: the **nasopharynx** behind the nose, the **oropharynx** behind the mouth, and the **laryngopharynx** opening into the larynx (see Figure 11-3 in Chapter 11).

   h. Make a median incision through the

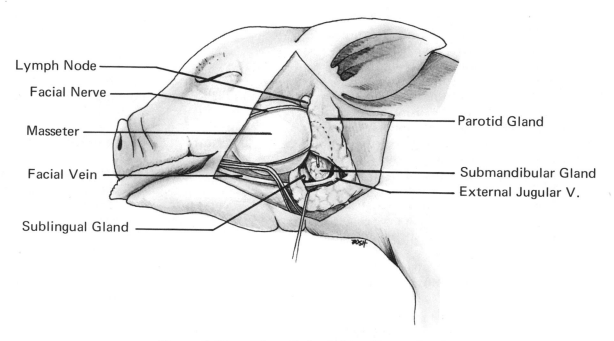

Lymph Node
Facial Nerve
Masseter
Facial Vein
Sublingual Gland
Parotid Gland
Submandibular Gland
External Jugular V.

Figure 9-11.   Dissection of the salivary glands.

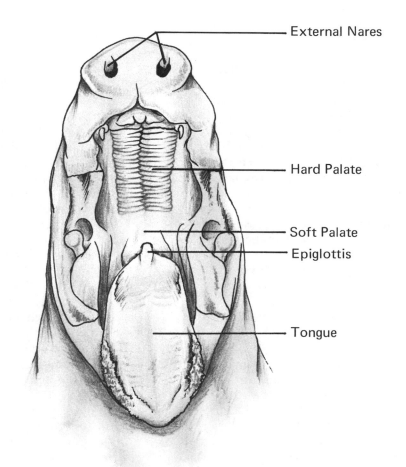

External Nares
Hard Palate
Soft Palate
Epiglottis
Tongue

Figure 9-12.   The oral cavity.

entire soft palate to expose the naso-pharynx. (Do not cut into the dorsal wall of the nasopharynx.)

i. Locate the two small slits, about 1 mm in diameter, in the lateral dorsal walls of the nasopharynx. These are the openings of the **Eustachian tubes** (auditory tubes). The **internal nares** also open into the nasopharynx.

j. Locate the opening of the pharynx into the **esophagus,** dorsal to the larynx.

k. Locate the **glottis,** opening into the larynx. The **epiglottis** can be seen as a small tonguelike flap at the entrance to the larynx.

8. Locate the esophagus again in the thoracic cavity to determine its position relative to the heart.

9. Locate the **diaphragm,** which separates the thoracic cavity from the abdominal cavity.

10. Use Figures 9-13 and 9-14 to assist you in locating the following organs. Compare these structures with those of the human shown in Figure 9-6.

a. Locate the large, reddish-brown colored liver posterior to the dia-phragm. Note that the superior sur-face of the liver is convex to match the concavity of the diaphragm.

b. Count the number of lobes in the liver. The pig liver is divided into five lobes: the **right lateral, right central, left central, left lateral,** and **caudate.** The human liver has four lobes.

c. Lift the right lobe of the liver and locate the **gall bladder,** the small, pear-shaped sac embedded in the right central lobe.

d. The umbilical vein can be found enter-ing the liver to the left of the gall bladder.

e. It is necessary to dissect carefully to avoid destroying the following struc-tures. The **cystic duct** from the gall bladder and the **hepatic duct** from the liver unite to form the **common bile duct,** which empties into the duo-denum (see Figure 9-14). To locate these structures, *gently* tease away the **lesser omentum** between the stomach and liver. First locate the green cystic duct from the gall bladder and the

common bile duct. To locate the hepatic duct, trace the common bile duct upward to the point where the cystic duct enters. The duct branching to the left is the hepatic duct.

11. Lift the liver to expose the **stomach,** which is located on the left side of the abdominal cavity.

a. Locate the entrance of the esophagus into the stomach.

b. Identify the following gross regions of the stomach: the **fundus, body, greater curvature, lesser curvature, cardiac region,** and **pyloric region** (See Figure 9-7).

c. Make an incision along the greater curvature of the stomach from the pyloric region to the cardiac region. Wash out the stomach. The green debris found here and elsewhere in the digestive tract is called **meconium.** It is bile-stained mucus, epithelial cells sloughed off from the skin and lining of the digestive tract, and amnionic fluid swallowed by the fetus. It is discharged in the first bowel move-ments of the newborn.

d. Observe the **gastric mucosa** lining the stomach and the **rugae,** the longitu-dinal folds visible in the interior of the stomach.

e. Continue the longitudinal incision through the **cardiac sphincter,** a cir-cular ring of smooth muscle surround-ing the opening of the esophagus into the stomach. Note that the sphincter is tightly closed. In this area there is a small **diverticulum** of the stomach near the esophagus. This is believed to be the rudiment of the complex chambering of the stomach of the cow. Humans lack this structure.

f. Continue the same longitudinal in-cision through the **pyloric sphincter,** the sphincter regulating the passage of food into the duodenum.

12. Locate the **small intestine,** beginning at the posterior end of the stomach. The small intestine is a long coiled tube divided into three regions: the **duodenum, jejunum,** and **ileum.**

a. The anterior curved portion of the small intestine leaving the stomach is the **duodenum.** This portion is

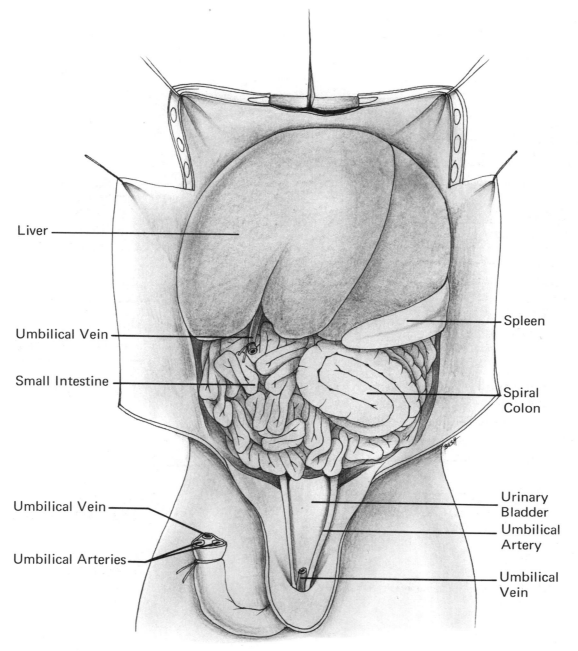

Liver

Umbilical Vein

Small Intestine

Umbilical Vein

Umbilical Arteries

Spleen

Spiral Colon

Urinary Bladder

Umbilical Artery

Umbilical Vein

Figure 9-13. Superficial view of digestive organs of the fetal pig.

approximately 1 cm long. The common bile duct can be seen entering the duodenum from the liver.

b. Open the duodenum by continuing the longitudinal incision through its wall from the pyloric sphincter, on the side away from the opening of the common bile duct. Note that the common bile duct empties into the duodenum through a small papilla, the **duodenal papilla.**

c. Observe the velvety texture of the interior of the small intestine. This texture is due to small fingerlike projections called **villi** that greatly increase the absorptive surface of the small intestine.

d. The two remaining, approximately equal, portions of the small intestine, the **jejunum** and the **ileum,** have no readily distinguishable boundary. The jejunum is the middle region of the

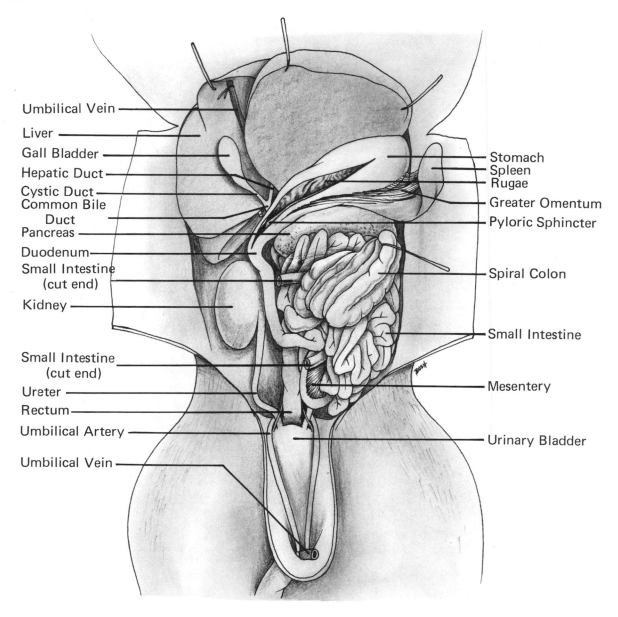

Umbilical Vein

Liver

Gall Bladder

Hepatic Duct

Cystic Duct
Common Bile
Duct
Pancreas

Duodenum

Small Intestine
(cut end)

Kidney

Small Intestine
(cut end)

Ureter

Rectum

Umbilical Artery

Umbilical Vein

Stomach
Spleen
Rugae

Greater Omentum

Pyloric Sphincter

Spiral Colon

Small Intestine

Mesentery

Urinary Bladder

Figure 9-14. Digestive organs of the fetal pig (with liver and spleen pulled back and small intestine removed on the right side).

small intestine and the ileum is the latter half that enters the large intestine.

13. Locate the **spleen,** the long dark organ to the left of the stomach. It is attached to the greater curvature of the stomach by means of the **greater omentum,** a specialized fold of the peritoneum. Compare the structure of the greater omentum in the pig with that in humans. The spleen is considered to be part of the circulatory system.

14. The **pancreas** lies in the angle between the curve of the stomach and the duodenum. The greater part of the gland is located behind the stomach. The pancreas is connected to the duodenum by the pancreatic duct. This duct is small and need not be dissected out.

15. Trace the ileum to its point of attachment with the **large intestine.**

   a. The ileum opens into the side of the colon, forming a blind pouch, the **cecum,** at the beginning of the **colon.**

In man, the vermiform appendix is located below the cecum. This is not present in the pig.

b. Cut into the cecum, wash out the contents, and observe the **ileocecal sphincter.**

c. The first part of the large intestine in the fetal pig is called the **spiral colon.** It is visible as a compact coiled mass on the left side of the abdominal cavity. This structure is not found in humans.

d. The posterior portion of the large intestine is the **rectum.** Locate this structure passing from the spiral colon as a straight tube into the pelvic cavity. The external opening of the rectum is the **anus.**

16. Locate the **peritoneum,** the double membrane lining the abdominal cavity.

a. The parietal layer of the peritoneum lines the body wall; the visceral layer covers the abdominal organs.

b. Locate the **mesentery,** the double layer of the peritoneum extending from the dorsal wall of the abdominal cavity to the small intestine. The mesentery contains blood vessels, lymphatics, and nerves (see Figure 9-14).

c. Observe the mesentery near its point of contact with the dorsal body wall and locate a row of small white bulges. These are **lymph nodes.**

d. If not done previously, locate the **greater omentum,** extending between the stomach and the spleen, and the **lesser omentum,** extending between the stomach and duodenum to the liver.

EXERCISE 9-C
ACTION OF SALIVARY AMYLASE

Objective

To determine the action of salivary amylase on starch.

Materials

Test tubes; saliva; 1% boiled starch; paper cups; Benedict's solution; Lugol's solution; graduate; beakers; thermometer; tripod; wire gauze; paraffin wax; distilled water; boiling water bath.

Discussion

Salivary amylase (or ptyalin) is produced by the parotid, submandibular, and sublingual glands, which empty their secretions by way of ducts into the mouth. Amylase acts on cooked starch and glycogen, hydrolyzing them to erythrodextrin, achromodextrin, and finally to maltose. Although the optimum pH of salivary amylase is 6.8 to 7.0, salivary digestion proceeds in the stomach until the acid gastric juice is mixed thoroughly with the bolus of food.

In this experiment, Benedict's test and the iodine test (Lugol's solution) will be used to follow the course of salivary digestion.

Benedict's test is one of the most commonly used tests for the detection of reducing sugars (sugars that contain a free aldehyde or ketone group). Glucose, or any other reducing sugar, reacts with Benedict's solution, which contains alkaline copper sulfate solution with sodium citrate. The sugar reduces the blue cupric ion, forming insoluble red cuprous oxide. The precipitate of cuprous oxide can usually be seen in the bottom of the tube after standing. Depending on the amount of reducing sugar present, Benedict's solution turns green, yellow, orange, or red.

Lugol's solution is a 1% solution of iodine and potassium iodide (1 part iodine, 2 parts potassium iodide, and 300 parts distilled water). Certain polysaccharides give characteristic colors when treated with iodine. Starch, for example, gives a deep blue to "black" color with Lugol's solution (the black is really a concentrated blue color). Glycogen gives a red-brown color with Lugol's solution, while erythrodextrin gives a red color. Cellulose, monosaccharides, and disaccharides do not react. A negative test is indicated by the yellow to brown color of the solution itself or by some other color (other than blue to black) resulting from pigments present in the substance being tested. The iodine test will not work in hot solutions.

Procedure

1. Collect some saliva by rinsing your mouth thoroughly with distilled water two or three times and then chewing a piece of paraffin wax. Expectorate about 5 ml of saliva into a paper cup.

2. Add 5 ml of 1% boiled starch solution to each of the two test tubes. Label these tubes 1 and 2.

3. Add 4 drops of Lugol's solution to each tube (or add Lugol's solution until the starch solution turns blue).
4. Add 8 drops of saliva to tube 1. Note the time at which the saliva is added. Add 8 drops of distilled water to tube 2.
5. Immediately place both tubes in a 37 °C water bath.
6. Observe the changes in color in the tubes. Note the time it takes tube 1 to become colorless (achromic).
7. After tube 1 becomes colorless, test both tubes with Benedict's solution (add 5 ml of Benedict's solution to each tube and place the tubes in a boiling water bath for 2 minutes).
8. Observe for any of the following color changes:
    -     Solution remains blue.
    +   Green solution.
    ++   Yellow solution.
    +++   Orange solution.
    ++++ Red solution or precipitate.
9. Tabulate your results under Results and Questions. Use the symbols in step 8 where appropriate.

EXERCISE 9-D
PROTEIN DIGESTION

Objectives

To demonstrate the effect of pepsin on protein; to study the effect of pH and boiling on the rate of action of pepsin.

Materials

0.5% pepsin; fibrin; 0.8% HCl; 0.5% NaOH; Hydrion paper (range 1-11); rack; beakers; graduate; thermometer; 40° water bath; boiling water; test tubes.

Discussion

Pepsin is the proteolytic enzyme secreted by the chief cells in the lining of the stomach. It digests proteins (fibrin in this experiment) to proteoses and peptones. The activity of pepsin depends on the pH of the solution, the optimum pH being 1.5 to 2.5. Pepsin is almost completely inactive in neutral or alkaline solutions. Pepsin is secreted in the inactive form,

pepsinogen; it is activated by HCl in the gastric juice.

Procedure

1. Prepare five test tubes, numbering them from 1 to 5, and add the following solutions to them (*measure the quantity of each solution carefully in this experiment*):
    Tube 1: 5 ml of 0.5% pepsin; 5 ml of 0.8% HCl.
    Tube 2: 5 ml of 0.5% pepsin; 5 ml of water.
    Tube 3: 5 ml of 0.5% pepsin; boiled for 10 minutes in a water bath; 5 ml of 0.8% HCl.
    Tube 4: 5 ml of 0.5% pepsin; 5 ml of 0.5% NaOH.
    Tube 5: 5 ml of water; 5 ml of 0.8% HCl.
2. Determine the approximate pH of each test tube with Hydrion paper (range 1-11) and include the data in the table under Results and Questions.
3. Place the same amount of fibrin (about the size of a pea) in each test tube. Shake well.
4. Place the tubes in a 40 °C water bath and shake them from time to time (do not erase the numbers on the tubes while shaking them). Maintain the temperature close to 40 °C.
5. Keep the tubes in the water bath for at least 1½ hours. Note the changes that the fibrin undergoes. The swelling (imbibition) that occurs in some tubes should not be confused with digestion. If the fibrin is digested, it becomes transparent and gradually disappears (dissolves) as the protein is digested to soluble proteoses and peptones.
6. Conclude the experiment when the fibrin is digested in one of the five tubes.
7. Record your observations under Results and Questions.

EXERCISE 9-E
EFFECT OF RENNIN ON MILK

Objective

To determine the effect of rennin on milk.

Materials

Rennin; milk; test tubes; beaker; thermometer; Benedict's solution; 40 °C water bath.

Discussion

The gastric juice of young animals contains rennin, an enzyme that causes milk to curdle. This enzyme, while not present in the gastric juice of human adults, is present in the stomach of young infants. Rennin is manufactured by the chief cells in the inactive form, prorennin, and is converted by HCl in the lumen of the stomach to the active form, rennin. Rennin converts casein (milk protein) to paracasein; the optimum pH for this reaction is 5.4. Calcium ions then react with the paracasein to form insoluble calcium paracaseinate (a white curd). Pepsin assumes this function in adults.

Procedure

1. Break a rennin tablet in half and use one piece.
2. Dissolve this piece in 3 ml of water.
3. Add the rennin to 10 ml of skimmed milk. Mix thoroughly and place the tube in a 40 °C water bath. Let the tube stand until it can be inverted without spilling the contents. Note the time needed for the curd to form.
4. Let the tube stand for an additional half hour or more, until liquid appears on the top of the tube. This supernatant fluid is called the whey, and the remainder of the tube's contents is the curd.
5. Perform Benedict's test on the whey. Remove, with a medicine dropper, approximately 1 ml of whey. Add an equal volume of Benedict's solution and boil.
6. Record your observations under Results and Questions.

EXERCISE 9-F
PANCREATIC DIGESTION OF FAT

Objectives

To determine the effect of pancreatic juice on fat; to determine the effect of cold on enzyme activity.

Materials

Pancreatin (1% solution of pancreatin in 0.1% Na_2CO_3); milk; test tubes; powdered litmus; beakers; graduate; thermometer; pipette; ice; 40 °C water bath.

Discussion

Pancreatin contains all of the enzymes present in pancreatic juice. Since the optimum pH of the pancreatic enzymes ranges between 7.0 and 8.8, the pancreatin is prepared in sodium carbonate. The enzyme active in this experiment is lipase, which digests fat to fatty acids and glycerol. The fatty acids produced change the color of blue litmus to red.

Procedure

1. Place 5 ml of litmus milk (milk to which powdered litmus has been added to give it a blue color) in a test tube, and place it in a 40 °C water bath.
2. Place another 5-ml portion of litmus milk in a second test tube and put it in an ice bath.
3. After these tubes have attained the temperature of the water baths, add 5 ml of pancreatin to each tube and replace the tubes in the water baths until a color change occurs in one tube.
4. Complete the table under Results and Questions.

EXERCISE 9-G
BILE

Objectives

To determine the effect of bile on surface tension; to demonstrate Gmelin's test for bile.

Materials

Bile; test tubes; concentrated nitric acid (HNO_3); sulfur; beakers; distilled water.

Discussion

Bile is the digestive juice secreted by the liver. Although bile contains no digestive enzymes, it is important in digestion since it contains bile salts, which emulsify fats. Emulsification of fats facilitates their digestion, since the very small fat droplets provide a greater surface area for the action of lipase on fat. Bile salts are also important in the absorption of digested fats. Bile also contains bile pigments, which are waste products from the breakdown of erythrocytes. Gmelin's test for bile involves the oxidation of bile pigments by nitric acid,

136

with a resultant formation of colored rings. This test can be used to test urine for the presence of bile pigments.

Procedure

1. Observe the color of bile.
2. To perform Gmelin's test for bile, place about 3 ml of concentrated nitric acid in a test tube.
3. Dilute 5 ml of bile with an equal volume of water. Carefully overlay the nitric acid with this dilute solution of bile by slowly pouring it down the side of the tube containing the acid.
4. If this test is properly performed, colored rings should appear at the interface between the two liquids: yellow nearest the acid, then red, violet, blue, and green nearest the top. These colored compounds constitute a positive result in Gmelin's test for bile.
5. To demonstrate the effect of bile on surface tension, place about an inch of distilled water in a clean beaker.
6. Sprinkle a small amount of sulfur on the surface of the water.
7. Observe the behavior of the sulfur. Do the particles fall to the bottom of the beaker through the water or do they remain floating on the surface?
8. Repeat the experiment by replacing the water with dilute bile (10 ml bile, 10 ml water). Compare the results of the addition of sulfur with those obtained when distilled water was used.

SELF-TEST—DIGESTIVE SYSTEM

Directions

See Chapter 1, Self-Test, page 9.

1. The hardest substance in the body is **enamel.**
2. The **root** is the part of the tooth that is embedded in bone.
3. The **periodontal** membrane attaches the tooth to the bone.
4. The major nerves and blood vessels supplying a tooth are found in the **periodontal membrane.**
5. The **crown** is the exposed surface of the tooth.
6. A complete human adult set of teeth normally contains **32** teeth.
7. Dental **caries** are decayed areas in teeth.
8. **Deciduous** teeth come in after the primary teeth are shed.
9. The eight teeth in the front of the mouth are called **incisors.**
10. The dental formula for the deciduous teeth is **2 1 0 2.**
11. Saliva is secreted by **three pairs** of salivary glands.
12. The enzyme present in saliva is called either **salivary amylase** or **ptyalin.**
13. Salivary amylase starts the digestion of **monosaccharides.**
14. An example of a polysaccharide is **galactose.**
15. Proteins are made up of large numbers of **amino acid units,** which are joined together by peptide linkages.
16. Benedict's test for reducing sugars provides a positive test with **starch.**
17. Table sugar is an example of a **monosaccharide.**
18. Fat molecules consist of **three molecules** of glycerol and **one molecule** of fatty acid.
19. A positive test for starch is provided by application of **Lugol's iodine solution.**

20. Proteoses and peptones are digested to polypeptides by **trypsin.**
21. The main enzymes found in protein digestion are pepsin in gastric juice, trypsin in pancreatic juice, and peptidases in **pancreatic juice.**
22. A chemical compound that increases the rate of reaction without actually entering into the reaction is called a **catalyst.**
23. Organic catalysts made by living cells are called **enzymes.**
24. Enzymes that catalyze the hydrolysis of proteins are called **proteases.**
25. Pancreatic juice is the **only** digestive juice with strong amylases, proteases, and lipase.
26. The enzyme **rennin** assists in the curdling of milk.
27. In the **small intestine** the enzyme pepsin acts to change proteins to peptones.
28. Pepsinogen is converted by **HCl** to pepsin.
29. Each disaccharide has its **own specific enzyme** for conversion to monosaccharides.
30. A portion of the roof of the mouth cavity is formed by the **hard palate.**
31. A baby with a **cleft palate** cannot take milk from a bottle because the mouth opens into the nasal cavities.
32. The esophagus is lined with **stratified squamous epithelium.**
33. The pyloric sphincter separates the **duodenum** from the stomach.
34. The vomiting center is located in the **medulla oblongata.**
35. A lesion of the inner wall of the stomach or first part of the small intestine is called a **peptic ulcer.**
36. Lining the small intestine are many fine, velvetlike or fingerlike projections called **rugae.**
37. Enlarged veins in the **stomach** are referred to as hemorrhoids.
38. The appendix is a cul-de-sac attached to the **descending colon.**
39. A **hernia** is a protrusion of part of an organ through an abdominal opening.
40. A hernia occurring through the navel is called **an umbilical hernia.**
41. The membrane lining the abdominal cavity is called the **pleura.**
42. The scientific name for the throat is the **larynx.**
43. **Peritonitis** is an inflammation of the lining of the abdominal cavity.
44. Peristalsis occurs in the stomach and intestines, **but not** in the esophagus.
45. The common bile duct enters the small intestine at the **ampulla of Vater.**
46. The temporary folds in the mucosa of the stomach are called **papillae.**
47. The **enzymes** in bile aid in the digestion of fats.
48. The production of bile by the liver represents both **secretory and excretory activities.**
49. The contents of the intestines are largely **fluid** upon entering the cecum.
50. **Hydrolysis** is the principal chemical reaction involved in the digestion of food.
51. Saliva has a **lower pH** than gastric juice.
52. **Bile salts** emulsify fat particles and thus increase their total surface area.
53. In the process of digestion, **bile** splits fats into fatty acids and glycerol.

138

54. The mouth cavity opens posteriorly into the **nasopharynx.**

55. The liver receives blood rich in food (which it processes and refines) from the **hepatic vein.**

56. The lining of the small intestine is the **only area** from which food is absorbed.

57. In the liver, urea is formed from **fat** metabolism.

58. In the absence of bile, one-third to two-thirds of ingested fat is lost in the **urine.**

59. The cystic duct leads from the gall bladder and opens into the **common bile duct.**

60. The colon is divided into segments called **haustra.**

61. **Kupffer cells** located in the stomach are responsible for the secretion of hydrochloric acid.

62. Constipation is a condition usually arising from a **lack of tonus** in the muscular layers of the colon.

63. **Saturated** fatty acid molecules contain all the hydrogen they are able to hold.

64. The most important processes in digestion and absorption take place in the **stomach.**

65. The first teeth of the permanent set to erupt are the **six-year molars.**

66. Weight-for-weight proteins provide **twice** as many calories as fats.

67. Gallstones are formed from substances in **bile.**

68. Parotitis, or "mumps," is an inflammation of the **parotid** gland.

69. **Cholelithiasis** is the formation of stones in the gall bladder or ducts.

70. Clay-colored stools are produced if the common bile duct is blocked, because the **bile pigments** are missing from the feces.

71. In the preceding case, the doctor might order a low-fat diet, because bile is important for **emulsification** of fats.

72. Lacteals are lymph vessels that absorb food from the **large intestine.**

73. The **longitudinal** layer of muscle in the large intestine forms the taenia coli.

74. The peritoneal cavity is the term used to describe the spaces between the **parietal** and **visceral** layers of peritoneum.

75. The **plasma proteins** formed by the liver play an important role in maintaining the osmotic pressure of the blood.

76. Bile has a **higher** pH than gastric juice.

77. Glycerol is one of the end products of **carbohydrate** metabolism.

78. Gastric lipase **is** essential for digestion of fats.

79. The greater omentum hangs from the **lesser** curvature of the stomach.

80. The mesentery of the **small intestine** serves as a support and holds blood vessels, lymphatics, and nerves.

81. Secretin is a hormone that stimulates the secretion of **pancreatic juice.**

82. The hormone that is specific for stimulating contraction of the gall bladder is **cholecystokinin.**

83. The stomach is concerned with digestion of **carbohydrates.**

84. The presence of sodium bicarbonate in **pancreatic juice** neutralizes the acid chyme.

85. **Osmosis** is involved in the absorption of water from the colon.

86. Proteins **are stored** in muscles and other parts of the body.

10

Metabolism

EXERCISE 10-A
BASAL METABOLIC RATE

Objective

To determine theoretical basal metabolic rate.

Materials

None.

Discussion

The surface of the body is the principal region from which heat is lost. This area varies with the height and weight of the individual. The relation between height and weight and body surface area is shown by means of a chart such as the Dubois Body Surface Chart in Appendix 3-A.

In health, the amount of heat lost over the surface of the body equals the amount of heat produced in excess of that required to maintain normal body temperature. Both age and sex affect rate of heat loss. No satisfactory reason has as yet been established for the difference between the sexes. The table below gives the average rate at which heat is lost in terms of calories per minute and per hour per square meter of body surface area. The figures provide a means of estimating basal metabolic rate.

Procedure

1. Record your height, weight, age, and sex under Results and Questions.
2. Using the Dubois Body Surface Chart (in Appendix 3-A), determine the approximate surface area of your body (BSA) and

record under Results and Questions. Follow the directions on the chart.
3. Using Table 10-1 (Heat Loss per Square Meter of Body Surface), determine your

TABLE 10-1
Heat Loss per Square Meter of Body Surface

Age	Males Calories per		Females Calories per	
	Min	Hr	Min	Hr
5	0.891	53.0	0.860	51.6
6	0.878	52.7	0.845	50.7
7	0.866	52.0	0.825	49.5
8	0.853	51.2	0.801	48.1
9	0.840	50.4	0.781	46.9
10	0.825	49.5	0.763	45.8
11	0.810	48.6	0.743	44.6
12	0.796	47.8	0.723	43.4
13	0.785	47.1	0.700	42.0
14	0.770	46.2	0.683	41.0
15	0.755	45.3	0.660	39.6
16	0.745	44.7	0.641	38.5
17	0.728	43.7	0.623	37.4
18	0.715	42.9	0.621	37.3
19	0.701	42.1	0.620	37.2
20-24	0.683	41.0	0.615	36.9
25-29	0.671	40.3	0.610	36.6
30-35	0.663	39.8	0.603	36.2
35-39	0.653	39.2	0.596	35.8
40-44	0.638	38.3	0.588	35.3
45-49	0.630	37.8	0.583	35.0
50-54	0.620	37.2	0.575	34.5
55-59	0.610	36.6	0.568	34.1
60-64	0.600	36.0	0.563	33.8
65-69	0.588	35.3	0.556	33.4
70-74	0.580	34.8	0.546	32.8
75-79	0.570	34.2	0.538	32.3

139

theoretical basal metabolic rate for 1 minute, 1 hour, and 1 day and record under Results and Questions. To do this, multiply the heat loss for your age and sex, in Calories per minute, times your body surface area.

EXERCISE 10-B
DIURNAL VARIATIONS IN BODY TEMPERATURE

Objective

To observe the variation in body temperature during a period of 24 hours.

Materials

Clinical thermometer (Fahrenheit); 70% alcohol; colored pencils.

Discussion

Body temperature is the result of metabolism. In fact, the oxidation of nutrients within body cells accounts for almost all of the heat produced. However, metabolic rate is greater in some tissues than in others, and it is in these that the major production of heat occurs. Muscles make up over half of the soft tissues of the body; oxidation in the muscles supplies the largest quantity of heat.

Body temperature varies with the external environment in **poikilothermic** animals, the cold-blooded animals, such as fish and reptiles. However, in **homoiothermic** (warm-blooded) animals, such as mammals and birds, temperature is maintained at a relatively constant level regardless of fluctuations in external temperatures. Animals of the latter type (including man) have a heat-regulating center located in the hypothalamus. This center consists of two distinct areas, one of which regulates loss of heat while the other regulates heat production.

A fever is thought to be due to the failure of the hypothalamus to function properly. This failure may result from the action of bacteria or viruses, or from dehydration.

PART 1. INSTRUCTIONS FOR USE OF THE THERMOMETER

1. Clean the thermometer in 70% alcohol.
2. Shake the thermometer to move the mercury below the 96 °F mark.
3. Place the thermometer under your tongue, with your lips closed, for at least 2 minutes. Be sure the lips are closed during the entire 2-minute period. If the reading on the thermometer is to be accurate, you should not attempt to talk until the thermometer has been removed. Furthermore, *the temperature should not be taken immediately after you have drunk any kind of beverage.*
4. Read the thermometer by holding it at or near eye level in a horizontal position, with the numbers down and the marks in a superior position. Slowly rotate the thermometer back and forth until the line of mercury is visible.
5. The distance between each short mark on the thermometer represents 0.2 °F, while the distance between long marks represents 1 °F. Most thermometers also use a long mark to indicate 98.6 °F, "normal" temperature.

PART 2. BODY TEMPERATURE VARIATIONS DURING A 24-HOUR PERIOD

1. Determine your **basal temperature** by taking your temperature upon waking but *before arising.* Record under Results and Questions.
2. Take your oral temperature at 4-hour intervals during a continuous 24-hour period (e.g., at 7 AM, 11 AM, 3 PM, 7 PM, 11 PM, 3 AM, and again at 7 AM). Record the data in the table provided under Results and Questions.
3. Collect the temperature measurements obtained by each member of the class during a 24-hour period at 4-hour intervals and record in the table under Results and Questions.
4. Plot your personal temperature data on the grid provided under Results and Questions, with time on the horizontal axis and temperature (starting at 96 °F) on the vertical axis. Use either blue or black ink (or blue or black pencil) in plotting these data.
5. From the data in the table, determine the average temperature of the class as a whole for each time interval indicated and plot the data on the grid using either red or green ink (or red or green pencil).

EXERCISE 10-C
EFFECT OF EXERCISE ON TEMPERATURE

Objective

To determine the effect of exercise on body temperature.

Materials

Clinical thermometers; 70% alcohol; (optional) bicycle ergometer.

Procedure

1. Enter all data from this experiment in the table under Results and Questions.
2. Take your temperature before exercising ("normal" temperature).
3. Take your temperature immediately following 1 minute of mild exercise (running in place for 1 minute).
4. Take your temperature immediately following severe exercise (running around the building rapidly or bicycling 2 minutes on the bicycle ergometer) (belt setting 2 for women, 3 for men, 35 kilometers per hour).
5. Wait 10 minutes (in resting position while seated working on other laboratory experiments) and again take your temperature.

EXERCISE 10-D
MAPPING OF SWEAT GLANDS

Objectives

To demonstrate the presence, activity, and distribution of sweat glands in the skin.

SELF-TEST—METABOLISM

Directions

See Chapter 1, Self-Test, page 9.

Materials

Iodine; 1-inch squares of bond paper; masking tape.

Procedure

1. Clean a 2-inch square on the forehead, neck, and arm with alcohol; let it dry, then paint the area with iodine. (Select areas of the skin that are not unduly hirsute [hairy] but where sweating readily occurs.) Allow the iodine to dry completely.
2. Hold a square piece of bond paper over the painted square for precisely 2 minutes. The paper should be held or taped firmly in place and not allowed to slip.
3. Remove the paper and count the number of blue (or purple) dots. Each dot represents the location of an active sweat gland pore. The dots appear when the iodine, diluted by sweat, reacts with the starch in the paper. The size of each dot varies with the amount of perspiration secreted by that sweat gland; the number of dots on the square gives the number of **active** sweat glands per square inch, at rest.
4. Repeat this experiment under conditions of mild exercise (running in place for 2 minutes) and severe exercise (running around the building or bicycling).
5. Enter all data in the table provided in Results and Questions.

1. **Muscle tone, along with metabolic rate,** is lowest while an individual is asleep.
2. **Catabolism** is the process of growth and repair of body tissues.
3. **Reduction** is the process by which body tissues release energy from food that has been digested.
4. The basic fuel of the body is **glucose or some other hexose.**
5. The source of energy for the body is the **chemical energy** obtained from the consumption of foods.

6. Changes in water temperature have a **greater** effect on body temperature than do changes in air temperature.

7. The ratio of carbon dioxide given off to the volume of oxygen consumed is of value because it indicates whether a carbohydrate, fat, or mixed diet is being **oxidized** by the body.

8. Normal basal metabolic rate is **higher** for women than for men.

9. Carbon dioxide and water are **end products** in the oxidation of proteins, carbohydrates, and fats.

10. The formation of glycogen from glucose is called **glyconeogenesis.**

11. **Exercise, food, and cold** are all powerful stimulators of metabolism.

12. A gram of carbohydrate, when oxidized in the body, yields about **4 Calories.**

13. A gram of fat oxidized in the body yields about **9 Calories.**

14. In protein metabolism, where an increase in the release of energy is greater than can be derived from protein alone, it has been shown that the "extra" energy is derived from simultaneous oxidation of other foodstuffs. This response is known as the **specific dynamic action of protein.**

15. A basal metabolism test indicates the amount of energy required to maintain body functions **when the person is at complete rest, but not sound asleep.**

16. The presence of food in the digestive tract **has no effect on** body temperature.

17. The energy produced by 1 g of protein is **considerably less than that** produced by 1 g of carbohydrate.

18. Basal metabolic rate **increases** with age.

19. The energy requirements of the body are usually measured in units of **small calories.**

20. Energy requirements of the body are **influenced by hormones.**

21. Measurements of metabolic rates are **almost always indirect** measurements.

22. The metabolic rate of **homoiothermic animals** increases as body temperature rises, due to the increase in the rate of chemical reactions that results with the increase in temperature.

23. **Variations between 98 and 99 °F may be normal,** when body temperature is taken orally, even if the variations occur in the same person.

24. Fever is a pathologic condition in which the hypothalamus (or "thermostat") is "set" at a **higher level.**

25. The **thalamus** is known to play a major role in the regulation of body temperature.

26. Daily variations in body temperature are referred to as **diurnal variation.**

27. Heat stroke is characterized by a **fall** in body temperature.

28. A normal rectal temperature is approximately **98.6 °F.**

29. Loss of heat in excretory products plays **an important role** in the control of body temperature.

30. Two external factors important in the regulation of body temperature are the **humidity** and the **movement of surrounding air.**

31. Successful efforts to reduce a fever result in **constriction** of skin capillaries.

32. Body temperature is **already well regulated** at birth.

33. In cool environmental temperatures, **conduction** accounts for most of the heat loss from skin.

34. Control of body temperature can be upset by **bacteria** or **viruses.**

35. Most of the heat of the body is produced by **smooth muscle tissue of the viscera.**

36. Heat production in the body is a **catabolic** process involving oxidation of nutrients during cellular respiration.

37. **Sunstroke** may occur as a result of high temperature and humidity. The body fails to lose excess heat and body temperature rises, along with the pulse and blood pressure.

38. The basal metabolic rate is related to **body surface area.**

11

The Respiratory System

EXERCISE 11-A
ANATOMY OF THE HUMAN RESPIRATORY SYSTEM

Objectives

To learn the location and function of the human respiratory organs.

Materials

Dissectable torso; anatomic charts; model of larynx; model of sagittal section of head; reference books.

Discussion

The respiratory system is concerned with the transportation of gases to and from the lungs and with the exchange of gases between the lungs and the pulmonary capillaries. Oxygen moves by diffusion from the air in the alveoli in the lungs into the pulmonary capillaries, and carbon dioxide moves in the reverse direction. The circulatory system transports these gases between the pulmonary capillaries and the systemic capillaries. Oxygen diffuses through the walls of the systemic capillaries, through the tissue fluid, into the cells. There it is used up in cellular respiration, the process by which energy is released from food. Carbon dioxide is a waste product of this reaction.

Breathing movements must occur for the gases to move along the respiratory tract into the lungs. Breathing is usually controlled automatically by the respiratory center in the medulla oblongata. The nerve impulses to the muscles in the thorax pass down the spinal cord to the cervical and thoracic regions. The phrenic nerve then carries these impulses to the diaphragm, and the intercostal nerves transmit the impulses to the external intercostal muscles. During inspiration, the size of the thorax increases, resulting in an increase in the size of the lungs, causing air to rush in. During expiration the reverse occurs.

Procedure

1. Use Figures 11-1 and 11-2, two views of the larynx, as self-tests.
2. Locate the thyroid cartilage on your own larynx.
3. Hold the larynx down and try to swallow. Now release the larynx and swallow. Relate this to the swallowing process.
4. Use Figure 11-3 as a self-test. The structures indicated in the key should also be located on the dissectable torso and the model of a sagittal section through the head.
5. Study Figure 11-4 showing pseudostratified ciliated columnar epithelial tissue of the respiratory tract. What is the primary function of this tissue? Note (in Figure 11-7) that alveoli are lined with simple squamous epithelium. Can you suggest a possible reason for this?
6. Study Figure 11-5, which shows the lobes in the lungs. How does the number of these lobes compare with the number in the fetal pig (see Exercise 11-B)?
7. Figures 11-6 and 11-7 show the relationship of alveoli to the lungs. Note the anatomic and histologic features which

Figure 11-1.   Larynx (anterior view).

Figure 11-2.   Larynx (posterior view).

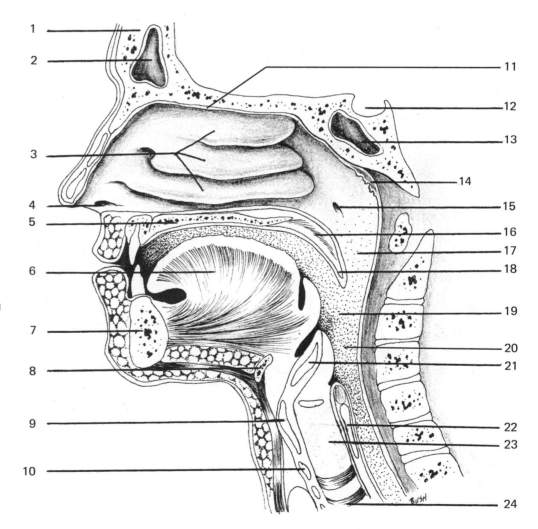

Figure 11-3.   Sagittal section through head.

Figure 11-4. Pseudostratified ciliated columnar epithelium of the respiratory tract.

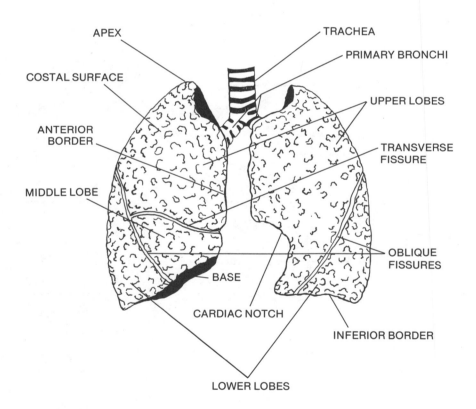

Figure 11-5. The lungs (showing division into lobes).

KEY TO FIGURE 11-6

1. thyroid cartilage
2. cricoid cartilage
3. trachea
4. right bronchus
5. secondary bronchi
6. apex (left lung)
7. rib
8. left bronchus
9. pulmonary artery
10. pulmonary vein
11. respiratory bronchiole
12. alveolar duct
13. alveoli
14. alveolar sac

Figure 11-6. Respiratory tract.

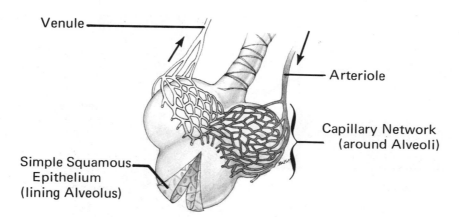

Figure 11-7. Microscopic view of alveoli showing
capillary network.

provide the mechanical basis for gas exchange. These figures may be used as self-tests.

EXERCISE 11-B
DISSECTION OF THE RESPIRATORY SYSTEM OF THE FETAL PIG

Objectives

To identify the respiratory organs of the fetal pig and to compare them with the corresponding human structures.

Materials

Fetal pig; dissecting board or tray; dissecting set.

Procedure

1. Make a median longitudinal incision through the muscles in the neck to expose the **larynx** and **trachea.** Do not sever the blood vessels or nerves located on either side of the trachea. Use Figure 11-8 as a guide for identification of these structures.
    a. The trachea contains rings of cartilage in its walls. Determine whether

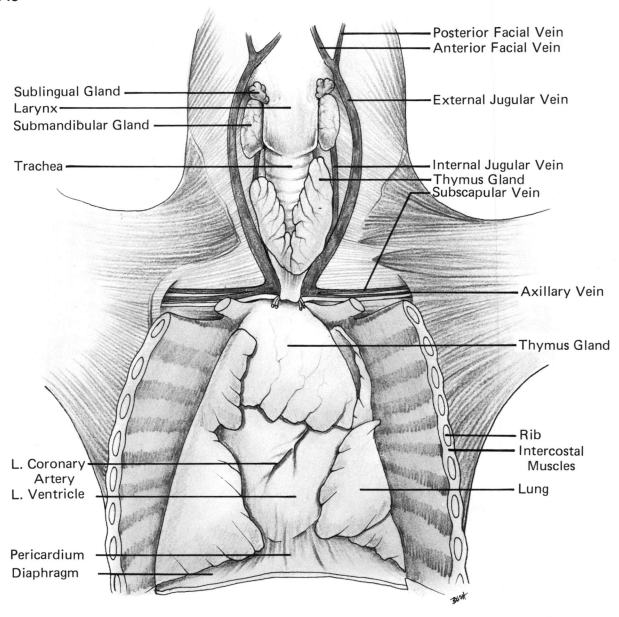

Figure 11-8.   Superficial view of thoracic cavity with neck dissected.

these rings are complete on the dorsal surface of the trachea.

b. Remove muscular tissue from the larynx. Make a longitudinal incision through the ventral wall of the larynx and locate the **vocal folds,** which are two small, shelflike membranes. These are poorly developed in the fetal pig.

c. Locate the **hyoid bone** anterior to the larnyx.

d. Remove the parotid gland. The sublingual and submandibular glands are

now visible adjacent to the larynx.

2. Identify the **thymus gland,** the large gland ventral to the heart. This gland consists of two major lobes which extend anteriorly into the neck region on either side of the trachea. The thymus is relatively large in the fetus.

3. The ventral neck muscles and the cervical part of the thymus gland cover the **thyroid gland,** the small, dark gland that lies on the upper trachea. Part the muscles and remove part of the thymus to expose this gland (see Figure 11-9).

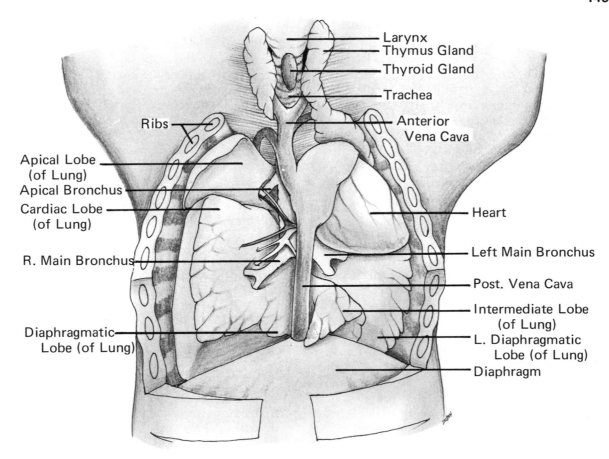

Larynx
Thymus Gland
Thyroid Gland
Trachea
Anterior
Vena Cava

Ribs

Apical Lobe
(of Lung)
Apical Bronchus
Cardiac Lobe
(of Lung)

R. Main Bronchus

Heart

Left Main Bronchus

Post. Vena Cava

Intermediate Lobe
(of Lung)

Diaphragmatic
Lobe (of Lung)

L. Diaphragmatic
Lobe (of Lung)

Diaphragm

Figure 11-9.   Dissection of the organs of the thoracic cavity of the fetal pig.

4. Observe the large right and left **common carotid arteries** and the **internal jugular veins** on each side of the trachea.

5. The **vagus nerve** is the conspicuous white band that is bound to the dorsal surface of the common carotid artery. This nerve supplies many of the thoracic and abdominal organs.

6. Free the trachea, laterally, from the preceding blood vessels and nerves. Lying along the trachea, and attached to it, are the two slender **inferior laryngeal nerves.** These nerves, which are essential for speech in humans, originate from the vagus nerve and, although small and delicate, they are easily seen against the trachea on either side.

7. Locate the **esophagus,** the muscular tube dorsal to the trachea.

8. Examine the interior of the thoracic cavity.

  a. Note that the thoracic cavity is divided into two lateral **pleural cavities,** which contain the lungs. The

pericardial sac, which contains the **heart,** is located in the space (mediastinum) between the lungs.

  b. The **pleura** is a double-layered serous membrane which lines the thorax. That portion of the pleura lining the thoracic wall is called the **parietal pleura;** that covering and adhering to the lungs is called the **visceral pleura.**

  c. The **pericardium,** the membrane surrounding the heart, is also composed of two layers: the outer parietal layer and the inner visceral layer. Much of the parietal pleura forming the medial walls of the pleural cavities is tightly bound to the parietal pericardium.

9. Remove thymus tissue in the thoracic cavity in order to study the **lungs.**

  a. Note that the lung is attached to other structures in the thorax only by the root. The **root of the lung** is formed by the bronchus, pulmonary artery and vein, bronchial arteries and veins, nerves, lymphatic vessels, and bronchial lymph nodes, all encircled by pleura.

b. Determine the number of lobes in each lung. Each lung is divided into three major lobes: **apical, cardiac,** and **diaphragmatic.** The right lung has an **intermediate lobe** beneath the apex of the heart (see Figure 11-9). In humans the right lung is divided into three lobes, the left into two lobes.

c. Cut off a small section of the left lung and note the density of the lung. The lungs have not yet filled with air, since they are nonfunctional before birth.

10. The trachea branches into a right and left **bronchus** dorsal to the heart. To locate the right bronchus, push the heart to the left side of the thoracic cavity (see Figure 11-9); then locate the inferior end of the trachea dorsal to the heart and right pulmonary blood vessels. Locate the **apical bronchus,** which leaves the trachea anterior to its termination and supplies the right apical lobe. Note the right **main (primary) bronchus,** which supplies the right cardiac and diaphragmatic lobes, and the small branch of the bronchus, which supplies the intermediate lobe. Then scrape away the right cardiac lobe of the lung, bit by bit, noting the organization of the bronchial tree and blood vessels. Leave the vessels intact. The branches of the bronchi can be distinguished from blood vessels because of the presence of cartilage in their walls and absence of colored latex.

11. Locate the **phrenic nerve,** the conspicuous white line that passes along the pericardium to the diaphragm on either the right or left side of the heart.

12. Lift the left lung and remove some of the parietal pleura dorsal to the lung to locate the esophagus. Follow the esophagus to the diaphragm.

EXERCISE 11-C
CHEST MEASUREMENTS DURING RESPIRATION

Objective

To determine the variation in chest measurements during respiration.

Materials

Calipers; lung demonstration model.

Discussion

In inspiration, due to contraction of muscles in the thorax, the size of the thoracic cavity increases. This causes an increase in the size of the lungs, lowering the air pressure inside the lungs. The decrease in air pressure inside the lungs causes air to enter the lungs, since air moves from a region of higher pressure to one of lower pressure. This constitutes inspiration. During expiration, the muscles of the thorax relax and the chest size decreases. This increases the air pressure inside the lungs, causing air to leave the lungs (see Figure 11-10).

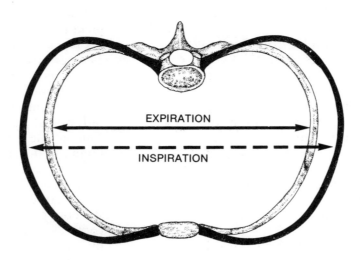

Figure 11-10. The mechanism of inspiration.

Procedure

1. To obtain the diameter of the chest, use the calipers. These instruments include a scale graduated in centimeters on one side and in inches on the opposite side. Learn how to read the scale using the side graduated in centimeters. Note that the number appearing before the long-division mark refers to the number of centimeters at that particular mark. For example, if the edge of the leg of the calipers was at the mark indicated by the arrow on the following diagram, the diameter of the chest would be recorded as 17 cm.

2. Measure the anteroposterior and lateral diameters of the chest, in centimeters, at the nipple line under the following conditions: at the end of a quiet inspiration, quiet expiration, forceful inspiration, and forceful expiration. Record the results in the table under Results and Questions.
3. Examine the lung demonstration model, which consists of a bell jar, rubber sheeting, two balloons, a rubber stopper, and glass tubing. Compare each of the parts of the model with the corresponding part of the human thorax.
4. Pull down on the rubber sheeting. Observe the change in the balloons.
5. Allow the rubber sheeting to return to its original position. Observe the results.

EXERCISE 11-D
RESPIRATORY VOLUMES

Objectives

To determine respiratory volumes with the spirometer and the respirometer.

Materials

Spirometer; Collin's 9-liter respirometer; disposable mouthpieces.

Discussion

The amount of air inhaled or exhaled from the lungs can be measured with a spirometer.

This instrument consists of a double set of tanks into which air can be inhaled or exhaled. The outer tank contains water and has a tube running through it to carry air above the water line. The inner tank is inverted over the air tube and rises a measured distance when air is exhaled into the tank. The amount of air inhaled or exhaled is indicated by the rise or fall of the pointer along the scale.

Respiratory volumes can also be determined with the Collin's respirometer. The principle involved is the same with both methods; however, the respirometer tank is connected to a pen and the volumes are recorded directly on chart paper.

Procedure with the Spirometer

1. Since a single measurement is usually not reliable, each determination should be made three times (unless other instructions are given) and an average calculated. Data should be recorded in the proper chart under Results and Questions.
2. Before beginning the experiment, determine how to read the scale on the spirometer. Use the scale graduated in liters. Each number from 1 through 6 indicates the number of liters. Each small mark between the liter marks indicates 0.1 liter. All answers should be recorded in milliliters (ml). To do this, multiply the answer in liters by 1000.
3. Do not let any air escape through the nose in any of these experiments. If necessary, hold the nostrils closed.
4. All measurements of respiratory volumes should be made with the subject standing.
5. At the conclusion of each measurement, return the pointer to the zero position by pressing down on the bell (remove the rubber stopper from the tank, if one is present, before applying pressure to the bell). Water will flow from the top of the instrument if this maneuver is not performed carefully.
6. Vital capacity.
   a. Vital capacity (VC) is the maximum amount of air that can be exhaled by the deepest possible expiration after the deepest possible inspiration. It averages 4500 ml in males, 3400 ml in females.
   b. To determine vital capacity, inhale as large a quantity of room air as possible.

c. Exhale into the spirometer to the fullest extent (try to empty the lungs completely). The exhalation should be done in a smooth, steady manner. The figure obtained is the vital capacity.

d. Repeat this determination two times.

7. Tidal volume (tidal air).

a. Tidal volume (TV) is the volume of air moved in and out of the lungs with each breath in normal quiet breathing. It averages approximately 500 ml in men and 400 ml in women.

b. Make certain that the indicator (pointer) is at the zero mark on the scale.

c. Take a normal quiet inspiration of room air.

d. Now exhale to the usual extent into the spirometer (do not look at the scale). The tank should rise slightly. Record the tidal volume.

e. Return the pointer to the zero position.

f. Make two additional determinations of the tidal air. Record all results under Results and Questions.

8. Expiratory reserve volume (supplemental air).

a. Expiratory reserve volume (ERV) is the amount of air that can be forcibly exhaled from the lungs after a normal quiet expiration (tidal air) following a normal inspiration. This averages about 1000 ml in males, 800 ml in females.

b. Inhale normally. Then immediately exhale a normal quiet breath into the room air. Now exhale as deeply as possible into the spirometer as much of the remaining air in the lungs as you can. This value is the ERV.

c. Return the pointer to the zero position.

d. Repeat the above procedure two times and record your data.

9. Inspiratory reserve volume (complemental air).

a. Inspiratory reserve volume (IRV) is the amount of air that can be forcibly inhaled after a normal quiet inspiration. It averages 3000 ml in males, 2200 in females. This measurement can be determined directly with the spirometer, or it can be calculated as follows:

$$IRV = VC - (TV + ERV)$$

b. To directly determine IRV, raise the bell of the spirometer to the 5-liter mark.

c. Inhale normally. Then insert the mouthpiece and inhale as much additional air as possible from the spirometer. Record this figure and subtract from the 5 liters. This is the IRV.

10. Determine the respiratory rate of the subject per minute by counting the number of breaths per minute. Record under Results and Questions. The respiration rate is usually 14 to 18 breaths per minute.

Procedure with the Respirometer

1. Study the diagram of the Collin's 9-liter respirometer (Fig. 11-11). Since the respirometer and spirometer are similar in principle, approximately the same figures for respiratory volumes should be obtained with both procedures.

2. In this exercise, respiratory movements are recorded directly on respirometer chart paper. This paper consists of a series of horizontal lines. The interval between two light-colored horizontal lines represents 50 ml. The interval between two dark-colored lines represents 1 liter (or 1000 ml).

3. Vital capacity.

a. Vital capacity (VC) is the maximum amount of air that can be exhaled by the deepest possible expiration after the deepest possible inspiration. It averages 4500 ml in males, 3400 in females.

b. To determine vital capacity, the bell of the respirometer should be pressed completely down, with the valve of the mouthpiece in the horizontal position. In this position, the respiration pen will be at (or very near) the top of the kymograph paper. The ventilograph pen should be removed from the surface of the kymograph paper.

c. Set the kymograph speed to 32 mm/min.

d. With the noseclip in position to prevent breathing through the nostrils, inhale as much room air into your lungs as possible, then forcibly exhale as much air as possible into the mouthpiece of the respirometer (try

Figure 11-11.   Collin's 9-liter respirometer.

to empty your lungs completely). The exhalation should be performed smoothly and steadily.

e.   Repeat two times. To lower the bell for the next determination, apply gentle pressure at the top of the bell.

4.   To measure tidal air, inspiratory reserve volume, and expiratory reserve volume (definitions in steps 7, 8, and 9 of the previous procedure), raise the bell of the respirometer by grasping the bell chain, with the mouthpiece valve in the horizontal position, and lifting until the respiration pen reaches the 2-liter mark on the kymograph paper. (The bell will stay in this position if the mouthpiece valve is moved to the vertical position.)

5.   With the nosepiece on your nose, a paper speed of 32 mm/min, and the mouthpiece valve in the horizontal position, breathe normally into and out of the respirometer five times. Follow a normal expiration by inhaling as deeply as possible. Then breathe normally five times. Inhale normally and then exhale as deeply as pos-

sible. Then return to normal breathing for five more breaths.

6.   Figure 11-12 is a sample record obtained by following these directions. Study the record carefully before making calculations of your own results. The graph was recorded from right to left. During expiration, the pen marks in a downward direction; during inspiration, the pen marks in an upward direction. Record all your results under Results and Questions, numbers 8 through 11.

EXERCISE 11-E
RESPIRATORY MOVEMENTS

Objective

To demonstrate respiratory movements with the pneumograph.

Materials

Paper cup or beaker *and* kymograph, bellows pneumograph; Marey tambour; ink

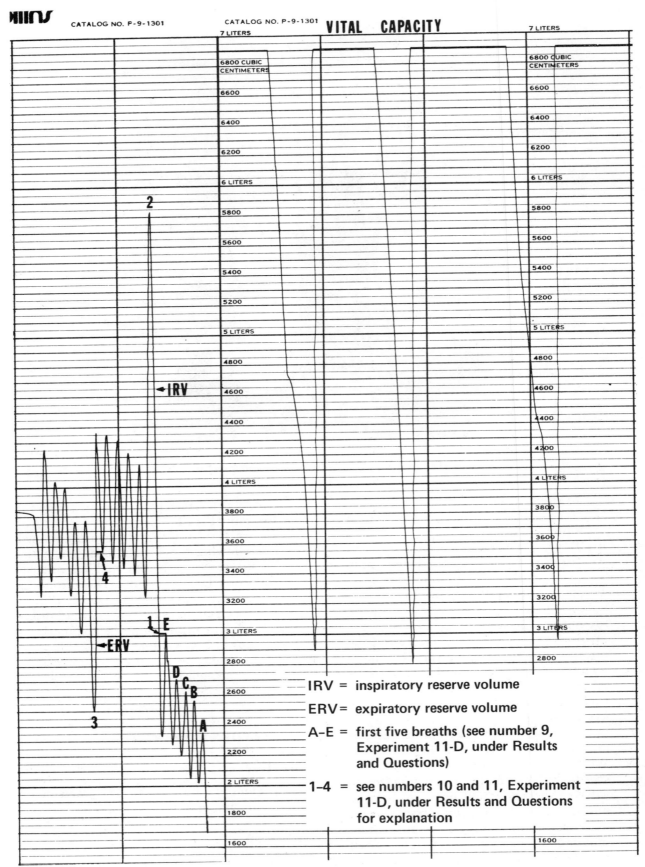

Figure 11-12. Sample record of respiratory volumes.

writing apparatus; semicircular stand; clamp *or* physiograph; transducer cable; transducer coupler *or* physiograph; adaptor cable AC-13; shielded input extension cable SC-13; impedance pneumograph coupler.

Discussion

The pneumograph and Marey tambour are used to record the rhythmical movements of the chest wall. The pneumograph consists of a coiled spring covered with a rubber tube, the ends of which are connected by an adjustable chain. The Marey tambour consists of a metal pan covered with a diaphragm of rubber, with a metal tube attached. The diaphragm rises whenever the air pressure increases within the tambour. As a subject breathes, the size of the chest varies and changes the air pressure within the pneumograph, which transmits these changes to the tambour. The same experiments can be performed with the bellows pneumograph and physiograph. The bellows pneumograph is a photoelectric transducer for recording rate and pattern of respiration.

In this experiment, the effects of mental calculation and drinking water (glossopharyngeal reflex) on breathing pattern will be demonstrated. Reading aloud will be performed to demonstrate during which phase of breathing (inspiration or expiration) talking occurs.

Procedure Using Marey Tambour and Kymograph

1. With the rubber tube in an anterior position, fasten the pneumograph around the chest of the subject at approximately the sixth or seventh rib (where the greatest amount of chest movement occurs).
2. Clamp the metal tube of the Marey tambour to the semicircular stand so that the diaphragm side of the tambour is up. Attach the yoke to the tambour (see Figure 11-13).
3. Attach the Marey tambour pen to the yoke (see Figure 11-13). The long arm of the stylus with the pen should extend out toward the kymograph. Insert the short end of the stylus through the hole in the axle. Tighten the check nut to hold it in position. The short arm of the stylus must rest in the notch on the metal glued to the diaphragm. The ink adapter must not touch the tambour.

4. Connect the rubber tubing extending from the pneumograph to one end of a Y tube. Connect a second arm of the Y tube to the tambour. At the end of a quiet inspiration, close the third arm with a clamp. It may be necessary to regulate the pressure in the pneumograph and tambour by letting air in or out by means of this clamp.
5. Throughout the experiment the subject should attempt to breathe naturally. The subject should not look at the drum as the record is being obtained.
6. Using drum speed 5, obtain a tracing of three normal breaths. Label inspiration and expiration on the record. Note that the pen falls during inspiration.
7. Calculate the duration of inspiration and that of expiration by dividing the length of the appropriate portion of the record, in centimeters, by the drum speed.
8. Using drum speed 9, make a tracing of the subject's respiratory movements under the following experimental conditions. (Precede and follow each event with normal breathing.)
    a. The subject breathes quietly for 1/2 minute, then hyperventilates 20 times, following the hyperventilation with a return to normal breathing for approximately another 1/2 minute.
    b. The subject breathes normally several times, then reads aloud from the textbook. The reading should continue for several minutes, with the subject trying to read for a lengthy period before taking a breath. At the conclusion of the reading, the subject should breathe normally several times.
    c. Record the respiratory pattern while the subject is mentally calculating the fifth power of some small number suggested by a nonsubject. The subject should not use paper or talk aloud while calculating.
    d. The subject breathes normally, then drinks an entire beaker of water without stopping, then breathes normally again for several breaths.
9. Label each record with the correct letter, a short title, and a brief explanation of the results.
10. Repeat the above procedure on each member of your group.

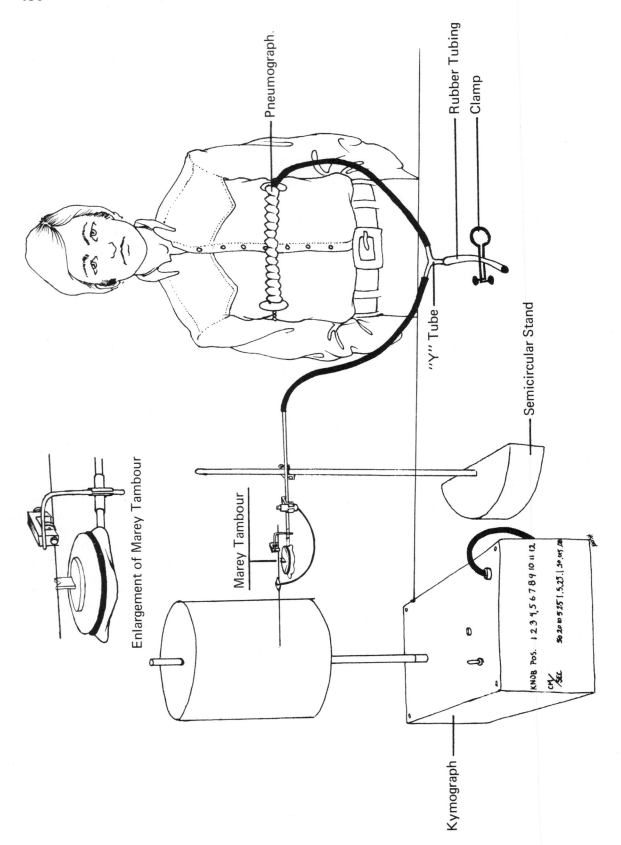

Pneumograph.

Rubber Tubing

Clamp

"Y" Tube

Semicircular Stand

Enlargement of Marey Tambour

Marey Tambour

Kymograph

KNOB POS. 1 2 3 4 5 6 7 8 9 10 11 12

50 20 10 5 2.5 1 .5 .25 .1 .50 .025 .010

CM/SEC

Figure 11-13. Diagram of pneumograph setup.

Procedure Using the Bellows Pneumograph and Physiograph

1. The subject must wear a shirt to prevent multiple grounding through the transducer.
2. Open the bellows pneumograph valve by turning the screw one-half turn counterclockwise. Fasten the strap around the chest (high up under the arms) with the transducer plug facing upward, positioned as shown in Figure 11-14. Tighten the strap sufficiently so that the bellows pneumograph remains in position under the arms but does not fit too tightly.
3. Connect the output of the bellows pneumograph to the 9-pin connector of the transducer coupler by means of the transducer cable. Refer to Exercise 7-F for operating instructions for the physiograph.
4. Compress the bellows slightly and close the transducer valve by rotating the wing screw clockwise. Release the bellows after the valve is closed to produce a slight internal negative pressure.
5. Place the channel amplifier controls in the following positions:
   a. Set the paper speed to 0.1 cm/sec.
   b. Set the time marker to 1 per second.
   c. Press the main frame RECORDER switch ON.
   d. Press the POWER switch ON.
   e. Press the RECORD switch OFF if it is glowing. This must be on only when actually recording.
   f. Set the filter to 10K.
   g. Set the mV/CM switch to the 50 mV/CM position. The amplitude may have to be readjusted later to produce a good height of contraction.
   h. Set the recording pen to the center dark-green line, using the POSITION control.
   i. Start the ink flowing in the pens associated with the transducer coupler and time event marker.
   j. Press the channel amplifier RECORD switch ON.
   k. Adjust the transducer coupler BALANCE control to restore the recording pen to the previously established baseline, if necessary.

Figure 11-14.   Diagram showing position of bellows pneumograph.

   l. If the signal cannot be returned to the baseline with the BALANCE control, open the valve on the bellows pneumograph and release the pressure. Then follow step 4 as before, compressing the bellows less than before or loosening the chest strap slightly.
   m. Adjust for the desired signal amplitude (height of the recording) by using the channel amplifier mV/CM control.
6. Using a paper speed of 0.1 cm/sec., make a tracing of the subject's respiratory movements under the following experimental conditions. (Precede and follow each event with normal breathing.)
   a. The subject breathes quietly for 1/2 minute, then hyperventilates 20 times, following the hyperventilation with a return to normal breathing for approximately another 1/2 minute.
   b. The subject breathes normally several times, then reads aloud from the textbook. The reading should continue for several minutes, with the subject trying to read for a lengthy period before taking a breath. At the conclusion of the reading, the subject should breathe normally several times.
   c. Record the respiratory pattern while the subject is mentally calculating the fifth power of some small number suggested by a nonsubject. The subject should not use paper or talk aloud while calculating.

d. The subject breathes normally, then drinks an entire beaker of water without stopping, then breathes normally again for several breaths.

7. Label each record with the correct letter, a title, and a brief explanation of the results.

8. Using a paper speed of 2.5 cm/sec and with the time event marker set to mark 1-second intervals, obtain a tracing of three normal breaths. Label inspiration and expiration on the record. Note that the pen rises on inspiration and falls during expiration (see Figure 11-15).

9. Calculate the duration of inspiration and that of expiration by dividing the length of the appropriate portion of the record, in centimeters, by the paper speed (2.5 cm/sec).

10. Repeat the above procedure on each member of the experimental team.

Alternate Procedure Using the Impedance Pneumograph

1. It is possible to perform the same experiments with the impedance pneumograph instead of the bellows pneumograph. A small alternating current of approximately 4 microamps is passed through the electrodes attached to the subject, with the voltage across the electrodes directly proportional to the subject impedance. (The impedance or conductivity to the passage of a current is reduced when air is brought into the lungs and increased as air is exhaled. The magnitude of the changes is proportional to the amount of air entering and leaving the lungs.) The small voltage variations resulting from impedance changes are amplified and detected as a signal for recording on the physiograph.

2. Apply a salt solution to two plate electrodes and attach them to the interspace between the fifth and sixth ribs near the sides of the chest, fastening them by means of the long rubber strap. Attach an additional plate electrode on the center of the subject's chest for grounding.

3. Insert the shielded input extension cable SC-13 to the input jack of the impedance pneumograph coupler.

4. Attach the long loose ends of the adaptor cable AC-13 to the subject, red on the left side, black on the right side, and green to the center plate electrode on the chest. Connect the short twisted ends of the adaptor cable AC-13 to the shielded input extension cable SC-13. Connect the red wire to the 1 position, the black to the 2 position, and the green to the G position.

5. Set the channel amplifier controls in the following positions (see Figure 11-16 and Exercise 7-F for general directions for the physiograph).
    a. Set the paper speed to 0.1 cm/sec.
    b. Set the time marker to 1 per second.
    c. Press the main frame RECORDER switch ON.
    d. Press the POWER switch ON.

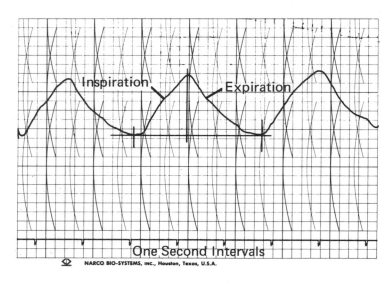

NARCO BIO-SYSTEMS, INC., Houston, Texas, U.S.A.

Figure 11-15. Tracing of three normal breaths at paper speed 2.5 cm/sec.

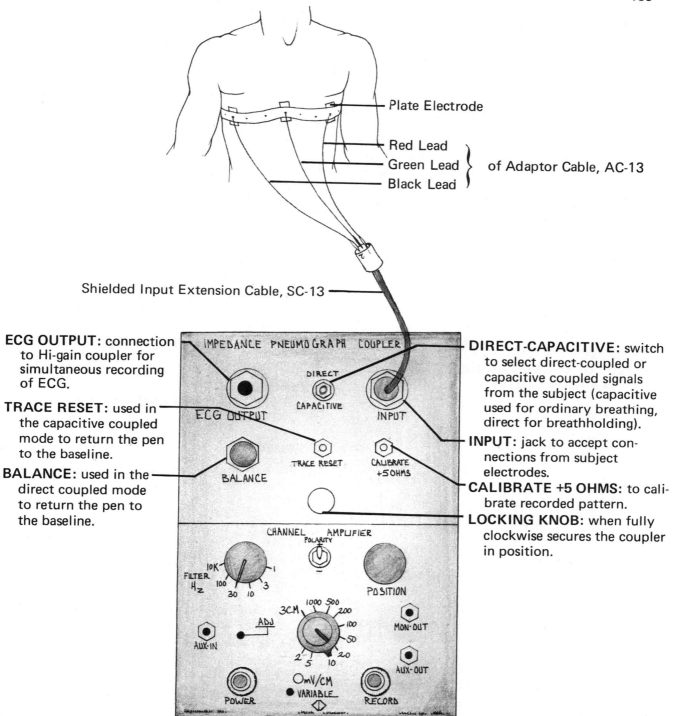

Figure 11-16.   Impedance pneumograph, with physiograph DMP-4B.

e. Press the RECORD switch OFF, if it is glowing.

f. Set the FILTER switch to 30.

g. Set the mV/CM switch to 10 mV/cm. The amplitude may have to be read-justed later to produce a good height of contraction.

h. Set the recording pen to the center dark-green line using the POSITION control.

i. Set the impedance pneumograph coupler DIRECT-CAPACITIVE switch to CAPACITIVE.
j. Start the ink flowing in the pens associated with the transducer coupler and time event marker.
k. Press the channel amplifier RECORD switch to ON.
l. Return the recording pen to the previously established baseline using the TRACE RESET button (the BALANCE control is not operative in the capacitive mode).

6. A tracing of the breathing pattern should now be obtained. To increase the amplitude of the recording, turn the mV/CM switch clockwise; to decrease the amplitude, turn the switch counterclockwise.
7. Follow steps 6 through 10 of the procedure with the bellows pneumograph.

EXERCISE 11-F
EFFECT OF CARBON DIOXIDE ON THE RESPIRATORY CENTER

Objective

To demonstrate the effect of carbon dioxide on the respiratory center.

Materials

Paper (or plastic) bag; straws; a beaker or paper cup; stopwatch.

Discussion

Hyperventilation washes much of the carbon dioxide out of the blood. The increase in oxygen content of the arterial blood after hyperventilation is negligible, but the carbon dioxide level may fall from a normal value of 44 mm Hg to as low as 15 mm Hg.

Hyperventilation may result in a feeling of dizziness because of cerebral anoxia (due to either decreased blood pressure, an increase in pH, or the constriction of cerebral vessels caused by the diminished carbon dioxide content of the blood).

Procedure

1. Breathe quietly for 1 minute and then note how long the breath can be held after a quiet inspiration.
2. Place a straw in your mouth, with the other end in a beaker of water. After a quiet inspiration, hold your breath as long as possible. Just before it is necessary to take a breath, begin to sip water. Continue timing and determine the total time elapsed after the original quiet inspiration until it is necessary to take a breath.
3. Hyperventilate ten times (breathe deeply and rapidly ten times) and then determine how long the breath can be held. Do not continue the experiment if a pronounced feeling of dizziness results.
4. Run around the building rapidly or bicycle for 1 minute on the bicycle ergometer (belt setting 2, speed 30). Determine how long the breath can be held immediately after the cessation of this exercise.
5. Enter all times in the table under Results and Questions. In explaining the results obtained in this experiment, make use of the fact that the respiratory center is very sensitive to slight changes in the carbon dioxide content of the blood.

EXERCISE 11-G
TEMPERATURE AND COMPOSITION OF EXHALED AIR

Objectives

To determine the temperature and composition of exhaled air.

Materials

Thermometer; glass plate; test tube; lime water; straw.

Discussion

When converting from Fahrenheit to Celsius, substitute the thermometer reading in the following formula:

$$Celsius = \frac{5}{9}(^\circ F - 32)$$

When converting from Celsius to Fahrenheit, substitute the thermometer reading in the following formula:

$$Fahrenheit = \frac{9}{5}\,^\circ C + 32$$

Procedure

1. Using a chemical thermometer, determine room temperature.
   Results in degrees Celsius. _____

2. Now, hold the bulb of the thermometer between the lips and approximately an inch into the mouth. The bulb should not be touching any part of your body.

3. Exhale air rapidly over the bulb of the thermometer and immediately take a reading of the temperature.
   Results in degrees Celsius. _____
   Results in degrees Fahrenheit. _____

4. Exhale air on a glass plate. Observe what collects on the surface of the plate.

5. Place a prepared solution of lime water in a test tube. Gently blow air into the lime water through a straw. A white precipitate of calcium carbonate should form in the test tube.

$$Ca(OH)_2 + CO_2 \rightarrow CaCO_3 \downarrow + H_2O$$

6. Record your observations under Results and Questions.

SELF-TEST—RESPIRATORY SYSTEM

Directions

See Chapter 1, Self-Test, page 9.

1. Carbon dioxide **is essential** to human life.

2. Mountain sickness at 15,000 feet above sea level occurs because the **oxygen content** of the blood is below normal.

3. Bends, or caisson disease, associated with high pressure, is due to an increased amount of **oxygen** in the blood.

4. **Cilia** aid in the movement of dust particles along the breathing passages.

5. The structure common to both the digestive and respiratory systems is the **trachea.**

6. The structures in cytoplasm containing the enzymes of cellular respiration are called **mitochondria.**

7. The **glottis** prevents food from entering the larynx.

8. The opening between the two vocal folds is called the **laryngeal aperture** or **glottis.**

9. Inspiration is **an active process** involving primarily the contraction of the diaphragm and external intercostal muscles.

10. The gaseous exchange across the respiratory membrane from the alveoli of the lungs to the capillary circulation is called **internal** respiration.

11. The hemoglobin picks up oxygen that has been **dissolved in the fluids of the lung tissue.**

12. **Sinus infection** is an extension of an infection from the nasal passages.

13. An illustration of a homeostatic reaction is the **increase in the rate of breathing** during exercise.

14. Bones making up the **lateral** wall of the nasal cavity include the inferior nasal concha, the maxilla, and the ethmoid.

15. The **pharyngeal** tonsils are also called the adenoids.

16. The tonsils are located within the **laryngeal aperture.**

17. The volume of air in excess of tidal air that can be inhaled by the deepest possible inspiration is called the **inspiratory reserve volume.**

18. Passive expiration is primarily due to the **contraction** of the muscles of inspiration.

19. The lungs expand during inspiration because the **two layers of the pleura adhere** to each other.

162

20. The site of greatest CO_2 concentration would be found in the **lungs.**

21. The **pulmonary veins** contain a greater concentration of oxygen than the **alveoli.**

22. Most of the oxygen carried in the body has combined with **hemoglobin** to form **oxyhemoglobin.**

23. Most of the carbon dioxide in the body is present in the form of sodium bicarbonate in the blood **plasma.**

24. The cartilaginous rings of the **trachea** are incomplete behind.

25. The **left** bronchus is shorter, larger in diameter, and more nearly vertical than the **right.**

26. The pleural cavities in which the lungs lie are formed by invagination of **two serous sacs.**

27. The maximum volume of air that can be exchanged in a single, voluntary respiratory cycle (i.e., inspiration and expiration) is called the **vital capacity.**

28. If an opening connects two volumes of gas, the gas will always flow from the area of **higher pressure** to the area of **lower pressure.**

29. **Intrapleural** pressure refers to either the absolute or relative value of pressure between the visceral and parietal layers of pleura.

30. **Intrapulmonary** pressure refers to the pressure within the respiratory passages of the lungs.

31. The **intrapleural** cavity is a true cavity only when accident or disease results in an opening between the potential **intrapleural** space and the atmosphere.

32. During inspiration, intrapulmonary pressure is **greater** than atmospheric pressure.

33. The partial pressure of oxygen in the lungs is approximately **100** mm Hg.

34. In combining with oxygen, hemoglobin is approximately **95%** saturated at an oxygen partial pressure of 100 mm Hg.

35. The speed of reaction of carbon dioxide with water is increased approximately 600 times by the enzyme **carbonic anhydrase.**

36. Carbon dioxide is much **less** soluble than oxygen in blood plasma.

37. Reduced oxygen tension in the blood stimulates **chemoreceptors,** which influence respiratory rates.

38. **Hypoventilation** may induce apnea.

39. Involuntary mechanisms of the control of respiration **may be taken over or modified** by the higher brain centers.

40. Normally the oxygen content of blood is approximately **20 cc per 100 cc** of arterial blood.

41. The principal **afferent** nerve in respiration is the phrenic nerve.

42. **Eupnea** is normal breathing.

43. The atmosphere contains from 0.03% to 0.049% carbon dioxide, but air exhaled from the lungs contains about **5%** carbon dioxide.

44. The respiratory center, which controls the breathing rate, acts primarily in response to the **amount of carbon dioxide** in the blood.

45. A substance that combines with the hemoglobin of the blood to form a stable compound and prevents oxygen from reaching the tissues is **carbon monoxide.**

46. The respiratory center is located in the **hypothalamus.**

47. Pleurisy is an inflammation of the **peritoneum.**

48. Bronchitis is an inflammation of the **lungs.**

49. A laryngectomy is the removal of the **vocal cords.**

50. A doctor may prescribe high percentage **oxygen** inhalations after surgery to increase the rate and depth of breathing.

51. A patient has tuberculosis of the left lung. To rest this lung and promote recovery, the doctor injects a measured amount of air into the **interpleural** space, inducing artificial pneumothorax.

52. Anoxia (hypoxia) is a **reduced** level of oxygen in the blood.

53. **Cheyne-Stokes** respiration consists of alternating periods of dyspnea and apnea.

54. **Atelectasis** refers to collapse of the lungs.

12

Blood Tests

EXERCISE 12-A
DETERMINATION OF ABO
AND RH BLOOD TYPES

Objectives

To determine the ABO and Rh blood types.

Materials

Sterile cotton; lancets; 70% alcohol; glass slides; wax pencil; toothpicks or applicators; anti-A, anti-B, group O (anti-A, B), and anti-Rho (anti-D) sera; light-heat box.

Discussion

The ABO and Rh blood type of each student will be determined in this exercise. The antigens (agglutinogens) that determine blood type are located on the plasma membrane of the erythrocytes, the antibodies (agglutinins) in the plasma. The antibodies cause agglutination (clumping) of the erythrocytes carrying the corresponding antigens.

To determine ABO blood type, anti-A and anti-B antisera (which contain the a and b antibodies, respectively) will be used. With blood type A, there should be agglutination of red blood cells by anti-A serum; with type B, agglutination of the cells by anti-B serum; with type AB, agglutination by both antisera; with type O, no agglutination by either antisera (see Figure 12-1).

The Rh blood type is determined in a similar manner. Although there are several Rh agglutinogens, the blood will be tested only for

the presence of the D (Rh_O) antigen, the most common antigen. If the blood reacts with the anti-D (Rh_O) serum, the blood type is called Rh positive (Rh+); if the antiserum does not cause agglutination of the cells, the blood is called Rh negative (Rh–). Approximately 85% of all Caucasians are Rh+ and approximately 15% are Rh–. For incidence of the ABO groups among selected races in the U.S., see Table 12-1. Exercise 21-A, Part 5, contains a discussion of the inheritance of blood types.

Procedure

1. Place the letter A at one end of a glass slide, B at the other end (Fig. 12-2).
2. Place 1 drop of anti-A serum at the A end; 1 drop of anti-B serum at the B end.
3. Clean the finger with 70% alcohol and allow to dry.
4. Puncture the fingertip with a sterile lancet.
5. Place 1 drop of blood next to each drop of antiserum.
6. Mix the blood with the antiserum by means of a toothpick or applicator. To avoid contamination, use a separate toothpick for each stirring operation.
7. Agglutination visible with the naked eye should begin almost immediately and should be complete by the end of 1 minute.
8. If the blood type is O, confirm this by using group O (anti-A, B) serum, which contains both the anti-A and anti-B agglutinins. Add 1 drop of the group O serum to the slide, followed by 1 drop of blood, and mix as before. No agglutination

165

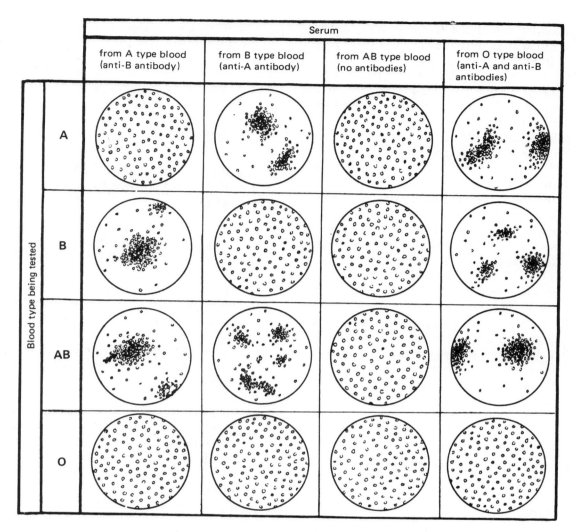

Figure 12-1.   Chart showing agglutination reactions.

Table 12-1. Incidence of Human Blood Groups in the U.S.

BLOOD GROUPS (PERCENTAGES)				
	O	A	B	AB
Caucasians	45	41	10	4
Blacks	48	27	21	4
Japanese	31	38	22	9
Chinese	36	28	23	13
American Indians	23	76	0	1
Hawaiians	37	61	2	0.5

Figure 12-2.   Preparation of slide for antisera.

should result if the blood is type O; the serum will agglutinate the cells of groups A, B, and AB.

9. To determine the Rh blood type, place 1 drop of anti-Rh₀ (anti-D) serum on a clean, dry slide that has been warmed on the light-heat box.
10. Add 1 drop of blood.
11. Mix the blood and antiserum thoroughly and spread over an area about an inch in diameter.
12. Place the slide on a warm (40 °C) light-heat box (or a microscope substage lamp) and tilt back and forth for no more than 2 minutes. The reaction usually appears within 30 seconds and is complete within 2 minutes. Readings should be taken only with the naked eye. The readings must be made before the preparation dries.
13. If the blood is Rh negative, the mixture will remain homogeneous. If the blood is Rh positive, coarse clumps will form promptly and increase in size with time.
14. Record the results of the entire class in the table under Results and Questions.

EXERCISE 12-B
DETERMINATION OF HEMOGLOBIN CONTENT OF BLOOD

Objectives

To determine the amount of hemoglobin in a personal sample of blood; to compare the results obtained with the use of the Tallquist scale with those obtained by means of a hemoglobinometer.

Materials

Sterile cotton; lancet; 70% alcohol; Tallquist scale; Spencer hemoglobinometer; hemolysis applicators.

Discussion

The Tallquist scale is used to estimate the grams of hemoglobin per 100 ml blood. This involves the comparison of the color of a drop of blood with a standard color chart. The Spencer Hb-meter, which is more accurate than the Tallquist scale, measures the oxyhemo-

globin directly as a result of its light absorption in the green portion of the spectrum. A suitable filter is used and the resulting color is matched with a colored glass standard. In both methods, 15.6 g/100 ml of blood is taken as 100%. The blood of the normal male usually contains 14 to 16 g of hemoglobin per 100 ml blood; that of the normal female 12 to 14 g per 100 ml.

Procedure A: The Tallquist Method of Determining Hemoglobin Content of Blood

1. Remove one square of absorbent paper from the Tallquist test booklet.
2. Clean the finger with 70% alcohol. *Let the alcohol evaporate.*
3. Puncture the finger with a sterile lancet.
4. Wipe away the first drop of blood with the edge of the absorbent paper (it contains excess tissue fluid).
5. Place the second drop of blood in the center of the paper. The drop must be free flowing. Do not squeeze the finger, as this forces out tissue fluid.
6. In a few seconds the blood stain will lose its glossiness and comparison should then be made immediately under direct (not artificial) light. *Do not let the blood dry to a brown color,* as inaccurate values will be obtained.
7. Place the specimen under the color comparison chart and move it along so that the blood stain appears at the apertures.
8. Compare the color of the drop with the colors on the Tallquist scale. Since the color differences on the chart represent 10% variations in the hemoglobin content, it will be necessary to estimate the intermediate percentages.
9. Record the data (in grams hemoglobin, percent hemoglobin, and stage of anemia) in the table under Results and Questions.

Procedure B: Determining Hemoglobin Content of Blood Using a Spencer Hb-Meter

1. To use the Spencer Hb-meter, assemble the following three parts: a double-sided chamber with an H-shaped moat, a cover plate, and a clip. If necessary, clean the

parts with distilled water and dry with lens paper.

2. Offset the chamber (which should be beneath the cover glass) from the cover glass so that half of the H is visible.

3. Obtain a drop of blood, using the method described in Procedure A.

4. Place a sizable drop of blood on the chamber surface.

5. Hemolyze the blood by agitating it gently with the tip of a hemolysis applicator, which has been treated with a hemolytic reagent. The blood will change from cloudy to transparent when hemolysis is complete. Thirty to 45 seconds are required for this.

6. Once hemolysis is complete, push the chamber into the clip.

7. Insert this chamber into the slot on the left side of the instrument.

8. Hold the instrument to the eye with the left hand in such a manner that the left thumb rests on the light switch on the bottom. When this button is pressed, a green split field appears in the instrument. With the other hand, move the slide button on the right side of the instrument until the two halves of the field appear as a single field.

9. The position of the index mark on the slider knob indicates the hemoglobin content. Record the grams of hemoglobin per 100 ml of blood and the percent hemoglobin, using the scale marked 15.6.

10. Clean and dry the chamber.

11. Record your data in the appropriate place under Results and Questions.

12. Obtain the results in grams of hemoglobin from each member of the class, using the results obtained with the Spencer Hb-meter. Average the sexes separately and record the averages under Results and Questions.

EXERCISE 12-C
COAGULATION TIME
AND BLEEDING TIME

Objectives

To determine the coagulation time of blood by the slide method and by the capillary tube method; to determine the bleeding time of blood.

Materials

Lancets; sterile cotton; 70% alcohol; glass slide; pins; filter paper; capillary tube.

Discussion

The bleeding time (normal range 1 to 3 minutes) is taken as the time elapsing before a small sharp incision stops bleeding. However, the time depends on the depth of the wound and the degree of hyperemia in the finger, as well as on the presence of adequate amounts of clotting factors. The coagulation (or clotting) time is the time required for a sample of blood removed from the body to clot. The usual way to determine coagulation time is to allow the blood to flow from an incision into a glass capillary tube. The tube is broken at 1/2-minute intervals to determine when the clot formed (normal clotting time 2 to 6 minutes). The diameter of the capillary tube influences the coagulation time.

Procedure A: Coagulation Time—
Slide Method

1. Clean the finger with 70% alcohol and allow it to dry.

2. Puncture the fingertip with a sterile lancet. Do not use the first drop of blood, since it clots abnormally fast.

3. *Note the time* that the drop of blood to be used first appears at the finger puncture. This time is used as the beginning of the experiment.

4. Place the drop of blood on a glass slide.

5. At 1/2-minute intervals, *slowly* draw a straight pin through the blood and observe the point of the pin.

6. Repeat step 5 until fine red threads can be detected on the end of the pin. This is the end point. Sometimes the entire mass forms a gel, which is also considered the end point.

7. The difference between the time the second drop of blood appeared and the first thread appeared is the coagulation time. Using this method of determination, the normal range of coagulation is 2 to 8 minutes.

8. Record coagulation time in the table under Results and Questions.

Procedure B: Coagulation Time— Capillary Tube Method

1. Use the method in Procedure A for obtaining the drop of blood. The drop of blood must be large.
2. Note the time the drop of blood to be used appears. This time is used as the beginning of the experiment.
3. Place one end of the capillary tube into the drop of blood (keep the other end of the tube open). Hold the tube horizontally (do not let the tip touch the skin) and allow the tube to fill by capillarity.
4. After exactly 1 minute (use a longer period of time if the blood took a long time to coagulate in the slide method), carefully break off a small piece (about 1 cm) of the capillary tube and determine whether a thread of coagulated blood is visible between the two pieces of tubing.
5. Repeat step 4 every 30 seconds until such a thread is obtained.
6. Record the coagulation time in the table under Results and Questions.

Procedure C: Bleeding Time

1. Puncture the finger as directed earlier. Secure a free flow of blood so that the first drop on the filter paper will be 1 cm or more in diameter.
2. Note the time of appearance of the first drop of blood. Blot the blood with filter paper every 30 seconds until the bleeding stops.
3. Divide the total number of drops on the filter paper by 2. This gives the bleeding time in minutes.
4. Record bleeding time in the table under Results and Questions.

EXERCISE 12-D
PREPARATION OF BLOOD SMEAR STAINED WITH WRIGHT'S STAIN

Objectives

To learn the technique of making a stained blood smear; to observe differentially stained blood.

Materials

Microscope; glass slides (plain and frosted at one end); sterile lancets; 70% alcohol; sterile cotton; paper towel; staining dish set containing Wright's stain; buffer (pH 6.4); distilled water.

Discussion

A differential count is a determination of the percentage of each type of leukocyte in a stained blood smear. In blood stained with Wright's stain, the erythrocytes stain pale red, the nucleus of the leukocytes blue. The granules in the cytoplasm of the leukocytes stain a variety of colors depending on the cell type. A description of the leukocytes and approximate percentages of each in normal blood is found in Exercise 3-D, Part 5 (Blood).

To make a differential white blood cell count, the technician would observe 100 WBCs stained with Wright's or Giemsa's stain and determine the type of each. The number of each type would be the percentage of each (since 100 cells are observed).

The percentage of each type of leukocyte varies in certain disease conditions. For example, the percentage of eosinophils is increased from approximately 1% to 3% in the normal person to 8% to 10% in certain allergic conditions and to as much as 25% to 50% in certain parasitic infections. The percentage of monocytes increases from 5% to 8% in the normal state to as high as 30% to 50% in certain chronic infections. Typical values in a differential count taken on a normal adult are as follows: 65% neutrophils, 25% lymphocytes, 6% monocytes, 3% eosinophils, 1% basophils.

Procedure

1. Place a small drop of blood near one end of a clean slide (frosted at one end) and *immediately* smear it with the end of a "spreader" slide (a plain glass slide) as follows (see Figure 12-3):
   a. Place the spreader slide in front of the drop of blood at an angle of about 45 degrees, as illustrated in Figure 12-3 A.
   b. Allow a moment for the blood to spread in the angle between the slides, as illustrated in Figure 12-3 B.
   c. Just before the blood spreads to the

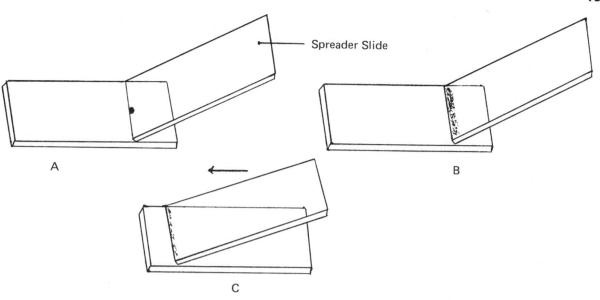

Spreader Slide

A

B

C

Figure 12-3.   Illustration of blood smear technique.

edges of the slide, push the spreader slide ahead of the drop of blood, as illustrated in Figure 12-3 C.

d. The slide should now be allowed to dry in the air.

2. Staining with Wright's stain:

a. As soon as the slide is dry, write your name on the frosted end and place it in the slide carrier.

b. Immerse the slide carrier into the container (staining dish) of Wright's stain for precisely 2 minutes.

c. Lift the slide carrier out of Wright's stain and immediately transfer it to the container of buffer solution. Leave the slide in the buffer for precisely 2 minutes.

d. Lift the slide carrier out of the buffer solution and dip it several times into the container of distilled water.

e. Place the slide carrier on a paper towel and allow it to air dry.

3. Examine the slide under the microscope (using high power or oil immersion).

4. Locate and identify a minimum of three different types of leukocytes. Draw each type identified. (The leukocytes are illustrated in Figure 3-16.)

EXERCISE 12-E
HEMATOCRIT AND THE COMPOSITION OF PLASMA

Objectives

To determine the hematocrit of blood and the composition of plasma.

Materials

Centrifuge; oxalated blood; centrifuge tube; pipette; Millon's solution; Benedict's solution; 10% acetic acid; filter paper; funnel; test tubes; beakers; distilled water.

Discussion

The hematocrit is the percentage of red blood corpuscles in the blood. It is determined by centrifuging a sample of whole blood and determining the percentage of packed red blood cells in the tube. Normal hematocrit values for a male are approximately 45 (range 38 to 53) and for a female 43 (range 38 to 48). It is possible to use the same tube to obtain an estimate of the percentage of white blood corpuscles in the blood. There are approximately 0.1% as many white blood corpuscles as there are red blood corpuscles.

A sample of the plasma will be removed from the hematocrit tube and analyzed. Plasma, the liquid portion of the blood, contains 90% water and 10% solutes. Plasma proteins are the most abundant constituent of the solutes in the plasma, making up 6% to 8% of the plasma. These plasma proteins include the albumins and globulins and the proteins essential for blood clotting. Glucose is also found in the plasma, in amounts ranging from 70 to 90 mg per 100 ml blood.

Procedure

1. Place exactly 15 ml of oxalated blood in a centrifuge tube and centrifuge for 1 hour.
2. The precipitate at the bottom of the tube is calcium oxalate. Above this are massed red blood corpuscles. Read the graduation and determine the percentage of RBCs.
3. A very thin layer of WBCs may be visible above the RBCs. Estimate the percentage of WBCs.
4. By means of a pipette, carefully remove as much of the plasma (the supernatant fluid) as possible. Do not disturb the layer of RBCs.
5. Place the plasma in a test tube and note its color.
6. Dilute 5 ml of the plasma with 10 ml of distilled water and boil.
7. When the plasma has reached the boiling point, add a drop or two of 10% acetic acid and filter. (Save the filtrate for use in step 9.) The coagulum consists of the common plasma proteins.
8. Place some of the coagulum in 5 ml of water and test for protein. To do this, add 10 drops of Millon's fluid and boil carefully. Observe the change in the color of the coagulum. The formation of a pink to red coagulum is positive for protein.
9. To 5 ml of the filtrate add an equal amount of Benedict's solution; boil. What is the color of the solution? The formation of a green, yellow, orange, or red color is positive for glucose in the plasma.

SELF-TEST—BLOOD TESTS

Directions

See Chapter 1, Self-Test, page 9.

1. A **hemocytometer** is used for blood counts.
2. The average number of RBCs per cubic millimeter is from 4½ to 5 million for **males**.
3. A symptom of leukemia is **a decrease** in the number of leukocytes in the blood.
4. Red bone marrow is the source of **erythrocytes, leukocytes,** and **thrombocytes**.
5. **Neutrophils** are the most abundant type of leukocyte.
6. **Vitamin K** is necessary for blood clotting because it catalyzes synthesis of **prothrombin** in the liver.
7. Calcium is **essential** in the conversion of prothrombin to thrombin.
8. Fibrin is the solid clot and is derived from **fibrinogen**.
9. Clotting is **slowed** when heat is applied to the wound.
10. **Coagulants** include heparin and dicumarol.
11. Type A blood may be given safely to a patient with **either type A or AB blood.**
12. Antigens are located in the plasma membrane of RBCs and **antibodies** are in the plasma.
13. The Rh factor is present in **most** Caucasians in the United States.
14. Women are Rh negative **more often** than men.
15. Hemophilia is a sex-linked hereditary disease occurring **primarily in males.**

16. The blood protein that contains antibodies opposing many pathogens is **globulin.**

17. Blood is **acid** in reaction.

18. Formed elements account for approximately **60%** of the volume of blood.

19. Cholesterol **is** a normal physiological constituent of the blood.

20. White cell counts of **5,000 to 10,000** per cubic millimeter of blood are in the normal range.

21. The **hemocytoblast** is the common stem cell from which both erythrocytes and leukocytes are developed.

22. The erythrocyte, in the mature stage, is **nucleated.**

23. Antibodies against the Rh factor are present in the blood of Rh-negative individuals **who have been exposed to Rh-positive blood.**

24. Blood serum is blood plasma minus **fibrinogen.**

25. A person with type AB blood may be called the universal **donor.**

26. The formation of a clot in a branch of the coronary arteries is called **cerebral vascular accident.**

27. Leukopenia is a **decrease** in the number of white blood corpuscles.

28. A reduction in number of erythrocytes or in the quantity of hemoglobin they contain is called **polycythemia.**

29. **Vitamin C** is needed for blood to clot.

30. **Leukocytes** are necessary for blood to clot.

31. In the blood clotting process, **thromboplastin** is formed from prothrombin.

32. The condition erythroblastosis fetalis occurs when the mother is **Rh+** and the baby is **Rh–.**

33. The normal thrombocyte count per cubic millimeter is **25,000 to 50,000.**

34. A thrombus is a **moving** blood clot.

35. Heparin and dicumarol may be given to a patient to **prolong** the clotting time.

36. The principal function of an erythrocyte is **to carry oxygen,** while that of a leukocyte is **to fight infection.**

37. **Erythrocytes** are phagocytic.

38. Hemopoiesis **in the embryo** occurs in the liver, spleen, red bone marrow, and lymph nodes.

39. The **inorganic salts** of the plasma aid in CO_2 transport.

40. A solution that has the same osmotic pressure as the blood is an **isosmotic** solution.

41. The pigment responsible for the color of red blood corpuscles is **myoglobin.**

42. Fluid located between the cells is called **intracellular** fluid.

43. **Leukocytosis** refers to the destruction of bacteria by leukocytes.

44. Hemoglobin carries **more** oxygen than carbon dioxide.

45. Leukocytes pass into the tissues through the walls of the **venules.**

46. The spleen is concerned with the destruction of worn-out **lymphocytes.**

47. **Proteins are** the most abundant compound in plasma.

48. Hemoglobin contains the mineral **copper.**

49. Approximately **10%** of the body weight is blood.

50. Lymph glands produce large numbers of **lymphocytes.**

13

Anatomy of the Circulatory System

EXERCISE 13-A
STRUCTURE OF AN ARTERY, A VEIN,
AND A LYMPH VESSEL VALVE

Objectives

To observe differences in the structure of an artery and a vein; to observe the structure of a valve in the wall of a lymphatic vessel.

Materials

Microscope; slides of a cross section of an artery and a vein; slide of longitudinal section of a lymphatic vessel containing valves.

Discussion

An artery may be defined as any vessel carrying blood away from the heart; a vein as any vessel returning blood from the capillary network to the heart. The lymphatic vessels form a different route for the return of fluid to the veins.

The wall of an artery is composed of three layers: the innermost **tunica intima**, a thin coat composed of one layer of endothelium, a small amount of connective tissue, and an internal elastic membrane; the thick **tunica media**, composed of smooth muscle arranged perpendicular to the length of the vessel and elastic connective tissue; and the outermost coat, the **tunica adventitia**, composed of loose connective tissue and adipose tissue. This external layer contains the vasa vasorum, the nutrient blood vessels nourishing the walls of all arteries and veins larger than 1 mm in diameter.

The veins contain the same three coats; however, the layers are thinner. The muscular and elastic tissues are much more poorly developed in the veins than in the arteries, while the connective tissue predominates in the veins. Many veins (and lymphatic vessels) contain valves in their walls that assist the return of fluid against gravity. Each valve consists of two semilunar pouches which open to let blood return to the heart and close to prevent backward flow of the blood.

Procedure

1. Examine the prepared slide of a cross section through an artery using the low power objective. Locate the three coats in the wall. Diagram the artery wall, showing the three layers in the correct proportions. Compare this slide with Figure 13-1, which shows the three layers in an artery and a vein.

2. Draw one small section through the entire wall in detail. (To see tissue in the tunica intima, it is necessary to use the high power objective of the microscope.) The innermost layer of the tunica intima is the endothelium. Observe the internal elastic membrane, the wavy purple line which forms the boundary between the tunica intima and tunica media.

3. Returning to low power, examine the tunica media. This layer contains both smooth muscle, which stains pink, and purple-staining elastic connective tissue. It is not necessary to draw cellular detail in the smoooth muscle. Locate the external elastic membrane, which separates the tunica media from the tunica adventitia.

4. Locate the vasa vasorum and adipose

Figure 13-1.   Cross section of artery.

tissue in the tunica adventitia. Include these in your drawing.

5. Examine a prepared slide of a cross section through a vein. Diagram the same three layers through the wall of the vein, showing differences in thickness of the wall. It is not necessary to include cells on this diagram.

6. Examine a slide of a longitudinal section of a lymphatic vessel with a valve. Diagram a section of the vessel with a valve; include the shape of the valve.

EXERCISE 13-B
GROSS ANATOMY OF THE
HUMAN CIRCULATORY SYSTEM

Objectives

To learn the locations and functions of major blood vessels in the body.

Materials

Anatomic charts; reference books.

Discussion

The circulatory system consists of the heart, blood vessels, and blood. Its primary function is to transport materials around the body. It transports food and oxygen to the cells, wastes away from the cells, hormones, antibodies, enzymes, etc.

The heart is a double pump located in the thoracic cavity. The right side of the heart pumps blood to the lungs, the left to the rest of the body. Be prepared in your study of the heart and blood vessels to trace the path of blood around the body.

Procedure

1. Use your text, charts, and references for orientation while studying the following figures.

2. Figure 13-2 shows the location and distribution of arteries. This figure may be used as a self-test.

3. Figure 13-3 shows the arteries supplying blood to the head and neck.

4. Study Figure 13-4, which shows the arteries supplying the trunk.

5. Figure 13-5 shows the location and distribution of veins. This figure may be used as a self-test.

6. Study Figure 13-6, which shows the azygos system of veins. These drain most of the body wall.

7. Figure 13-7 shows portal circulation. This figure may be used as a self-test.

8. Study Figure 13-8, which shows coronary circulation. The right and left coronary arteries originate from the ascending aorta. Determine the parts of the heart supplied by each coronary artery.

9. Figure 13-9 shows the pathway of blood through the heart.

10. Figure 13-10 shows the interior of the heart in detail and includes the major blood vessels carrying blood to and from the heart. This figure may be used as a self-test.

Left common carotid artery

Brachiocephalic artery

KEY TO FIGURE 13-2

1. RIGHT INTERNAL CAROTID ARTERY
2. EXTERNAL CAROTID
3. RIGHT COMMON CAROTID
4. VERTEBRAL
5. SUBCLAVIAN
6. CELIAC
7. COMMON HEPATIC
8. GONADAL
9. INFERIOR MESENTERIC
10. COMMON ILIAC
11. EXTERNAL ILIAC
12. DEEP ARTERIAL ARCH
13. LATERAL FEMORAL CIRCUMFLEX
14. FEMORAL
15. PERONEAL
16. LEFT SUBCLAVIAN ARTERY
17. AORTIC ARCH
18. BRACHIAL
19. THORACIC AORTA
20. DIAPHRAGM
21. GASTRIC
22. SPLENIC
23. SUPERIOR MESENTERIC
24. RENAL
25. RADIAL
26. ULNAR
27. INTERNAL ILIAC
28. SUPERFICIAL ARTERIAL ARCH
29. POPLITEAL
30. ANTERIOR TIBIAL
31. POSTERIOR TIBIAL
32. DORSALIS PEDIS

Figure 13-2.   Major arteries of the body.

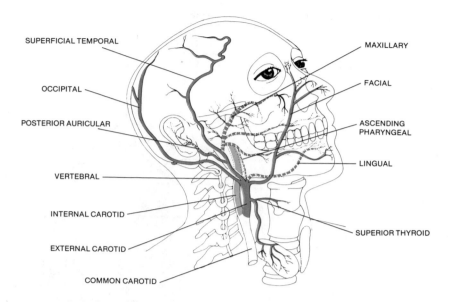

Figure 13-3.   Arteries supplying the head and neck.

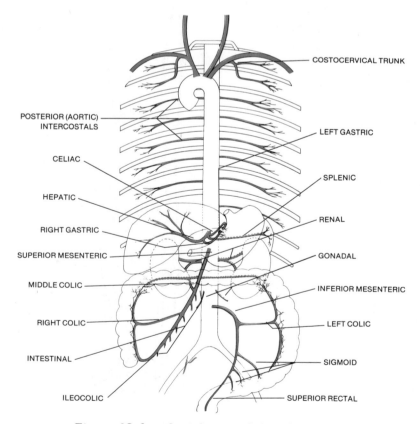

Figure 13-4.   Arteries supplying the trunk.

176

KEY TO FIGURE 13-5

1. SUPERIOR SAGITTAL SINUS
2. INFERIOR SAGITTAL SINUS
3. RIGHT EXTERNAL JUGULAR VEIN
4. INTERNAL JUGULAR
5. BRACHIOCEPHALIC
6. SUPERIOR VENA CAVA
7. HEPATIC
8. PORTAL
9. SUPERIOR MESENTERIC
10. MEDIAN CUBOIDAL
11. INTERNAL ILIAC
12. GREAT SAPHENOUS
13. LEFT SUBCLAVIAN VEIN
14. AXILLARY
15. CEPHALIC
16. BRACHIAL
17. BASILIC
18. SPLENIC
19. RENAL
20. INFERIOR MESENTERIC
21. COMMON ILIAC
22. EXTERNAL ILIAC
23. FEMORAL
24. POPLITEAL
25. SMALL SAPHENOUS
26. PERONEAL
27. POSTERIOR TIBIAL
28. ANTERIOR TIBIAL
29. DORSAL VENOUS ARCH

Figure 13-5.   Major veins of the body.

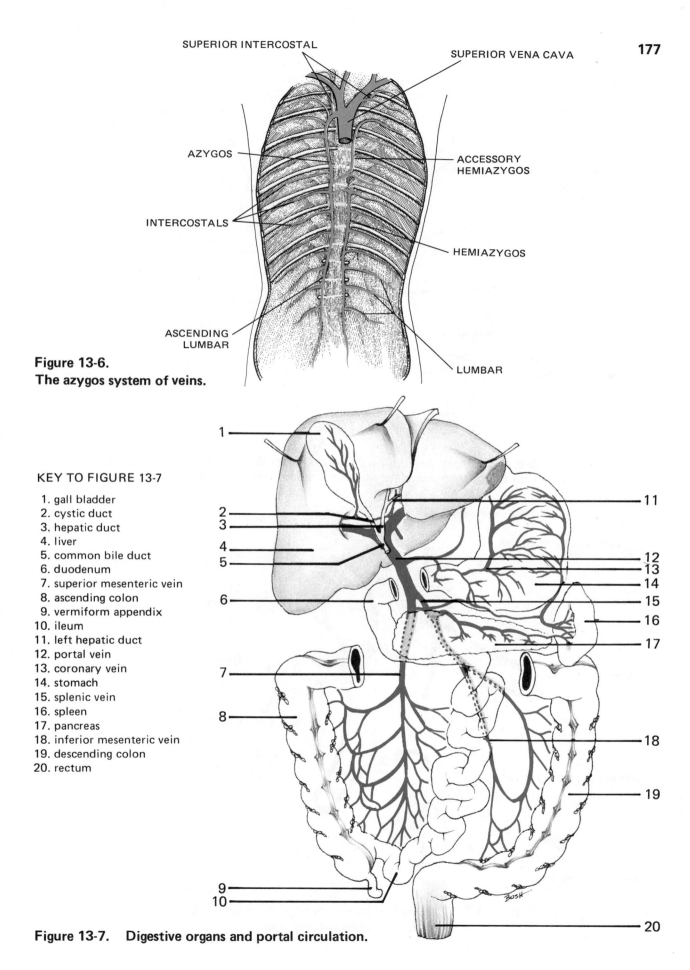

Figure 13-6.
The azygos system of veins.

SUPERIOR INTERCOSTAL

SUPERIOR VENA CAVA

AZYGOS

ACCESSORY
HEMIAZYGOS

INTERCOSTALS

HEMIAZYGOS

ASCENDING
LUMBAR

LUMBAR

KEY TO FIGURE 13-7

1. gall bladder
2. cystic duct
3. hepatic duct
4. liver
5. common bile duct
6. duodenum
7. superior mesenteric vein
8. ascending colon
9. vermiform appendix
10. ileum
11. left hepatic duct
12. portal vein
13. coronary vein
14. stomach
15. splenic vein
16. spleen
17. pancreas
18. inferior mesenteric vein
19. descending colon
20. rectum

Figure 13-7.   Digestive organs and portal circulation.

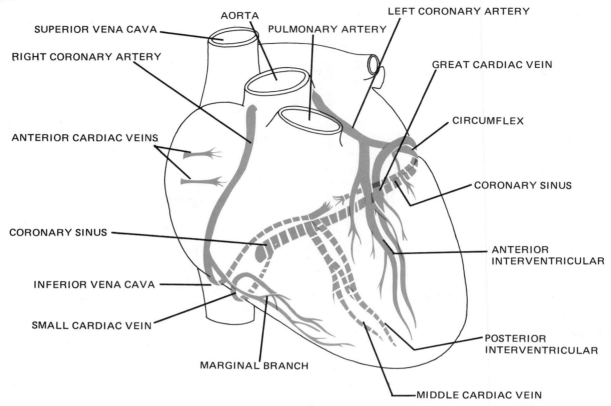

Figure 13-8. Coronary circulation (anterior view—the dotted lines represent vessels on the posterior surface; arteries colored red, veins colored blue).

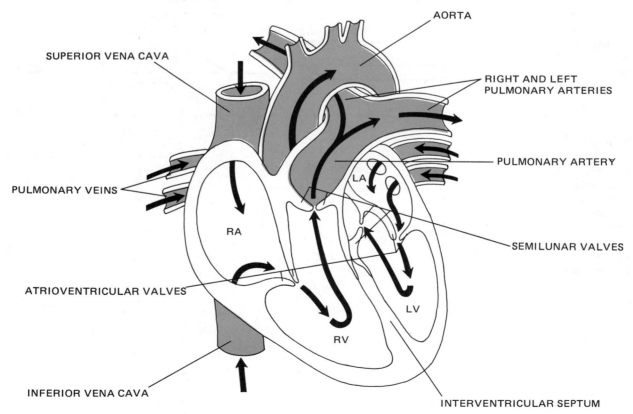

Figure 13-9. Pathway of blood through the heart (arteries colored red, veins colored blue).

KEY TO FIGURE 13-10

1. external jugular vein
2. internal jugular vein
3. common carotid artery
4. brachiocephalic artery
5. right pulmonary artery
6. right pulmonary veins
7. superior vena cava
8. aortic semilunar valve
9. right atrium
10. tricuspid valve
11. right ventricle
12. inferior vena cava
13. axillary vein
14. subclavian vein
15. brachiocephalic vein
16. aortic arch
17. L. pulmonary artery
18. pulmonary artery
19. L. pulmonary veins
20. pulmonary semilunar valve
21. left atrium
22. mitral valve
23. chordae tendineae
24. left ventricle
25. papillary muscle
26. interventricular septum

Figure 13-10.   Blood vessels of the neck and interior of the heart (arteries colored red, veins colored blue).

EXERCISE 13-C
DISSECTION OF THE SHEEP HEART

Objectives

To dissect the sheep heart; to compare the sheep heart with the human heart.

Materials

Preserved sheep, human, and horse hearts; dissecting set; dissecting pan; models of the human heart.

Discussion

The anatomy of the sheep heart is very similar to that of the human. In Exercise 13-D, the anatomy of the fetal pig heart will be compared with that of the adult sheep heart.

Observe carefully in this exercise the remnants of structures important in fetal circulation. Directions for this exercise are given with the heart in anatomic position.

Procedure

1. Locate the following structures on the models of the human heart:
   a. Aorta.
   b. Aortic semilunar valve.
   c. Bicuspid (mitral) valve.
   d. Chordae tendineae.
   e. Inferior vena cava.
   f. Left atrium.
   g. Left auricle.
   h. Left ventricle.
   i. Papillary muscle.
   j. Pulmonary artery.

k. Pulmonary semilunar valve.
l. Pulmonary vein.
m. Right atrium.
n. Right auricle.
o. Right ventricle.
p. Superior vena cava.
q. Tricuspid valve.
r. Moderator band (if present).

2. The same structures should also be located on the sheep heart. Rinse the sheep heart in water to remove as much preservative as possible.

3. The **pericardium** (the fibroserous membrane surrounding the heart) has been largely removed in preparing the sheep heart. Observe the remnants of this membrane attached to the large vessels above the heart.

4. Separate a small portion of the **epicardium** (the visceral layer of the pericardium) from the **myocardium** by careful dissection with a scalpel. The third layer of the heart, the **endocardium**, will be visible when the heart is opened.

5. Determine which is the ventral surface of the sheep heart by comparing the sheep heart with that shown in Figure 13-11. Locate the **pulmonary artery** on the ventral surface of the heart. This artery emerges from the anterior ventral surface of the heart, medial to the **left auricle**. The auricles are the earlike outpocketings of the **atria**, the upper chambers of the heart. Locate the **right** and **left auricles**.

6. Note the **anterior longitudinal sulcus** separating the **right ventricle** from the **left ventricle**. The **coronary blood vessels** can be seen in this sulcus.

7. Compare the thickness of the wall of the **right ventricle** with that of the **left ventricle** by pressing the wall of each ventricle between your thumb and forefinger.

8. If a demonstration dissected sheep heart is on display, observe the incisions before proceeding. Using great care, make an incision through the ventral wall of the pulmonary artery and the right ventricle parallel to, and 3/4 of an inch to the right of, the anterior longitudinal sulcus. Do not dissect so deeply that you cut into the dorsal surface of either the pulmonary artery or right ventricle. Continue the incision forward anteriorly to the point where the pulmonary artery branches into the **right and left pulmonary arteries**. Remove as much adipose tissue as necessary to expose the branches of the pulmonary artery.

9. Open the pulmonary artery and note the **pulmonary semilunar valve**. Observe the number of pouches in this valve. Remove any coagulated blood present in the blood vessels or heart.

10. Continue the original incision through the right ventricle wall (keeping parallel to the anterior longitudinal sulcus) around and through the dorsal wall of the right ventricle until reaching the **interventricular septum**.

11. Examine the dorsal surface of the heart. The thin-walled **superior vena cava** can be seen above the right auricle, extending straight down into the right atrium. Make a longitudinal incision through the dorsal wall of the superior vena cava, continuing down through the right atrium (immediately to the left of the right auricle). Continue this incision down the dorsal wall of the right ventricle to the point of juncture with the first incision.

12. If the incisions were properly made, it should now be possible to spread open the superior vena cava, right atrium, and right ventricle. Compare your dissection with Figure 13-12.

13. Determine whether a valve is present at the entrance of the superior vena cava into the right atrium.

14. Observe the internal structure of the right auricle. The muscle visible in the interior of the auricle is called the **pectinate muscle**, since it resembles a comb (pecten).

15. Locate the large opening of the **inferior vena cava** on the left side of the interior of the right atrium. Insert a finger or probe through the mouth of this vein to locate the external opening on the dorsal surface of the heart. Compare the location of this vein with the corresponding vein in humans.

16. Locate the orifice of the **coronary sinus** posterior to the opening of the inferior vena cava. Locate this vessel on the dorsal surface of the heart.

17. Locate the **interatrial septum**, the wall that separates the two atria. Examine this septum from the interior of the right

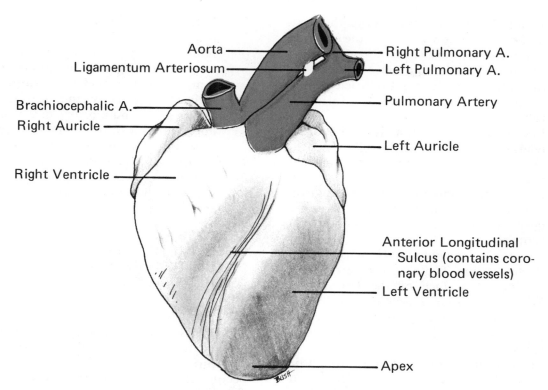

Figure 13-11. Ventral view of sheep heart (arteries colored red).

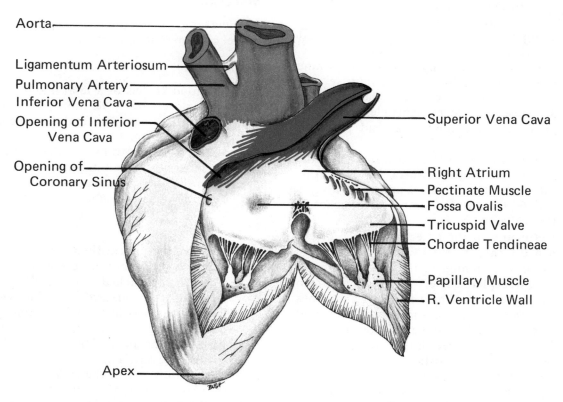

Figure 13-12. Right side of sheep heart (arteries colored red, veins colored blue).

atrium. Locate the **fossa ovalis**, the oval-shaped depression ventral to the entrance of the inferior vena cava.

18. Examine the **tricuspid valve** between the right atrium and the right ventricle. Determine the number of cusps that form this valve.

19. Locate the **papillary muscles** and **chordae tendineae** in the wall of the right ventricle. Determine the number of papillary muscles.

20. Locate the **moderator band** crossing the lumen of the right ventricle. This is believed to prevent overdistension of the ventricle.

21. Locate the four **pulmonary veins** entering the **left atrium**. These vessels are visible on the dorsal surface of the left atrium. Whether all four vessels can be located depends on how they were cut. It is not likely that you will see all four pulmonary veins.

22. Make a longitudinal incision through the most lateral of the pulmonary veins. Continue this down through the wall of the left atrium and the left ventricle to the **apex** of the heart.

23. Spread open the left side of the heart. Compare the wall thickness of the left ventricle with that of the right.

24. Observe the **bicuspid valve**. Determine how many major cusps comprise this valve. Determine which of the following are present in the left ventricle: moderator band, chordae tendineae, and papillary muscles.

25. Insert a finger up along the midline of the left ventricle into the **aorta**. Cut along this line until the **aortic semilunar valve** is visible. Count the number of pouches in this valve.

26. Returning to the external surface of the heart, locate the thick-walled aorta above the heart, arching to the left. Locate the **brachiocephalic artery** that branches from the aortic arch. This vessel later branches into the subclavian and common carotid arteries, which supply the arms and head. In humans, three large blood vessels branch from the aortic arch.

27. Open the aorta as it emerges from the network of blood vessels anterior to the heart. Observe the smooth lining of this vessel.

28. If the pulmonary artery was not severed too close to the heart when the heart was removed from the sheep you will be able to locate the **ligamentum arteriosum**, the remnant of the **ductus arteriosus**. Carefully dissect away the adipose tissue between the pulmonary artery and the aorta anterior to the heart. Be careful not to sever the ligamentum arteriosum when removing the adipose tissue.

29. Locate all the preceding structures on the preserved horse and human hearts.

EXERCISE 13-D DISSECTION OF THE CIRCULATORY SYSTEM OF THE FETAL PIG

Objectives

To dissect the circulatory system of the fetal pig and to compare it with the corresponding structures in the human circulatory system; to become familiar with the pathway of blood in fetal circulation.

Materials

Fetal pig; dissecting set; dissecting tray; model of human fetal circulation.

Discussion

The blood vessels of a fetal mammal, such as the pig, closely resemble those of the human adult. Modifications for fetal life include a placental circulation by way of the umbilical cord and two devices to bypass the lungs, since the lungs are not functional before birth. The arteries of the fetal pig have been injected with red latex; the veins with blue.

Procedure

1. Observe the **pericardium** surrounding the heart. After determining the structure to which it is attached, remove the parietal layer of the pericardium. The visceral layer of the pericardium forms the **epicardium**, the outermost layer of the heart.

2. Note that the **apex** of the heart is directed toward the left. The heart is tilted so that the greater part of the **right ventricle** lies directly in front, along the ventral surface of the heart. The **left ventricle** forms the apex of the heart.

3. The atria lie anterior to the ventricles. Each atrium has a conspicuous earlike appendage called the **auricle** on the ventral surface.

4. A groove, the **coronary sulcus**, separates the right atrium from the right ventricle. The **anterior longitudinal sulcus** is the groove that separates the right ventricle from the left ventricle. Dorsal to this sulcus is the **interventricular septum**. The **coronary blood vessels** are located in these grooves (the right coronary artery in the coronary sulcus, the left in the anterior longitudinal sulcus).

5. Observe the **anterior vena cava** (precaval vein), the large vessel entering the anterior part of the right atrium. (This vein is called the superior vena cava in humans.) The anterior vena cava drains the head, neck, and arms.

6. Trace this vessel forward and note that it is formed by the union of the two **brachiocephalic veins** (see Figure 13-13).

7. Trace the left brachiocephalic vein forward. This vein is formed by the union of three veins: the small **left internal jugular vein**, which lies next to the **left common carotid artery**; the larger **left external jugular vein**, which lies lateral to this; and the **subclavian vein**, which drains the arm. In humans, the internal jugular is larger than the external jugular.

8. Trace the subclavian vein through the chest wall. In the axillary region this vein

Figure 13-13.   Veins of the thorax and neck.

is known as the **axillary vein**. On the arm it becomes the **brachial vein**. To follow the vein on the arm, slit the skin and muscles on the ventral surface of the arm.

9. Locate the **posterior vena cava** (postcaval vein) posterior to the heart and trace it forward to the point where it drains into the right atrium. This large vein, called the inferior vena cava in humans, drains the lower portion of the body.

10. Trace the postcaval vein back through the **diaphragm** into the abdominal cavity, where it lies to the right of the aorta. To see the vein and its tributaries, it will be necessary to dissect away the peritoneum, since the posterior vena cava and the aorta are retroperitoneal.

11. The **hepatic veins** drain blood from the liver into the posterior vena cava. To locate these veins, gently scrape away tissue on the right anterior surface of the liver. Several hepatic veins may be located in this manner. The **umbilical vein** (carrying fresh oxygenated blood from the placenta) passes through the liver and connects with one of the larger hepatic veins.

12. Locate the **renal veins**, which carry blood from the kidneys into the posterior vena cava.

13. Returning to the thoracic cavity, push the left lung toward the right side of the body. Locate the **hemiazygos vein**, which lies next to the vertebral column and receives blood from the **intercostal veins**. The hemiazygos vein enters the dorsal surface of the right atrium.

14. The other major veins will be dissected with the arteries.

15. Locate the **pulmonary artery** on the ventral surface of the heart. Trace it down to its origin in the right ventricle; then follow it toward the lungs, noting that it branches into a **right** and **left pulmonary artery**.

16. At the point of branching of the pulmonary artery, the large **ductus arteriosus** passes anteriorly to connect to the aorta. The ductus arteriosus is larger than either the right or left pulmonary artery.

17. The **dorsal aorta** arises from the left ventricle. Locate this vessel dorsal and anterior to the pulmonary artery. The first branches of the dorsal aorta are the small **right** and **left coronary arteries**, which arise from the base of the aorta. The left

coronary artery is visible on the ventral surface of the heart in the anterior longitudinal sulcus, the right coronary artery in the coronary sulcus.

18. The dorsal aorta passes anteriorly for a short distance and then turns to the left. This region of the aorta is called the **aortic arch**.

19. To enable you to see the arteries branching off the aortic arch, free the anterior vena cava from the arteries beneath.

20. The first branch off the aortic arch is the **brachiocephalic artery**. This artery first gives off the **right subclavian artery** and then the **right** and **left common carotid arteries**.

21. Trace the common carotids toward the head along each side of the trachea. These arteries branch to form the **external** and **internal carotid arteries** at the anterior border of the larynx.

22. Returning to the aortic arch, locate the left **subclavian artery**, which supplies the left side of the chest and the left arm. Locate the **right** and **left internal mammary (sternal) arteries**, which supply the pectoralis muscles and mammary glands. These vessels arise from the subclavian arteries on either side of the sternum.

23. The subclavian artery becomes the **axillary artery** after exiting through the chest wall into the axillary space, and then becomes the **brachial artery** on the upper arm. Follow the brachial artery until it branches to form the **radial** and **ulnar arteries**, which supply the forearm. It may not be possible to locate the latter two arteries.

24. Pull the viscera in the thorax gently to the right to expose the dorsal aorta. As this vessel passes through the thorax, it is called the **thoracic aorta**. Remove the pleura to expose the aorta in the thorax.

25. Note the **intercostal arteries** emerging from the thoracic aorta. These supply the intercostal muscles.

26. Trace the descending aorta through the diaphragm. The first major branch from the abdominal aorta is the **celiac artery** (see Figure 13-14). To locate this artery, it will be necessary to remove the peritoneum covering the anterior end of the abdominal aorta immediately beneath the diaphragm. This large artery branches and supplies the liver, pancreas, spleen,

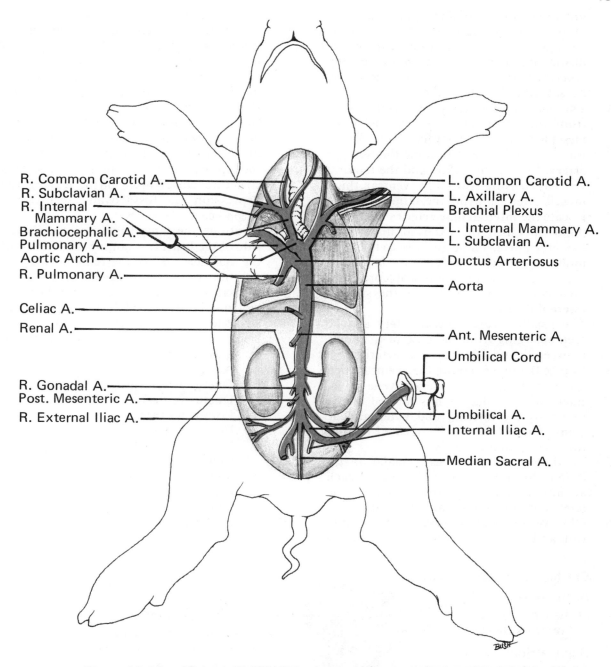

R. Common Carotid A.
R. Subclavian A.
R. Internal
  Mammary A.
Brachiocephalic A.
Pulmonary A.
Aortic Arch
R. Pulmonary A.

Celiac A.
Renal A.

R. Gonadal A.
Post. Mesenteric A.
R. External Iliac A.

L. Common Carotid A.
L. Axillary A.
Brachial Plexus
L. Internal Mammary A.
L. Subclavian A.
Ductus Arteriosus
Aorta

Ant. Mesenteric A.
Umbilical Cord

Umbilical A.
Internal Iliac A.

Median Sacral A.

Figure 13-14. Major arteries of the fetal pig (heart pulled to the right).

and duodenum.

27. Locate the **anterior mesenteric artery**, the unpaired vessel located a short distance posterior to the origin of the celiac. This vessel is also retroperitoneal. It supplies the small intestine and a portion of the large intestine.

28. Locate the **renal arteries** (which supply the kidney) posterior to the anterior mesenteric artery.

29. The right and left genital arteries (**testicular** or **ovarian**) are small vessels that emerge from the ventral surface of the aorta, posterior to the renals near the base of the aorta. If your specimen is a male, follow the testicular artery to the **inguinal canal**.

30. Turn the descending portion of the colon to one side to see the **posterior mesenteric artery**. The posterior mesenteric is a small,

unpaired vessel, arising from the aorta immediately posterior to the ovarian or testicular arteries. It divides almost immediately, with one branch proceeding anteriorly and one posteriorly along the dorsal surface of the colon.

31. The paired **external iliac arteries** arise from the aorta lateral to the posterior mesenteric artery. They continue downward on each side to become the **femoral artery**. Locate this vessel and the femoral vein by teasing away the ventral thigh muscle after removing the skin.

32. Locate the **internal iliac arteries** below the point at which the external iliacs arise from the aorta. These give rise to the large **umbilical arteries**, which pass lateral to the bladder, to the umbilical cord, and then continue downward as the smaller **internal iliac arteries**.

33. The small, **median sacral artery** can be seen emerging from the base of the aorta between the two internal iliac arteries.

34. Locate the two **common iliac veins**, which unite to form the posterior vena cava. Each common iliac vein is formed by the union of the **internal** and **external iliac veins**. These veins can be located next to the corresponding artery.

35. To dissect the **fetal heart**, make an incision through the lateral wall of each atrium and auricle. Carefully remove the latex and any blood that is present.

36. Observe the point of entrance of the anterior and posterior venae cavae into the right atrium.

37. Locate the **foramen ovale** (the hole in the **interatrial septum**) near the dorsal wall of the heart, just anterior to the entrance of the posterior vena cava. At this late time in fetal life, the opening is quite small. Pass a probe through the foramen ovale (see Figure 13-15). Blood returning to the heart by way of the posterior vena cava passes from the right atrium directly to the left atrium, bypassing the lungs. This structure closes after birth, leaving the depression, the fossa ovalis, seen in the sheep heart.

38. Continue the lateral incision down each side of the heart to examine the interior of the ventricles. Since the remainder of the anatomy of the fetal pig heart is the same as that of the sheep and human heart, it will not be described further. Locate all structures listed in Exercise 13-D.

39. Locate the following on the model of human fetal circulation:
    a. Aorta.
    b. Ductus arteriosus.
    c. Ductus venosus.
    d. Foramen ovale.
    e. Inferior vena cava.
    f. Internal iliac artery.
    g. Pulmonary artery.
    h. Superior vena cava.
    i. Umbilical artery.
    j. Umbilical cord.
    k. Umbilical vein.

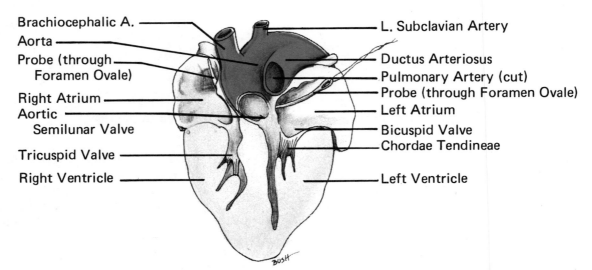

Figure 13-15. **Anterior aspect of coronal section through fetal pig heart (arteries colored red).**

SELF-TEST—ANATOMY OF THE CIRCULATORY SYSTEM

Directions

See Chapter 1, Self-Test, page 9.

1. The right and left common iliac veins unite to form the **superior vena cava.**
2. The blood vessel that carries blood from the fetus to the placenta is the **umbilical artery.**
3. Two fetal structures that allow blood to bypass the lungs are the **foramen ovale** and the **ductus arteriosus.**
4. Lymph from the thoracic duct drains into the **left subclavian vein.**
5. An artery is a vessel that leads **from** the heart, while veins lead **toward** it.
6. Small arteries are called **arterioles.**
7. The **endocardium** is a sac surrounding the heart.
8. Narrowing and stiffening of a valve of the heart, making it difficult for blood to get through, is called **cardiac thrombosis.**
9. The internal carotid artery, the vertebral artery, and the Circle of Willis are involved in supplying blood to the **brain.**
10. The **internal jugular** veins drain the brain.
11. The common iliac veins drain the **legs** and **pelvis.**
12. The brachial artery supplies the **leg.**
13. The **great saphenous** vein drains the legs.
14. The **celiac** artery supplies the stomach, liver, spleen, and pancreas.
15. The hepatic **vein** carries oxygen to the liver.
16. Veins contain valves—arteries **do not.**
17. Arteries **always** carry oxygenated blood.
18. Blood is pumped to the lungs by the **left ventricle.**
19. **Endocarditis** is an inflammation of the lining and valves of the heart.
20. Congenital heart disease **appears during old age.**
21. Swelling, or edema, of the feet and legs is a common symptom of **heart failure.**
22. An important function of the spleen is to produce **erythrocytes** in the adult.
23. The heart muscle is called the **endocardium.**
24. Cardiac muscle has **striated** myofibrils.
25. The heart and portions of the great vessels fill the **pericardial cavity.**
26. The membrane surrounding the heart is a **serous** membrane.
27. The blood in the pulmonary **artery** is fully oxygenated.
28. Blood entering the left atrium of the heart comes directly from the **inferior** and **superior venae cavae.**
29. Venous sinuses are found in the **skull** and **heart.**
30. The inner layer of tissue in the arterial wall is called the **endocardium.**
31. An **anastomosis** is a passageway or connection between two vessels.

32. The aorta arches to the **right**.

33. The coronary arteries are the **only** branches from the ascending aorta.

34. The **right** and **left common carotid arteries** divide into the internal and external carotid arteries.

35. There are **more** veins than arteries in the body.

36. The myofibrils in the walls of arteries are **striated**.

37. There are **two** umbilical arteries and **one** umbilical vein which provide circulation between the placenta and the embryo.

38. The umbilical vein carries **oxygenated** blood.

39. The prominent superficial vein in the neck is the **external carotid**.

40. The carotid sinus is located at the bifurcation of the **common carotid artery**.

41. The azygos vein drains blood from the intercostal veins into the **inferior vena cava**.

42. The basilic vein drains the **brain**.

43. In making a complete circuit through the human body, blood passes through the heart **once**.

44. Muscle cells are present in the layer of an artery wall known as the **tunica intima**.

45. Capillaries may be present in the walls of the **larger arteries**.

46. The coronary sinus opens into the **right atrium**.

47. The nutrient artery of the lungs is the **bronchial artery**.

48. The artery that brings oxygen to the liver is the **portal artery**.

49. Apoplexy is a term used for a **heart attack**.

50. The thoracic duct receives **blood** from the digestive tract.

51. Lymph flow is aided by **valves** in lymphatic vessels.

52. Lymph glands produce large numbers of **lymphocytes**.

14

Physiology of the Frog Heart

Objectives

To observe the parts of the frog heart and the sequence of contraction of each part.

Materials

Frog; dissecting set; frog board; clips; beaker of frog Ringer's solution; medicine dropper.

Discussion

In this series of experiments the frog heart will be used to observe the action of the heart and to demonstrate some of the properties of cardiac muscle. Although the frog has a three-chambered heart, it is similar in action to the human heart. The frog heart consists of the **sinus venosus**, a thin-walled, dorsal sac, which receives blood from the **anterior** and **posterior caval veins**; the **right atrium**, into which the sinus venosus empties; the **left atrium**, which receives blood from the lungs; and the **ventricle**, which receives blood from both atria. The blood is then pumped out the **truncus arteriosus**, the large ventral artery that arises from the ventricle.

Procedure

1. Pith the brain of the frog. This destroys the brain and as a result the frog does not feel pain.

2. To pith the frog, hold it in your left hand (as illustrated in Figure 14-1). The fingers and thumb should hold the arms to the trunk. Place the index finger on top of the head and press the head downward. With the nail of the right index finger, locate the junction between the occipital bone and the vertebral column. Indent the skin at this point.

3. Insert a probe through the skin at this junction. As soon as the probe enters the cord between the bones, the frog should become flaccid. This condition is called spinal shock.

4. When it is certain that the probe has entered the cord, turn and direct the probe forward through the foramen magnum inside the cranial cavity. Twist the probe until the brain is destroyed. It should be possible to feel bone on all sides of the probe if the probe is positioned correctly in the cranial cavity.

5. To minimize movement of the frog during the experiment, destroy the spinal cord as well as the brain. Insert the probe into the spinal cord at the site of entry of the probe and turn it downward to destroy the cord. The frog is now referred to as double pithed. Place the frog on its back on the frog board and pin all four legs down.

6. Using scissors, make an incision in the skin from the abdomen up to the jaw, slightly to one side of the midline.

7. Now, cut through the body wall along the same line, from the abdomen through the shoulder girdle. Use a lifting action on the

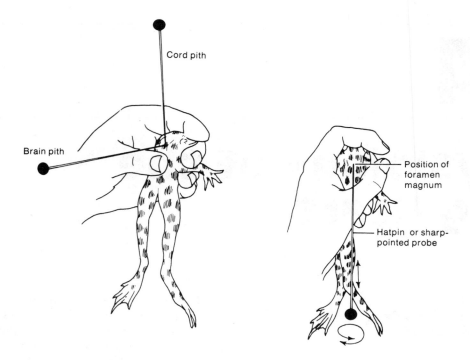

Figure 14-1. Procedure for pithing a frog.

lower blade of the scissors to avoid damaging the viscera. Open the thoracic cavity, exposing the heart and lungs.

8. By making several lateral incisions, some of the skin and musculature can be pinned aside, thus more clearly exposing the internal organs.

9. Keep the skin and the internal organs moist with frog Ringer's solution. The skin should not be allowed to touch the internal organs, since it contains secretions that are toxic to them.

10. Note the absence of a diaphragm. Occasionally the lungs may be distended with air. They can be gently pushed back into the pleural cavity or deflated by a snip with the scissors.

11. In the thoracic cavity, note the pericardium surrounding the heart. Wipe away any blood near the heart with filter paper or a paper towel.

12. Determine to which structures the pericardium is attached.

13. Observe the size of the heart.

14. Make an incision in the pericardium. Is any moisture present between the pericardial sac and the heart?

15. Note the size of the heart, after removing the pericardium, and compare it with the size before the pericardium was cut.

16. Moisten the heart with Ringer's solution.

17. Using Figures 14-2, -3, and -4 as guides, locate the sinus venosus (by lifting the apex of the ventricle), the right atrium, the left atrium, and the truncus arteriosus.

18. Observe the sequence of contraction of the atria and the ventricle.

19. Determine the rate of the atria and of the ventricle for 30 seconds. Multiply each figure by 2 to determine the heart rate per minute.

EXERCISE 14-B
EXTRASYSTOLE

Objectives

To demonstrate the occurrence of extrasystole, the compensatory pause, and the absolute refractory period.

Materials

Frog board; stand; clips; thread; beaker of frog Ringer's solution; pin hook; medicine dropper; dissecting set; frog; *either* kymograph, heart lever, induction stimulator, signal magnet, two double clamps, and platinum electrodes *or* physiograph, pin electrodes, stimulator output extension cable, transducer cable, and myograph B.

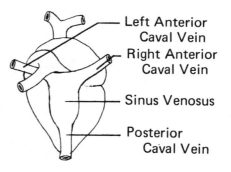

Left Anterior
Caval Vein

Right Anterior
Caval Vein

Sinus Venosus

Posterior
Caval Vein

Truncus
Arteriosus
Right Atrium
Left Atrium

Ventricle

Figure 14-2. Ventral view of frog heart.

Figure 14-3. Longitudinal section of frog heart.

Figure 14-4. Dorsal view of frog heart.

Discussion

The absolute refractory period, the time during which an excitable tissue will not respond to a stimulus, occurs with cardiac muscle tissue all during systole. The relative refractory period, the time during which it takes a greater amount of stimulus than usual to stimulate the tissue, occurs during early diastole. During diastole, the heart responds to an adequate stimulus by giving an extrasystole, which is followed by a longer pause, a compensatory pause. In this experiment you will stimulate the heart at various times during the cardiac cycle, noting when the heart responds to a stimulus.

Procedure Using Kymograph

1. Connect the platinum electrodes and the signal magnet to the induction stimulator. Attach the platinum electrodes to the terminals marked STIM, and the signal magnet to the two terminals marked MAG (refer to Figure 14-5).
2. Prepare the kymograph. Place the frog heart preparation from the previous experiment to the right of the kymograph with the writing facing the operator. Place the semicircular base of the stand toward the kymograph.
3. The heart lever is used for recording heart action. It consists of an aluminum stylus with an ink pen and an adapter, a yoke with a check nut to hold the stylus in any position, and a yoke handle (see Figure 14-6). Screw the yoke handle into the yoke.
4. Attach the yoke handle with a two-way clamp to the semicircular stand so that the check nut is up. Place the arm that protrudes from the adapter of the ink pen through the hole next to the check nut on the yoke (see Figure 14-6). Tighten the check nut. Check to make sure that the aluminum stylus, the pen, and the adapter do not touch the yoke handle at any point in the excursion of the heart lever. If necessary, readjust the position of the arm in the check nut to achieve this goal.
5. Attach the signal magnet to the stand below the heart lever. Align the tip of the signal magnet pen immediately below that of the pen of the heart lever.
6. Use the same frog heart as in the preceding experiment. Pass a v-shaped pin hook (made from a straight pin) through the tip of the apex of the ventricle. Do not puncture the ventricle, since a better record is obtained if the heart is full of blood. Tie a piece of thread to the pin hook.
7. Connect the thread from the pin hook to the aluminum stylus (short arm) of the heart lever with a small piece of colophonium cement. Adjust the length of the thread so that the ventricle is raised from the body of the frog. The thread between the heart and the lever must be vertical.
8. Make sure that the frog heart lever is horizontal. The magnitude of the response on the record may be varied by adjusting the heart lever.
9. Line up the signal magnet so that the signal magnet pen writes immediately beneath the pen of the heart lever.
10. Use drum speed 7. Check that the equipment writes correctly on the drum.
11. Hold the stimulating electrodes so that they constantly touch the ventricle.
12. Record six to eight normal beats of the

Figure 14-5.   Diagram of setup for stimulation of frog heart using kymograph.

Figure 14-6.   Heart lever.

heart. The ink pen rises upon contraction of the ventricle and returns to the baseline during diastole.

13. Using a weak, single stimulus (approximately 25 volts), stimulate the ventricle at 7- to 10-second intervals (make the circuit, *hold it for 7 to 10 seconds,* then break the circuit). Some of the stimuli should be administered during systole and others during diastole (both early and late). Continue the experiment until the heart record shows several extrasystoles.

14. Include the record under Results and Questions.

Figure 14-7. Setup for stimulation of the frog heart with the DMP-4B.

Procedure Using the Physiograph

1. Connect the myograph to the stand with the mounting rod and clamp. Attach the frog board to the base of the stand (see Figure 14-7). See Exercise 7-F for detailed

operating instructions for the physiograph. Pens should be in the time and event channel and in the appropriate channel amplifier.

2. Attach the transducer cable to the myograph B and to the 9 pin connector on the

transducer coupler of the physiograph.

3. Attach the stimulator output extension cable to the RF Isolated Output on the stimulator, red to red, black to black. Then, using the clip at the opposite end of the extension cable, attach the cable to the stand where the frog will be used.

4. Use the same frog as in the previous experiment.

5. Pass a v-shaped pin hook (made from a straight pin) through the tip of the apex of the ventricle. Do not puncture the ventricle, since a better record is obtained if the heart is full of blood. Tie a piece of thread to the pin hook.

6. Tie the other end of the thread in a fixed loop (not a slip knot) and slip the loop over the myograph leaf spring hook. Adjust the vertical position of the myograph (or use the myograph tension adjuster) to maintain a constant slight tension on the thread connected to the heart. The tension may need to be decreased later if the atrial contraction is visible on the record.

7. Attach a set of pin electrodes (blue and yellow) to the clip electrodes attached to the stand. Insert the pin electrodes into the ventricle of the heart.

8. Set the channel amplifier controls as follows:
   a. Set the paper speed to 1 cm/sec.
   b. Set the time marker to 1 per second.
   c. Press the main frame RECORDER switch ON.
   d. Press the POWER switch ON.
   e. Press the RECORD switch OFF if it is glowing.
   f. Set the FILTER switch to 10K, the mV/CM switch to 100.
   g. Set the recording pen on the center dark-green line for that channel with the POSITION control.
   h. Start the ink flowing in the pen associated with the transducer coupler and in the pen attached to the time event marker.
   i. Press the RECORD switch ON. Reset the baseline to the center dark-green line with the BALANCE control.
   j. Adjust the amplitude (mV/CM switch) to produce a deflection of the

desired height (about 3/4 inch with each beat of the heart). The tension on the myograph may have to be readjusted.

9. Start the paper moving. Record six to eight normal beats of the heart. The pen rises upon systole of the ventricle and returns to the baseline upon diastole.

10. Turn on the stimulator. Set the duration to 7, multiplier to X1. Set the voltage to 10, multiplier to X1. Using a weak, single stimulus (start with 10 volts and gradually increase the strength of the stimulus until a result occurs during diastole), stimulate the ventricle at 7- to 10-second intervals. Some stimuli should be administered during systole and others during diastole (both early and late). Continue the experiment until the heart record shows several extrasystoles and compensatory pauses.

11. Include the record, fully labeled, under Results and Questions.

EXERCISE 14-C
PHASES OF THE CARDIAC CYCLE

Objective

To determine the length of each phase of the cardiac cycle.

Materials

Frog; frog board; pin hook; Ringer's solution; stand; beaker; medicine dropper; dissecting set; *either* kymograph, heart lever, and two double clamps *or* physiograph, pin electrodes, stimulator output extension cable, transducer cable, and myograph B.

Discussion

In this exercise, the duration of each phase of the cardiac cycle will be determined. At a fast paper speed, the contractions of the atria and the ventricle are separated sufficiently from each other so that each can be measured. The contraction of the atria raises the pen a slight distance; the contraction of the ventricle raises the pen still higher. It may be possible to detect the contraction of the sinus venosus preceding that of the atria. A record of the frog heart beat will usually resemble the diagram in Figure 14-8.

ab = atrial systole
be = atrial diastole
cd = ventricular systole
dg = ventricular diastole

Figure 14-8.   Phases of the cardiac cycle.

Procedure with the Kymograph

1. Use the same frog heart preparation as in the previous experiments.
2. Record three consecutive heartbeats at drum speed 4 (each student).

Procedure with the Physiograph

1. Use the same frog heart preparation and physiograph setup as in the previous experiments.
2. Record three consecutive heartbeats at paper speed 10 cm/sec (each student).

EXERCISE 14-D
EFFECT OF TEMPERATURE ON HEART RATE

Objectives

To demonstrate the effect of temperature on the rate of the heart beat; to calculate the Q_{10} for the rate of the heart beat.

Materials

Dissecting set; beakers; frog Ringer's solution; ice; water baths of various temperatures; medicine dropper; thermometer; frog; frog board and clips; tripod; coarse salt; wire gauze. For alternate procedure use the kymograph or physiograph setup from the previous experiment.

Discussion

An increase in temperature speeds up the rate of chemical reactions. The rate of the heartbeat will be determined at several temperatures to verify that an increase in temperature produces an increase in heart rate. The temperature coefficient, or Q_{10}, of a reaction is the rate of that reaction (rate of heartbeat in this experiment) at one temperature divided by the rate of the same reaction at a temperature 10 °C below the first temperature.

$$Q_{10} = \frac{\text{Rate at a higher temperature}}{\text{Rate at a temperature } 10° \text{ lower}}$$

The Q_{10} is often 2 to 3 for biological reactions.

Procedure

1. Use the same frog heart preparation as in the previous experiments. Remove the pin hook from the frog heart.
2. Keep the frog board over the sink and use paper towels to absorb any excess Ringer's solution.
3. Ringer's solution of various temperatures, ranging from 2 to 32 °C, will be needed.
4. To cool Ringer's solution to approximately 2 °C, place ice cubes, salt, and water in a large beaker. Place a small beaker containing Ringer's solution inside the large beaker.
5. Heat additional Ringer's solution. By combining very cold Ringer's solution and hot Ringer's solution, prepare baths (as needed) at the following temperatures: 2, 12, 22, and 32 °C. (Other temperatures may be used but they should be in a series with 10° intervals between them. Do not use a temperature above 35 °C.)
6. Flood the heart with the coldest solution. This must be done for *a sufficient length of time to allow the heart to attain the temperature of the solution.*
7. After the temperature of the heart is stabilized (determine this by counting and

checking for stability of the rate), count the heart rate for 1/2 minute and multiply by 2.

8. Repeat the above procedure, increasing the temperature of the Ringer's solution 10 °C each time. Record the rate of the heartbeat in the table under Results and Questions.

9. Calculate and record (under Results and Questions) the Q_{10} for at least three successive 10 °C increases in temperature, such as the increase between 2 and 12 °C, 12 and 22 °C, and 22 and 32 °C.

Alternate Procedure

1. Using the same frog heart preparation as in the previous experiment (using either the kymograph or physiograph), prepare the solutions and arrange the frog board over the sink as described in steps 1 to 7 above.

2. If using the kymograph, use drum speed 7. After the heart rate is stabilized at the lowest temperature Ringer's solution obtainable, record the heart rate at that temperature, starting at the bottom of the piece of kymograph paper, for one entire turn of the drum. Then lower the drum. Before beginning the next recording, stabilize the heart at a temperature 10 °C higher; then record. Repeat the above procedure, increasing the temperature of Ringer's solution 10 °C each time. Calculate the rate of the heartbeat at each temperature by counting the number of beats in 15 cm and multiplying by 2. (At a drum speed of 7, the paper moves 0.5 cm/sec.)

3. The procedure is the same if the physiograph is used (use paper speed 0.5 cm/sec). Record the heartbeat at each temperature on a separate entire sheet of paper, cut out the strips, and superimpose them on one sheet of paper.

4. Calculate the heart rate per minute at each temperature with the physiograph by counting the number of beats in 15 seconds and multiplying by 4, or in 30 seconds and multiplying by 2.

5. Calculate and record under Results and Questions the Q_{10} for three successive 10 °C increases in temperature, such as the increase between 2 and 12 °C, 12 and 22 °C, and 22 and 32 °C.

EXERCISE 14-E
HEART BLOCK

Objective

To demonstrate the occurrence of heart block.

Materials

Frog board and string; frog; beaker; frog Ringer's solution; medicine dropper; thread; dissecting set.

Discussion

Pressure applied to the conducting system by means of a ligature in the atrioventricular groove decreases the rate of the heartbeat, resulting in heart block. After release of the pressure, the ventricle may resume its normal beat. However, if the conducting system was permanently damaged by the ligature, the ventricle may beat at a much slower rate than the atria. This demonstrates that the automaticity of the ventricle is less than that of the remainder of the heart.

Procedure

1. Expose the heart of a frog or use the same frog as in the previous experiment. This experiment must be the last experiment in any series as the heart often will not resume beating.

2. Count the rate of the whole heart. Since the atria and the ventricle beat at the same rate, record this figure under Results and Questions in the columns for "Rate before experiment" for both the atria and the ventricle.

3. Moisten a thread in Ringer's solution and pass it around the heart in the atrioventricular groove (see Figure 14-9). Tie a loose, single knot so that pulling the ends will tighten the thread in the groove.

4. Tighten the thread slightly and count and tabulate the rates of both the atria and ventricle. Continue tightening the thread and tabulate the rates of both parts. (One student should count the rate of the atria while another student simultaneously counts the rate of the ventricle, for the same length of time.)

5. Continue tightening the thread until the ventricle stops beating. Count the contrac-

Figure 14-9.   Ligature in atrioventricular groove.

tions of the atria and record their rate and that of the ventricle (which is zero) in the row in the table headed "Rate during ventricular arrest" under Results and Questions.

6. Cut or untie the thread in the atrioventricular groove. Now count the rate of both the atria and the ventricle and record these figures in the table. If the ventricle does not resume its beat, stimulate it. Record the rate of beat of the ventricle if it resumes beating.

EXERCISE 14-F
AUTOMATICITY OF THE HEART

Objectives

To demonstrate the degree of automaticity possessed by individual parts of the frog heart and the gradual decrease in irritability from the sinus venosus to the apex.

Materials

Dissecting set; frog; beaker of frog Ringer's solution; watch glass; induction stimulator; platinum electrodes.

Procedure

1. Use the same frog if the ventricle resumed a normal beat in Exercise 14-E, or prepare a fresh heart.
2. Determine the rate of heartbeat when the heart is still within the body of the frog.
3. Remove the heart by first cutting through the arteries and veins near the heart. Lift up the heart and, to remove the sinus venosus, cut deep, dorsal to the heart.
4. Place the heart in a watch glass containing Ringer's solution.
5. After 1 minute, count the rate of beat of the entire heart.
6. Determine the location of the sinus venosus on the dorsal surface of the right atrium; then carefully separate the sinus venosus from the remainder of the heart.
7. After several minutes, count the rate of beat of each of the two separated parts of the heart (the sinus venosus and the combined atria-ventricle).
8. Now separate the atria from the ventricle and determine the rate of beat of each part after several minutes. If the ventricle does not initiate its own beat, stimulate it. Record in the chart (under Results and Questions) the initial rate (zero) and the rate after stimulation.
9. If the ventricle begins to beat, cut off the apex. The apex generally will not beat by itself. If the apex does not initiate its own beat, stimulate it and record the rate of the beat obtained.

Note: The self-test of Chapter 14 has been combined with that for Chapter 15 and is located at the end of Chapter 15.

15

Physiology of Circulation

EXERCISE 15-A
MICROCIRCULATION IN THE
FISH OR FROG

Objective

To demonstrate circulation in the tail of a fish or the web of a frog.

Materials

Goldfish (or frog); microscope; balsa wood (or frog board and frog web board); thumbtacks; cotton; cover glass.

Discussion

The tail of a fish or the web of a frog can be used to demonstrate microcirculation, since the tail or web is thin enough for light to pass through, allowing the blood vessels to be observed with a microscope. The vessels in the web or tail can be distinguished on the basis of the rate of flow of blood, the pulsations, and the direction of flow of blood.

Procedure A (Using Fish)

1. Cut a hole approximately 1/2 inch in diameter near one end of a piece of balsa wood approximately 3 inches wide, 6 inches long, and 1/4 inch thick.
2. Saturate with water two pieces of cotton, each slightly larger than the fish and from 1/4 to 1/2 inch thick, and place these near the hole in the board.
3. Lay the fish on the first cotton pad.

(Handle the fish with care. Hold it firmly enough to prevent it from dropping, but do not crush it.) Orient the tail of the fish over the hole.
4. Lay the second wet cotton pad on top of the fish. (This pad has sufficient weight to hold the fish in position.)
5. Spread the tail over the hole in the balsa wood, and pin it in this position by applying a thumbtack at the margin of the tail on either side. Do not puncture the tail.
6. Place the fish so that the hole in the balsa wood is in position on the stage of the microscope for viewing with the low power objective. Cover the tail with a cover glass. Keep the tail moist with tap water.
7. Examine the vessels in the tail under low power of the microscope. Distinguish between an artery and a vein by noting the direction of blood flow (toward or away from a bifurcation—branch).
8. Locate a capillary. The erythrocytes (nucleated) can be seen passing through the capillary in single file. Note the twisting movement of some of the red blood cells in the capillaries.
9. Observe the difference in rate of blood flow in the three types of vessels.
10. Note in which type of blood vessels pulsations are observed.
11. The microcirculation may be observed for up to 30 minutes in this manner without damage to the fish. When you complete the experiment, release the fish into its container.

Procedure B (Using Frog)

1. Pith the frog. Place the frog (ventral surface up) on a frog board. Tie both forelegs and one hindleg loosely to the frog board, leaving the other hindleg free to extend over the web board.
2. Spread the web of the free leg over the hole in the web board and fasten the web to the web board with pins. Do not stretch the web too tightly.
3. Keep the frog and the web moist with tap water throughout the experiment. It may be necessary at intervals throughout the experiment to massage the hindleg to restore circulation. Select a light area of the web and examine this with the low power of the microscope, following steps 7 to 11 in the procedure outlined above with the fish.

EXERCISE 15-B
HEART SOUNDS AND
PULSE RATE

Objectives

To listen to heart sounds and to determine the effect of exercise on these sounds; to determine the effect of body position and running on heart rate.

Materials

Stethoscope; bicycle ergometer. For Alternate Procedure: physiograph; photoelectric pulse pickup.

Discussion

As the heart beats, it makes certain characteristic sounds that can be heard through the stethoscope. These sounds are described as lub-dup. The first sound is caused by the contraction of the ventricle and the snapping shut of the atrioventricular (AV) valves; the second by the closing of the semilunar valves. These sounds furnish information concerning the condition of the heart valves. Heart murmurs are caused by defects in the heart valves.

The pulse reflects the rate of the heartbeat. It can be felt at points where an artery lies near the surface over a bone; however, the radial artery is customarily used in taking the pulse.

The position of the body has an effect on heart rate. The rate is usually lower when the person is lying down, slightly higher when sitting, and higher when standing. Exercise markedly increases the heart rate.

Procedure

1. Place the stethoscope in the ears so that the top of the earpiece points inward and upward into the ear.
2. Hold the bell of the stethoscope firmly against the chest of the seated subject at the fifth intercostal space, about 3 inches to the left of the midline.
3. Listen to and describe the two heart sounds.
4. Have the subject run in place for 2 minutes. Again listen to the heart sounds. Describe any change in the sounds.
5. Practice taking your pulse at the radial artery by placing the tips of your fingers in the groove medial to the styloid process of the radius (on the thumb side of the forearm). Determine the pulse rate for an entire minute each time.
6. Count your pulse for *one full minute* under each of the following conditions and include your values in the appropriate place under Results and Questions.
   a. Reclining for 1 minute.
   b. Sitting for 1 minute.
   c. Standing for 1 minute.
   d. While exercising (running in place or bicycling with a belt setting of 2 for females and 3 for males and pedaling 35 kph) for 1 minute.
   e. Immediately after exercising for 2 full minutes.
7. Obtain the resting, sitting pulse rate (6b) from each member of the class and average the sexes separately.

Alternate Procedure Using the Physiograph

1. Perform steps 1 through 4 as outlined above.
2. Refer back to Exercise 7-F for detailed directions for the physiograph.
3. Connect the photoelectric pulse pickup to the physiograph and to the ventral surface of a finger of the left hand (Fig. 15-1) so that the photoconductor is next to the

JACK: accepts mating plug from certain specialized instruments

9-PIN CONNECTOR: accepts transducer cable; myograph and bellows pneumograph connect here

BALANCE: used for returning pen to its central position after RECORD button is pushed

7-PIN CONNECTOR: accepts Photoelectric Pulse Transducer

LOCKING KNOB: when fully clockwise secures coupler in position

Figure 15-1. Photoelectric pulse pickup with DMP-4B.

skin. Fit the foam rubber band over the photoelectric pulse pickup and wrap the band snugly around the finger. The pulse pickup is light sensitive and must be shielded with the black band.

4. Have the subject recline on the laboratory table.

5. Adjust the controls of the physiograph as follows:
   a. Start the ink flowing in the pens attached to the transducer coupler and the time event channel.
   b. Press the RECORDER switch on the main frame ON.
   c. Set the paper speed to 0.5 cm/sec and the time marker to 1 per second.

   d. Press the POWER switch ON.
   e. Press the RECORD switch OFF (if it is glowing).
   f. Set the FILTER switch to 10K and the mV/CM switch to 20.
   g. Set the recording pen to the center dark-green line using the POSITION control.
   h. Press the RECORD switch ON. Adjust the transducer coupler BALANCE control to reposition the recording tracing around the center dark-green line for that channel.
   i. Start the paper moving. Adjust the mV/CM switch for the desired amplitude. An amplitude of no more than 1

Figure 15-2. **Record of pulse with photoelectric pulse pickup.**

inch is desirable, since the amplitude will increase after exercise. It may be necessary to reposition the pulse pickup on the finger if no record is obtained.

6. Record the pulse for *one full minute* under each of the following conditions (the time marker omits the second mark each minute):
   a. Reclining for 1 minute.
   b. Sitting for 1 minute.
   c. Standing for 1 minute.
   d. Exercising on the bicycle ergometer for 1 minute. Use a belt setting of 2 for females, 3 for males, at 35 kph. Rest the hand with the photoelectric pulse pickup on the handlebar.
   e. Immediately after exercising for 2 minutes.

7. Calculate the pulse rate during the last 30 seconds of each minute and multiply by 2 to obtain the heart rate per minute. See the sample record (Fig. 15-2) for method. At a paper speed of 0.5 cm/sec, 5 seconds elapse between each two dark-green vertical lines. Include your results under Results and Questions.

8. Obtain the before-exercise resting, sitting pulse rate (6b) from each member of the class and average the sexes separately.

EXERCISE 15-C
BLOOD PRESSURE

Objectives

To determine blood pressure and the effect of exercise on blood pressure and heart rate.

Materials

Sphygmomanometer; stethoscope; bicycle ergometer. For Alternate Procedure: physiograph; electrosphygmograph coupler; transducer coupler; photoelectric pulse pickup; electrosphygmograph.

Discussion

Since direct measurement of blood pressure involves instruments that enter the blood vessel, the indirect method, which depends on the amount of pressure required to close off the flow of blood through the brachial artery, is most commonly used. The brachial artery, located in the upper arm, lies close to the ventral surface of the humerus.

The sphygmomanometer consists of (1) a compression bag surrounded by an unyielding cuff for application of extra-arterial pressure, (2) a mercury manometer or pressure gauge by which the applied pressure is read, (3) a bulb for inflation of the cuff to create pressure in the system, (4) a valve to release the air from the cuff, and (5) attachments for connecting the cuff to the manometer and bulb. The manometer is used to measure the pressure within the cuff in millimeters of mercury.

Exercise results in an increase in heart rate, blood pressure, and respiration rate. The amount of increase and the rate of return to normal depend the physical condition of the individual and the intensity of the exercise.

Procedure

1. This experiment requires the collaboration of three students. One student should take blood pressure, one should take pulse rate, and the third is the subject. (Pulse must be taken in the arm not used for determination of blood pressure.)

2. The subject should sit in a quiet room for 5 minutes in a relaxed position with the right arm on the table. After 5 minutes, determine the blood pressure and pulse. (Always take the pulse simultaneously with the blood pressure reading.)

3. Wrap the cuff around the arm approximately 1 inch above the antecubital space (elbow). The cuff should fit snugly. If a hook cuff is used, circle the arm so that the correct arrow is over the artery. Pull the tail end of the cuff snugly over the arm and hook the metal buttonhole over the metal button.

4. Place the stethoscope over the brachial artery just below (and not touching) the cuff. The stethoscope should be applied firmly throughout the experiment but not so tightly that the pressure compresses the brachial artery. No sound should be heard in the artery at this time. Verify this.

5. Pump air into the cuff until the mercury column or pressure reading on the gauge is 200 mm. If the pressure is high enough, the brachial artery is compressed, and no sound should be heard through the stethoscope.

6. Release the pressure slowly (the pressure should fall 2 to 3 mm per heart beat) by means of the valve on the bulb, while listening through the stethoscope for the first sound. This sound, which indicates that blood is again flowing through the artery, is heard with each beat of the heart and is taken as the systolic pressure. The height of the column of mercury or pressure on the gauge should be read at this point.

7. Continue reducing the pressure carefully. The sound becomes louder, then dull and muffled, and then ceases. The point of complete cessation of sound is taken as the diastolic pressure. If no cessation of sound occurs, the point of muffling should be taken as diastolic pressure, and should then be recorded as the point of muffled sounds. (On the average, dulling of sounds appears 5 to 10 mm above the point of cessation of sounds.) Diastolic sounds may persist all the way down to zero in certain clinical states, such as aortic insufficiency, hyperthyroidism, and anemia, and occasionally even in normal persons.

8. Rapidly release the pressure once the diastolic pressure is determined.

9. With blood pressure readings taken in this manner, a mean error of ± 8 mm Hg may be expected in individual readings of systolic and diastolic pressure (the systolic pressure tends to be too low and diastolic too high). Variations in auditory acuity are important causes of error. Errors are also likely when subjects have unusually large or small arms; here the error may exceed 30 mm Hg.

10. Determine systolic pressure, diastolic pressure, and pulse two additional times. (Allow 2 minutes between readings since, due to relaxation of arterial tone, the last readings may be lower than the previous ones.) Average these, if the determinations agree reasonably well, and record the value in the "Before Exercise" column in the table under Results and Questions.

11. Subtract diastolic pressure from systolic pressure to obtain pulse pressure.

12. The subject should exercise by running vigorously around the building (if possible, with blood pressure cuff attached— consult instructor) or by bicycling 2 minutes on the bicycle ergometer (belt setting

2 for women, 3 for men, at 35 kph). Immediately after cessation of exercise, repeat all measurements.

13. Repeat all measurements 2 minutes after exercise, 4 minutes after exercise, and 6 minutes after exercise. Try to be exact about the times. Record all results under Results and Questions.

Alternate Procedure with the Physiograph

1. The same experiments on the effect of exercise on circulation may be performed with the physiograph, using two channels to simultaneously record blood pressure and heart rate. See Exercise 7-F for detailed directions for the operation of the physiograph and the photoelectric finger pulse pickup. The electrosphygmograph is a transducer/preamplifier for recording indirect systolic and diastolic blood pressures (range 0 to 300 mm Hg). The electrosphygmograph combines a pressure transducer and a preamplifier to produce single-channel recordings of occluding cuff pressure and superimposed Korotkoff sounds. These sounds are the sounds heard as blood passes through a partially occluded blood vessel.

2. The electrosphygmograph coupler and the transducer coupler are needed in this experiment. Calibrate the channel amplifier connected to the electrosphygmograph as follows:
   a. Press the main frame RECORDER switch ON.
   b. Press the POWER switch ON on the channel amplifier.
   c. Press the RECORD switch OFF (if it is on).
   d. Set the mV/CM switch to 1000.
   e. Using the POSITION control, set the recording pen 1.5 cm (three green lines) below the center dark-green line.
   f. Set the mV/CM switch to 3 cm ADJ. The recording pen should write 1.5 cm (three green lines) above the center dark-green line.
   g. If the pen does not deflect a total of 3 cm, adjust the inset multiturn control (with a screwdriver) until the pen writes 1.5 cm below the center line when the mV/CM switch is in the

1000 position, and 1.5 cm above the center line when the mV/CM switch is in the 3 cm ADJ position. This adjustment should not have to be changed throughout the experiment.
   h. Press the POWER switch OFF.

3. Have the subject sit on the bicycle. Place the photoelectric pulse pickup on the ventral surface of a finger on the right hand and connect the other end to the 7-hole input connector on the transducer coupler (see Figure 15-1).

4. Using Figure 15-3 as a guide, position the cuff on the left arm of the subject so that the microphone is over the brachial artery approximately 1 inch above the elbow. Check that the words "place distally over artery" on the inner surface are on the middle of the ventral surface of the arm above the elbow (next to the surface of the arm) on the brachial artery.

5. Following Figure 15-3, connect the plug on the cuff to the input marked MIC on the electrosphygmograph coupler. Connect the plastic tube on the cuff to input marked CUFF on the electrosphygmograph. Connect the plastic tube on the bulb to the input marked BULB on the electrosphygmograph coupler.

6. Start the ink flowing in the pens attached to the photoelectric pulse pickup, the electrosphygmograph, and the time event marker.

7. Set the time marker to 1 per second and the paper speed to .5 cm/sec. Start the paper moving.

8. Initial settings for the channel for the photoelectric pulse pickup:
   a. Press the POWER switch ON.
   b. Press the RECORD switch OFF (if it is on).
   c. Set the mV/CM switch to 20 and the filter to 10K.
   d. Set the pen to the center dark-green line with the POSITION control.
   e. Press the RECORD switch ON. Reposition the pen (if necessary) with the BALANCE control to record symmetrically around the center dark-green line.
   f. Increase or decrease the amplitude with the mV/CM switch as necessary to obtain a tracing approximately 1 inch high.

9. Initial settings for the channel amplifier

CUFF: accepts tubing from the cuff

BULB: accepts tubing from the hand pressure bulb

PRESSURE RANGE SWITCH: 3 positions (0–200 will be used)

MIC: jack which accepts plug from microphone in cuff

100 mm Hg CAL: pushbutton switch to provide a signal equal to 100 mm pressure

BALANCE: used to restore pen to its original baseline

LOCKING KNOB: when fully clockwise, secures coupler in position

Figure 15-3.   Setup for electrosphygmograph with the DMP-4B.

and coupler for the electrosphygmograph:

a. Press the POWER switch ON.

b. Press the RECORD switch OFF if it is glowing, the mV/CM switch to 2, the filter to 10K.

c. Set the recording pen to a baseline 2.5 cm (five lines) below the center dark-green line using the POSITION control.

d. Set the ESG coupler PRESSURE switch to the 0-200 mm range.

e. Press the channel amplifier RECORD switch ON.

f. Adjust the ESG coupler BALANCE control to set the recording pen to the original baseline 2.5 cm (five lines) below the center dark-green line. With this calibration, five squares

173412

Systolic Pressure
(118 mm)

Diastolic Pressure
(70 mm)

SQUARES 5 MM. X 5 MM.

Figure 15-4. Tracing of blood pressure with electrosphygmograph.

equal 100 mm Hg; therefore, each square equals 20 mm and 1 cm equals 40 mm.

10. Close the screw on the bulb. Inflate the cuff to 160 mm Hg and slowly decrease the pressure (by opening the screw slightly) until sound marks appear. Then adjust the amplitude of the marks by varying the mV/CM switch until the marks are at least 2 cm in amplitude. If the Korotkoff sounds are not clearly defined on the record (see Figure 15-4), the cuff and microphone may need repositioning to a more medial position. Always turn the RECORD switch OFF before making any changes in equipment.

11. Position each pen so that it does not interfere with the tracing of the pen from another channel. The hand with the photo-electric pulse pickup should rest on a pillow on the handlebar or on the handlebar itself. The subject should not grip the handlebar with this hand. During readings of the blood pressure, the arm with the cuff attached should hang down at the side. The recording should resemble that shown in Figure 15-5. (The bellows pneumograph may also be connected [see Experiment 11-F] to simultaneously record respirations.)

12. The experiment will last 11 minutes. Mark the beginning of the first minute of recording. Take the subject's blood pressure near the beginning of the first minute of recording. With the bulb, inflate the cuff above

the expected systolic pressure (to at least 160 mm Hg on the resting subject and to at least 200 mm Hg after exercise). Slowly lower the cuff pressure (usually 2 to 3 mm Hg/heartbeat) by means of the valve on the bulb, slowly passing through the systolic and diastolic pressure ranges. The microphone picks up the sounds in the artery. The first sound heard as the pressure is lowered is taken as the systolic pressure. The sound becomes louder as the pressure is lowered, as more blood passes through the partially occluded artery with each beat of the heart, and then becomes dull and finally ceases when the pressure in the artery is above the pressure in the cuff.

13. Where the first vertical line intersects the diagonal descending line is the systolic pressure; where the last vertical line intersects the diagonal descending line is the diastolic pressure (see Figure 15-4).

14. Rapidly release the pressure once the diastolic pressure is determined.

15. Calculate the blood pressure. Write the pressure on your record, indicating where you made each calculation. Enter the results under Results and Questions.

16. Determine systolic and diastolic pressure two additional times near the beginning of the second and third minutes of recording. Subtract diastolic pressure from systolic pressure to obtain pulse pressure.

17. Turn OFF the channel amplifier connected to the electrosphygmograph while

Figure 15-5. Tracing of respiration, blood pressure, and pulse.

the subject is exercising. The subject should grip the handlebar with the hand connected to the electrosphygmograph.

18. Have the subject pedal the bicycle ergometer for 2 minutes (belt setting 2 for women, 3 for men, at 35 kph), continuing the recording of the pulse during and after exercise.

19. Immediately after cessation of exercise, the subject should drop his left arm to his side. Press the RECORD button for the channel amplifier connected to the electrosphygmograph and take the blood pressure immediately after exercise and at 2 minutes, 4 minutes, and 6 minutes after exercise.

20. Calculate heart rate (optional: respiration). Write this (these) on your record (marking where you made each calculation of rate per minute) and also enter on the data chart under Results and Questions.

EXERCISE 15-D
ELECTROCARDIOGRAPHY

Objectives

To demonstrate the recording of an electrocardiogram (ECG); to demonstrate the effect of activity on the heart tracing.

Materials

Beck-Lee Electrocardiograph, EKG Sol.

Discussion

The electrocardiograph records the electrical activity of the heart. As the wave of excitation passes through the heart, electrical currents spread into the tissues surrounding the heart; a small proportion of these spread all the way to the surface of the body. If suitable electrodes are placed on the body on opposite sides of the heart, the electric potential generated by the heart can be recorded.

Electrodes are usually attached to the arms and legs of the subject and connected to the electrocardiograph. The right arm, left arm, left leg, and chest electrodes, in various combinations, are referred to as electrocardiograph leads. The right leg is included in the circuit as a neutral reference point. Certain designations, by convention, always indicate certain electrode combinations. Only the limb leads will be used in this laboratory exercise. To increase the diagnostic value of the electrocardiogram (ECG), numerous other leads are taken from the chest.

Limb Leads

Lead 1: Right arm and left arm
Lead 2: Right arm and left leg
Lead 3: Left arm and left leg

Lead Marking Code

One dot   •
Two dots   ••
Three dots   •••

A normal ECG, showing three beats of the heart, is reproduced in Figure 15-6. Note that each beat is composed of several waves. These waves are due to changes in the electrical potential of the heart as the wave of depolarization (excitation wave), which precedes the contraction, spreads from the SA node over the heart in a definite manner. When the wave of depolarization is moving toward the recording electrode, an upward deflection occurs; when the wave is receding from the same electrode, a downward deflection occurs. From an ECG it is possible to determine the magnitude, duration, and direction of the potential changes occurring within the heart.

The electrical events represented on the ECG are labeled on the normal record (see Figure 15-6). The P wave is caused by the wave of excitation spreading from the SA node over the atria. The P wave immediately precedes the contraction of the atria. The duration of the P wave does not normally exceed 0.11 seconds.

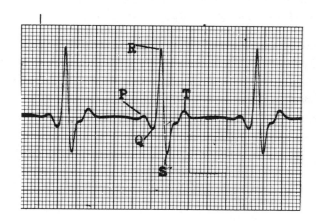

Figure 15-6. Normal electrocardiogram showing three beats of the heart.

The QRS complex is caused by the depolarization of the ventricles. Ventricular systole immediately follows this event. This is a complex wave with three distinct components. It consists of the downward deflection Q, the upward deflection R, and the negative deflection S. The normal range of duration of the QRS complex is 0.06 to 0.10 seconds.

The T wave is caused by the repolarization of the ventricles. (Atrial repolarization usually occurs during the QRS complex and therefore does not show up on the record.)

The distance between P and R indicates the delay in transmission of the impulse at the AV node. The P-R interval (sometimes called the P-Q interval) starts with the beginning of the P wave and ends with the beginning of the Q wave, if one is present, or the R wave. The upper limits of normal for the P-R interval for cardiac rates above 70 beats per minute is 0.20 seconds. Any time longer than that indicates some delay in conduction.

The clinical value of the ECG lies in the fact that many functional abnormalities can be detected from these records, such as a defective valve, a defect in the conducting mechanism, a myocardial infarction, etc. If the tracing is definitely abnormal, the patient has heart disease. However, a patient may have a normal ECG and still have heart disease.

The following is a brief description of the operating procedure for the Beck-Lee Cardi-O-Mite. For a more complete discussion of operating technique, refer to the instruction manual. This instrument uses special paper that does not require ink in the recording stylus. The paper turns black when it is exposed to heat; the stylus itself is made very hot by an electrical current flowing through its tip.

Do not look for abnormalities in the ECG, as it will not be taken under standard conditions.

Procedure

1. Plug the power cord into the left side of the Cardi-O-Mite.
2. With the off-ground switch in the off position, plug the other end of the power cord into the wall outlet. Check to be certain the input switch is at the AC position.
3. Place the lead selector switch in the stand-by (dash) position between STD and CF.
4. Turn the instrument on by sliding the off-ground switch from the off position to the center position opposite the lower arrow. Allow the instrument to warm up for 2 minutes. This is necessary to prevent drifting of the baseline.
5. Place the graph-monitor switch in the top G (for graph) position for recording. This switch is moved to visual or audible only when the instrument is used for monitoring the heart.
6. Place the speed switch in the 25 position. The paper speed in this position is 25 mm/sec. The light vertical lines on the paper are time lines, separated from each other by an interval of 0.04 seconds. The distance between two dark vertical lines is 0.20 seconds. The light horizontal lines are 1 mm apart and each represents 0.1 millivolt when the electrocardiograph is properly standardized.
7. Set the sensitivity switch at 1.
8. Using the position control, move the recording stylus to the center of the recording chart.
9. Squeeze approximately 1/2 inch of the EKG Sol on the fleshy inside portion of both forearms and calves (see Figure 15-7).
10. Vigorously rub the EKG Sol into the skin.
11. Attach four electrodes to the subject. Attach one end of the rubber strap to one of the rectangular electrodes by slipping the contact post of the electrode through one of the holes near the end of the strap. Then squeeze about 1/2 inch of the EKG Sol into the center of the rectangular electrode and place it directly over the reddened skin area, then press it into position with a slight circular motion to eliminate any small air pockets.
12. Fasten the electrode into position by drawing the strap around the arm or leg and slipping the proper hole over the contact post so a firm contact is made, but not so tight as to cause discomfort (see Figure 15-8). Somatic tremor will result if the strap is too tight. However, if the strap is too loose, it may move during the taking of the ECG, resulting in an unsatisfactory tracing.
13. After the four electrodes have been attached in this manner, connect the ends of the patient cable leads to their corre-

Figure 15-7. Diagram showing position of electrodes.

sponding electrode. Each lead wire has been color coded.

RA Lead (white) to right arm electrode.
LA Lead (black) to left arm electrode.
RL Lead (green) to right leg electrode.
LL Lead (red) to left leg electrode.

14. Avoid any tension on the patient cable while placing the junction of the cable on the subject's body.

15. Insert the patient cable plug into the Cardi-O-Mite patient cable socket.

16. Turn the lead selector switch to the STD position, adjust the stylus heat control for proper baseline width, and standardize the instrument by depressing the standardization button. When the stylus heat control is properly adjusted, the baseline will appear black with a uniform density and will be approximately 1 mm in width with sharp and distinct edges. Depression of the standardization button should result in a deflection by the stylus of exactly 10 mm.

17. Now place the lead selector switch in the standby position between STD and 1. In this position (note that there is a standby position before each lead selector switch position), the chart motor is automatically stopped and the instrument is prepared for the following lead.

18. Have the subject lie down and remain motionless.

19. Record the ECG using leads 1, 2, and 3. Insert a standardization pulse in each lead and code each lead by means of the lead marker for future identification (one, two, or three dots).

20. After recording these three leads, return the lead selector switch to the standby position between STD and 1.

21. In steps 22 to 25, a normal record on lead 1 will precede the experimental variable. Code the normal record with one dot. Code the variable as described.

22. Record a few normal beats on lead 1, then have the subject clench his fist several times. Mark this section of the record with one dash. Note the effect that clenching the fist has on the record.

23. Record a few normal beats on lead 1, then have the subject lift his left leg. Mark this section of the record with two dashes. What effect is noted on the record?

Figure 15-8. Diagram showing attachment of an electrode.

24. Record a few normal beats on lead 1, then have the subject lift his left arm. Mark this section of the record with three dashes. What effect is noted on the record?
25. Record a few normal beats on lead 1, then have the subject stand and perform 20 knee bends (after which he should quickly resume the prone position), and continue the recording. Mark this section of the record with a dash and a dot.
26. Include your results under Results and Questions.

EXERCISE 15-E
ELECTROCARDIOGRAPHY WITH THE PHYSIOGRAPH

Objectives

To record the electrocardiogram; to simultaneously record the electrocardiogram and respiratory pattern.

Materials

Physiograph; plate electrodes; strap; hi-gain coupler; impedance pneumograph coupler; adaptor cable AC-13; impedance pneumograph/ECG preamplifier coupling cable; shielded input extension cable SC-13.

Discussion

The hi-gain preamplifier is used in recording a wide range of bioelectric potentials. It can be used to record the ECG, the electroencephalogram (EEG), the electromyogram (EMG), and heart sounds. The impedance pneumograph can be used with the hi-gain preamplifier to simultaneously record respiration and ECG from the same set of electrodes.

Refer to the discussion in Exercise 15-D for the interpretation of the waves of the ECG and to study the illustration (Fig. 15-6) of a normal ECG. Only two chest leads will be used in this laboratory exercise, since the ECG will be recorded in conjunction with breathing rate. Do not look for abnormalities in the ECG, as it will not be recorded under standard conditions.

Procedure

1. Apply a salt solution (such as EKG Sol) to three plate electrodes. Attach two of them to the interspace between the fifth and sixth ribs near the sides of the chest, fastening them by means of the long rubber strap. Attach an additional plate electrode on the center of the subject's chest for grounding (see Figure 15-9). Attach the long loose ends of the adaptor cable AC-13 to the subject, red lead on the left side of the chest, black on the right, and green to the ground in the middle. Connect the short twisted ends to the shielded input extension cable SC-13. Connect the red wire to the 1 position, the black to the 2 position, and the green to the G position.
2. Set up the equipment as in Figure 15-9. Insert the shielded input extension cable SC-13 to the INPUT jack of the impedance pneumograph coupler. Connect the impedance pneumograph/ECG preamplifier coupling cable to the ECG OUTPUT on the impedance pneumograph. Insert the other end in the INPUT jack on the hi-gain coupler.
3. If it is not necessary to obtain a tracing of the respiratory pattern of the subject, connect the shielded input extension cable SC-13 directly to the INPUT jack of the hi-gain coupler (see Figure 15-10). Set the paper speed to .5 cm/sec while setting up the experiment and start the paper moving.
4. Initial settings for the channel amplifier to be used with the hi-gain coupler:
   a. Press the main frame RECORDER switch ON.
   b. Start the ink flowing in channels connected to the time event marker, hi-gain coupler, and impedance pneumograph coupler.
   c. Press the POWER switch on the channel amplifier connected to the hi-gain coupler ON.
   d. Set the FILTER switch to 30, the mV/CM switch to 5, and the recording pen on the center dark-green line (set with the POSITION control).
5. Initial settings for the hi-gain coupler:
   a. Set the time constant switch to 3.2.
   b. Set the INPUT switch to OFF/CAL.
6. Initial settings for the channel amplifier to be used with the impedance pneumograph:
   a. Press the POWER switch ON.
   b. Set the FILTER switch to 30, the mV/CM switch to 10, and the record-

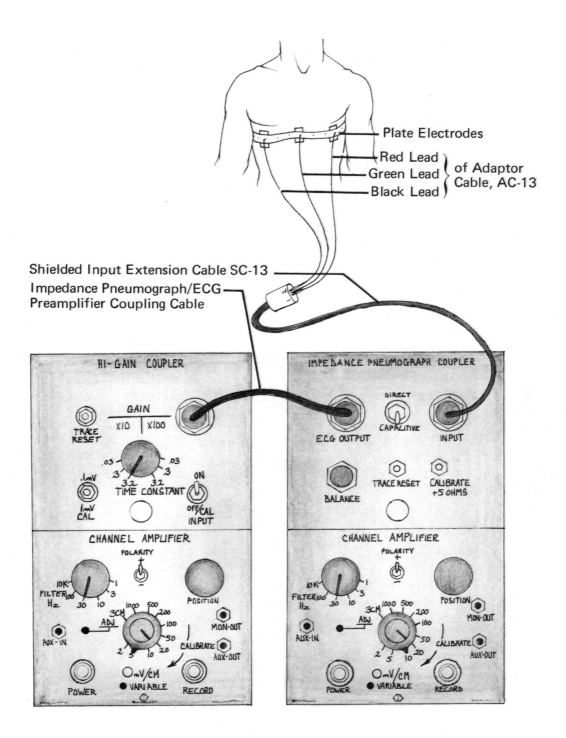

Figure 15-9. Equipment setup for simultaneously recording ECG and respiration with the Physiograph DMP-4B.

ing pen on the center dark-green line (set with the POSITION control).

7. Initial setting for the impedance pneumograph coupler: DIRECT-CAPACITIVE switch on CAPACITIVE.

8. Set the hi-gain coupler INPUT switch to ON and press both channel amplifier RECORD switches on. A tracing of both the ECG and breathing should be obtained. To increase the amplitude of either

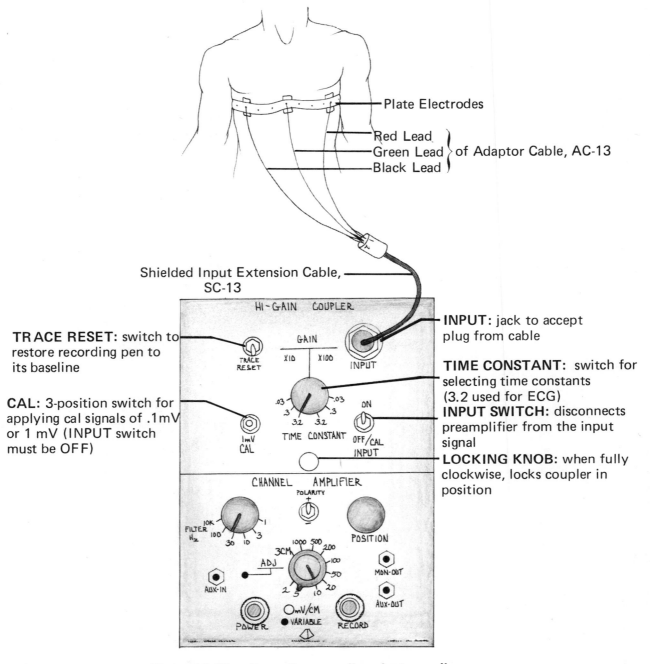

Figure 15-10. **Setup for recording electrocardiogram.**

recording, turn the appropriate mV/CM switch clockwise; to decrease the amplitude, turn the switch counterclockwise. With either record, return the pen to the baseline by pressing the TRACE RESET button on the coupler. If the recording is reversed, move the POLARITY switch to negative.

9. Set the paper speed to 2.5 cm/sec. Set the time marker at 1 second.

10. Record the ECG and respirations for one complete piece of recording paper at paper speed 2.5 cm/sec. The record should be similar to that shown in Figure 15-11.

11. Increase the paper speed to 10 cm/sec. Record the ECG and respiration for one complete piece of chart paper.

Figure 15-11.   Tracing of ECG and respiration.

SELF-TEST—PHYSIOLOGY OF CIRCULATION

Directions

See Chapter 1, Self-Test, page 9.

1.   The pulse is usually taken at the **radial** artery.
2.   The **aorta** has the highest blood pressure of any blood vessel.
3.   The average pulse rate before birth is **160**.
4.   The vagus nerve **accelerates** the heart.
5.   Between heartbeats, the elasticity of the arterial walls **maintains** blood pressure.
6.   Blood pressure is determined by **peripheral resistance** and **cardiac output**.
7.   After a hemorrhage, the pulse will be **slower**.
8.   The vasomotor center, located in the **cerebellum**, regulates blood pressure.
9.   Low blood pressure is called **hypotension**.
10.   The left atrium receives **deoxygenated** blood.
11.   Contraction of the heart is called **systole**, and relaxation is called **diastole**.
12.   The **atrioventricular** node is the pacemaker of the heart.
13.   **Heart block** results from a defect in the conducting system.
14.   The portal vein carries the **end products of digestion** to the sinusoids of the liver.
15.   **Hypertension** is the term designating hardening of the arteries.
16.   When an individual lacks sufficient oxygen to burn fuel and remove wastes, he develops an **"oxygen debt."**
17.   The **mitral (biscuspid) valve** is located between the right atrium and the right ventricle.
18.   Rheumatic fever frequently affects the **heart**.
19.   Receptors sensitive to changes in blood pressure are located in the right **atrium**, the **carotid sinus**, and the **aortic arch**.

20. A slow, strong heart rate would result from nerve impulses arising mainly from the **thoracolumbar (sympathetic)** portion of the nervous system.

21. The usual effect of cold is to **constrict** superficial blood vessels and so to help control hemorrhage.

22. The heartbeat is initiated by the **Bundle of His.**

23. **Systole** of the atria lasts longer than **diastole.**

24. There is a slight delay in transmission of the impulse at the **atrioventricular node.**

25. A unique feature of the portal system is that blood from the digestive tract is detoured through the **kidney** instead of being returned directly to the inferior vena cava.

26. The pulse pressure is the **sum of** the systolic and diastolic blood pressures.

27. Systolic blood pressure is **higher** than diastolic blood pressure.

28. Hemorrhage from an artery results in a **steady** flow of blood.

29. Blood flows least rapidly through **veins.**

30. Blood pressure in **veins** normally exceeds that in capillaries.

31. The vessels that contribute the greatest resistance to blood flow are the **venules.**

32. Syncope or fainting results from **an increase** in blood pressure.

33. Dilated veins of the rectum produce a condition known as **hemorrhoids.**

34. Studies show that vigorous exercise **enlarges** the heart.

35. During the beating of the heart, sounds are produced by the closing of the **semilunar valves.**

36. Blood pressure increases when the ventricles are in **diastole.**

37. Vasodilation is controlled by a center in the **medulla oblongata.**

38. The vagus nerve carries impulses that **stimulate** the heart.

39. Localized death of cardiac tissue due to obstruction of a coronary artery is known as a **myocardial infarction.**

40. Elephantiasis is a condition caused by **excessive production of lymph.**

41. **Bradycardia** is an abnormally slow heartbeat.

42. In hypothermia, the heart rate would **increase.**

43. Essential hypertension is that which results from a **known cause.**

16

The Nervous System

ANATOMY OF THE NERVOUS SYSTEM

Objectives

To become familiar with the gross and microscopic anatomy of the nervous system.

Materials

Prepared slides of cross sections of the spinal cord and a nerve; models of the brain; charts; reference books.

Discussion

For convenience of study, the nervous system may be divided into a central (CNS) portion, a peripheral portion, and an autonomic (ANS) portion. The latter is usually subdivided into sympathetic and parasympathetic divisions. The central nervous system is composed of the brain and the spinal cord, the peripheral nervous system of the spinal and cranial nerves.

The nervous system serves to coordinate body activities by receiving, integrating, and transmitting messages. The structural units of the nervous system are neurons. A neuron is the name used for a single nerve cell. A nerve is a group of axons and dendrites bound together by connective tissue outside the central nervous system. (The structure of the neuron and medullated nerve fiber was described in Exercise 3-E.)

Procedure

PART 1. STRUCTURE OF A NERVE

1. Obtain a slide of a cross section through a nerve. Examine the slide with the low power objective.
2. Observe the connective tissue sheath called the epineurium surrounding the entire nerve. This sheath contains connective tissues, cells, collagenic fibers, adipose tissue, and nutrient blood vessels called the vasa nervorum.
3. Note that the nerve fibers comprising the nerve are arranged in bundles; each bundle (funiculus) is surrounded by connective tissue called the perineurium.
4. Locate the endoneurium, the connective tissue that surrounds each nerve fiber.
5. Make a diagram of the entire cross section of the nerve showing the preceding structures. Label the epineurium, perineurium, endoneurium, nerve fibers, vasa nervorum, and adipose tissue. It is not necessary to draw any cells in this diagram.
6. Now, examine the slide with the high power objective. Locate a nerve fiber that contains a nucleus in the neurilemma. Draw this fiber below the diagram of the nerve. Include on this drawing the axis cylinder, located in the center of the fiber; the thick myelin sheath; the thin neurilemma surrounding the fiber; and the nucleus of the neurilemma.

PART 2. THE SPINAL CORD

1. Obtain a slide of a cross section through the spinal cord. First, study this slide with the naked eye to observe the shape and size of the cord. Since the cord was mounted upside down on the slide (so that it will appear right side up when using the microscope), be certain to hold the slide

so that the printing is at the bottom and upside down while examining the slide with the naked eye.

2. Diagram the shape of the entire cord and adjacent roots of the spinal nerve on a full sheet of paper. This drawing should include the shape of the central gray matter.

3. Now, study the slide under low power of the microscope. (Return the slide to the usual position for microscope viewing.)

4. Observe the shape of the central canal, the dorsal median septum, and the ventral median fissure. Determine whether the latter two touch the central gray matter. Include these on the diagram. Use your text and/or other references to aid you in this study. Compare with Figure 16-1.

5. Include the following labels on your diagram: dorsal root; dorsal root ganglion; ventral root; dorsal horn; ventral horn; dorsal, lateral, and ventral funiculi; dorsal median septum; ventral median fissure; central canal; white matter; and gray matter.

PART 3. GROSS STRUCTURE OF THE BRAIN

Study Figures 16-2, 16-3, and 16-4 showing the structure of the brain including the ventricles of the brain. These cavities within the brain are filled with cerebrospinal fluid. The lateral ventricles (within the cerebral hemispheres) are the largest. The third ventricle is within the diencephalon and communicates with the fourth ventricle by way of the cerebral aqueduct. The fourth ventricle is located in the hindbrain between the cerebellum and the medulla oblongata.

EXERCISE 16-B DISSECTION OF THE SHEEP BRAIN

Objectives

To study the structure of the sheep brain; to compare the sheep brain with the human brain.

Materials

Sheep brains (whole and sagittal sections); human brain; dissecting set.

Discussion

The structure of the sheep brain is very similar to that of the human brain. Note any differences as you study the brains. The brain is surrounded by three layers of **meninges**. The outermost, the **dura mater**, was removed in

KEY TO FIGURE 16-1

1. dura mater
2. arachnoid
3. pia mater
4. subarachnoid space
5. denticulate ligament
6. posterior (dorsal) gray horn
7. lateral gray horn
8. anterior (ventral) gray horn
9. anterior (ventral) white column
10. gray commissure
11. lateral white column
12. central canal
13. posterior (dorsal) white column

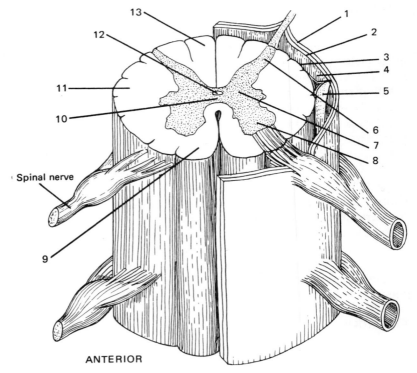

Figure 16-1. Cross section of the spinal cord showing meninges on the right.

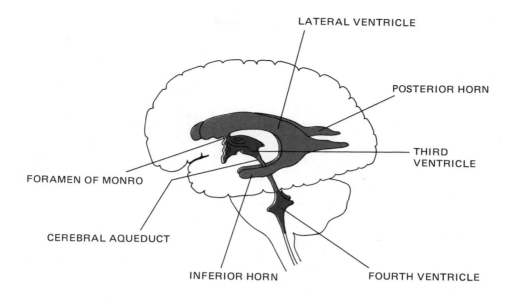

Figure 16-2. Ventricles of the brain.

KEY TO FIGURE 16-3

1. corpus callosum
2. septum pellucidum
3. thalamus
4. mammillary body
5. hypothalamus

6. infundibulum
7. hypophysis (pituitary)
8. pons (pons Varolii)
9. medulla oblongata
10. fornix

11. splenium
12. pineal body
13. corpora quadrigemina
14. superior colliculus
15. inferior colliculus

16. cerebral aqueduct
17. cerebral peduncles
18. cerebellum
19. fourth ventricle

Figure 16-3. Sagittal section of the brain.

218

KEY TO FIGURE 16-4

1. optic chiasma
2. hypothalamus
3. pons (pons Varolii)
4. medulla oblongata
5. olfactory bulb
6. olfactory tract
7. optic nerve (II)
8. infundibulum
9. optic tract
10. mammillary body
11. oculomotor nerve (III)
12. motor root
13. sensory root
14. trigeminal nerve (V)
15. abducens nerve (VI)
16. vagus nerve (X)
17. cerebellum

Figure 16-4.   Inferior surface of the brain.

preparing the sheep brains. This layer may be seen surrounding the brain of the pig if the surrounding cranial bones are carefully cut away with scissors.

Procedure

1. Obtain a sagittal section of the sheep brain and an entire sheep brain and rinse both with tap water. Use the entire brain for steps 2 to 15.
2. The inner two layers of the meninges can be seen covering the brain. The **arachnoid**, the middle layer, lies between the **dura mater** and the **pia mater**, the innermost, vascular layer of the meninges. The arachnoid is most easily distinguished from the pia mater in the region overlying the grooves on the brain surface, since the pia mater dips into the grooves and the arachnoid does not.
3. Observe the anterior paired **cerebral hemispheres** and the posterior **cerebellum** on the dorsal surface of the brain. The cerebral hemispheres are separated from each other by the **longitudinal fissure**; the cerebellum is separated from the cerebral hemispheres by the **transverse fissure** (see Figure 16-5).

4. Spread the cerebral hemispheres apart and observe deep in the longitudinal fissure the thick transverse band of fibers, the **corpus callosum**, that connects the cerebral hemispheres.
5. The surface of each hemisphere is composed of numerous convolutions. The raised area of each convolution is called a gyrus, the depression a sulcus.
6. The roof of the midbrain (mesencephalon) can be seen by spreading the cerebral hemispheres and cerebellum apart (see Figure 16-5). Four prominent round swellings, the **corpora quadrigemina**, form the roof of the midbrain. The larger, anterior pair is called the **superior colliculi**, the smaller, posterior pair the **inferior colliculi**. The **pineal body** can be seen between the superior colliculi. The **trochlear nerve** appears as a thin white strand, directed ventrally, slightly posterior to the inferior colliculi (see Figure 16-6).
7. Posterior to the cerebral hemispheres is the **cerebellum**. The cerebellum is connected with the brain stem by three prominent fiber tracts or peduncles. Lift up the lateral edge of the cerebellum. The middle **cerebellar peduncle** can be seen connecting the cerebellum with the pons.

Figure 16-5. Dorsal view of sheep brain (with cerebellum separated from cerebral hemispheres).

Labels in figure:
- Longitudinal Fissure
- Cerebral Hemisphere
- Pineal Gland
- Superior Colliculus
- Inferior Colliculus
- Transverse Fissure
- Cerebellum
- Medulla Oblongata

Slightly posterior to this is the **inferior cerebellar peduncle** connecting the cerebellum to the medulla. Locate the **superior cerebellar peduncle**, which is composed of the fibers connecting the midbrain to the cerebellum.

8. Observe the ventral surface of the sheep brain. A pair of **olfactory bulbs** can be seen beneath the cerebral hemispheres. These bulbs lie over the cribriform plate of the ethmoid and receive the olfactory neurons from the nose (see Figure 16-6).

9. A white band, the **olfactory tract**, extends from each bulb along the ventral surface of the cerebral hemispheres.

10. The **hypothalamus** makes up the ventral surface of the diencephalon. It is located posterior to the olfactory tract. The hypothalamus forms the floor of the third ventricle. The hypothalamus consists of many nuclei in the interior of the white matter visible from the ventral surface of the brain, the mammillary bodies, the optic chiasma, and the infundibulum (stalk of the pituitary).

11. Locate the **optic chiasma**, the x-shaped structure at the anterior border of the hypothalamus (see Figure 16-6). The optic nerves undergo a partial crossing over (decussation) at the anterior border of the hypothalamus, forming the optic chiasma.

12. The remainder of the hypothalamus is the oval area lying posterior to the optic chiasma, covered by the **pituitary gland** (hypophysis). Do not remove the gland. The **infundibulum** can be seen connecting the pituitary to the hypothalamus.

13. Posterior to the infundibulum is the rounded **mammillary body** (there are two in humans).

14. Observe the **cerebral peduncles** on the ventral surface of the midbrain. The large **oculomotor nerves**, covered by the pituitary gland, arise from the cerebral peduncles posterior to the mammillary body.

15. Posterior to the midbrain is the **pons**. This

Figure 16-6. Ventral view of sheep brain.

is composed primarily of white fibers, many of which run transversely across the pons out to the cerebellum.

16. The **medulla oblongata** is posterior to the pons. The longitudinal bands of tissue at each side of the **ventral median fissure** on the ventral surface of the medulla are known as the pyramids.

17. To see the remaining parts of the brain, use the sagittal section of the sheep brain. (Compare the specimen with Figure 16-7, a sagittal section of a sheep brain.) Relocate the **corpus callosum**, which consists of the white fibers connecting the two cerebral hemispheres.

18. A thin, vertical septum of tissue, the **septum pellucidum**, lies ventral to the corpus callosum. The **lateral ventricle** lies behind this septum and may be seen by breaking the septum.

19. The **fornix**, a band of white fibers, lies ventral to the septum.

20. The **third ventricle** and the **thalamus** lie ventral to the fornix. The narrow third ventricle, the walls of which are covered by a shiny layer of epithelium, is in the midline. The thalamus forms the lateral walls of the third ventricle.

21. The **foramen of Monro**, the opening through which each lateral ventricle communicates with the third ventricle, lies in the depression anterior to the massa intermedia. Find this connection by passing a dull probe through it.

22. Relocate the **hypothalamus.** This lies ventral to the third ventricle.

23. Note the **pineal body** dorsal to the midbrain, near the **superior colliculus.**

24. Observe the narrow **cerebral aqueduct** leading through the midbrain, connecting the third and fourth ventricles.

25. The **fourth ventricle** lies above the pons and medulla, below the cerebellum.

26. The beginning of the spinal cord may be seen connected to the medulla. A canal known as the **central canal**, which is connected to the fourth ventricle, is present in the center of the cord.

27. Note the treelike arrangement of gray and white matter in the cerebellum. This arrangement is known as the **arbor vitae** (tree of life). The gray matter of the cere-

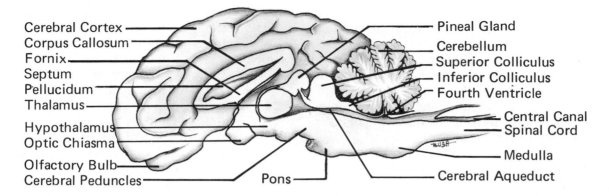

Cerebral Cortex
Corpus Callosum
Fornix
Septum
Pellucidum
Thalamus
Hypothalamus
Optic Chiasma
Olfactory Bulb
Cerebral Peduncles
Pons
Pineal Gland
Cerebellum
Superior Colliculus
Inferior Colliculus
Fourth Ventricle
Central Canal
Spinal Cord
Medulla
Cerebral Aqueduct

Figure 16-7.   Sagittal section through sheep brain.

bellum is on the outside, the white is toward the center.

28. The outer layer of the cerebral hemispheres, the **cortex**, is also composed of gray matter. Make a shallow incision through the cortex to see the white matter beneath.

29. Examine the human brain and locate as many of the preceding structures as possible. Note the paired mammillary bodies, the larger size of the cerebral hemispheres, and the deeper convolutions.

EXERCISE 16-C
DISSECTION OF THE BRAIN AND SPINAL CORD OF THE FETAL PIG

Objectives

To study the structure of the brain and spinal cord of the fetal pig; to compare the brain and spinal cord of the fetal pig with the human brain and spinal cord.

Materials

Fetal pig; dissecting board or pan; dissecting set.

Procedure

1. The brain and spinal cord of the fetal pig are very similar in structure to those of the human and the sheep, although smaller. Since the cranial bones and vertebral column are not fully ossified, it is relatively easy to remove the brain and to expose the spinal cord of the fetal pig.

2. Make an incision through the skin of the fetal pig from the shoulders to the pelvis. Separate the skin from the muscles and pin it to the side.

3. Cut through the muscles on each side of the vertebral column from the mid-thoracic region to the pelvis to expose the vertebral column.

4. With fine, sharp scissors cut off the tops of the vertebral arches. Then insert the tip of the scissors in the vertebral cavity and cut lengthwise through the bones of the vertebral column, just lateral to the center of the column. It may be easier to cut the bone if the other hand is placed under the abdominal region of the pig, arching the back of the pig. Remove the bone and expose the spinal cord.

5. Examine the **spinal cord**. The **dura mater** surrounds the cord. The **dorsal roots** of the spinal nerves should be visible emerging from the cord. The **spinal nerves** are visible as fine white threads running out to the muscles.

6. Place the pig on its back and examine the interior of the thoracic cavity. A white thread should be visible running lengthwise, parallel to each side of the vertebral column. This is the **sympathetic trunk.** The swellings on the trunk are the **ganglia** of this lateral chain of ganglia.

7. Remove the skin from the entire dorsal surface of the skull, from the eyes to the neck.

8. Chip away the skull bones, starting with the fontanels. Use scalpel and fingers until the brain is completely exposed.

9. Separate the spinal cord from the medulla

at the foramen magnum by making a cut through the spinal cord caudal to the medulla.

10. Carefully lift out the brain from the cranial cavity, severing each cranial nerve and the stalk of the pituitary as far from the brain as possible. The **olfactory bulbs** usually tear off from the brain and may be visible in the floor of the cranial cavity. Identify the stalk of the pituitary in the floor of the cranial cavity.

11. Remove the dura mater; then follow steps 2 to 28 of the procedure for the sheep brain, Exercise 16-B.

EXERCISE 16-D
REFLEX ACTION IN THE NORMAL, SPINAL, AND DOUBLE-PITHED FROG

Objective

To demonstrate which reflexes require the presence of the brain and which merely require the presence of the spinal cord.

Materials

Frog; dissecting set; beakers; tripod; wire gauze; stand; thermometer; clamp; frog board; string.

Discussion

A reflex is an involuntary response to a stimulus. Reflexes are purposeful, predictable, and persistent. That is, they are useful (often protective), a given stimulus always produces the same response, and they last throughout the lifetime of the animal. Some reflexes, such as the photopupil reflex, require the presence of the brain; others, such as the withdrawal of the leg if the toes are dipped in acid, require only the spinal cord.

Procedure

1. Make all the following tests and observations upon
   a. a normal frog
   b. a spinal frog, and
   c. a double-pithed frog.
2. On completion of the tests, record all data in the chart under Results and Questions.
3. Normal frog:
   a. Place the frog on the deck. Note the position of the head and legs.
   b. Determine the rate of respiration by observing the closing and opening of the nostrils or by the raising and lowering of the floor of the mouth.
   c. Place the frog on its back and observe to see if it rights itself.
   d. Place the frog on the frog board, right side up, and secure it gently around the midtrunk region with string. Tip the frog board so the head is depressed. Note whether the frog elevates its head.
   e. Place the frog in a sink full of water. Can it stay afloat and swim? A spinal frog may make swimming movements.
   f. Let the toes of the right foot of a suspended frog dip into a beaker of water at 50 °C. Does it withdraw its foot?
   g. Pinch the toes of the right hind leg. Does the frog withdraw its leg?
   h. Test for the presence of the corneal reflex by observing if the frog blinks when the cornea is touched.
   i. Observe the frog's response to a loud noise (drop a book on the table near the frog).
4. Spinal frog:
   a. Pith the frog.
   b. Wait until the frog emerges from the period of spinal shock, then perform all the tests in step 3.
5. Double-pithed frog:
   a. To double-pith the frog, insert the probe into the occipitovertebral junction. Direct the probe downward into the spinal cavity and destroy the cord.
   b. Repeat all the tests in step 3.

EXERCISE 16-E
DEMONSTRATION OF INDIVIDUAL HUMAN REFLEXES

Objectives

To determine the responses obtained in various common reflexes.

Materials

Rubber reflex hammers.

Discussion

A variety of human reflexes will be demonstrated in this exercise. The first two (knee and ankle jerks) are stretch reflexes.

Stretching the tendon (in this experiment caused by striking the tendon with a reflex hammer) stimulates stretch receptors. An impulse travels to the cord, then back (by way of the same nerve) to the muscle in which the impulse originated. The muscle contracts, thus resisting further stretch. This type of reflex is important in maintaining an upright position.

Procedure

PART 1. PATELLAR REFLEX (KNEE JERK)

1. Have the subject sit on a table so that the leg hangs free.
2. Strike the patellar ligament just below the knee with the edge of the hammer. This should result in the reflex contraction of the quadriceps femoris muscle, resulting in extension of the leg.
3. Have the subject clasp his or her hands behind the back and pull, just prior to and during the striking of the tendon. What effect does this have on the extent of the knee jerk?
4. Give the subject a column of figures to add and while he is doing this, tap the patellar ligament. What effect does this have on the extent of the knee jerk?

PART 2. ACHILLES REFLEX (ANKLE JERK)

1. The subject should kneel on a chair, feet hanging free over the edge of the chair.
2. Tap the tendon of Achilles. The gastrocnemius muscle should now contract, resulting in plantar flexion of the foot.

PART 3. PHOTOPUPIL REFLEX

1. The subject should close his eyes for 2 minutes while facing a bright light (the microscope lamp).
2. Have the subject open his eyes and note the large pupil, which should constrict shortly after the light strikes the eye.
3. After the initial constriction, a lesser dilation of the pupil occurs, which is then followed by another constriction.
4. See if you can observe the preceding theoretical results in the subject.

PART 4. ACCOMMODATION REFLEX

1. Have the subject look at a distant object 20 or more feet away. (Do not let subject look into bright light.)
2. Examine the size of the pupil.

3. Now have the subject look at a pencil held about 10 inches from the face (without changing the illumination) and observe the size of the pupil.

PART 5. CONVERGENCE REFLEX

1. Observe the position of the eyeball while the subject is looking at a distant object.
2. Now have the subject focus on a pencil held about 10 inches from the face.
3. Observe the change in the position of the eyeballs.

EXERCISE 16-F
REACTION TIME

Objective

To determine the length of human reaction time to sight, sound, and touch.

Materials

Two keys; wire; *either* a kymograph, semicircular stand, clamp, signal magnet, and two dry cells *or* a clock graduated in hundredths of seconds (Lafayette model no. 54019).

Discussion

Reaction time is the length of time required for a voluntary response to the stimulation of a sense organ. It varies with the particular sense organ stimulated and is affected to some extent by practice and by the intensity of the stimulus.

Procedure

1. Use a drum speed of 4 throughout the experiment.
2. Connect the two dry cells, the signal magnet, and the two keys in series (see Figure 16-8).
3. The subject whose reaction time is to be measured operates key A. The investigator operates key B.
4. To determine reaction time to sight, key B must be a silent key.
5. Start the drum rotating.
6. Have the subject close key A and, while the drum is rotating, watch for deflection of the signal magnet.
7. Close key B. This completes the circuit; the pen of the signal magnet should descend.
8. As soon as the subject sees the pen descend on the paper, he or she should

Figure 16-8. Diagram of setup for measuring reaction time.

open key A, breaking the circuit. This causes the pen to return to its original position.

9. Repeat the test at least three times and calculate the average reaction time to sight. Do this by measuring the length of the deflection of the signal magnet tracing and dividing by the drum speed (5 cm/sec). Record the reaction time in hundredths of seconds. Show all calculations.

10. To measure the reaction time to <u>sound</u>, key B must make an audible noise when it closes.

11. The subject should close his eyes throughout the experiment.

12. Have the subject close key A. Then close key B.

13. As soon as the subject hears the click of key B, he should open key A, breaking the circuit.

14. Repeat this action at least three times and calculate the reaction time to sound.

15. To determine the reaction time to <u>touch</u>, key B must again be silent. The subject must close his eyes throughout this experiment.

16. Have the subject close key A.

17. Close key B with one hand and touch the subject on the shoulder with the other hand at exactly the same time.

18. As soon as the subject feels the touch, he should open key A, breaking the circuit.

19. Repeat this action at least three times and calculate the reaction time to touch.

20. Record all results in the table under Results and Questions.

Alternate Procedure

1. Plug in the clock. The clock and keys should be wired as shown in Figure 16-9. Determine how the clock is read. The clock should read to hundredths of seconds.

2. The subject whose reaction time is to be measured operates key A. The investigator operates key B. To determine the reaction time to sight, key B must be a silent key.

3. Set the clock to zero time by depressing the lever on the front. Have the subject close key A and watch the clock. Then close key B. This completes the circuit; the clock should begin to move. As soon as the subject sees the movement of the hand of the clock, he should open key A, breaking the circuit. This causes the clock

Figure 16-9. Diagram of setup for measuring reaction time

to stop. Record the time in hundredths of seconds. Reset the clock to zero.

4. Repeat the procedure three times. Record each time in the chart under Results and Questions and calculate the average reaction time for sight.

5. To measure the reaction time to sound, key B must make an audible noise when it is closed. The subject should close his eyes throughout the experiment. Have the subject close key A. Then close key B, completing the circuit. As soon as the subject hears the click of key B, he should open key A, breaking the circuit. Record the time. Reset the clock to zero.

6. Repeat this procedure three times and calculate the average reaction time to sound.

7. To determine the reaction time to touch, key B must again be silent. The subject must close his eyes throughout this experiment. The subject should close key A. The investigator should then close key B with one hand and touch the subject on the shoulder with the other hand at exactly the same time. As soon as the subject feels the touch, he should open key A, breaking the circuit. Record the time and reset the clock to zero.

8. Repeat this procedure three times and calculate the average reaction time to touch.

SELF-TEST—NERVOUS SYSTEM

Directions

See Chapter 1, Self-Test, page 9.

1. When a nerve is stimulated by a number of subliminal stimuli in a short space of time, **summation** may occur.

2. At the synapse, impulses pass from the axon of one neuron to the **axon** of the next neuron.

3. A threshold stimulus results when energy is **just sufficient** to initiate the response of normally excitable tissue.

4. **White matter** of the spinal cord contains the long ascending or descending motor and sensory pathways.

5. The radial nerve is a branch of the **cervical plexus.**

6. The **phrenic** nerve is a branch of the plexus that is formed by the first four cervical nerves.

7. Depolarization is associated with excitation of a membrane, while **hyperpolorization** is associated with inhibition.

8. The **reflex arc** is the functional unit of the nervous system.

9. In the reflex arc, impulses pass from the internuncial neuron to the **afferent** neuron.

10. The motor area of the cerebral cortex lies in the **post-central** gyrus.

11. The spinal cord extends to the base of the **first sacral** vertebra.

12. The **hypothalamus** is an important relay station for sensory pathways between the brain stem and the cerebral cortex.

13. Temperature regulation is under the control of the **thalamus.**

14. The aggregations of nerve cell bodies located deep in the brain and spinal cord may be called **nuclei.**

15. A **synapse** is the small gap between a nerve and muscle.

16. The surface of the brain contains raised parts called convolutions or **sulci.**

17. The cortex of the brain consists of **white** matter.

18. Inflammation of a membrane of the brain or spinal cord is called **meningitis.**

19. Injury to a speech center affecting speech and word understanding is called **aphasia.**

20. Motor nerves to one side of the body originate, for the most part, in the **same** side of the brain.

21. The major control mechanisms for balance and posture are located in the **cerebellum.**

22. The cranial nerve conveying impulses concerned with equilibrium is the **acoustic.**

23. The cranial nerve conveying impulses to most of the viscera of the body is the **oculomotor** nerve.

24. The nerve carrying impulses causing us to shrug our shoulders and turn our head is the **accessory.**

25. The cranial nerve carrying impulses that would warn you if the coffee were hot is the **trigeminal.**

26. The cranial nerve that carries impulses giving you information about decaying substances is the **acoustic.**

27. In general, the craniosacral division of the autonomic system is concerned with conservative and restorative processes, while the **thoracolumbar** division is concerned primarily with processes involving energy exchange.

28. A lumbar puncture is done between **L5** and **S1** to avoid hitting the spinal cord, which ends at L1 and L2.

29. In a lumbar puncture, cerebrospinal fluid may be removed from the **subarachnoid space.**

30. A red color of the cerebrospinal fluid may indicate bleeding somewhere in the **central nervous system.**

31. An amputee sometimes has sensations in the missing extremity because the nerve fiber may be stimulated at any point along its **course.**

32. Intramuscular injections should be given in the **upper outer quadrant** of the buttocks.

33. It is important to give injections in the correct quadrant to avoid the **blood vessel** that courses through the buttocks.

34. Tic douloureux is a spasmodic neuralgia of the **glossopharyngeal** nerve.

35. A reflex is a **voluntary** response to a harmful stimulus.

36. The Nissl bodies in neuroplasm are related to **the metabolism of the cell.**

37. Axons carry nerve impulses **toward** the nerve cell body.

38. Gray matter of the brain and spinal cord is predominantly made up of **nonmyelinated** nerve cell processes.

39. The **myelin sheath** is responsible for regeneration of injured peripheral nerve tissues.

40. The **central nervous system** is composed of the brain and spinal cord.

41. The connective tissue cells of the central nervous system are called **neuroglial cells.**

42. The myelin sheaths of spinal and cranial nerves are broken into segments at sites known as **nodes of Ranvier.**

43. The outer surface of nerve cell membrane is electrically **negative** with respect to the interior of the cell at rest.

44. **White** matter of the brain consists of masses of nerve cell bodies.

45. The localization area for voluntary motion is in the **frontal lobe** of the cerebrum.

46. The **great longitudinal fissure** divides the cerebrum into right and left hemispheres.

47. The **thalamus** is responsible for conscious motor activity and conscious sensations.

48. Normal control of vital mechanisms of the viscera is mediated by the **autonomic nervous system.**

49. A rapid heart rate, an increase in respiratory rate, and an increase in blood pressure would result from stimulation of the **parasympathetic** division of the autonomic nervous system.

50. The pupil of the eye dilates in response to stimulation of the **craniosacral** division of the autonomic nervous system.

51. The **dura mater** is the inner layer of the meninges at the surface of the spinal cord and brain.

52. The agent liberated at the terminals of all preganglionic neurons and at the postganglionic neurons of the parasympathetic divisions is called **acetylcholine.**

53. The passage of a nerve impulse from one neuron to another is due to the presence of **acetylcholine** at the synapse.

54. The region of the spinal cord that contains cell bodies of motor neurons is the **posterior** horn.

55. The vagus nerve emerges from the **medulla.**

56. Control of the rate of the heartbeat is a function of the **pons varolii.**

57. The **arachnoid** forms the floor of the subarachnoid space.

58. The rate of respiration is controlled by a center in the **cerebellum.**

59. The cerebellum has a cortex composed of **white matter.**

60. The nerve that carries impulses resulting in the action of chewing is the **trigeminal.**

61. The nerve carrying impulses causing us to frown is the **glossopharyngeal.**

17

Sense Organs

INTRODUCTION

Stimuli from both the external and internal environment are received by a variety of receptors. Specific stimuli are received by specific receptors which are, for the most part, modified histologically for their particular function. Receptors may be classified functionally, depending on the particular kind of stimulus they respond to, as photoreceptors, mechanoreceptors, chemoreceptors, pressoreceptors, or osmoreceptors. A classification of receptors, with the type of stimulus received, follows.

A. Exteroceptors

These are receptors that are sensitive to stimuli arising at the surface of the body as well as to those coming from the external environment. Included are the following:

1. Rods and cones in the retina of the eye (photoreceptors).
2. Hair cells of the Organ of Corti in the inner ear.
3. Nasal membrane receptors on the superior concha (chemoreceptors).
4. Taste receptors in the tongue (chemoreceptors).
5. The following skin receptors:
   a. Meissner's corpuscles—touch (mechanoreceptors).
   b. Krause's end bulbs—cold (mechanoreceptors).
   c. Organ of Ruffini—warmth (mechanoreceptors).
   d. Pacinian corpuscle—deep pressure (mechanoreceptors).

   e. Bare (unencapsulated) nerve endings —pain (respond to a variety of stimuli).

B. Interoceptors

Interoceptors are receptor end organs that are located in and transmit impulses from the viscera. Stimulation of these receptors may give rise to sensations of discomfort or internal pain that may be the result of hunger, thirst, cramping pains accompanying disorders of the gastrointestinal tract, the sharp pain of acute appendicitis, etc. Other interoceptors, based on their functions, may be classified as follows:

1. Pressoreceptors are sensitive to changes in blood pressure. When stimulated, the following responses result:
   a. Right heart (Bainbridge) reflex— Pressoreceptors in the superior and inferior venae cavae, as they enter the right atrium, when stimulated by increased pressure, convey impulses to the cardiac center in the medulla along vagus nerve fibers. This results in an accelerated heartbeat.
   b. Aortic reflex—Pressoreceptors in the aortic sinus (located in the aortic arch) are sensitive to changes in pressure. Increased pressure slows the heart rate (impulses to cardiac center via vagus nerve).
   c. Carotid sinus reflex—Pressoreceptors in the carotid sinus, which is a slightly dilated area of the internal carotid artery at the point where the common carotid artery divides (bifurcates) into

the internal and external carotid arteries, respond to fluctuations in pressure. Impulses are conveyed to the cardiac center of the medulla by the glossopharyngeal nerve. Increased pressure slows the heart rate.

2. Osmoreceptors are sensitive to changes in osmotic concentrations in the blood (extracellular fluid), especially as influenced by sodium and chloride ions. They are found in the hypothalamus and are important in regulating fluid balance within the body.

C. Proprioceptors

These are receptors that give information concerning movements and position of the body. They are located primarily in muscles, tendons, joints, and the nonauditory portion of the inner ear.

The action of many of these receptors will be demonstrated in the exercises that follow.

EXERCISE 17-A
GROSS ANATOMY OF THE HUMAN EYE

Objectives

To locate and identify the structures of the human eye.

Materials

Text; reference books; models; wall charts.

Discussion

Before proceeding to other exercises concerning the eye, it is usually advantageous to become thoroughly familiar with the gross features of the eye. Much of this learning activity may be accomplished outside the laboratory.

Procedure

1. Use Figures 17-1, 17-2, and 17-3 of the eye as self-tests.
2. When you have become familiar with the indicated structures on the figures, locate them on the models of the eye and on wall charts.

EXERCISE 17-B
DISSECTION OF THE SHEEP EYE

Objectives

To locate and identify the structures of the mammalian eye by examining and dissecting a sheep eye.

Materials

Preserved sheep eye; dissection instruments.

Discussion

The size and structures of the sheep eye compare favorably with those of the human eye. This, coupled with their availability, makes them ideal for studying the anatomical structures of the eye.

Procedure

PART 1. EXTERNAL ASPECT OF THE SHEEP EYE

1. Note the fat on the surface of the eye. This cushions the eye from shock in its bony orbit.

KEY TO FIGURE 17-1

1. superior oblique	9. excretory ducts
2. medial rectus	10. lateral rectus
3. lacrimal duct	11. sclera
4. lacrimal sac	12. pupil
5. lacrimal puncta	13. iris
6. nasolacrimal duct	14. inferior rectus
7. superior rectus	15. inferior oblique
8. lacrimal gland	

Figure 17-1.   Anterior view of eye showing lacrimal apparatus.

230

KEY TO FIGURE 17-2

1. posterior cavity
   (contains vitreous humor)
2. fovea centralis
3. optic disc
4. retinal blood vessels
5. optic nerve
6. nerve sheath
7. canals of Schlemm
8. posterior chamber
9. anterior chamber
10. anterior cavity
11. aqueous humor
12. pupil
13. cornea
14. crystalline lens
15. iris
16. conjunctiva
17. suspensory ligaments
18. ciliary body
19. sclera
20. choroid
21. retina

Figure 17.2.   Midsagittal section through the eye.

KEY TO FIGURE 17-3

1. levator palpebrae
   superioris
2. pulley
3. superior oblique
4. superior rectus
5. cornea
6. medial rectus
7. lateral rectus
8. sclera
9. inferior oblique
10. inferior rectus

Figure 17-3.   Extrinsic muscles of the right eye.

2. Identify the following structures:
    a. The **sclera**, the tough external white coat.
    b. The **conjunctiva**, reflected over the anterior surface of the eye and attached to the eyeball a short distance from the edge of the cornea.
    c. The **cornea**, the anterior, transparent (opaque in your specimen, due to action of the preservative) portion of the sclera.
    d. The **optic nerve**, located on the posterior surface. The nerve has the appearance of a solid white core and is approximately 3 mm thick.
3. Carefully dissect away the connective tissue (fat, etc.) from the posterior surface of the eyeball to free the six **extrinsic eye muscles.** These resemble flattened straps.

PART 2. INTERNAL ASPECT OF THE SHEEP EYE

1. Hold the eye so that the cornea is in a superior position.

Figure 17-4. Dissecting a sheep eye.

2. Make an incision (see Figure 17-4) into the eyeball about 1/2 cm from the edge of the cornea and cut completely around the eye (parallel to the cornea), separating the eye into anterior and posterior portions.

3. Turn the eyeball so that the cornea is in an inferior position. Separate the two portions of the eyeball. If the incision was made correctly, it should be possible to carefully loosen the vitreous humor from the lens and to keep the vitreous humor in the posterior portion of the eyeball and the lens in the anterior third of the eye.

4. Examine the interior of the anterior part of the eye.
    a. Observe the **ciliary body,** the black structure that has the appearance of narrow, radial folds.
    b. Locate the **suspensory ligaments,** the very delicate fibers connecting the ciliary body to the lens. They hold the lens in position.
    c. Free the lens from the ciliary body and remove it. Remnants of the suspensory ligaments can be seen attached to the lens.
    d. The **iris** is now visible anterior to the

former position of the lens. The iris also appears black. Try to distinguish between the **circular** and **radial** fibers comprising the iris.
    e. Hold the lens up to the light. Does any light pass through? The lens in your specimen may be opaque due to the action of the preservative.

5. Examine the external surface of the anterior third of the eye. It is now relatively easy to distinguish the iris, **pupil,** and cornea.

6. Examine the posterior two-thirds of the eye and observe the following structures:
    a. The **vitreous humor** (in life, this substance is perfectly clear). Remove it from the eyeball.
    b. The **retina,** the white inner coat that was covered by the vitreous humor. Determine the point at which the retina is attached dorsally.
    c. The **choroid coat.** The retina covers this coat, and the two are easily separated. The irridescent appearance of the choroid is due to the presence of the **tapetum lucidum,** a special structure not present in the human

eye. The function of the tapetum lucidum is to reflect some light back onto the retina. This reflecting device is found in vertebrates that live under conditions of low light intensity. This causes the animal's eyes to shine in the dark.

d. The **sclera,** the outer white coat.

EXERCISE 17-C
ACCOMMODATION

Objective

To demonstrate accommodation.

Materials

Pins; 3 x 5 cards.

Discussion

The ability of the eye to focus on far objects and then to rapidly adjust and focus on near objects is referred to as accommodation. Ability to accommodate depends on changes in the shape of the crystalline lens.

Procedure

1. Face the window and hold your hand, with the fingers outspread, about 6 inches in front of your eyes.
2. Close your eyes for a moment, then open them and note which seems to be in focus—your fingers or some distant object such as a bush or tree or some other item. Record your observations under Results and Questions.
3. With a pin, prick two holes in a 3 x 5 card that are approximately 3 mm apart (a distance less than the diameter of the pupil).
4. Look through the pinholes and bring a pin into the line of vision so that it appears in the overlapping part of the luminous circles.
5. Now, look at a distant object in the back of the room and note whether the pin appears double or single.
6. Accommodate for the pin. Note whether the pin now appears double or single. Record your observations and answer the questions under Results and Questions.

EXERCISE 17-D
MEASURING THE NEAR POINT OF ACCOMMODATION

Objectives

To measure the near point of vision; to determine if the value is more or less for the dominant eye; to determine which eye is the dominant one.

Materials

Pin; 3 x 5 card; meter stick.

Discussion

Since accommodation depends on the resiliency of the lens, the near point of accommodation will vary as resiliency varies. The shape of the eyeball will also influence the measurement.

Procedure

1. Hold a pin, or a 3 x 5 card with a well-defined letter printed on it, at arm's length.
2. While holding a meter stick just under the eye, gradually bring the pin (or card) closer to the eye by drawing it along the margin (or on the surface) of the meter stick.
3. When the pin appears to be double, or the letter on the card becomes distorted, the item is within the near point and your eye can no longer accommodate for it.
4. Move the pin (or card) away to the precise point where it appears single (or undistorted) again. This is your near point of vision.
5. Determine the near point for each eye in centimeters.
   Right eye _____
   Left eye _____
6. On Table 17-1, locate the age group to which your near point corresponds for each eye. Record in the spaces provided under Results and Questions.
7. To determine your dominant eye, make a small hole (about this size ◯) in a piece of paper.
8. Place a coin at your feet on the floor.
9. Hold the paper with the hole in it at waist level.
10. Locate the coin through the hole in the

Table 17-1. Relationship
between Age and Near Point of Vision

Age	Near Point	
	cm	in.
10	7.5	2.95
20	9.0	3.54
30	11.5	4.53
40	17.2	6.77
50	52.5	20.67
60	83.3	32.80

paper and close your right eye. If the coin disappears you are right-eyed.

11. Now close your left eye. If the coin disappears you are left-eyed. Which eye was dominant? _____

EXERCISE 17-E
SNELLEN CHART TEST FOR VISUAL ACUITY

Objective

To measure visual acuity.

Materials

Snellen chart; illiterate "E" chart; 3 x 5 card.

Discussion

The Snellen method for measuring visual acuity is based on the fact that certain sized letters can be clearly seen by eyes with normal acuity at specific distances. The first line (letter E) is of such a size that it can be clearly seen by a normal-sighted individual standing 200 feet away from the chart. Another line on the chart contains letters of a size that should be clearly readable by the same individual at a distance of 20 feet. $V = d/D$, where V stands for vision and d is the distance at which certain letters can be read by the subject. D is the distance at which the letters can be read by the normal eye. For example, if an individual reads a line of letters at a distance of 20 feet which the "normal" eye could read at a distance of 30 feet, his or her visual acuity = 20/30. The Snellen chart is used to detect myopia (nearsightedness).

Procedure

1. Have the subject stand 20 feet from the Snellen chart, while you stand near the chart.
2. Have the subject cover one eye with a 3 x 5 card but not close the eye.
3. Indicate to the subject the lines to be read. The subject should read the chart as far down as possible with each eye separately and then with both eyes (without glasses). Note: d/D can be read off the chart next to the last line that can be read successfully by the subject. Record your data in the table under Results and Questions.
4. If the subject usually wears glasses, have him or her repeat the test with glasses on.
5. Repeat the above procedure with the illiterate "E" chart. Record your data in the table.

EXERCISE 17-F
TEST FOR ASTIGMATISM

Objective

To test for the presence of astigmatism.

Materials

Astigmatism chart.

Discussion

Astigmatism is a condition in which the refracting surfaces of the cornea and crystalline lens are not perfect. A chart for the detection of this condition consists of a series of parallel lines arranged like the spokes of a wagon wheel. If the refracting surfaces are not distorted, all the spokes will be seen with equal distinctness and none will appear darker than others. If astigmatism is present, the horizontal spokes may be properly focused and seen while the vertical spokes are focused either in front of or behind the retina. They will, therefore, be more or less blurred. Of course, other spokes than the ones mentioned may be involved—distortion will vary with the location of the eye defect.

Astigmatism is corrected by means of a cylindrical lens. To test a lens (such as those in your glasses) designed to correct astigmatism, rotate the lens or glasses 90 degrees, keeping the center of the lens fixed on some slender vertical or horizontal object (such as the window blinds). Any change in shape of the object indicates a cylindrical lens has been added to the glasses for the correction of astigmatism.

Procedure

1. Stand 10 feet away from a well-lighted astigmatism chart.
2. Cover the left eye and observe the lines on the chart. Note if some of the lines (e.g., vertical or horizontal) appear to be in sharper focus than others.
3. Move toward the chart, one step at a time, repeating your observations.
4. Repeat the preceding procedure with the right eye covered.
5. Record your data under Results and Questions.

EXERCISE 17-G
THE BLIND SPOT

Objective

To demonstrate the occurrence of the blind spot.

Materials

None.

Procedure

1. Hold this page approximately centered, about 20 inches in front of the face, with the left eye closed.
2. Focus on the cross seen below. At this distance both the cross and the circle

should be seen.
3. Gradually bring the paper closer until the circle cannot be seen (look steadily at the cross the entire time).
4. Bring the paper still closer to the face. Now the circle should reappear.
5. Repeat the above procedure with the right eye closed, but this time the opened eye should focus on the circle.

EXERCISE 17-H
COLOR BLINDNESS

Objective

To determine whether the subject is color-blind.

Materials

Ishihara's color plates.

Procedure

1. Using sunlight whenever possible, hold the plates of the test book 75 cm (approximately 30 inches) from the subject.
2. Tilt the plates so that the plane of the paper is at right angles to the line of vision.
3. Each answer should be given without more than 3 seconds' delay. The correct answer for each plate is given in the front of the test book.
4. Record how many errors the subject makes.

EXERCISE 17-I
ANATOMY OF THE EAR

Objectives

To become familiar with the structures of the ear and their functions.

Materials

· References; models; wall charts; ear ossicles.

Discussion

Unlike light rays, which may travel through a vacuum, sound waves require some medium, such as air or water, to be conducted. In the ear, both air and water are involved in the transmission of sound waves to the auditory receptors located within the cochlea. A knowledge of the anatomy of the ear is essential if these principles, which relate to its physiology, are to be understood.

Procedure

1. Use Figures 17-5 and 17-6 as self-tests.
2. Compare the structures indicated on Figures 17-5 and 17-6 with those found on models of the ear, on wall charts, and in references.
3. Using your text or other current references, determine the functions of the structures of the ear.
4. Demonstration: examine the auditory ossicles (malleus, incus, and stapes) that have been placed under the stereoscopic microscope.
5. Obtain a slide of the **cochlea** labeled Internal Ear, Cochlea. Since the cochlea makes two-and-a-half spiral turns around a pillar of spongy bone, the **modiolus**, the

slide contains approximately five views of the canals of the cochlea. Selecting one portion that resembles some model of the cochlea (refer to Figures 17-7 and 17-8), diagram a radial section through the canals and label the following structures: **basilar membrane, tectorial membrane, vestibular membrane, scala vestibuli, scala media (cochlear duct), scala tympani, hair cells of the organ of Corti, supporting cells,** and **cochlear nerve.** Indicate the location of the **perilymph** and **endolymph.**

EXERCISE 17-J
BONE CONDUCTION OF SOUND WAVES

Objective

To demonstrate bone conduction.

Materials

Tuning fork; 70% alcohol.

Procedure

1. To demonstrate bone conduction of sound waves, hold a ticking watch or the handle of a vibrating tuning fork (these may first be cleaned with 70% alcohol) between the

KEY TO FIGURE 17-5

1. posterior semicircular canal
2. lateral semicircular canal
3. fenestra vestibuli (ovalis)
4. fenestra cochlea (rotunda)
5. superior semicircular canal
6. vestibule
7. cochlea
8. modiolus

Figure 17-5. Osseous labyrinth.

236

Figure 17-6.   The ear.

KEY TO FIGURE 17-7

1. scala vestibuli
2. vestibular membrane
3. tectorial membrane
4. organ of Corti
5. scala tympani

Figure 17-7.   Axial section through entire cochlea showing canals.

KEY TO FIGURE 17-8

1. hair cells of
   organ of Corti
2. supporting cells
3. basilar membrane
4. scala tympani
5. scala vestibuli
6. vestibular membrane
7. cochlear duct
8. tectorial membrane
9. cochlear nerve

Figure 17-8.   Radial section through one coil of the cochlea.

teeth. If a tuning fork is used, start it vibrating by striking it against the palm of the hand (never against a hard surface).
2. With the watch or tuning fork in position, cover first one ear, then both. Compare the intensity of the sound heard with both ears open, one ear covered, and both ears

covered. Record your observations under Results and Questions.
3. Now perform the Rinné test for middle-ear deafness by holding the handle of a vibrating tuning fork against the mastoid process (the "bump" located just behind the ear). The tuning fork should be

pointed back away from the ear and only the handle should touch the head.

4. When the sound can no longer be heard, hold the tuning fork (by the handle) just outside the external ear. In middle-ear deafness, no sound is heard by air conduction after it ceases to be heard by bone conduction.

5. Simulate middle-ear deafness by plugging the ear to be tested with cotton (or closing it with a finger) and then repeat the test.

6. Record your data and answer the questions under Results and Questions.

EXERCISE 17-K
LOCALIZATION OF SOUNDS

Objective

To demonstrate localization of sounds.

Materials

Watch or tuning fork.

Procedure

1. Have the subject close both eyes.
2. Now hold a ticking watch or vibrating tuning fork (or use some other sound-making device such as snapping fingers) approximately 6 inches (a) in front of the head, (b) above the head, (c) behind the head, (d) on either side of the head. Record your observations concerning localization of the sounds under Results and Questions.

EXERCISE 17-L
LOCALIZATION OF TOUCH SENSATION

Objectives

To determine whether the ability to localize a point of stimulation varies on different parts of the body; to determine whether there is a difference in the ability to discriminate between two points of stimulation applied simultaneously to different parts of the body.

Materials

Pencil; ruler; esthesiometer.

Discussion

Both tactile localization and tactile discrimination are demonstrated in this exercise. Tactile localization involves the ability to tell more or less accurately which portion of skin is touched. In the brain is a field that corresponds to the field of the periphery of the body. By tactile discrimination, we mean the power to discern two distinct sensations when the skin is stimulated at two points. When the stimulated points are close enough together, only one sensation is felt by the subject.

Procedure

PART 1. LOCALIZING A STIMULUS

1. Have the subject close his or her eyes.
2. Touch the palm of the subject's hand with a pencil.
3. The subject should then try to place the point of a pencil on the precise spot stimulated.
4. Measure, in millimeters, the distance (if any) by which he missed the precise point of stimulation. Repeat the procedure two more times. Average the results of the three determinations and record the values in the table under Results and Questions.
5. Repeat the foregoing procedure on the back of the hand, fingertip, ventral surface of the forearm, ventral surface of the upper arm, and upper back.

PART 2. TWO-POINT DISCRIMINATION

1. The esthesiometer resembles a compass with two sharp points.
2. The eyes of the subject should be closed throughout this exercise.
3. The observer should touch the subject in a random manner with either one point or two points of the esthesiometer to prevent guessing.
4. Measure (in millimeters) how close the two points of an esthesiometer can be and yet be felt as two points when applied to the skin on the ventral surface of the thumb. Make each determination three times. Average the results and record all values in the table under Results and Questions.

5. Repeat the experiment on the palm and back of the hand, ventral surface of the forearm, ventral surface of the upper arm, back, and tip of the tongue.

EXERCISE 17-M
CUTANEOUS SENSATIONS

Objective

To demonstrate the punctiform distribution of cutaneous sense receptors.

Materials

Bristle; hot nails; cold nails; pins; rubber stamp grid; stamp pad.

Discussion

The cutaneous sensations include heat, cold, touch, and pain. Receptors for heat, cold, and touch are lacking in the internal organs. Pain receptors are quite general in distribution, and this sensation can be elicited from most organs.

Procedure

1. Stamp a grid on the ventral surface of the forearm or, if too hairy, on the arm (on the biceps brachii).
2. Touch each square in the grid on your forearm in at least six different spots with a bristle to determine the location of the **touch** receptors. Apply just sufficient pressure to bend the bristle. Use the same pressure each time. Don't assume you are feeling a touch sensation merely because you see the bristle touching. Indicate the location of each receptor with a "T" in the appropriate location on the grid under Results and Questions.
3. To locate the **cold** receptors, use nails cooled in ice water. Dry the nails and then lightly touch just the tip of the nail to at least six different sites in each square of the grid. Change nails at frequent intervals. Mark the site of each cold receptor located by this procedure with a "C" on the grid under Results and Questions.
4. Using nails heated in water to 40 or 50 °C and dried, locate the **heat** receptors in accordance with the procedure of step 3

and indicate their location on the grid with an "H."
5. To locate **pain** receptors, explore the same area of skin as before with a pin. The sensation perceived when a pain receptor is stimulated by slight pressure resembles a slight electric shock, not a definite pain. Indicate the sites of these receptors on the grid with the letter "P."
6. Relocate a touch receptor and stimulate the site with a cold nail. Record your observation under Results and Questions.

EXERCISE 17-N
PRESSURE SENSATION

Objective

To determine if sensitivity to pressure varies from one site to another in the body.

Materials

Bristle; piece of glass plate (or other perfectly smooth, hard surface); about 50 sheets of smooth paper.

Discussion

The receptors for this sensation are located immediately below the skin. A related sensation occurs when the urinary bladder or the rectum is filled with urine or feces (sensation of fullness).

Procedure

1. Place a bristle (or hair) on a smooth, hard surface (e.g., a piece of glass) and cover it with from 10 to 50 sheets of paper (count them). Do this while the subject has his eyes closed or is looking elsewhere.
2. The subject should now attempt to determine the location of the bristle by lightly passing the tips of the fingers across the surface of the papers. Determine the maximum number of sheets of paper under which the subject could feel the bristle.
3. Repeat the test having the subject use the knuckle of the index finger, the proximal portion of the palm of the hand, the elbow, the chin, and the nose. Record your data under Results and Questions.

EXERCISE 17-O
RECEPTOR ADAPTATION

Objective

To demonstrate adaptation of receptors to stimuli.

Materials

Coins; paper cups; warm water; ice water; tincture of iodine or perfume.

Discussion

Disappearance of a sensation is due to the fact that the receptors adapt to stimuli and thus initiate no more nerve impulses until a change takes place in the stimulus.

Procedure

PART 1. TOUCH STIMULATION

1. Place an object (e.g., a coin) on the skin of the ventral surface of the forearm. How many seconds does the touch sensation last?
2. Repeat the experiment at a new spot on the skin. After the sensation disappears, add two more coins of the same size on top of the first coin. If the sensation returned, how many seconds did it last? Record your data under Results and Questions.

PART 2. TEMPERATURE STIMULATION

1. Immerse an index finger in warm water for 2 minutes. Now dip the other index finger into the same container of warm water. Note the difference between the sensations in each of the fingers.
2. Now immerse one index finger in warm water and the other in ice water. After 2 minutes immerse both fingers in the same container of cold tap water. Record your observations under Results and Questions.

PART 3. CHEMICAL STIMULATION

1. With one nostril held closed, sniff (breathe relatively deeply) a bottle containing tincture of iodine or perfume. Note the beginning time and the time it takes for the odor to disappear.

Beginning time _____ Time required for odor to disappear _____

2. As soon as the odor disappears, release the other nostril and attempt to smell the tincture of iodine with it. If you can still detect the odor in the single nostril after 5 minutes, release the other nostril and smell the iodine with it. Note any difference in intensity. Record your observations under Results and Questions.
3. Figure 17-9 shows the basis for chemical stimulation of olfactory (nasal) epithelium. The impulses transmitted to the brain as a result of such stimulation cause the sensation of smelling.

EXERCISE 17-P
REFERRED PAIN

Objective

To experience referred pain.

Materials

Enamel pan; ice water.

Discussion

Referred pain is a common sensory phenomenon in which stimulation in one part of the body gives rise to a sensation (often pain) that seems localized in a different or remote part of the body.

Procedure

1. Place your elbow in a tray of ice water deep enough to cover it.
2. Keep your elbow in position long enough to feel the following progression of sensations: first, a feeling of some discomfort in the region of the elbow; later, pain sensations that are felt elsewhere. Record your observations under Results and Questions.

EXERCISE 17-Q
LOCATION OF TASTE BUDS

Objective

To determine where the greatest concentration of receptors (taste buds) for each of the four basic taste sensations is located.

241

Cribriform plate of ethmoid bone

Olfactory epithelium

Lamina propria

Substance being smelled

(b)

Frontal lobe of cerebrum

Cribriform plate of ethmoid bone

Superior nasal concha

Middle nasal concha

Inferior nasal concha

KEY TO FIGURE 17-9

1. olfactory tract
2. olfactory bulb
3. olfactory nerve fibers
4. supporting cell
5. olfactory cell
6. olfactory hair

(a)

Figure 17-9.   Olfactory receptors.

242

Materials

5% sucrose; 1% acetic acid or 5% un-sweetened lemon juice; 5% NaCl; 0.5% quinine sulfate; cotton-tipped applicators; paper cups.

Procedure

1. Figure 17-10 shows the structure of a taste bud. Which cranial nerves are sensory for the taste buds?
2. An outline of the tongue appears under Results and Questions. As you obtain data from the activities below, record on this outline the site where each substance was tasted using the following symbols to represent each spot where a specific taste receptor was stimulated; x for sweet, o for salt, s for sour, and b for bitter.
3. Before doing a given test, thoroughly dry the tongue with a paper towel.
4. With a cotton-tipped applicator, apply a small amount of 5% sucrose to the back, sides, and tip of the tongue. Record the results on your drawing.
5. Rinse your mouth with water and dry the tongue before using each of the remaining three solutions.
6. Repeat step 3, in the following sequence, for each of the remaining solutions: 5% NaCl, 1% acetic acid, 0.5% quinine sulfate. Record your results on the drawing.

KEY TO FIGURE 17-10

1. gustatory pore
2. gustatory hair
3. gustatory cell
4. supporting cells

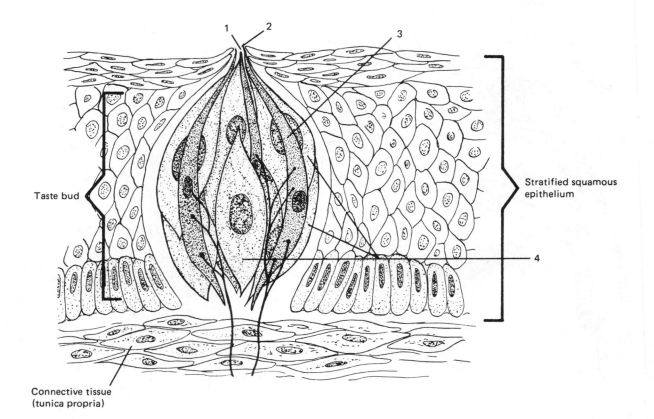

Figure 17-10. Structure of a taste bud.

SELF-TEST — SENSE ORGANS

Directions

See Chapter 1, Self-Test, page 9.

1. A **detached retina** occurs when the tissue lining the eyeball is pulled loose in one area and causes blurred vision.

2. **Conjunctivitis** is an inflammation of the membrane that lines the eyelids and covers the cornea.

3. **Glaucoma** is a disease of the eye characterized by increased tension within the eyeball and progressive loss of vision.

4. .If you look into an eye with an **ophthalmoscope** you may observe the retina, macula lutea, optic disc, and the retinal blood vessels.

5. **Myopia,** or farsightedness, is caused when the eyeball is too short or the refractive power too little, which causes the rays to focus behind the retina.

6. A patient with **nystagmus** will have involuntary oscillations, or "to and fro" movements, of the eyeball.

7. **Otitis media** is usually a complication of a severe cold and sore throat, because the infection ascends through the eustachian tube.

8. A **myringotomy** (an incision in the tympanic membrane) is sometimes performed in severe otitis media to allow pus to escape.

9. Our ears become "stopped up" with sudden changes in altitude because the eustachian tubes are **usually closed;** thus changing air pressure causes bulging of the tympanic membrane.

10. Cutaneous sensations are **equally** distributed over the body.

11. The brushes of Ruffini receive sensations of **heat.**

12. Pressure sensations are received by **Pacinian corpuscles.**

13. The end bulbs of Krause receive **cold** stimuli.

14. Hearing and balance are localized in the **frontal** lobe of the cerebrum.

15. The conscious awareness of heat, cold, and pressure is localized in the **parietal** lobe of the cerebrum.

16. The perception of objects seen is localized in the **occipital** lobe of the cerebrum.

17. The olfactory cells are **modified hair cells.**

18. Taste buds to detect sweetness are most numerous on the **lateral parts** of the tongue.

19. Injury to the right optic tract behind the optic chiasma would destroy the nasal visual field sight of the **left** eye and the temporal visual field sight of the **right** eye.

20. The shape of the crystalline lens is regulated by the **ciliary muscle.**

21. A pigment that is thought to be associated with the cones is called **iodopsin.**

22. The brown pigment (melanin) that causes eye color is found in the **pupil.**

23. The **vitreous** humor of the eye circulates through the anterior and posterior chambers and is drained by the canal of Schlemm.

24. The ability of the eye to adapt for near vision and far vision is known as **accommodation.**

25. Astigmatism is due to irregularities in the **cornea.**

26. Tears aid in keeping bacteria out of the eye due to the presence of **lysozyme.**

27. **Conduction** deafness may be caused by cerumen in the ear canal.

28. The stapes is attached to the **fenestra cochlea** or **round window.**

29. Hair cells in contact with the **tectorial** membrane (in the inner ear) are stimulated when the membrane vibrates.

30. The receptors for hearing are located on the **organ of Corti** within the inner ear.

31. The utricle is generally associated with **static posture** or the orientation of the body in relation to gravity, while the semicircular canals are concerned with **dynamic equilibrium.**

32. The eustachian tube leads from the pharynx to the **internal** ear.

33. The **semicircular canals** contain hair cells that move when the head is moved.

34. **Ossicles** of the middle ear transmit sound waves to the inner ear.

35. The **round** window serves as an escape valve for sound waves.

36. The fibers of the cochlear nerve pass through the **modiolus** to reach the organ of Corti.

37. The organ of Corti is located on the **basilar membrane.**

38. The **cornea** is the clear transparent tissue covering the anterior portion of the sclera.

39. The area where the optic nerve leaves the eye is **devoid of rods and cones** and is, therefore, insensitive to light stimuli.

40. The iris of the eye and ciliary body constitute the **extrinsic** muscles of the eye.

41. The white of the eye is the **choroid** portion of the eye.

42. The area of keenest vision of the eye is located at the **fovea centralis.**

43. The blind spot of the eye is located in the **fovea centralis.**

44. The right side of the cerebrum receives the nerve fibers from the **right side** of both eyes.

45. The **rods** are responsible for color vision.

46. Vitamin A, frequently associated with night vision, is an essential part of **rhodopsin.**

47. When the point of focus of your eyes is in front of the retina, you are **nearsighted.**

48. Visual purple, which aids in twilight vision, is not regenerated after being bleached by light if the diet is deficient in **vitamin C.**

49. Accommodation, or the focusing of an object on the retina, is brought about by the **change of shape in the lens.**

50. With advancing years the lens becomes firmer and the ability to alter its curvature decreases. This condition is called **hypermetropia.**

51. In vision, accommodation is brought about by action of the **ciliary muscle.**

52. **Cataract** involves opaqueness of the lens.

53. The parts of the ear concerned with balance include **otoliths** and **hair cells.**

54. In the order of their occurrence from the outside inward, the bones of the middle ear are the **incus, malleus, and stapes.**

18

The Urinary System

EXERCISE 18-A
ANATOMY OF THE
HUMAN URINARY SYSTEM

Objectives

To become familiar with the location, structure, and function of the organs in the urinary system.

Materials

Dissectable torso; anatomic charts; reference books; models; slide of nephron.

Discussion

The urinary system consists of the kidneys, ureters, urinary bladder, and urethra. The ureters conduct urine from the kidneys to the bladder; the urethra conducts urine from the bladder to the outside (and sperm from the testes in the male).

The primary function of the kidneys is to preserve homeostasis. This term refers to the maintenance of a constant internal environment. The kidneys maintain homeostasis through the excretion of various toxins and metabolic wastes as well as other substances present in the blood in surplus amounts (e.g., sugar eaten in excess or present in excess because of the disorder known as diabetes mellitus). Fluid and electrolyte balance, as well as acid-base balance, depends primarily on the proper functioning of the kidneys. Malfunction of these organs results in a failure of homeostasis; unless corrected, such failure finally results in death.

The structural and functional unit of the kidney is the nephron; there are approximately one million nephrons in each kidney. The blood is filtered in these units, and urine is produced as a result of selective transport (which is partially under the influence of hormones) of water and other substances from the uriniferous tubules of the nephrons.

Procedure

1. Using your text, charts, and reference books for orientation, locate the following organs on the dissectable torso. Be prepared to describe the location of each organ in anatomic terms (see Figure 18-1).
   a. Kidneys.   c. Urethra.
   b. Ureters.   d. Urinary bladder.
2. On the model of a longitudinal section through the kidney, locate the structures indicated in the keys to Figures 18-2 and 18-3.
3. Examine a slide of the kidney showing nephrons. Compare an observed nephron with Figure 18-4 showing a magnified view of a renal corpuscle and with Figure 18-5 showing (schematically) a complete nephron and its relationship to the circulatory system.

EXERCISE 18-B
DISSECTION OF THE URINARY
SYSTEM OF THE FETAL PIG

Objectives

To identify the urinary organs in the fetal pig; to compare them with the corresponding human structures.

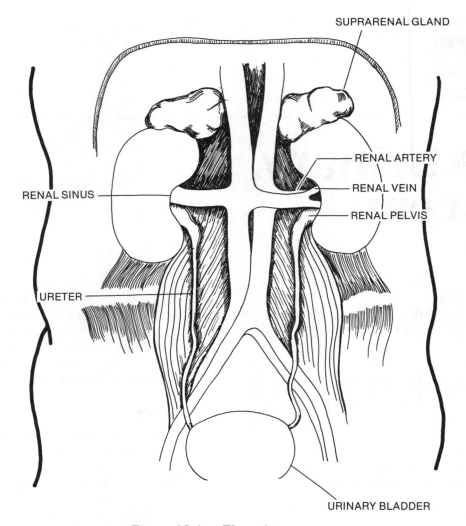

Figure 18-1. The urinary tract.

KEY TO FIGURE 18-2

1. adipose tissue
2. renal pelvis
3. major calyx
4. minor calyx
5. ureter
6. pyramid
7. calyces
8. renal medulla (the semicircle of pyramids)
9. renal papilla
10. renal cortex
11. renal column
12. renal capsule

Figure 18-2. Longitudinal section through the kidney.

247

KEY TO FIGURE 18-3

1. renal artery
2. renal vein
3. renal pelvis
4. ureter
5. calyces
6. arcuate artery and vein
7. interlobar artery and vein
8. interlobular artery and vein

KEY TO FIGURE 18-4

1. afferent arteriole
2. efferent arteriole
3. glomerulus
4. Bowman's capsule
5. uriniferous tubule (proximal convoluted tubule)

Figure 18-3.   Renal blood supply.

Figure 18-4.   The renal corpuscle.

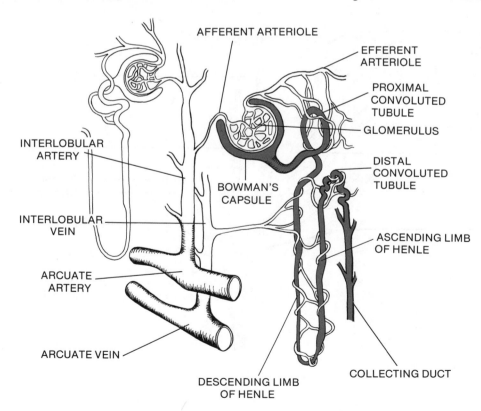

AFFERENT ARTERIOLE

EFFERENT ARTERIOLE

PROXIMAL CONVOLUTED TUBULE

GLOMERULUS

DISTAL CONVOLUTED TUBULE

ASCENDING LIMB OF HENLE

COLLECTING DUCT

INTERLOBULAR ARTERY

INTERLOBULAR VEIN

ARCUATE ARTERY

ARCUATE VEIN

BOWMAN'S CAPSULE

DESCENDING LIMB OF HENLE

Figure 18-5.   The nephron.

248

Materials

Fetal pig; dissecting board or tray; dissecting set.

Discussion

The organs in the urinary system of the fetal pig are very similar to those in the human. As you dissect the organs, be prepared to trace the path of urine from its site of production to the point at which it passes to the outside. The pig

kidney will be sectioned so that you can study its internal structure, since it is a good example of a typical mammalian kidney.

Procedure

1. Observe the paired kidneys on the dorsal body wall of the pig. Use Figure 18-6 as a guide.
2. Remove the peritoneum, which covers only the ventral surface, from the left kidney. Since the kidneys are separated

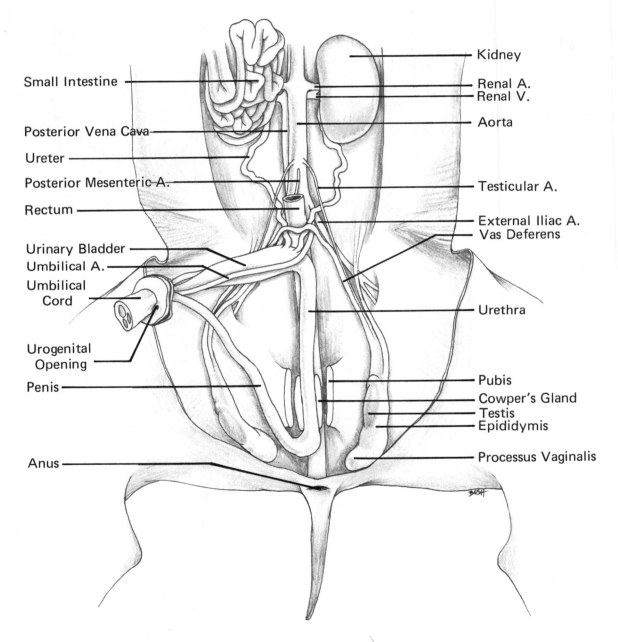

Figure 18-6. Ventral view of urinary system (with intestine pushed to the right) of the male fetal pig. (See Figure 20-12 for female fetal pig.)

from the abdominal organs by a layer of peritoneum, their location is described as being retroperitoneal.

3. Identify the **renal artery** and **renal vein,** which carry blood to and from the kidney.

4. Locate the **adrenal gland,** a narrow band immediately above and medial to each kidney.

5. Observe the **ureter,** the narrow, white, convoluted tube which drains the urine from each kidney. Trace the ureter from the **hilum,** the opening on the medial border of each kidney, to the **urinary bladder,** freeing it from the peritoneum. The urinary bladder is attached to the reflected ventral strip of the abdominal wall.

6. Observe the **umbilical arteries,** which lie lateral to the urinary bladder.

7. Locate the **urethra,** the duct that conducts urine from the posterior end of the bladder to the outside. The remainder of the urethra will be freed when the reproductive system is dissected.

8. Remove one kidney. Make a longitudinal (coronal) section through the kidney.
   a. The **renal capsule** is the thin layer of connective tissue around the outside of the kidney.
   b. The **renal cortex** is the outer light-brown layer of the kidney immediately beneath the capsule. This layer contains renal corpuscles.
   c. The next layer of the kidney, the **renal medulla,** contains the **pyramids.**
   d. Locate the **renal pelvis,** the funnel-shaped expansion of the ureter inside the **renal sinus,** which is the hollow interior of the kidney.
   e. Identify the **papillae** of the pyramids, which open into the **calyces** of the pelvis.
   f. Trace the renal artery into the kidney. Locate the **interlobar, arcuate,** and **interlobular** arteries. The corresponding veins should also be identified.

9. Replace the kidney in the abdominal cavity of the fetal pig.

EXERCISE 18-C
URINALYSIS

Objectives

To determine some of the characteristics of urine; to test for some abnormal constituents which may be present in urine; to use the tests in determining unknowns in urine specimens.

Materials

Cylinder (or large-diameter test tube); beakers; hydrometer; test tubes; test tube holder; concentrated nitric acid; Benedict's solution; Clinitest reagent tablets; powdered sulfur; Ketostix; Clinistix; stopwatch; Bili-Labstix.

Discussion

Specific gravity is an expression of the weight of a substance relative to the weight of an equal volume of water. Pure water, by definition, has a specific gravity of 1.000. The urinometer is a float containing a scale that indicates directly the specific gravity of the urine into which it is placed. It is necessary to correct the specific gravity for temperature, since the hydrometer is calibrated to read correctly only at 15 °C.

The color of normal urine varies from a light straw color to dark amber. Usually freshly voided urine is clear, but it may become cloudy on standing. The presence of certain drugs, bile pigments or their products, and blood will affect the color. A cloudy appearance of freshly voided urine is usually caused by the presence of pus or phosphates.

This exercise will also demonstrate the use of several common tests for the presence of albumin and glucose in urine. Although a slight amount of albuminuria is normal in approximately 5% of the population, it also occurs abnormally in many renal diseases, in pregnancy, in patients with hypertension, etc. Glycosuria occurs in diabetes mellitus as well as in certain other diseases. Benedict's solution in the form of Clinitest tablets is commonly used to detect the presence of reducing sugars in urine. This solution, however, is not specific for glucose, since it will give a positive reading with any reducing sugar. There are tests specific for the presence of glucose. For example, Bili-Labstix contains an enzyme that reacts specifically with glucose.

Ordinarily, ingested fats are oxidized in the body and form ketones (acetone and others). Upon further oxidation, they become carbon dioxide and water. If diabetes mellitus is present and the patient is unable to use glucose, a larger quantity of fat is oxidized to produce energy. As a result, ketones are produced in greater quantities than is normal and are usually excreted into the urine. Ketone bodies may also be found in the urine during starvation.

Hay's test for bile salts involves the addition of sulfur to urine. Since bile salts lower the surface tension of the water in urine, the presence of bile salts will cause the sulfur to sink.

PART 1. ANALYSIS OF A URINE SPECIMEN

Procedure

1. Place a portion of the urine specimen in a cylinder or a large-diameter test tube. The hydrometer must float freely.
2. By means of the hydrometer (see Figure 18-7), determine the specific gravity of the sample. Study Figure 18-7 to learn how to read the hydrometer. The top number (1.000) on the hydrometer is the specific gravity of water. Each horizontal line below the top represents one thousandth (0.001). Note that each number, such as 10 (really 1.010), is *above* the line for that number. Some hydrometers, such as the one pictured here, drop the 1.0 and just indicate 10 on the line; others indicate 1.010 for the same line. Take a reading to three decimal places.
3. Take the temperature of the urine specimen with a chemical thermometer. The hydrometer is calibrated to be ready at 15 °C. It is necessary to add 0.001 to the specific gravity reading for every 3 °C the temperature of urine is above 15 °C; subtract 0.001 from the specific gravity reading for every 3 °C it is below 15 °C. Record your determinations under Results and Questions. Pour the urine back into the original container for use in later tests.
4. Note the color and transparency of the urine specimen.
5. If the urine is cloudy, add a drop of concentrated nitric acid to a 5-ml portion of the urine specimen. This will dissolve

the phosphates of calcium and magnesium, which may cause cloudiness but not pus. Therefore, this test may be used to distinguish between a phosphate precipitate and pyuria.

6. Benedict's Test.
   a. To test for the presence of glucose, place 5 ml of Benedict's solution in a test tube.
   b. Add exactly 8 drops of urine and boil the solution for 2 minutes (or for about 5 minutes in a boiling water bath).
   c. A high concentration of phosphates may produce a white precipitate, whereas the precipitate of cuprous oxide in a positive Benedict's test is red and the solution may be green, yellow, orange, or red.
   d. If the solution remains blue, the test is negative; green is recorded as +, yellow as ++, orange as +++, and red as ++++.
7. Clinitest reagent tablets.
   a. Place 10 drops of water and 5 drops of urine in a test tube.
   b. Add one Clinitest tablet. The concentrated sodium hydroxide in the tablet generates heat so that the liquid will boil in the test tube. The color of the solution is graded as in Benedict's test.
8. Clinistix.
   a. Dip the test end of the strip briefly into the fresh urine. Tap the edge of strip against the side of the urine container to remove excess urine.
   b. Exactly *10 seconds* after removing the strip from the urine, compare the reagent side of the strip with the color chart.
   c. If the test is negative, the test area remains red. A positive test is indicated by a purple color in the test area. This test is specific for glucose in the urine.
   d. The presence of large amounts of ascorbic acid in the urine will interfere

Figure 18-7.   The hydrometer.

with this and the other dip tests for glucose.

9. Hay's Test for Bile Salts in Urine.
   a. Sprinkle a little finely powdered sulfur on the surface of cool urine.
   b. If the sulfur sinks at once, bile salts are present in the amount of 0.01% or more.
   c. If the sulfur sinks only after gentle agitation, bile salts are present in the amount of 0.0025% or more.
   d. If the sulfur remains floating even after gentle shaking, bile salts are absent.

10. Ketostix.
    a. Dip the test end of the strip in fresh urine and remove immediately. Tap the edge of the strip against the side of the container to remove excess urine.
    b. After exactly *15 seconds,* compare the color of the dipped end with the color chart.
    c. The strip will remain unchanged or will appear cream colored from wetting if the test is negative.
    d. In a positive test, the color will vary from pink to purple, depending on the amount of ketone bodies (aceto-acetic acid and acetone) present.

11. Bili-Labstix.
    This test detects the presence of protein, glucose, ketone bodies, bilirubin, and blood in urine as well as the pH of the specimen.
    a. Dip the strip into the urine, remove it immediately, and start the stopwatch or begin timing with a clock.
    b. Tap the edges of the strip against the side of the urine container to remove excess urine. This is necessary to prevent run-over of reagents.
    c. Compare test areas closely with the corresponding color charts on the bottle label. The test area farthest from the fingers is for blood. Be especially careful to compare the colors at the correct time.
       (1) Blood—read *25 seconds* after wetting. The blood test is highly sensitive to hemoglobin. It also gives a positive result if intact erythrocytes are present.
       (2) Bilirubin—read *20 seconds* after wetting.
       (3) Ketone bodies—read *15 seconds*

after wetting.
       (4) Glucose—read *30 seconds* after wetting. This test is specific for glucose.
       (5) Protein—read *immediately* or at any time up to 1 minute after dipping.
       (6) pH—read *immediately* or at any time up to 1 minute after dipping.

PART 2. ANALYSIS OF URINE SPECIMENS FOR UNKNOWNS

Discussion

In chemistry, when the composition of a specimen is not known, it may be designated an unknown. In this experiment, the unknowns will be urine specimens to which glucose, blood, ketone bodies, and albumin may be added. The glucose, blood, ketone bodies, and albumin may be added to any or all of three urine specimens, and in any combination. The student will analyze each of the specimens to determine which contain(s) the additives.

If the tests in Part 1 on the student's urine gave positive results for the presence of glucose, blood, ketone bodies, and/or albumin, the instructor should be informed; the urine of some other student should then be used for this experiment.

Procedure

1. Number three clean test tubes (1, 2, and 3) near the top.
2. Add 10 ml of urine to each tube.
3. Take the tubes to the instructor to have glucose, blood, ketone bodies, and/or albumin introduced into the specimens.
4. Test your specimens to determine to which tube, if any, the glucose, blood, ketone bodies, and albumin have been added. Record your results in the table provided under Results and Questions.

EXERCISE 18-D
MICROSCOPIC EXAMINATION OF SEDIMENT OBTAINED FROM URINE

Objective

To examine sediment obtained from centrifuged urine.

Materials

Centrifuge tubes; centrifuge; slide; cover glass; Sedi-Stain; microscope.

Discussion

The normal sediment in urine varies considerably with the sex of the subject, the time the specimen was taken, the manner in which the specimen was collected, the pH, and how the specimen was handled following collection. To be of clinical significance, the specimen should be obtained by catheterization because of the possibility of contamination by any other means of collection.

To examine the sediment, the urine is centrifuged to concentrate all solids. By adopting a standard amount of urine (usually 10 ml), it is possible to report the results in a meaningful manner.

The urine sediment will usually contain some squamous epithelial cells. These originate primarily in the mucosa of the bladder and urethra, but may also originate in the vaginal mucosa of females. Various crystals may also be present. Calcium oxalate and yellow uric acid crystals are common in acid urine. Usually a few leukocytes are seen in the sediment; however, amounts greater than 6 to 10 per high power field *in the male* are regarded with suspicion and may be diagnostic of a urinary tract infection. Slightly higher amounts are considered normal in the female because of sloughing from the vaginal mucosa. Erythrocytes are usually not present.

Bacteria are not normally present in freshly voided, properly handled urine; however, if the specimen is not obtained in a sterile manner (catheterization and a sterile container), contamination results. If a contaminated specimen is left standing at room temperature for any length of time, bacteria will multiply rapidly. It is possible that both motile and nonmotile bacteria will be observed in this experiment. If bacteria are found in large amounts in a freshly voided specimen that is examined immediately, a urinary tract infection should be suspected.

Casts are the result of solidification of albumin that has entered the uriniferous tubule; they are subsequently washed out by the urine. They are hollow, retain the shape of the tubule, and may contain any material which was lying free in the tubule or loosely attached to its wall. Types of casts include: hyaline, granular, RBC, WBC, epithelial, and others. Casts may be recognized by their parallel sides and rounded ends. Casts are usually associated with albuminuria and may indicate the presence of kidney disease.

Ova of parasites, sperm, trichimonads, yeasts, hair, and paper fibers may also be present in the urine.

Procedure

1. Place 10 ml of fresh urine in a centrifuge tube and centrifuge for 5 minutes. (Precaution: Make certain the centrifuge is balanced with another tube containing 10 ml of urine or water.)
2. Pour out all the urine possible (do this quickly without shaking the tube or inverting it for more than a moment).
3. Add 2 drops of stain (such as Sedi-Stain) to the sediment in the tube. Thoroughly mix the contents of the tube with the stain by tapping briskly on the bottom of the tube with the index finger.
4. Transfer 1 drop of the stained sediment onto a clean glass slide.
5. Cover the drop of sediment with a cover glass and examine it under the microscope, using both the low and high power objectives.
6. Make sketches of the substances observed in the sediment.
7. Identify as many of the substances in the sediment as possible by comparing them with Figures 18-8 through 18-11. Answer the questions under Results and Questions.

Figure 18-8. Urine sediment: (a) squamous epithelial cells, (b) blood corpuscles (leukocytes and erythrocytes), and (c) bacteria.

Figure 18-9.   Crystals common to acid urine: (a) uric acid crystals and (b) calcium oxalate crystals.

Figure 18-10.   Casts: (a) finely granular cast and (b) epithelial cell.

Figure 18-11.   Triple phosphate crystals (common to alkaline urine).

SELF-TEST — URINARY SYSTEM

Directions

See Chapter 1, Self-Test, page 9.

1.   The term "glycosuria" refers to the presence of **sugar** in the urine.

2.   Inflammation of the urinary bladder is called **cystocele.**

3.   Anuria means **scanty** urine production.

4.   **Oliguria** refers to frequency of urination at night.

5.   The general function of a diuretic drug is to **decrease** the excretion of urine.

6.   The pyramids are located in the **medulla** of the kidney.

7.   The renal pelvis opens directly into the **urinary bladder.**

8.   The components of urine enter Bowman's capsule from the blood by the process of **osmosis.**

9.   Urea is formed in the **kidneys.**

10.   Sugar is normally **excreted** by the kidneys after its removal from the blood.

11.   The formation of urea is accomplished by the breakdown of **amino acids.**

12.   If the **pancreas** is malfunctioning, sugar might be found in the urine.

13. Renal blood vessels enter the kidney at the **hilus.**

14. The kidneys lie between the **periosteum** and the posterior body wall.

15. Urination is termed **micturition.**

16. The smooth muscle in the wall of the bladder is called the **detrusor** muscle.

17. **Stones** are materials (often albumin) that have been the form of the tubules in which they are molded.

18. The kidneys excrete **only a small** amount of the water and other substances they receive from the blood.

19. The tuft of capillaries in Bowman's capsule is known as the **glomerulus.**

20. The efferent arteriole has a **larger** diameter than the afferent arteriole.

21. Urine contains a **higher** concentration of urea than blood plasma.

22. The wastes of metabolic processes include **salts** that pass out of the body through the lungs.

23. The **urinary bladder** is superior in location to each kidney.

24. Glucose and amino acids are reabsorbed by the part of the nephron known as the **glomerulus.**

25. The connective tissue surrounding the outside of the kidney is called the **capsule.**

26. The urinary bladder serves to **concentrate** urine.

27. The function of the loop of Henle is to reabsorb **water.**

28. The fundamental microscopic unit of structure of the kidney is the **calyx.**

29. Protein is present in blood but absent from the **glomerular filtrate.**

30. The term albuminuria refers to the presence of **pus** in the urine.

31. Because of the size of the molecules, fats are usually **found** in urine.

32. The kidneys filter approximately **300** quarts of fluid each day.

33. The pressure of blood is **higher** in the glomerulus than in other systemic capillaries.

34. The renal **veins** rapidly subdivide to form arterioles.

19

The Endocrine System

EXERCISE 19-A
ENDOCRINE GLANDS

Objectives

To learn the locations and functions of endocrine glands.

Materials

Dissectable torso; brain model showing hypophysis and pineal gland; anatomical charts; text and other references; fetal pig; embalmed cat.

Discussion

The secretions of endocrine glands (containing hormones) diffuse into the blood, which transports them to the structures acted upon. In contrast to these ductless glands, exocrine glands have ducts which convey the glandular secretions to a surface inside or outside the body. For example, the secretions of the salivary glands are carried by ducts to the buccal cavity.

To be classed as a hormone, a compound must meet the following criteria: (1) It is produced by a particular endocrine gland; (2) removal of the gland, or the part of the gland producing the compound, results in failure of some other organ to develop or function normally; (3) in the absence of the endocrine gland, artificial replacement of the hormone in the body restores the target organ to its normal size and functional capacity. Chemically, hormones are either steroids or proteins or are derived from proteins.

In the autonomic nervous system, impulses traveling over preganglionic fibers stimulate the secretion of acetylcholine at the synapses with ganglion cells. The compound is also released at postganglionic parasympathetic terminals and by most of the postganglionic sympathetic fibers that supply smooth muscle and sweat glands in the skin. All such fibers are known as cholinergic fibers; these fibers inhibit the action of certain target organs, such as the heart and the sphincters of the gastrointestinal tract, and stimulate the action of others, such as the muscle in the gastrointestinal tract, bronchioles, the urinary bladder, and the gall bladder. Sympathin, which is the same as norepinephrine (noradrenalin), is released at the postganglionic sympathetic terminals (with the exceptions noted above). These fibers are known as adrenergic fibers; they are excitatory in certain areas, such as the heart, blood vessels in the abdominal viscera, and sphincters, and inhibitory in the gastrointestinal tract and urinary bladder. While these fibers are not endocrine glands, the compounds secreted are chemical coordinators which act in a manner similar to hormones. The endocrine and nervous systems are the two main integrating mechanisms of the body. The normal functioning of these two systems results in the parts of the body working together as an integrated whole.

Procedure

1. Using your text, references, and anatomical charts as resource materials, lo-

255

cate the glands shown on the following page on the disectable torso and the model of the brain:
   a. Hypophysis (pituitary)
   b. Ovaries
   c. Pancreas
   d. Parathyroids
   e. Pineal gland
   f. Suprarenals (adrenals)
   g. Testes
   h. Thymus
   i. Thyroid
2. Locate the following glands in the fetal pig and, in the space provided, give a brief, precise anatomical description of their location:
   a. Hypophysis

   b. Ovaries

   c. Pancreas

   d. Parathyroids

   e. Suprarenals (adrenals)

   f. Testes

   g. Thymus

   h. Thyroid

3. An embalmed cat will be dissected to show each of the glands listed under step 2. The location of each will be pointed out by the instructor. Following the demonstration, compare the glands of the fetal pig with those of the cat. Note similarities and differences in the sizes and locations of the glands. Use care to avoid damaging the glands in the cat.
4. Answer the questions and complete the tables under Results and Questions. Figure 19-1 may be used as a self-test.

EXERCISE 19-B
EFFECTS OF INSULIN ON A FISH

Objective

To observe the effects of insulin on a fish.

Materials

Commercial insulin; two 500-cc beakers; glucose; 1½- to 2-inch fish ("sunfish" or "blue-gill" of genus *Lepomis* are preferred; goldfish may also be used, but results are more variable).

Discussion

A fish is a convenient animal in which to observe the effects of insulin and, since the action of this hormone on the fish involves the same mechanism as that in humans, the results obtained in the following experiment should provide insights concerning administration of insulin to humans.

Insulin aids in maintaining the physiological balance between glycogen stored in the liver and muscles and glucose in the blood. When insufficient insulin is produced by the islets of Langerhans (found in the pancreas), as is the case in diabetes mellitus, injections of insulin are usually administered. Care must be exercised to avoid giving too much insulin, since this results in such a decrease in the level of blood glucose that the patient goes into shock. If the nervous system is to function properly, the blood glucose level must be adequate.

Procedure

1. Place a small (1½ to 2 inches in length) fish in a beaker containing 200 cc of water to which 10 drops of commercial insulin have been added.
2. Observe the fish for the following symptoms that occur as a result of diffusion of the insulin through the gill membranes of the fish into its circulatory system: extreme irritability, convulsive motions, and finally coma (state of insensibility).
3. When the fish goes into a coma, place it in a second beaker containing 200 ml of water to which a half teaspoon of glucose has been added.
4. The fish should return to normal, and it may then be placed back in the aquarium.

257

KEY TO FIGURE 19-1

1. pituitary
   (hypophysis)
2. thyroid
3. thymus
4. suprarenals
   (adrenals)
5. pancreas
6. ovaries
7. testes
8. parathyroids
9. pineal

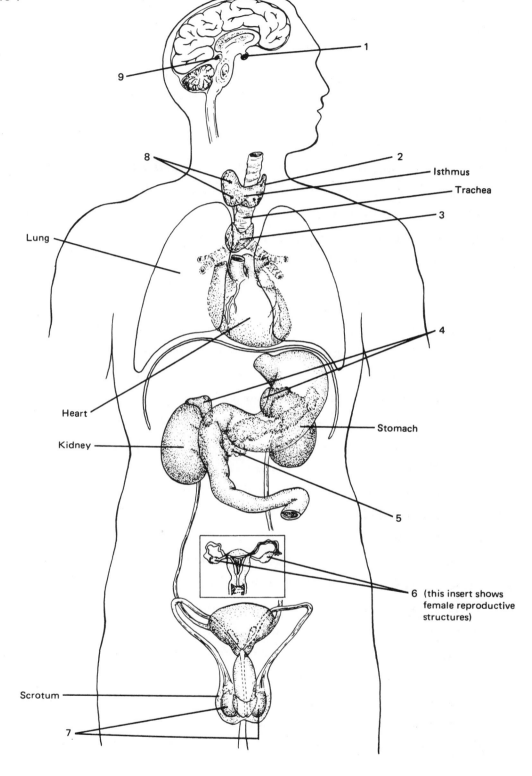

Figure 19-1.   Location of endocrine glands and associated structures.

SELF-TEST — ENDOCRINE SYSTEM

Directions

See Chapter 1, Self-Test, page 9.

1. Hypofunction of the thyroid gland in infancy is called **myxedema.**
2. Diabetes insipidus is caused by hypofunction of the **anterior pituitary gland.**
3. Tetany is caused by hyposecretion of the **thyroid gland.**
4. Insulin is not given by mouth because it is **digested by enzymes in the alimentary canal.**
5. The somatotropic hormone is produced by the **anterior pituitary gland.**
6. Goiter is a condition characterized by excessive growth of the **thymus.**
7. **ADH** stimulates the production of the adrenal cortical hormones.
8. A disease resulting from failure of the nephrons to reabsorb water is called **diabetes mellitus.**
9. Secretions of the **adrenal** glands control calcium metabolism.
10. An exophthalmic goiter is a result of **hyperthyroidism.**
11. The **pineal** gland is located in the sella turcica.
12. **Hypertrophy** means an increase in the size of a structure.
13. True dwarfism results from lack of the **parathyroid** hormone.
14. Protruding eyeballs may indicate **hyperthyroidism.**
15. Steroids are formed by the **adrenal cortex.**
16. As a person grows older, the thymus **remains the same size.**
17. Adrenalin **decreases** the consumption of oxygen.
18. The PBI test is a measure of **thyroid** function.
19. The hormone that causes the gall bladder to contract is **secretin.**
20. A symptom of diabetes mellitus is **alkalosis.**
21. ACTH is produced by the **adrenal cortex.**
22. Iodine is needed for the production of **parathormone.**
23. Acromegaly is caused by **a lack of thyroxin.**
24. Increased secretion of ADH may result in **diuresis.**
25. The **lactogenic hormone** causes the ejection of milk from the mammary glands.
26. Oxytocin is stored by the **posterior pituitary gland.**
27. The hormone controlling male secondary sex characteristics is **FSH.**
28. The adrenal **medulla** is essential for life.
29. Epinephrine stimulates **glycogenesis.**
30. A lack of **parathormone** can cause muscle twitches.
31. Dwarfism, gigantism, and acromegaly result from a defect in the **thyroid gland.**
32. The interstitial cells produce **ICSH.**
33. The hormones of the adrenal medulla have the same function as the **parasympathetic** nervous system.
34. The absence of insulin results in the formation of **ketone bodies.**
35. **Cretinism** is more common where there is a lack of iodine in the soil.

20

The Reproductive System

EXERCISE 20-A
THE HUMAN MALE
REPRODUCTIVE SYSTEM

Objectives

To identify the location and function of the structures of the male reproductive system.

Materials

Dissectable torso; anatomic charts; references; slides of the testis and epididymis.

Discussion

The male reproductive system consists of the two male gonads (testes), the ducts that conduct the sperm to the outside, and the accessory structures (glands and penis). Spermatogenesis begins at puberty under the influence of hormones and continues throughout life.

Procedure

1. Examine a slide of a cross section through the human testis under both low and high power of the microscope. To locate the testis, compare the slide with Figure 20-1 (since some slides contain the epididymis on the same slide). The seminiferous tubules (one of which is illustrated in Figure 20-1) should fill the field.
2. Examine the shape of the seminiferous tubules. These are approximately circular, since each is a cross section through a long tubule (see Figure 20-3).
3. Draw a portion of the field that includes three seminiferous tubules with the interstitial cells in between.
4. Study the wall of one seminiferous tubule. The cells here are in various stages of meiosis. The cells near the outside of the tubule are called **spermatogonia.** These

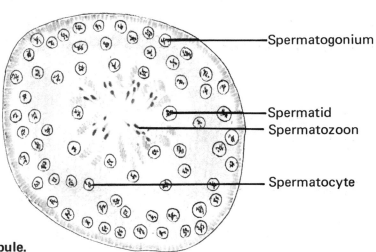

Figure 20-1.
Cross section through a seminiferous tubule.

Spermatogonium

Spermatid
Spermatozoon

Spermatocyte

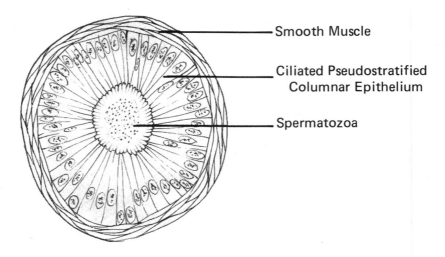

Figure 20-2.   Cross section through the epididymis.

KEY TO FIGURE 20-3

1. vas efferens
2. tunica vaginalis
3. tunica albuginea
4. seminiferous tubule
5. septum
6. epididymis
7. vas deferens
8. rete testis

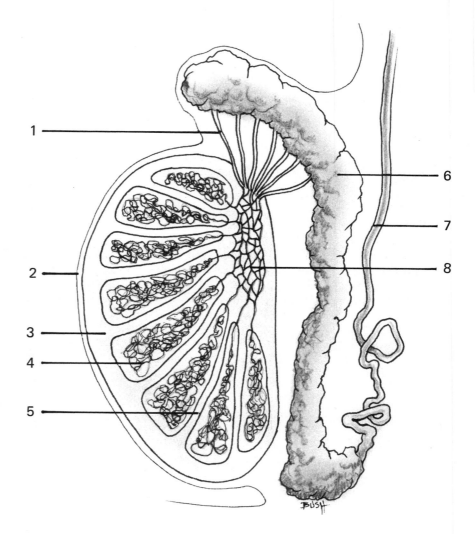

Figure 20-3.   Vertical section through the testis and adjacent structures.

cells begin the process of spermatogenesis (sperm production) by dividing by mitosis several times and enlarging to form **primary spermatocytes,** located closer to the center of the tubule. The primary spermatocytes undergo meiosis and form **secondary spermatocytes,** and finally **spermatids.** (Study Figure 20-5, which compares spermatogenesis and oogenesis.) The spermatids are the cells closest to the lumen of the tubule. These mature into **spermatozoa** (sperm) located in the vicinity of the spermatids.

5. Draw a strip of cells from the outside to the center of one seminiferous tubule on your drawing of the seminiferous tubule.
6. Study the slide of the epididymis (or use the portion of the epididymis on the slide of the testis). Identify each of the parts listed in Figure 20-2. Note the sperm in the lumen of the tubule. Compare the structure of the wall of the epididymis with that of the wall of the seminiferous tubule.
7. The testis, the epididymis, and the beginning of the vas deferens are located in the scrotum. These structures and some of their parts are indicated on Figure 20-3, which may be used as a self-test.
8. Using your text or other references, locate the structures on the key to Figure 20-4 on the dissectable torso and compare them with Figure 20-4, which may be used as a self-test.

EXERCISE 20-B
THE HUMAN FEMALE REPRODUCTIVE SYSTEM

Objectives

To become familiar with the location and function of the structures in the female reproductive system.

Materials

Dissectable torso; anatomic charts; references; slides of the ovary.

Discussion

The female reproductive system consists of female gonads (ovaries), Fallopian tubes, uterus, vagina, and accessory structures. The process of oogenesis (egg production), which actually begins before birth, ceases at the time of climacteric, usually between ages 45 and 50 years.

Procedure

1. Obtain two slides of the human ovary, one showing the Graafian follicle and the other containing the corpus luteum.
2. First study the slide of the ovary showing the Graafian follicle. This slide shows various stages in the development of the follicle. Locate a **primordial follicle** under high power. This structure contains a large immature ovum with a conspicuous nucleus and is surrounded by a single layer of follicle cells. Mark off a sheet of drawing paper into fourths. Draw the primordial follicle in the first area.
3. Returning to low power, locate an **immature follicle.** The follicle cells have divided many times and secreted follicular fluid. The immature ovum (which may not be visible, depending on how the follicle was sectioned) is located at one end of the follicle and is surrounded by follicle cells. Draw this structure in the second area on your paper.
4. On the same slide, locate a **mature (Graafian) follicle** and draw it in the third area of your paper. This is a very large follicle filled with clear fluid.
5. On the second slide of the ovary, locate the **corpus luteum.** This structure appears after ovulation. The wall of the follicle collapses and is thrown into folds. The cavity assumes an irregular stellate shape. The cells become filled with a yellow fluid. Draw this structure in the fourth area of your drawing paper.
6. The stages in oogenesis are similar to those in spermatogenesis. The oogonia multiply before the birth of a female child. At the time of birth, the primordial follicles contain the primary oocytes. These mature at various times during the reproductive years of the woman. Approximately twenty primordial follicles begin to develop each menstrual month; however, usually only one matures into a Graafian follicle and releases an egg.
7. Compare the appearance of structures on your slides with Figure 20-6, which may be used as a self-test.

262

1. vas deferens
2. pubis
3. prostate gland
4. corpus cavernosum urethrae
5. urethra
6. corpus cavernosum

7. prepuce
8. glans penis
9. ureter
10. sacrum
11. urinary bladder
12. seminal vesicle
13. ejaculatory duct

14. rectum
15. Cowper's (bulbourethral) gland
16. external anal sphincter
17. anus
18. tunica vaginalis
19. testis
20. scrotum

Figure 20-4.   Parasagittal section through male pelvis.

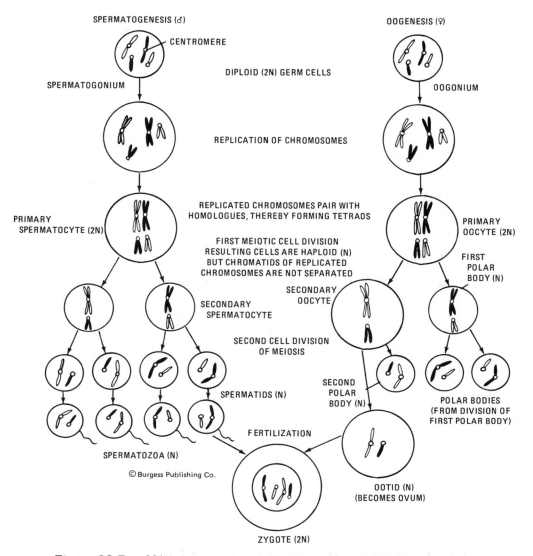

Figure 20-5. Meiosis: a comparison of spermatogenesis and oogenesis.

KEY TO FIGURE 20-6

1. primordial follicles
2. blood vessels
3. immature follicle
4. follicular fluid
5. corpus luteum
6. Graafian follicle
7. immature ovum

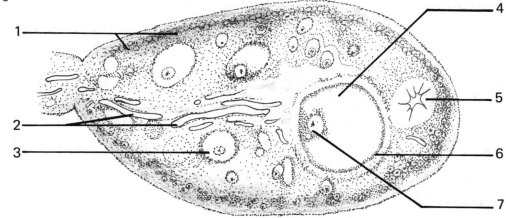

Figure 20-6. Diagrammatic section through human ovary.

8. Using a model, wall chart, your text, or other references, identify each of the structures indicated in the key to Figure 20-7 and compare with Figure 20-7, which may be used as a self-test.

9. Using your text or other references, locate the structures listed in the keys to Figures 20-8, 20-9, and 20-10 on the dissectable torso (where possible) and compare with the figures.

KEY TO FIGURE 20-7

1. fimbriated opening
2. ovary
3. Fallopian tube
4. fundus
5. uterine cavity

6. urinary bladder
7. urethra
8. labium minus
9. labium majus
10. sacrum

11. rectum
12. cervix
13. rectouterine
   excavation
   (cul-De-sac of Douglas)

14. external os
15. fornix
16. vagina
17. external anal sphincter
18. anus

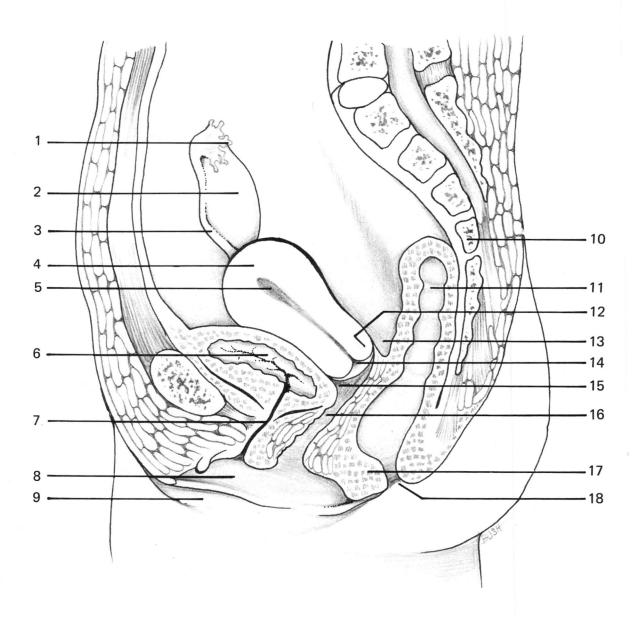

Figure 20-7. Median sagittal section through female reproductive organs.

KEY TO FIGURE 20-8

1. fundus
2. ovary
3. ovarian ligament
4. endometrium
5. body (uterine) cavity
6. myometrium
7. Fallopian tube
8. fimbriated opening

9. ovary (sectioned)
10. internal os
11. cervical canal
12. external os (mouth of uterus)
13. cervix
14. fornix
15. vagina

Figure 20-8.   Coronal section through female reproductive organs.

KEY TO FIGURE 20-9

1. prepuce of clitoris
2. external urethral orifice
3. labium minus
4. labium majus
5. mons pubis
6. clitoris
7. vestibule
8. vaginal orifice
9. hymen
10. perineum
11. anus

Figure 20-9.   Female external genital organs (perineal view).

266

KEY TO FIGURE 20-10

1. clavicle
2. pectoralis major
3. adipose tissue
4. skin
5. intercostal muscles
6. rib
7. tubuli lactiferi (milk ducts)
8. nipple
9. areola
10. glandular tissue

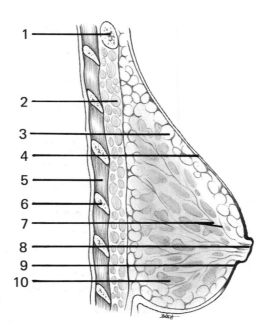

Figure 20-10.   Sagittal section through the female breast.

EXERCISE 20-C
THE ENDOMETRIAL
(MENSTRUAL) CYCLE

Objectives

To identify the phases of the endometrial cycle; to learn the origins and the functions of the hormones involved in the endometrial cycle.

Materials

Textbook and/or other references.

Discussion

Menarche, the beginning of a functional menstrual cycle, usually starts between ages 12 and 15 years. Menstruation is the periodic disintegration of the highly vascular endometrial lining of the uterus. The endometrial tissue is discharged along with blood through the vagina about every 28 days. The period of discharge lasts an average of 4 to 5 days. Normally, menstruation does not occur during pregnancy, and it stops permanently at menopause (which usually takes place between 45 and 50 years of age).

In the endometrial cycle (see Figure 20-11), the preovulatory phase (the time before ovulation) is often from days 6 to 13. However, this phase may be much longer. The time of ovula-

tion depends on the duration of the preovulatory phase. For example, in a 32-day cycle, the preovulatory phase would probably last until cycle day 17 or 18 and ovulation would then take place on the 18th or 19th cycle day (instead of day 14 or 15). The length of the postovulatory or premenstrual phase, on the other hand, is fairly constant and usually lasts 14 cycle days. For example, in the 28-day cycle illustrated in the diagram (Figure 20-11), the postovulatory phase is from days 15 to 28. Thus, any differences in the length of the total menstrual cycle are due primarily to differences in the duration of the preovulatory, rather than the postovulatory, phase.

During the preovulatory phase, a follicle containing an immature ovum (egg) begins to develop in response to the presence of follicle stimulating hormone (FSH), a secretion of the anterior lobe of the pituitary gland. The follicle soon begins to secrete the hormone estrogen, which stimulates the initial formation of the endometrium. After ovulation (during the postovulatory phase), the anterior pituitary secretes luteinizing hormone (LH), which causes the follicle to thicken into the corpus luteum. This structure produces the hormone progesterone (and estrogens), which continues the development of the endometrium (and maintains it for about seven or eight months in the event of pregnancy). An ovum will die if it is not

Figure 20-11. Diagram of the endometrial cycle.

fertilized within about 24 hours after ovulation. It fertilization does not occur, the pituitary gland (a few days after ovulation) does not provide enough hormones (e.g., LH) to maintain the corpus luteum which, in turn, ceases to provide hormones for maintaining the endometrium. The result is menses.

In Figure 20-11, the slanted line between days 5 and 28 represents the buildup of the endometrium. The slanted line between days 1 and 5 represents the disintegration of the endometrium. The dotted line with the word "pregnancy" represents the maintenance of the endometrium during pregnancy.

Procedure

1. Using your text and/or some other references, define each of the following:
   a. Menses. _____
   _____
   b. Preovulation. _____
   _____
   c. Premenstrual. _____
   _____
   d. Postovulation. _____
   _____
   e. Endometrium. _____
   _____
   f. Graafian follicle. _____
   _____
   g. Corpus luteum. _____
   _____
   h. Anterior pituitary. _____
   _____
   i. Ovulation. _____
   _____

2. Determine which hormones are secreted during the preovulation phase and record them on Figure 20-11.

3. Determine which hormones are secreted during the postovulation phase and record them on Figure 20-11.

EXERCISE 20-D
THE PLACENTA

Objectives

To identify and learn the structures of the placenta.

Materials

Model of placenta; preserved fetus with umbilical cord and placenta; text and/or other references.

Discussion

The placenta serves as an organ of nutrition, respiration, and excretion for the developing individual. It also serves as a temporary endocrine gland. The chorionic portion (see Figure 20-12) of the placenta secretes chorionic gonadotropin, a hormone that maintains the functioning of the corpus luteum. The placenta also produces estrogens and progesterone.

Procedure

1. Study Figure 20-12, which shows a portion of the placenta.
2. Compare Figure 20-12 with the model of the placenta, with the preserved fetus, and with drawings of this organ in your text and/or other references. As you study the placenta, note the following:
   a. The **trophoblast,** which develops an outer and an inner layer.

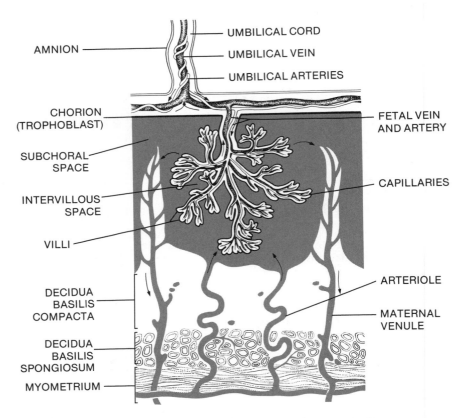

Figure 20-12. Section of placenta (arrows indicate direction of flow of blood). Maternal blood is shaded.

b. The **placental villi,** which grow from the inner layer of the trophoblast.

c. The **chorion,** which includes the trophoblast and its villi; it is the outer fetal membrane.

d. The **umbilical arteries,** which lead into capillaries in the chorionic villi and which carry waste materials from the embryo.

e. The **marginal sinuses** and **intervillous spaces,** where the mother's blood surrounds the villi.

f. The **maternal arterioles** and **venules,** which carry blood to and from the marginal sinuses and intervillous spaces.

g. The **umbilical vein,** which carries oxygenated blood and nutrients from the placenta to the embryo.

h. The **umbilical cord,** which contains the umbilical blood vessels. Note that it does not contain any nerves.

i. The **amnion,** which is a fetal membrane that rests against the chorion.

The amnion is filled with amnionic fluid in which the embryo floats.

EXERCISE 20-E DISSECTION OF THE REPRODUCTIVE SYSTEM OF THE FETAL PIG

Objectives

To identify the reproductive organs of the fetal pig and to compare them with the corresponding human structures.

Materials

Fetal pig; dissecting set; dissecting pan.

Discussion

The reproductive organs of the fetal pig are similar to those of the human. Note, however, the differences in the structure of the uterus and the lack of an ejaculatory duct in the male.

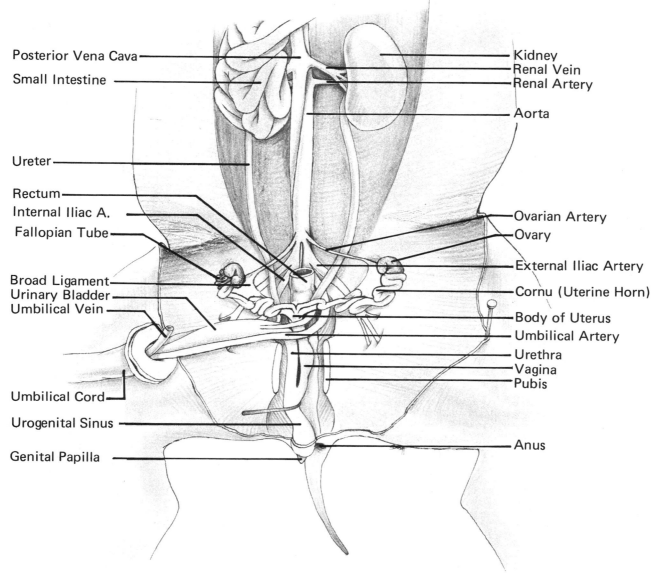

Figure 20-13.   Reproductive organs of the female fetal pig (with intestine and urethra pulled to the right and right ovary turned to the left).

Although you will dissect the reproductive system of only one sex, you are responsible for that of both sexes. Therefore, carefully study the reproductive structures on a fetal pig of the opposite sex.

Procedure

PART 1. THE FEMALE REPRODUCTIVE SYSTEM

1. Use Figure 20-13 as a guide in your dissection. Identify the **ovaries,** a pair of

small, light-colored oval bodies located posterior to the kidneys.

2. The **uterine tubes (Fallopian tubes)** are very small, highly convoluted tubes lying on the dorsal surface of the ovaries. The expanded end of the Fallopian tube, which partially covers the ovary and picks up the eggs from the ovary, is called the **ostium.**

3. Trace the Fallopian tubes until you reach a larger tube immediately next to each ovary. These tubes, the **uterine horns** or **cornua,** are the beginning of the uterus. The eggs are carried through the Fallopian

tubes to the uterine horns where they develop. The fetuses tend to be equally spaced throughout the two horns.

4. The two horns unite in the midline to form the **body of the uterus**, which lies dorsal to the urethra. The **broad ligament** can be seen running laterally from the body of the uterus to the uterine horns.

5. To dissect the rest of the female reproductive system, the pelvic cavity must be exposed. Remove the skin from the ventral pelvis and cut through the pelvic muscles and the pubic symphysis in the midventral line. Cut with care, since the urethra lies immediately beneath the pubis.

6. Locate the **urethra,** the tube carrying urine from the urinary bladder.

7. Dorsal to the urethra identify the **vagina,** the tube leading from the posterior end of the uterus.

8. Separate the urethra from the vagina. Toward the posterior end, the vagina and urethra unite to form a common passage called the **urogenital sinus (vulva),** which opens to the outside. An external **genital papilla** is located on the external surface at the opening of the urogenital sinus.

9. The lateral boundaries of the urogenital sinus are folds called the **labia.** These unite ventrally to form the genital papilla.

10. Locate the **rectum,** the continuation of the large intestine, dorsal to the vagina.

PART 2. THE MALE REPRODUCTIVE SYSTEM

1. Locate the **scrotum,** the sac visible under the skin ventral to the anus. Early in fetal development the testes are located below the kidneys; however, they migrate before birth through the inguinal canal into the scrotum.

2. Locate the **inguinal canals,** two openings in the abdominal wall, by tracing the internal spermatic (testicular) arteries posteriorly until they pass through the canals.

3. To expose the remainder of the male reproductive organs, cut through the skin in the midventral line ventral to the pubic symphysis. Cut through the scrotum carefully, to avoid damaging the structures contained within.

4. Using Figure 20-14 as a guide, locate both the left and right **processus vaginalis,** large white sacs on each side that contain the testes; these may not completely fill the processus vaginalis at this stage of development. This structure is an evagination of the peritoneum that precedes the descent of the testes and surrounds them.

5. Pass a probe from the abdominal cavity through the inguinal canal and note that this emerges inside the processus vaginalis.

6. Cut open one of the sacs to expose the **testis.** The **epididymis** should be located along the medial side of the testis. This begins at the cranial end of the testis and extends to its caudal end. Identify the **gubernaculum,** the band of tissue that extends from the posterior end of the epididymis to the scrotal wall. This helps pull the testis posteriorly.

7. The **vas deferens** carries the sperm from the epididymis through the inguinal canal to empty into the urethra. Trace the vas deferens through the inguinal canal to the urethra, noting how it loops over the ureter and enters the dorsal surface of the urethra.

8. Locate the **penis,** the long muscular tube lying just under the skin immediately posterior to the umbilical cord and the urogenital opening in the midventral strip of the abdominal wall. Remove the overlying skin so that the penis is exposed.

9. Now move the penis to one side of the midventral line and cut through the midventral portion of the pelvic muscles and the pubic symphysis. Spread the legs apart to expose the pelvic cavity. The **urethra** should now be visible emerging from the bladder.

10. Separate the **rectum** from the urethra and trace both tubes to the outside.

11. Identify the large pair of **bulbourethral** or **Cowper's glands,** each of which is located at one side of the urethra near the anus.

EXERCISE 20-F EMBRYOLOGY

Objective

To study various stages of development before birth.

Materials

Slides of starfish embryology; series of preserved human fetuses.

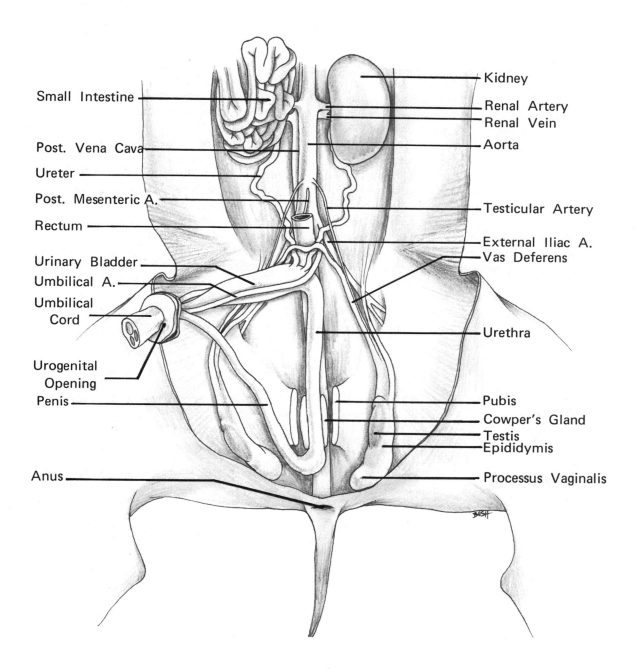

Figure 20-14. Ventral view of urinary system and reproductive organs of the male fetal pig (with intestine pushed to the right).

272

Discussion

The stages in early embryology will be studied in the starfish. The stages in human embryology are similar, although not identical.

Procedure

1. Obtain three slides of starfish embryology (cleavage stages, blastula, and gastrula). Compare all structures observed with those in Figure 20-15.
2. After fertilization occurs, the fertilized egg divides repeatedly by mitosis. These cells normally remain attached together. The slide entitled "Cleavage stages" contains the fertilized egg and the early cleavage stages. Locate the **zygote,** the 2-, 4-, 8-, and 16-cell stages. Observe the **fertilization membrane** surrounding the fertilized egg and the early stages of cleavage. Observe the size of the fertilized egg and the size of the young embryo.

3. After a number of cleavage divisions, a solid ball of cells (the **morula**) is formed. Locate this structure on the slide.
4. The cells in the solid ball soon move to the outside, forming a hollow ball or blastula. On the slide entitled "Starfish blastula," locate a sectioned **blastula** showing the cavity in the center.
5. Soon after the formation of the blastula, the ball becomes indented at one end. This invagination produces a two-layered embryo. Locate this stage **(gastrula)** on the slide entitled "Starfish gastrula."
6. Study the stages of human development exemplified by specimens present in the laboratory. Note the age at which the nails and hair develop. Study Figures 20-16 through 20-19, which show stages in human development.
7. Examine Figure 20-20, which shows the position of a full-term fetus in the uterus.

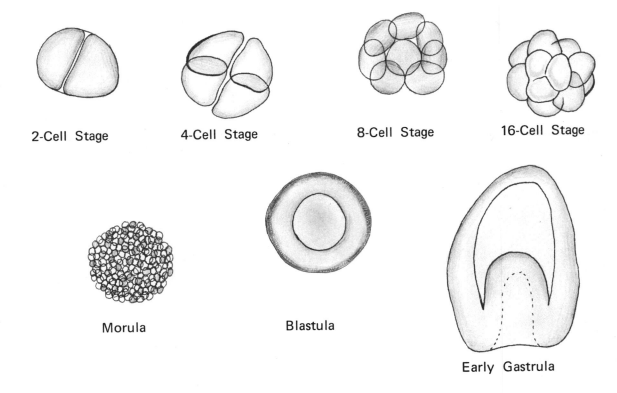

2-Cell Stage   4-Cell Stage   8-Cell Stage   16-Cell Stage

Morula   Blastula   Early Gastrula

Figure 20-15. Stages of starfish embryology.

Figure 20-16.   Twenty-six day old embryo.

Figure 20-17.   Thirty-four day old embryo.

Figure 20-18.   Forty-three day old embryo.

Figure 20-19.   Fifty-six day old embryo.

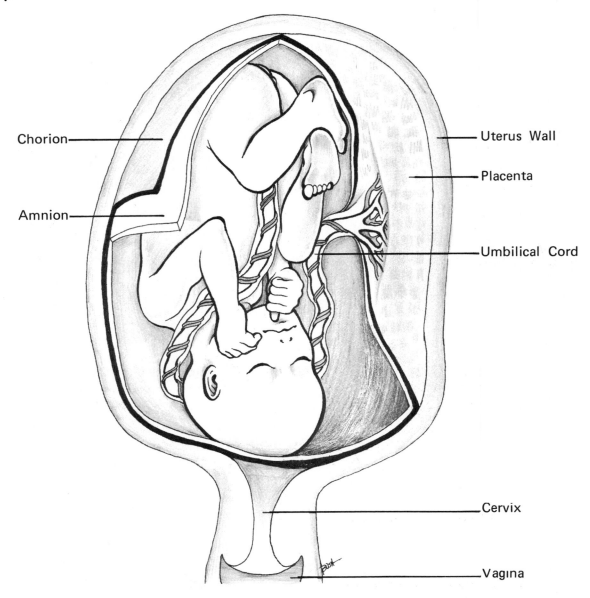

Chorion

Amnion

Uterus Wall

Placenta

Umbilical Cord

Cervix

Vagina

Figure 20-20.   Full-term human fetus.

SELF-TEST — REPRODUCTIVE SYSTEM

Directions

See Chapter 1, Self-Test, page 9.

1. The sperm cell on its way to the exterior of the male body follows this course: **seminiferous tubule, vas deferens, epididymis, urethra.**

2. An ovum on its way to the exterior of the female body follows this course: **ovary, Fallopian tube, uterus, vagina.**

3. A zygote is a **follicle.**

4. The term **"implantation"** means blastula being imbedded in the mucous lining of the uterus.

5. The **menopause** is the cessation of menstruation.

6. Unless fertilization occurs, the human ovum usually **disintegrates** before reaching the uterus.

7. The vagina normally has an **acid** pH.

8. Spermatozoa are formed in the **epididymis.**

9. **Androgens** are produced by the interstitial cells.

10. A surgically sterilized female **may** menstruate normally.

11. Ovulation involves the rupture of the **corpus luteum** with the release of the egg.

12. The upper rounded part of the uterus is called the **fundus.**

13. The female homologue of the penis is the **clitoris.**

14. The seminal vesicles produce a secretion giving an **acid** reaction to the semen.

15. Testosterone is produced by the **follicle** cells.

16. **Fraternal** twins are always of the same sex.

17. Fertilization usually occurs in the **vagina.**

18. Another name for the womb is the **uterus.**

19. Dysmenorrhea means **menstrual pain.**

20. The placenta serves for **transport** of material between mother and child.

21. Salpingitis is an inflammation of the **uterus.**

22. A **mastectomy** is surgical removal of the uterus.

23. **Amenorrhea** means the absence of menstruation.

24. Cleavage of the zygote begins in the **uterus.**

25. The notochord is the precursor of the **spinal cord.**

26. The first division of the fertilized ovum results in **two identical cells,** each containing the same amount of male and female chromosome elements.

27. The skin is formed from the **entoderm.**

28. Ovulation usually occurs **five** days after the onset of menstruation, in a 28-day menstrual month.

29. Progesterone is secreted by **both the corpus luteum and the placenta.**

30. The **areola** is the pigmented area around the nipple.

31. The cul-de-sac of Douglas is the pocket between the **rectum** and the uterus.

32. The hormone responsible for ovulation is follicle stimulating hormone **(FSH).**

33. Circumcision is the surgical excision of the **prepuce, or foreskin.**

34. The testes descend through the **inguinal canal** before birth.

35. The umbilical **artery** contains deoxygenated blood.

36. The **chorion** is the inner of the two fetal membranes.

37. The cervix is the lower part of the **Fallopian tube.**

38. Pregnancy is not possible after a hysterectomy, **but ovulation still occurs.**

39. The normal position of the uterus is with the fundus tilted **forward over the urinary bladder.**

40. Sperm cells are produced in the **vasa efferentia.**

41. A mature sperm cell contains the **haploid** number of chromosomes as a result of **meiosis.**

42. The **diploid** number of chromosomes results from the fertilization of an ovum by a sperm cell.

43. Sperm cells are stored in the **epididymis and the vas deferens.**

44. Failure of the male gonads to descend into the scrotum is known as **a hernia.**

45. The common passageway for both sperm and urine is the **ureter.**

46. The enzyme **hyaluronidase,** if present in sufficient amounts, apparently enables sperm to penetrate the corona radiata during fertilization.

47. An ovum dies within approximately **24 hours** after ovulation unless fertilized.

48. The secretions of the **bulbourethral (Cowper's)** glands lubricate the urethra in males during sexual excitation.

49. Another name for the birth canal is the **uterine cavity.**

50. Progesterone is produced in the nonpregnant body by **only the corpus luteum.**

51. Ovulation cannot occur with a low blood level of **luteinizing hormone (LH).**

52. Contraceptive pills contain **ovarian hormones or related substances.**

53. Contraceptive pills prevent **ovulation.**

21

Genetics

Objectives

To become familiar with basic principles of heredity; to learn how to work selected genetics problems.

Materials

Text and/or other references containing information on elementary genetics.

Discussion

Only a few genetic principles will be discussed in this chapter. It is assumed that the instructor will supplement this discussion with lecture material and appropriate reading assignments. See Appendix 4 for definitions of the terms used in this chapter.

The chromosomes in the nuclei of the cells of higher plants and animals occur in matched pairs, which are referred to as **homologous** chromosomes. One member of a homologous pair of chromosomes is derived from the male parent, while the other member of the pair is derived from the female parent. A typical human cell contains 23 pairs of chromosomes. During meiosis (see Figure 20-5 in Chapter 20), which occurs during the formation of the ovum and sperm **(gametes)**, the pairs separate, and each gamete then contains one member of each of the 23 pairs of chromosomes. The latter cells are said to contain the **haploid** (n) number of chromosomes, which is an indication that they

have half the species number of chromosomes. The species number of chromosomes in humans is 46 (23 pairs) and is referred to as the **diploid** (2n) number of chromosomes. When a sperm fertilizes an ovum, the species (or diploid) number of chromosomes is reestablished in the **zygote** (fertilized ovum). With the exception of the sex chromosomes (to be discussed later), the two members of a pair of homologous chromosomes are indistinguishable.

Genes, the fundamental units of heredity, are arranged in a linear sequence on the chromosomes. The number of different genes in humans has been estimated at 10,000 to 50,000. Genes are composed primarily of protein and a nucleic acid called **deoxyribonucleic acid (DNA)**. The DNA transmits the genetic information, since it contains in coded form all the information required to build new cells. Each DNA molecule is composed of two strands of nucleotides wound in a double helix. Each nucleotide consists of one phosphate molecule, one sugar (deoxyribose), and one base (either the purine adenine or guanine or the pyrimidine thymine or cytosine). Weak hydrogen bonds join the two strand together at the bases. Each base in one strands pairs with its complementary base in the second strand. (Adenine pairs only with thymine, and guanine only with cytosine.) This structure (see Figure 21-1) may be compared with a ladder. The rungs of the ladder are the bases and the backbone (or sides) the alternating sugar and phosphate groups. Since the sugar and phosphate remain the same in each nucleotide and only the bases change, each gene must be determined by the changing sequence in which the four bases are arranged. This may

277

278

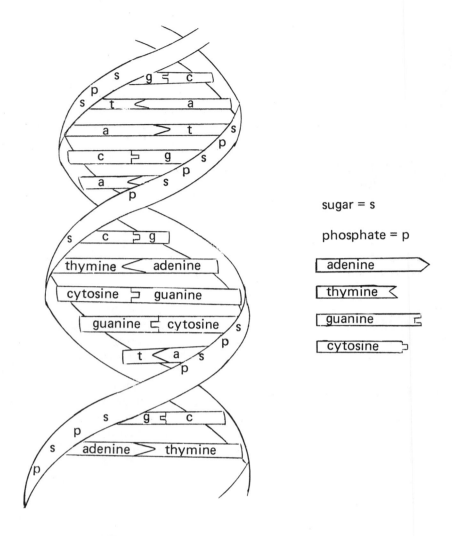

sugar = s

phosphate = p

adenine

thymine

guanine

cytosine

Figure 21-1.   The structure of DNA.

be compared with a four-letter alphabet which spells out the genetic information.

When a cell divides, the DNA of each chromosome produces an exact copy of itself (replication). The two strands that compose the DNA molecule separate and each strand duplicates its former member from chemical building blocks available in the cell. As a result of this replication of the DNA, each daughter cell (at the end of mitosis) contains the same genetic material as the parent cell.

The specialized nature of a cell depends on the type and quantity of protein in the cell. DNA functions in protein synthesis by controlling the formation of a second nucleic acid, **RNA (ribonucleic acid)**; RNA then serves as a pattern for protein synthesis. The structure of RNA is much like that of DNA, but it consists of only a single strand, the sugar is ribose, and the base uracil replaces thymine. Several types of RNA are produced in the nucleus. One type of RNA, called messenger RNA, carries the genetic message from its storage site in DNA out to the ribosomes (which contain ribosomal RNA) in the cytoplasm. Here proteins are synthesized from amino acids deposited at the correct site on the ribosome by "transfer" RNA. Every three bases in a particular sequence in DNA form the code for the placement of one particular amino acid in a protein. So a gene might be defined as a segment of DNA in which are encoded the complete instructions ordering the sequence of amino acids in one protein chain.

Genes occur in pairs, one gene on one chromosome, the other gene on the corresponding, or homologous, chromosome. If the two genes of a homologous pair of chromosomes are for the same expression of a trait, the condition is called **homozygous**. However, if one gene provides a different expression of the trait than the gene on the other chromosome of the pair, the condition is called **heterozygous**. The term **allele** is applied to alternate forms of a gene for a given trait. Alleles are genes borne at the same **locus** (location on the chromosome) on homologous chromosomes. Each allele produces a different expression of the same trait. For example, the gene for brown eyes is an allele of the gene for blue eyes.

The transmission of many hereditary traits seems to be under the influence of a single pair of genes. If the two genes are heterozygous, usually only one gene will exert an effect. A gene is called **dominant** if it is fully manifested in the heterozygous state. If the gene is manifested only in the homozygous state, meaning that two identical genes are needed to produce the effect, the gene is called **recessive**. Occasionally the heterozygote is intermediate between the homozygous dominant and recessive. This lack of dominance occurs, for example, in some types of flower coloration and cattle coat color.

The **genotype** is the genetic makeup of an individual. It is an indication of the genes present, whether they are expressed or not. Usually symbols, such as letters of the alphabet, are used to express the genotype. The capital form of the letter is used as a symbol for a dominant trait, and the lower case form of the same letter is used to symbolize the recessive gene for the same trait. The **phenotype** is that which can be observed about an individual, such as hair color, eye color, or blood type, and it is usually described with words rather than symbols. As a result of the interaction between genes and the environment, the phenotype is potentially variable.

PART 1. WORKING GENETICS PROBLEMS INVOLVING A SINGLE PAIR OF GENES (MONOHYBRID CROSS)

Discussion

The method of working simple genetics problems involving a monohybrid cross will be illustrated by using **astigmatism** (which is due to irregularities of the cornea or the lens of the eye). This is the same method used by Gregor

Mendel (sometimes referred to as the father of genetics) in the study of pea plants.

A single pair of genes is involved. The gene for astigmatism is dominant over that for the normal condition. When two parents heterozygous for astigmatism have children, approximately 3/4 of the offspring would be expected to have astigmatism and 1/4 would be expected to be normal. Use the following procedure in working all problems of this type.

Procedure

1. Select and record symbols for each trait. In this problem, the symbol A = the allele for astigmatism (since this symbol represents the dominant gene) and a = the allele for normal (since this symbol represents the recessive trait).
2. Write the genotype of each parent. In this problem, since each parent is heterozygous, each parent would have the genotype Aa. Remember to use two genes for each trait, since each cell in the gonads, prior to meiosis, contains the diploid number of chromosomes.
3. Determine the number of different gametes each parent can produce by using the following rule: the number of different gametes = 2^n, where n = the number of heterozygous pairs. Therefore, a parent of genotype Aa could produce two different types of gametes (2^1), while a parent of genotype AaBb could produce four different types (2^2) and one of genotype AaBbCCdd could also produce only four, since the latter parent has only two heterozygous pairs of genes.
4. Write down all of the possible different gametes that could be produced. Each gamete must have one gene of each pair of genes; it can never have both members of one pair of genes and one of the other pair. For example, a person with genotype AA would produce only one type of gamete, A. In a dihybrid cross (a cross involving two pairs of genes), a person with genotype AABB would produce only a single type of gamete, AB. The person would not produce a gamete containing AA (both genes for astigmatism) or BB (both genes of the second characteristic). Be sure to consider all possible combinations. The number of gametes arrived at

should agree with the theoretical number in step 3. In our example of a cross between two parents having the genotype Aa, each parent can produce two kinds of gametes (in equal numbers): A and a.

5. Make a checkerboard (Punnett square) with the different gametes from one parent on one side and the gametes from the other parent on the top, and complete the squares as shown below.

♂

	A	a
A	AA	Aa
a	Aa	aa

(♀ labels the left side)

6. Determine the phenotype and genotype of each of the resulting offspring. In this example, 3/4 of the offspring would be expected to have astigmatism and 1/4 would be expected to be normal. The phenotypic ratio is, therefore, 3:1 (3 astigmatism: 1 normal). The genotypic ratios of the offspring would be 1:2:1, as follows:

1/4 A A
1/2 Aa
1/4 aa

7. Check to make sure that each new individual has two genes for each trait and that the total number of genes in each offspring is the same as that in the original parents.

PART 2. WORKING PROBLEMS INVOLVING TWO PAIRS OF GENES (DIHYBRID CROSS)

Discussion

A dihybrid cross involves two different traits, each due to a pair of genes borne on a different pair of chromosomes. The gene for farsightedness is dominant over that for normal vision. If a person heterozygous for astigmatism and farsightedness is married to a person with the same genotype, the problem can be solved by following the same general procedure as that for a monohybrid cross.

Procedure

1. Symbols: A = astigmatism, a = normal, F = farsighted, f = normal.

2. Genotypes of parents: AaFf.
3. The number of different gametes for each is four, since AaFf contains two heterozygous pairs and $2^2 = 4$.
4. Each parent, since the two have identical genotypes, would form these four gametes, in equal numbers: AF, Af, aF, and af.
5. Checkerboard:

♂

	AF	Af	aF	af
AF	AAFF	AAFf	AaFF	AaFf
Af	AAFf	AAff	AaFf	Aaff
aF	AaFF	AaFf	aaFF	aaFf
af	AaFf	Aaff	aaFf	aaff

(♀ labels the left side)

6. Phenotypic ratios of the offspring:
    9/16 with astigmatism and farsighted
    3/16 with astigmatism and normal
    3/16 normal but farsighted
    1/16 normal/normal
These ratios are obtained in a typical dihybrid cross.

PART 3. WORKING PROBLEMS INVOLVING A LACK OF DOMINANCE

Discussion

In crosses involving a lack of dominance, both genes of the heterozygote express themselves in the offspring. Problems are worked in the same way as those in Part 1, but the heterozygous progeny show the interaction of both genes. For example, if a person with straight hair (HH) marries a person with curly hair (hh), the resulting offspring have wavy hair (Hh). If two parents have wavy hair, approximately 1/4 of the offspring would be expected to have straight hair, 1/2 wavy hair, and 1/4 curly hair.

Procedure

1. Symbols: HH = straight, Hh = wavy, hh = curly.
2. Parental genotypes: Hh x Hh
3. Types of gametes; H, h and H, h
4. Place the gametes on the Punnett square

(checkerboard); then complete the rest of the squares as follows:

	♂	
♀	**H**	**h**
H	HH	Hh
h	Hh	hh

5. Determine the phenotypic ratio: 1:2:1 (1 straight: 2 wavy: 1 curly).
6. Determine the genotypic ratio: 1:2:1 (1/4 HH:1/2 Hh:1/4 hh).

PART 4. WORKING SEX-LINKED PROBLEMS

Discussion

Of the 23 pairs of chromosomes in a human, one pair is called the **sex chromosomes** and the other 22 pairs are called **autosomes**. In the human female, the sex chromosomes look alike and are called X chromosomes, whereas in the male, the two chromosomes differ from each other. The male has one X chromosome and a smaller chromosome called the Y chromosome. During meiosis these two chromosomes separate. Therefore, the male produces two types of sperm, half containing the X chromosome and half the Y. All the ova of the female contain the X chromosome. Therefore, it is the male that determines the sex of the child.

The X chromosome, since it is larger than the Y, contains many genes not on the Y chromosome. These genes, located *only* on the X chromosome, are called **sex-linked** genes. Hemophilia and color blindness are both inherited as sex-linked recessives. Using color blindness as an example, if a woman has either one or two genes for normal vision, she will have normal vision. A woman having two genes for color blindness will be color-blind. However, since a man does not have a gene for color vision on the Y chromosome, he will be color-blind if he has only one gene for color blindness.

Procedure

Cross a woman who is heterozygous for color blindness with a man having normal color vision.

1. The genotype for the woman (who has normal color vision but is a carrier of a gene for color blindness) may be written as follows: $X^C X^c$, wherein C = normal color vision, c = color-blind, and the X's represent the X chromosome where the genes for this trait are borne.
2. The genotype of a male, normal for color vision, may be written as follows: $X^C Y$ (a color-blind male would have the genotype: $X^c Y$). Therefore, the problem could be set up as follows:

$$\text{Parents:} \quad X^C X^c \ \times \ X^C Y$$
$$\text{Gametes:} \quad X^C, X^c \quad X^C, Y$$

The gametes are then placed on the Punnett square and the rest of the squares are completed in the following manner:

	♂	
♀	X^C	Y
X^C	$X^C X^C$	$X^C Y$
X^c	$X^C X^c$	$X^c Y$

3. From the preceding it is possible to answer the following questions:
   a. From such a cross, what are the chances of a color-blind male being produced? (Answer: 1/2, or 50/50.)
   b. What are the chances of a color-blind female being produced? (Answer: none.)

   A key fact to remember is that half of all the sons produced as a result of such a union might be expected to be color-blind.

PART 5. WORKING PROBLEMS INVOLVING MULTIPLE ALLELES

Discussion

The preceding problems assume that each gene exists in only two alternative forms; however, many genes have more than two forms. These are referred to as multiple alleles. This is exemplified by the three different genes, borne at the same locus, involved in the determination of the ABO blood types. No individual will have more than two of these genes, since he has only two chromosomes and no more than one gene can occupy a given locus at a time.

The Rh factor also involves more than a single pair of genes (e.g., C, D, and E), although for elementary problem solving only a single pair of genes may be considered wherein Rh+ is dominant to Rh−.

The MN blood type series is due to a pair of genes, neither of which shows dominance over the other. While this series is not important as far as transfusions are concerned (no antibodies are produced in response to introduction of the antigens), it may be of significance (along with the ABO and Rh types) in establishing possible paternity cases. In such cases it may be possible to prove that a certain man could not have been the father of the child in question, but it is not possible to prove that a particular man is the father of the child (only that he may be).

Procedure

1. The phenotypes and genotypes that follow are necessary for working genetics problems involving blood types:

Phenotype	Genotype
O	OO
A	AO, AA
B	BO, BB
AB	AB
Rh+	++, +−
Rh−	−−
M	MM
N	NN
MN	MN

2. In the above genotypes, genes A and B (responsible for producing antigens A and B) are both dominant over O but are not dominant over each other. Rh+ is dominant over Rh−. M and N show no dominance over each other.
3. Once the parents' genotypes are established, problems are solved in the same manner as that shown for monohybrid and dihybrid crosses.

PART 6. PROBABILITY

Discussion

The solution of genetics problems involves the use of probability. We are asking what the chances are that a particular event will occur. Based on the genotypes of two heterozygous brown-eyed parents (see monohybrid crosses), it is possible to predict that there is one chance in four (1/4) that such parents may produce a blue-eyed child. It is not possible to say they will produce such a child.

Probability is defined as:

$$p = \frac{\text{Number of favorable cases}}{\text{Total number of cases}}$$

If an event is certain to happen, its probability is 1; if the event is impossible, its probability is 0. Other probabilities are expressed as fractions between 0 and 1. For example, the probability of drawing a king from a deck of cards is 4/52, or 1/13, since there are four kings in the deck. The probability of throwing heads in one toss of a coin is 1/2.

Procedure

1. To determine probability, ask what is the number of favorable cases or chances of a particular event occurring. The answer to this question in the case of the kings in the deck (mentioned in the discussion) was four.
2. Also, ask what is the total number of cases. The total cases in the deck of cards was 52.
3. Put the results of steps 1 and 2 in the form of a fraction. In the case under consideration, the resulting fraction was 4/52, which reduces to 1/13. Therefore, the probability that a king would be drawn from a shuffled deck of cards is 1 in 13, or 1/13.
4. Another point to consider in such problems is that the probability that one or the other of two (or more) mutually exclusive events will occur is the **sum** of the separate probabilities. For example, the probability of drawing either an ace or a king from a standard deck of cards is 4/52 + 4/52 = 8/52 or 2/13.
5. The probability that both of two independent events will occur together is the **product** of the two separate probabilities. This can be extended to any number of different events. For example, the probability of drawing first an ace (then replacing it) and then a king from a standard deck of cards is 1/13 x 1/13 = 1/169.

EXERCISE 21-B
GENETICS PROBLEMS

Objective

To learn how to solve some of the basic types of genetics problems.

Materials

None.

Procedure

The following are practice problems involving the principles found in Exercise 21-A. On a separate piece of paper try to solve these problems without reference to the key at the end of the exercise. After completing the practice problems, solve those assigned by the instructor under Results and Questions.

1. How many different types of gametes can be produced by an individual of genotype AabbCcDDEe?

2. The gene for brown eyes is dominant over that for blue eyes. A woman with blue eyes marries a brown-eyed man whose mother had blue eyes. What proportion of the children would be expected to have blue eyes?

3. Curly hair shows lack of dominance over straight hair, the heterozygote possessing wavy hair. If two people with wavy hair marry, what hair types would you expect to find among their offspring?

4. Two children in a family have blood type O. Their mother has type B blood, their father type A. What is the genotype of the mother? What is the genotype of the father?

5. In humans the gene for farsightedness is usually inherited as a dominant. A man who is heterozygous for farsightedness marries a woman with normal vision. What fraction of their children would be expected to be farsighted?

6. The gene for astigmatism is inherited as a dominant. Two people heterozygous for astigmatism marry. What is the probability that they will have two normal children in a row?

7. What is the probability of having two boys in a row?

8. Two brown-eyed parents have a blue-eyed child. What is the probability that their next child will be blue-eyed?

9. Two normal parents are each heterozygous for a recessive gene for feeblemindedness. What is the probability that they will have four feebleminded children in a row?

10. In humans the gene for the ability to taste phenylthiocarbamide (PTC) is dominant over that for the inability to taste PTC. The gene for brown eyes is dominant over that for blue eyes. What proportion of the offspring of two parents, each heterozygous for both traits, would be blue-eyed tasters?

11. Red-green color blindness in humans results from a sex-linked recessive gene. Two normal parents (the mother blue-eyed, the father heterozygous for brown eyes) produce a color-blind son.
   a. What are the genotypes of the parents?
   b. What proportion of their sons would you expect to be color-blind?
   c. What is the probability that two daughters in a row will be color-blind?

12. A woman carrying the genes for both color blindness and hemophilia (she inherited both of these sex-linked recessive traits from her father) marries a man who is color-blind but not hemophilic.
   a. What is the probability that the first two children will be normal boys?
   b. What is the probability of having a hemophilic daughter?

13. In each of the following situations, state whether it is possible or impossible for these parents to have had the child indicated and give a reason for your answer.

Mother	Father	Child
a. A, MN, Rh+	O, M, Rh+	AB, MN, Rh−
b. AB	A	O

14. In humans, normal pigmentation is due to a dominant gene, albinism to its recessive allele. These are not sex-linked. A normal man marries an albino woman. Their first child is an albino. Use this information to solve the following problems:
   a. What is the genotype of the father?
   b. What is the probability that their next child will be an albino?

KEY TO PRACTICE PROBLEMS

1. $2^3 = 8$
2. 1/2
3. 1/4 straight hair
   1/2 wavy hair
   1/4 curly hair
4. mother's genotype = BO
   father's genotype = AO
5. 1/2
6. 1/16
7. 1/4
8. 1/4
9. 1/256
10. 3/16
11. a. bbX^{C}X^c x BbX^{C}Y
    b. 1/2
    c. 0
12. a. 1/16
    b. 0
13. a. impossible; no B from parents
    b. impossible; no O from mother
14. a. Aa (A = normal, a = albino)
    b. 1/2

EXERCISE 21-C
VARIABILITY IN MAN

Objective

To observe genetically determined variability in man.

Materials

PTC-impregnated papers.

Discussion

Because of the almost infinite possible combination of traits in humans, every individual, with the exception of identical twins, is unique. Even identical twins are not absolutely alike due to the modification of genes influenced by their environment. A study of the traits in this exercise exemplifies, in a limited way, human variability.

PART 1. HEREDITARY BASIS FOR TESTING PHENYLTHIOCARBAMIDE

Procedure

1. Place a strip of phenylthiocarbamide (PTC) test paper on your tongue. If you experience no taste sensation, chew the paper.
2. Determine your genotype and record it under Results and Questions. Note: The ability to taste PTC is dominant to inability to taste the chemical (about 70% of subjects report a strong bitter taste, while approximately 30% report no taste). Use T for taster and t for nontaster. If you are a taster, you will not know (unless a study is made of your family) whether you are homozygous or heterozygous for the trait, and you should, therefore, record it as T_.

PART 2. HEREDITARY BASIS FOR PIGMENTED IRIS

Discussion

Pigmentation for eye color is located in the front part of the iris. A person with blue eyes has no pigment in the front of the eyes. The eyes become increasingly dark with increasing amounts of pigment in the front of the iris (passing through hazel or green or gray to brown or dark brown). Geneticists feel certain that there are several genes involved in determining eye color; however, to simplify, we shall group all types with a pigmented iris together.

Procedure

1. A blue-eyed individual is homozygous recessive (bb) for nonpigmented iris. A person with a pigmented iris may be either homozygous (BB) or heterozygous (Bb) for the trait.
2. Determine your genotype for eye color and record it under Results and Questions.

PART 3. HEREDITARY BASIS FOR MIDDIGITAL HAIR

Discussion

The complete absence of hair from the middle segments of the fingers is a form of genetic variability in man.

Procedure

1. Absence of middigital hair is due to a recessive trait (dd). Presence of hair on one or more middle segments may be due to multiple alleles, each of which is dominant to the recessive gene. Group all of the multiple alleles with the symbol D.
2. Determine your genotype for this trait and record it under Results and Questions.

PART 4. HEREDITARY BASIS FOR EAR LOBES

Procedure

1. Free hanging ear lobes are dominant (E_) to adherent (ee) lobes (in the latter there is no gap between the lobe and the cheek).
2. Determine your genotype for ear lobes and record it under Results and Questions.

PART 5. HEREDITARY BASIS FOR BENT LITTLE FINGER

Discussion

The distal (terminal) segment of the little fingers may be straight or turned inward (toward the ring finger).

Procedure

1. Bent is dominant (F_) to straight (ff) for the terminal segment of the little finger.
2. Determine your genotype for the terminal segment of your little finger and record it under Results and Questions.

PART 6. HEREDITARY BASIS FOR BLOOD GROUPS

Procedure

1. Use the results obtained in Exercise 12-A for your ABO and Rh blood types.
2. Determine your genotypes for ABO and Rh blood types by referring to the genotypes listed under Exercise 21-A, Part 4, and record them under Results and Questions.

PART 7. HEREDITARY BASIS FOR SINGING VOICE

Procedure

1. Singing voice is due to one pair of alleles, which may be symbolized by V^1 and V^2. The expression of the genes is different in males and females. The genotype of bass and soprano is V^1V^1; of baritone and mezzo-soprano V^1V^2; of tenor and alto V^2V^2.
2. Determine the genotype of your singing voice and record it under Results and Questions.

PART 8. HEREDITARY BASIS FOR DOUBLE-JOINTED THUMBS

Procedure

1. Ability to throw the thumb out of joint is usually dominant (J_) to its allele (jj), which determines tight ligaments.
2. Determine your genotype for double-jointed thumb (actually loose ligaments that permit the thumb to be thrown out of joint) and record it under Results and Questions.

PART 9. HEREDITARY BASIS FOR THE LONG PALMAR MUSCLE

Procedure

1. Clench and flex your fist. You will observe either two or three tendons running

from your forearm to the center of the heel of the palm. If three tendons are present, the prominent middle one is the tendon of the long palmar muscle. If only two tendons are present, the long palmar muscle and its tendon are absent.
2. The presence of the muscle in both arms is determined by recessive alleles (pp). The presence of the muscle in only one arm is probably an expression of the heterozygous condition (Pp). The absence of the muscle in both arms is probably an expression of the homozygous condition (PP).
3. Determine your genotype for the presence or absence of the long palmar muscle and its tendon.

PART 10. HEREDITARY BASIS FOR HAIR COLOR

Discussion

Hair color seems to be determined by several factors; however, by considering only the larger categories, hair color may be analyzed in terms of two gene pairs. The brown pigment, melanin, provides either a brown, black, or blond hair color (if red is not present). The darker shades are dominant. Red hair color is determined by a homozygous recessive condition of another pair of alleles.

Procedure

1. Symbolize dark hair color with (D_) and blond with (dd). Red pigmentation is symbolized (rr) and lack of pigment is (R_). A person with genotype ddrr would have sandy red hair; one with ddRR or ddRr would have blond hair; one with DDrr or Ddrr would have red hair or dark hair with tints of red; one with DDRR, DdRR, DdRr, or DDRr would have dark hair.
2. As accurately as possible, determine your genotype for hair color and record it under Results and Questions.

SELF-TEST — GENETICS

Directions

See Chapter 1, Self-Test, page 9.

1. Intellectual performance of some mentally deficient children has been improved by administering **thyroxin**.

2. If a person comes from a lineage showing epilepsy, **it is important** that the hereditary background of the proposed marriage mate be studied.

3. Color blindness is a sex-linked trait and is inherited **only by males.**

4. **All** color blindness is inherited.

5. **All** inherited conditions are apparent at birth.

6. A child with both parents showing allergy **is likely** to exhibit allergy early in life.

7. A frightening experience to an expectant mother **will** cause her child to become nervous later in life.

8. A man may genetically transmit hypersensitivity, or allergy, to his offspring **without himself showing the condition.**

9. Consanguineous marriages **always result** in inferior offspring.

10. Sex-linked disorders occur **only in males.**

11. A person who inherits a predisposition to a disorder **is certain to have** that disorder.

12. Hereditary factors result from the action of **genes found in chromosomes** of cells.

13. A certain organic disorder first appeared at the age of 50. This disorder **could not possibly** have been hereditary.

14. An organic disorder was present at birth. Therefore, this disorder **must have been** hereditary.

15. Consanguineous marriages tend to produce a greater tendency toward a **heterozygous** condition.

16. The only hereditary bridge between parents and offspring is the **blood.**

17. A person with a pair of genes that produce brown eyes **is always heterozygous** for eye color.

18. If a certain trait appears only when the person is homozygous for that trait, the gene is **recessive.**

19. If a person has one pair of genes for a trait, **only one** of these genes can be transmitted to an offspring.

20. A person with a pair of genes that produce blond hair is **homozygous** for hair color.

21. A person who inherits a condition resulting in pernicious anemia actually inherits a deficiency **of the stomach.**

22. The constitutional factor resulting in hardening of the arteries **appears to have a genetic basis.**

23. **All** feeblemindedness is inherited.

24. Parents of average intelligence **may have** children of superior intelligence.

25. Parents of average intelligence **may have** children with inherited feeblemindedness.

26. Parents of superior intelligence **may have** children of average intelligence.

27. Mature sex cells are called **gametes.**

28. The chromosome number of a female is **44 + XX**; of a male **44 + XY.**

29. A recessive sex-linked characteristic in a man might be transmitted to some of his **son's daughters.**

30. So-called acquired characteristics of living organisms are **never** inherited.

Appendix 1

Formulas Used in Preparation of Solutions

Benedict's Solution

Copper sulfate (pure crystallized)	17.3 g
Sodium or potassium citrate	173.0 g
Sodium carbonate (crystallized)	200.0 g
(or 100 g anhydrous sodium carbonate)	
Distilled water, to make	1.0 liter

Dissolve the citrate and carbonate in 700 cc of water with the aid of heat, and filter. Dissolve the copper sulfate in 100 cc of water and pour slowly into the first solution, stirring constantly. Cool, and make up to 1 liter. The reagent keeps indefinitely.

Blood Anticoagulant Solution

Dissolve 12 g of sodium oxalate in 100 cc of 0.9% sodium chloride. To this add 4000 cc of freshly drawn blood; mix thoroughly.

Buffer Solution for Use with Wright's Stain

A solution of pH 6.4 is made by dissolving 6.63 g of monobasic potassium phosphate and 3.20 g of dibasic sodium phosphate in 1 liter of distilled water.

Lugol's Iodine Solution

Iodine	1.0 g
Potassium iodide	2.0 g
Distilled water	300.0 cc

Millon's Solution

Dissolve 100 g of mercury in 200 g of concentrated nitric acid; dilute the solution with two volumes of water.

Ringer's Solution

Sodium chloride	7.000 g
Potassium chloride	0.075 g
Calcium chloride	0.100 g
Sodium carbonate (crystallized)	200.0 g
Distilled water, to make	1.000 liter

The sodium bicarbonate must be completely dissolved before the calcium chloride is added.

Appendix **2**
Weights and Measures

Linear Measurements

1 meter (m)	= 100 centimeters (cm) = 1000 millimeters (mm) = 39.37 inches (in.) = 3.2808 feet (ft) = 1.09 yards (yd)
1 inch (in.)	= 2.540 cm
1 millimeter (mm)	= 0.001 m = 0.1 cm = 1/25 in (approximately)
1 micron (μ)	= 0.000001 m = 0.001 mm = 10,000 Angstrom units (Å) = 1/25,000 in
1 millimicron (mμ)	= 0.000000001 m = 0.000001 mm = 10 Å = 1/25,000,000 in

Volumetric Measurements

1 liter	= 1000 milliliters (ml) = 1000 cubic centimeters (cc) = 0.9 dry quart = 1.0567 liquid quarts (U.S. liquid)
1 fluid ounce (fl oz)	= 8 fluid drams (fl dr) = 29.573 cc
1 minim (min.)	= 1/60 fluid dram (fl dr) = 1/480 fluid ounce (fl oz)

Weight

1 kilogram (kg)	= 1000 grams (g) = 2.20462 pounds (lb) (avoirdupois) = 35.27 ounces (oz)
1 ounce (oz)	= 28.3495 g
1 gram (g)	= 1000 milligrams (mg) = 15 grains (gr) = 0.03527 oz (avoirdupois)
1 milligram (mg)	= 1000 micrograms (mcg) = 0.001 g = 1/60 gr
1 microgram (mcg), (μg), or gamma	= 0.001 mg = 1/28,000,000 oz (approximately)
1 grain (gr)	= 0.0648 g
1 dram (dr) (Apothecary)	= 60 gr = 3 scruples (scr)

Pressure

1 atmosphere (atm)	= 14.696 lb per sq in. = 2116.3 lb per sq ft
1 atmosphere	= 29.92 in. mercury (Hg) = 760 mm of Hg

Appendix 3

Respiration and Metabolism

APPENDIX 3-A. DUBOIS BODY SURFACE CHART*

Directions

To find body surface of a patient, locate the height in inches (or centimeters) on Scale I and the weight in pounds (or kilograms) on Scale II and place a straightedge (ruler) between these two points. The ruler will intersect Scale III at the patient's surface area.

*As prepared by Boothby and Sandlford of the Mayo Clinic.

APPENDIX 3-B. PREDICTED VITAL CAPACITY — MALES*

Height in Centimeters

Age	146	148	150	152	154	156	158	160	162	164	166	168	170	172	174	176	178	180	182	184	186	188	190	192	194
16	3765	3820	3870	3920	3975	4025	4075	4130	4180	4230	4285	4335	4385	4440	4490	4540	4590	4645	4695	4745	4800	4850	4900	4955	5005
18	3740	3790	3840	3890	3940	3995	4045	4095	4145	4200	4250	4300	4350	4405	4455	4505	4555	4610	4660	4710	4760	4815	4865	4915	4965
20	3710	3760	3810	3860	3910	3960	4015	4065	4115	4165	4215	4265	4320	4370	4420	4470	4520	4570	4625	4675	4725	4775	4825	4875	4930
22	3680	3730	3780	3830	3880	3930	3980	4030	4080	4135	4185	4235	4285	4335	4385	4435	4485	4535	4585	4635	4685	4735	4790	4840	4890
24	3635	3685	3735	3785	3835	3885	3935	3985	4035	4085	4135	4185	4235	4285	4330	4380	4430	4480	4530	4580	4630	4680	4730	4780	4830
26	3605	3655	3705	3755	3805	3855	3905	3955	4000	4050	4100	4150	4200	4250	4300	4350	4395	4445	4495	4545	4595	4645	4695	4740	4790
28	3575	3625	3675	3725	3775	3820	3870	3920	3970	4020	4070	4115	4165	4215	4265	4310	4360	4410	4460	4510	4555	4605	4655	4705	4755
30	3550	3595	3645	3695	3740	3790	3840	3890	3935	3985	4035	4080	4130	4180	4230	4275	4325	4375	4425	4470	4520	4570	4615	4665	4715
32	3520	3565	3615	3665	3710	3760	3810	3855	3905	3950	4000	4050	4095	4145	4195	4240	4290	4340	4385	4435	4485	4530	4580	4625	4675
34	3475	3525	3570	3620	3665	3715	3760	3810	3855	3905	3950	4000	4045	4095	4140	4190	4225	4285	4330	4380	4425	4475	4520	4570	4615
36	3445	3495	3540	3585	3635	3680	3730	3775	3825	3870	3920	3965	4010	4060	4105	4155	4200	4250	4295	4340	4390	4435	4485	4530	4580
38	3415	3465	3510	3555	3605	3650	3695	3745	3790	3840	3885	3930	3980	4025	4070	4120	4165	4210	4260	4305	4350	4400	4445	4495	4540
40	3385	3435	3480	3525	3575	3620	3665	3710	3760	3805	3850	3900	3945	3990	4035	4085	4130	4175	4220	4270	4315	4360	4410	4455	4500
42	3360	3405	3450	3495	3540	3590	3635	3680	3725	3770	3820	3865	3910	3955	4000	4050	4095	4140	4185	4230	4280	4325	4370	4415	4460
44	3315	3360	3405	3450	3495	3540	3585	3630	3675	3725	3770	3815	3860	3905	3950	3995	4040	4085	4130	4175	4220	4270	4315	4360	4405
46	3285	3330	3375	3420	3465	3510	3555	3600	3645	3690	3735	3780	3825	3870	3915	3960	4005	4050	4095	4140	4185	4230	4275	4320	4365
48	3255	3300	3345	3390	3435	3480	3525	3570	3615	3655	3700	3745	3790	3835	3880	3925	3970	4015	4060	4105	4150	4190	4235	4280	4325
50	3210	3255	3300	3345	3390	3430	3475	3520	3565	3610	3650	3695	3740	3785	3830	3870	3915	3960	4005	4050	4090	4135	4180	4225	4270
52	3185	3225	3270	3315	3355	3400	3445	3490	3530	3575	3620	3660	3705	3750	3795	3835	3880	3925	3970	4010	4055	4100	4140	4185	4230
54	3155	3195	3240	3285	3325	3370	3415	3455	3500	3540	3585	3630	3670	3715	3760	3800	3845	3890	3930	3975	4020	4060	4105	4145	4190
56	3125	3165	3210	3255	3295	3340	3380	3425	3465	3510	3550	3595	3640	3680	3725	3765	3810	3850	3895	3940	3980	4025	4065	4110	4150
58	3080	3125	3165	3210	3250	3290	3335	3375	3420	3460	3500	3545	3585	3630	3670	3715	3755	3800	3840	3880	3925	3965	4010	4050	4095
60	3050	3095	3135	3175	3220	3260	3300	3345	3385	3430	3470	3500	3555	3595	3635	3680	3720	3760	3805	3845	3885	3930	3970	4015	4055
62	3020	3060	3110	3150	3190	3230	3270	3310	3350	3390	3440	3480	3520	3560	3600	3640	3680	3730	3770	3810	3850	3890	3930	3970	4020
64	2990	3030	3080	3120	3160	3200	3240	3280	3320	3360	3400	3440	3490	3530	3570	3610	3650	3690	3730	3770	3810	3850	3900	3940	3980
66	2950	2990	3030	3070	3110	3150	3190	3230	3270	3310	3350	3390	3430	3470	3510	3550	3600	3640	3680	3720	3760	3800	3840	3880	3920
68	2920	2960	3000	3040	3080	3120	3160	3200	3240	3280	3320	3360	3400	3440	3480	3520	3560	3600	3640	3680	3720	3760	3800	3840	3880
70	2890	2930	2970	3010	3050	3090	3130	3170	3210	3250	3290	3330	3370	3410	3450	3480	3520	3560	3600	3640	3680	3720	3760	3800	3840
72	2860	2900	2940	2980	3020	3060	3100	3140	3180	3210	3250	3290	3330	3370	3410	3450	3490	3530	3570	3610	3650	3680	3720	3760	3800
74	2820	2860	2900	2930	2970	3010	3050	3090	3130	3170	3200	3240	3280	3320	3360	3400	3440	3470	3510	3550	3590	3630	3670	3710	3740

*Baldwin, E. DeF., Cournand, A., and Richards, D. W., Jr., Pulmonary Insufficiency 1, Physiologic Classification, Clinical Methods of Analysis, Standard Values in Normal Subjects/Medicine, 27:243, 1958.

APPENDIX 3-C. PREDICTED VITAL CAPACITY — FEMALES*

Height in Centimeters

Age	146	148	150	152	154	156	158	160	162	164	166	168	170	172	174	176	178	180	182	184	186	188	190	192	194
16	2950	2990	3030	3070	3110	3150	3190	3230	3270	3310	3350	3390	3430	3470	3510	3550	3590	3630	3670	3715	3755	3800	3840	3880	3920
17	2935	2975	3015	3055	3095	3135	3175	3215	3255	3295	3335	3375	3415	3455	3495	3535	3575	3615	3655	3695	3740	3780	3820	3860	3900
18	2920	2960	3000	3040	3080	3120	3160	3200	3240	3280	3320	3360	3400	3440	3480	3520	3560	3600	3640	3680	3720	3760	3800	3840	3880
20	2890	2930	2970	3010	3050	3090	3130	3170	3210	3250	3290	3330	3370	3410	3450	3490	3525	3565	3605	3645	3695	3720	3760	3800	3840
22	2860	2900	2940	2980	3020	3060	3095	3135	3175	3215	3255	3290	3330	3370	3410	3450	3490	3530	3570	3610	3650	3685	3725	3765	3800
24	2830	2870	2910	2950	2985	3025	3065	3100	3140	3180	3220	3260	3300	3335	3375	3415	3455	3490	3530	3570	3610	3650	3685	3725	3765
26	2800	2840	2880	2920	2960	3000	3035	3070	3110	3150	3190	3230	3265	3300	3340	3380	3420	3455	3495	3530	3570	3610	3650	3685	3725
28	2775	2810	2850	2890	2930	2965	3000	3040	3070	3115	3155	3190	3230	3270	3305	3345	3380	3420	3460	3495	3535	3570	3610	3650	3685
30	2745	2780	2820	2860	2895	2935	2970	3010	3045	3085	3120	3160	3195	3235	3270	3310	3345	3385	3420	3460	3495	3535	3570	3610	3645
32	2715	2750	2790	2825	2865	2900	2940	2975	3015	3050	3090	3125	3160	3200	3235	3275	3310	3350	3385	3425	3460	3495	3535	3570	3610
34	2685	2725	2760	2795	2835	2870	2910	2945	2980	3020	3055	3090	3130	3165	3200	3240	3275	3310	3350	3385	3425	3460	3495	3535	3570
36	2655	2695	2730	2765	2805	2840	2875	2910	2950	2985	3020	3060	3095	3130	3165	3205	3240	3275	3310	3350	3385	3420	3460	3495	3530
38	2630	2665	2700	2735	2770	2810	2845	2880	2915	2950	2990	3025	3060	3095	3130	3170	3205	3240	3275	3310	3350	3385	3420	3455	3490
40	2600	2635	2670	2705	2740	2775	2810	2850	2885	2920	2955	2990	3025	3060	3095	3135	3170	3205	3240	3275	3310	3345	3380	3420	3455
42	2570	2605	2640	2675	2710	2745	2780	2815	2850	2885	2920	2955	2990	3025	3060	3100	3135	3170	3205	3240	3275	3310	3345	3380	3415
44	2540	2575	2610	2645	2680	2715	2750	2785	2820	2855	2890	2925	2960	2995	3030	3060	3095	3130	3165	3200	3235	3270	3305	3340	3375
46	2510	2545	2580	2615	2650	2685	2715	2750	2785	2820	2855	2890	2925	2960	2995	3030	3060	3095	3130	3165	3200	3235	3270	3305	3340
48	2480	2515	2550	2585	2620	2650	2685	2715	2750	2785	2820	2855	2890	2925	2960	2995	3030	3060	3095	3130	3160	3195	3230	3265	3300
50	2455	2485	2520	2555	2590	2625	2655	2690	2720	2755	2785	2820	2855	2890	2925	2955	2990	3025	3060	3090	3125	3155	3190	3225	3260
52	2425	2455	2490	2525	2555	2590	2625	2655	2690	2720	2755	2790	2820	2855	2890	2925	2955	2990	3020	3055	3090	3125	3155	3190	3220
54	2395	2425	2460	2495	2530	2560	2590	2625	2655	2690	2720	2755	2790	2820	2855	2885	2920	2950	2985	3020	3050	3085	3115	3150	3180
56	2365	2400	2430	2465	2495	2525	2560	2590	2625	2655	2690	2720	2755	2790	2820	2855	2885	2920	2950	2980	3015	3045	3080	3110	3145
58	2335	2370	2400	2430	2460	2495	2525	2560	2590	2625	2655	2690	2720	2750	2785	2815	2850	2880	2920	2945	2975	3010	3040	3075	3105
60	2305	2340	2370	2400	2430	2460	2495	2525	2560	2590	2625	2655	2685	2720	2750	2780	2810	2845	2875	2915	2940	2970	3000	3035	3065
62	2280	2310	2340	2370	2405	2435	2465	2495	2525	2560	2590	2620	2655	2685	2715	2745	2775	2810	2840	2870	2900	2935	2965	2995	3025
64	2250	2280	2310	2340	2370	2400	2430	2465	2495	2525	2555	2585	2620	2650	2680	2710	2740	2770	2805	2835	2865	2895	2925	2955	2990
66	2220	2250	2280	2310	2340	2370	2400	2430	2460	2495	2525	2555	2585	2615	2645	2675	2705	2735	2765	2800	2825	2860	2890	2920	2950
68	2190	2220	2250	2280	2310	2340	2370	2400	2430	2460	2490	2520	2550	2580	2610	2640	2670	2700	2730	2760	2795	2820	2850	2880	2910
70	2160	2190	2220	2250	2280	2310	2340	2370	2400	2425	2455	2485	2515	2545	2575	2605	2635	2665	2695	2725	2755	2780	2810	2840	2870
72	2130	2160	2190	2220	2250	2280	2310	2335	2365	2395	2425	2455	2480	2510	2540	2570	2600	2630	2660	2685	2715	2745	2775	2805	2830
74	2100	2130	2160	2190	2220	2245	2275	2305	2335	2360	2390	2420	2450	2475	2505	2535	2565	2590	2620	2650	2680	2710	2740	2765	2795

*Baldwin, E. Def., Cournand, A., and Richards, D. W., Jr., Pulmonary Insufficiency 1, Physiologic Classification, Clinical Methods of Analysis, Standard Values in Normal Subjects/Medicine, 27:243, 1958.

Appendix 4

Definitions for Genetics

Acquired character   A change from the normal type brought about by environmental influence.

Allele   One of normally two alternate forms of a gene, one being the normal type, the other the mutant type. When three or more alleles exist for any given locus (site) in the chromosome, they form a multiple allele series. This occurs less frequently than two alleles at a locus.

Autosomes   Chromosomes other than sex chromosomes.

Backcross   A cross of an F_1 hybrid to either of its parents.

Carrier   An individual heterozygous for a recessive gene that is not expressed. In appearance the individual is indistinguishable from the homozygous dominant.

Chromosome   A deep-staining, rodlike body in the nucleus of cells, visible at cell division. Chromosomes contain the genes, the hereditary determiners. All species have a characteristic chromosome number.

Cumulative effect   The more pronounced effect caused by two genes in the homozygous condition as compared with the effect in the heterozygous condition. Probably one allele supplies insufficient enzyme for a reaction so that there is less product produced. The hybrids are distinguishable from the parents. The effect is sometimes referred to as **incomplete dominance.**

Dihybrid cross   A cross of two pairs of genes, one pair for one trait and the other pair for a different trait.

Diploid (2n) (the species number of chromosomes)   The chromosome number just twice the haploid gametic number (n). At meiosis, homologous chromosomes form pairs; hence the name, meaning double or twofold (see **Haploid**).

Dizygotic twins   Fraternal twins produced by the fertilization of two separate eggs by two different spermatozoa.

Dominance   Complete suppression of the expression of one allele by another allele at the same locus in the homologous chromosome.

Egg   The female germ cell; in animals, an ovum.

Eugenics   The science concerned with improvement of the heredity of the human race.

F_1   Abbreviation for first filial generation, usually the hybrid between two homozygous types.

F_2   Abbreviation for the second filial generation, usually produced by intercrossing two F_1's or by self-fertilizing an F_1, as is possible in plants.

Fertilization   The union of a male gamete (sperm) with a female gamete (ovum) to form a zygote, which develops into an embryo.

Fraternal twins   See **Dizygotic twins.**

Gamete   A mature reproductive male or female germ cell, sperm, or egg.

Gene   The discrete, particulate hereditary determiner located in the chromosome in linear order; the "element" of Mendel and "factor" of early genetic terminology. The gene is composed mostly of DNA. It was discovered by Mendel and named by Johannsen.

Genetics   The science of heredity of the similarities and differences among organisms.

Genotype   The genetic constitution or gene makeup of an organism.

Germ cell   A mature sex cell; a gamete, capable of uniting in fertilization with another gamete to reproduce the organism.

Germ plasm   A special kind of protoplasm transmitted from generation to generation. The chromosomes and genes constitute the germ plasm; this is the physical basis of heredity.

Gonad   A gland, such as an ovary or testis, in which gametes (sex cells) are produced.

Haploid   Having half the number of chromosomes (gametic number) found in diploid organisms (half the species number of chromosomes).

Hemizygous   Only one gene (or chromosome) is present; there is no homologous allele. Genes on the X chromosome and Y chromosome of human males are hemizygous.

Heredity   Transmission of traits from parent to offspring.

Heritability   The extent to which a given trait is determined by inheritance.

Heterozygous   The chromosome of one parent provides one form of allele for a trait, while the homologous chromosome (from the other parent) contains a different allele (a different form of the gene) at the same locus for the same trait.

Homologous chromosomes   A pair of chromosomes that are similar in size, shape, structure, and function. One of the pair is provided by the male parent, the other by the female parent. In humans, the male spermatozoon contains 23 chromosomes that are homologous to the 23 chromosomes in the ovum (except for the X chromosome, which pairs with the Y chromosome or another X chromosome).

Homozygous   The homologous chromosome of one parent contains an allele for a trait that is exactly like the allele contained at the same locus on the homologous chromosome provided by the other parent.

Hybrid   A cross of unlike organisms (i.e., organisms with different traits. Usually they are of the same species, but crosses have been made between closely related species, the offspring of which are usually sterile).

Identical twins   See **Monozygotic twins.**

Inbreeding   Mating of related types; **consanguineous** mating (mating of relatives).

Incomplete dominance   Lack of dominance. See **Cumulative effect.**

Lethal gene (lethal mutation)   A gene that renders the gamete nonviable (gametic lethal) or one that prevents the complete development of a zygote (zygotic lethal). Zygotic lethals may produce their effects at any time from fertilization of the egg on.

Linkage   The association of two or more characters in inheritance caused by two genes associated in the same chromosome. The nearer the genes to each other, the closer the linkage.

Linkage group   A group of characters all showing linkage with others in the same group. The genes for these characters are arranged linearly in one chromosome, the genes close together showing close linkage.

Locus (pl. loci)   The physical location of a gene in the chromosome. Genes, normally, have two (sometimes more) alleles which may occur at a given locus (only one allele may occupy the locus at any given time).

Meiosis   A special type of cell division found in gamete production. It consists of two divisions, one of which is reductional. Homologous chromosomes pair and assort at random to produce gametes with the haploid (n) number of chromosomes.

Mendel's law   The principle that hereditary characters are determined by discrete particles (genes) that segregate at random in gamete formation (see **Linkage**).

Mitosis   Cell division in which chromosomes are divided equally in such a manner that daughter cells have exactly the same number and composition of genes as do the original chromosomes in the original cell.

Monohybrid   A cross involving a single pair of genes for a given trait. (Also known as a monogenic cross.)

Monozygotic twins   Twins that have developed from a single fertilized ovum (egg) that divided to form two zygotes wth identical genotypes; identical twins.

Multiple alleles   Three or more alleles occurring at a single locus on a chromosome. All relate to the same trait (they may not occupy the same locus at the same time).

Mutable gene   An unstable gene that mutates frequently.

Mutagen   Any substance, chemical or physical, that causes genes to mutate.

Mutant   A variant from the normal gene, inherited in a Mendelian manner.

Mutation   A change that is inherited (see **Mutant**).

n, 2n   The gametic (haploid or n) and zygotic (diploid or 2n) chromosome numbers, respectively.

Outbreeding   Mating of unrelated individuals or of individuals not closely related; the opposite of inbreeding.

Ovum   See **Egg**.

P   Abbreviation for parent.

Parthenogenesis   Reproduction without fertilization.

Pedigree   1. The genotype of an individual. 2. A chart showing the ancestral history of an individual.

Phenotype   The appearance of an individual. The appearance is produced by the genotype in combination with the environment.

Predisposition   A condition of special susceptibility to a disease.

Probability   The chance or likelihood of a given possible event.

Progeny   Offspring; individuals resulting from a mating.

Punnett square   After R.C. Punnett; the conventional checkerboard with male gametes on one axis and female gametes on the other. Zygotes are obtained by multiplying all male gametes by all female gametes.

Recessive   Producing little or no effect when occurring with an allele dominant for the same trait.

Sex chromosome   A chromosome, usually designated X or Y, particularly concerned with sex determination; e.g., in *Drosophila* (fruit flies) and mammals, including man, the female is XX (has two X chromosomes) and the male is XY.

Sex linkage   An unusual type of inheritance caused by genes located in the X chromosome. The Y chromosome is practically devoid of genes, and those present are not homologous with those located on the X chromosome. The Y chromosome is not a carrier of alleles in sex-linked problems.

Sex-promoting alleles   Certain alleles concerned with sex determination. Females are always heterozygous, males homozygous or hemizygous.

Sib mating   The mating of sisters and brothers (s - sister, i - with, b - brother, thus, sib).

Syndrome   A group of symptoms that occur together and characterize a disease.

Test cross   A cross of the heterozygote with an individual containing only recessive alleles of the gene in question.

Appendix 5

Determination of pH

The concentration of hydrogen ion, H^+, in the environment (e.g., in food, water, solutions, etc.) and in living organisms (both plant and animal) is of great physiological importance. This ion is universally present in aqueous systems and has marked influence on the functions of living systems. It affects the solubility of all other elements as well as the availability and absorption of ions, the stability of proteins and enzyme systems, and numerous other functions of plants and animals.

The concentration of this ion is so important that a special scale (the pH scale) has been established to simplify its expression. The pH is the negative logarithm of the hydrogen ion concentration in a solution:

$$pH = - \log (H^+)$$

In pure water the concentration of H^+ is equal to the concentration of OH^- (hydroxyl ion) and each is equal to 1×10^{-7} moles/liter. Since pH is defined as the negative logarithm of the hydrogen ion concentration, then in pure water, at 25 °C, pH = $- \log (1 \times 10^{-7})$ = $\log 10^7$ = 7.0.

The pH scale of commonly used solutions extends from 0 to 14, with a pH of 7 representing neutrality. Pure water (lacking minerals and carbon dioxide) would have a pH of 7. As the pH goes up, the hydrogen ion concentration decreases, and the solution becomes more alkaline (basic). As the pH of a solution goes down, the hydrogen ion concentration increases, and the solution becomes more acidic. Since the pH scale is a logarithmic scale, a pH of 6 (10^{-6} moles/liter) would indicate an acid solution with a concentration of hydrogen ions ten times greater than that at a pH of 7.0 (10^{-7} moles/liter). The hydrogen ion concentration would be a hundred times greater at pH 6 (10^{-6} moles/liter) than at pH 8 (10^{-8} moles/liter).

Thus we see that acidity and alkalinity can be expressed in terms of pH. A pH less than 7.0 indicates an acid solution, while a pH greater than 7.0 indicates an alkaline solution.

METHODS FOR DETERMINING HYDROGEN ION CONCENTRATION (pH)

Taste

In general, acids have a sour taste while alkaline substances have a more or less bitter taste. For example, a soda cracker may have a pH as high as 8.5 (alkaline) and lemon may have a pH as low as 2.2 (acid). It is well to remember, however, that sourness may be masked by sugar. Thus, a ripe apple may taste sweet but have a pH as low as 2.9.

Litmus Paper

Litmus paper is paper impregnated with the organic dye, litmus, obtained from several species of lichens. This paper is ordinarily provided in short strips, and one end of the strip is immersed in the solution to be tested. Blue litmus paper turns red in an acid medium, while red litmus paper turns blue in an alkaline medium.

Hydrion Paper

This paper comes in a special dispenser from which strips of 1 to 2 inches at a time may be removed. A portion of the strip is placed in the sample to be tested and then compared with a color scale. This is a quantitative measurement (the foregoing methods are qualitative) and is accurate to within a single unit of the pH scale.

Indicators

These are dyes that are used to test the pH of a solution. As the hydrogen ion content of the solution changes, rearrangement of the indicator molecule occurs, which results in a change in color. Indicators may also provide quantitative measurements of pH, though not as accurately as hydrion papers.

pH Meters

These are instruments designed for rapid and accurate pH measurements of solutions, pastes, and semisolids. They are accurate, when properly standardized, to 0.10 pH unit, and determinations may be made in the 0 to 14 pH range.

KEYS TO SELF-TESTS

CHAPTER 1

1. Transverse
2. Transverse
5. Superior
6. Distal
8. Frontal (coronal)
9. Distal
10. Dorsal
11. Lateral
15. Posterior and dorsal
18. Abdominal cavity
21. Bilateral
22. Dorsal
25. Prone
27. Lateral
29. Distal
30. Lateral
31. Lower right
32. Pelvic cavity

CHAPTER 2

4. Smaller
6. Resolving
8. 100
9. Fine adjustment knob
11. 250
12. Lower
15. Electron beams
16. L.s.
18. 50

CHAPTER 3

1. A tissue
3. Conducts
5. Columnar epithelium
6. Chondrocytes
9. An organ
10. Endothelium
14. Ciliated columnar cells
18. Canaliculi
19. Compact (dense)
22. Smooth (visceral)
24. Stratum corneum
25. Dermis
27. Melanin
32. Mainly water and a little salt
33. Sebaceous
34. Dermis
37. Metaphase
38. Prophase
43. Cytoplasm
44. Only in the cytoplasm
45. Mitochondria
48. The nucleus

CHAPTER 4

2. Have
4. Compound
6. True
7. The same
8. Diaphysis; epiphyses
12. Compact
13. Proximal epiphyses
14. Neck
16. Femur
19. Endosteum
20. Pelvic (sacral)
26. Pelvis
28. Female
31. Vertebral foramina
38. Meatus
39. Fossa
40. Tubercle
41. Diarthroses
45. Hinge
49. Abduction
52. Abduction
53. Supination
55. Thorax
57. Scoliosis
60. Not a clean break
61. Splinter
66. Kyphosis or hunchback
67. Red

CHAPTER 5

1. Passive
4. Not the same
7. Hypertonic
8. Differentially (semi) permeable
10. Less; more
12. Hypotonic
13. Water
15. Hypotonic
17. Higher; lower
19. Isotonic
21. Indirectly
22. Starch
23. NaCl, glucose (crystalloids)
24. True solutions and colloids
25. Emulsions
28. Concentration
32. Diffusion and osmosis
34. By freezing
35. Isomers

CHAPTER 6

1. Cardiac
2. Movable
3. On the posterior thigh
4. Gastrocnemius
5. Radius
9. Rectus abdominis
12. Quadriceps femoris
14. Downward
16. Sarcoplasm
20. Hereditary
21. Latissimus dorsi
22. Medial rectus
23. Scapula and clavicle
24. Subscapularis
27. Flexes
28. Flexes
29. Hamstring
31. Extends
34. Flexes

CHAPTER 8

1. Recovery
2. Cholinesterase
9. Tonus
10. Less
11. Produce
12. Acetylcholine
17. The same (approximately) time as
18. Efferent
19. Related
20. Is not
22. Cannot
23. Myoglobin

CHAPTER 9

4. Root canal (pulp cavity)
8. Permanent
13. Polysaccharides
14. Starch, cellulose, or glycogen
16. Monosaccharides and most disaccharides
17. Disaccharide
18. 1 molecule; 3 molecules
21. Intestinal juice
27. Stomach
36. Villi
37. Rectum
38. Cecum
41. Peritoneum
42. Pharynx
44. As well as
46. Rugae
47. Bile salts
51. Higher pH

53. Lipase
54. Oropharynx
55. Portal vein
56. Major area
57. Protein
58. Feces
61. Parietal cells
64. Small intestine

66. Half
72. Small intestine
77. Fat
78. Is not
79. Greater
83. Proteins
86. Are not stored

CHAPTER 10

2. Anabolism
3. Oxidation
8. Lower
10. Glycogenesis
16. Tends to elevate
17. Approximately the same as that
18. Decreases
19. Large Calories

25. Hypothalamus
27. Rise
28. 99°F
29. A limited role
31. Dilation
32. Poorly regulated
33. Radiation
35. Skeletal muscles

CHAPTER 11

3. Nitrogen
5. Pharynx
7. Epiglottis
10. External
16. Pharynx
18. Relaxation
20. Cells
21. Alveoli — pulmonary veins
25. Right — left

32. Less
36. More
38. Hyperventilation
41. Efferent
46. Medulla oblongata
47. Pleura
48. Bronchi
49. Larynx
50. Carbon dioxide
51. Intrapleural

CHAPTER 12

3. An increase
9. Speeded up
10. Anticoagulants
14. No more often
17. Alkaline (basic)
18. 45%
22. Non-nucleated (anucleate)
25. Recipient
26. Coronary thrombosis
28. Anemia
29. Vitamin K
30. Thrombocytes

31. Thrombin
32. Rh–, Rh+
33. 250,000 - 500,000
34. Stationary
37. Leukocytes
41. Hemoglobin
42. Intercellular (tissue)
43. Phagocytosis
45. Capillaries
46. Erythrocytes
47. Water is
48. Iron
49. 7

CHAPTER 13

1. Inferior vena cava
7. Pericardium
8. Stenosis
12. Arm
15. Artery
17. Do not always
18. Right ventricle
20. Appears at birth
22. Leukocytes (lymphocytes)
23. Myocardium
27. Veins
28. Pulmonary veins

30. Endothelium
32. Left
36. Nonstriated
39. External jugular
41. Superior vena cava
42. Arm
43. Twice
44. Media
48. Hepatic
49. Stroke (cerebral vascular accident)
50. Lymph

CHAPTERS 14 AND 15

4. Slows down
7. Faster
8. Medulla oblongata
10. Oxygenated
12. Sinoatrial
15. Arteriosclerosis
17. Tricuspid

20. Craniosacral (parasympathetic)
22. Sinoatrial node
23. Diastole, systole
25. Liver
26. Difference between
28. Pulsating

29. Capillaries
30. Arteries
31. Arterioles
32. A decrease
36. Systole

38. Depress
40. Blockage of lymphatic vessels
42. Decrease
43. An unknown cause

CHAPTER 16

2. Dendrite
5. Brachial plexus
9. Efferent
10. Precentral
11. First lumbar
12. Thalamus
13. Hypothalamus
15. Myoneural junction
16. Gyri
17. Gray
20. Opposite
23. Vagus
26. Olfactory
28. L3-L4
33. Sciatic nerve
34. Trigeminal

35. An involuntary
37. Away from
39. Neurilemma
43. Positive
44. Gray
47. Cerebrum
49. Sympathetic
50. Thoracolumbar (sympathetic)
51. Pia mater
54. Anterior (ventral)
56. Medulla oblongata
57. Pia mater
58. Medulla oblongata
59. Gray matter
61. Facial

CHAPTER 17

5. Hyperopia
10. Unequally
14. Temporal
18. Tip
19. Right—left
22. Iris
23. Aqueous
28. Fenestra ovalis, or oval window

32. Middle
38. Conjunctiva
40. Intrinsic
41. Sclera
43. Optic disc
45. Cones
48. Vitamin A
50. Presbyopia
54. Malleus, incus, and stapes

CHAPTER 18

2. Cystitis
3. Lack of
4. Nocturia
5. Increase
7. Ureter
8. Filtration
9. Liver
10. Reabsorbed
14. Peritoneum
17. Casts

20. Smaller
22. Gases
23. Adrenal gland
24. Uriniferous tubule
26. Store
28. Nephron
30. Protein (albumin)
31. Not found
32. 190
34. Arteries

CHAPTER 19

1. Cretinism
2. Posterior pituitary (or hypothalamus)
3. Parathyroids
6. Thyroid
7. ACTH
8. Diabetes insipidus
9. Parathyroid
11. Pituitary
13. Somatotropic
16. Decreases in size
17. Increases
19. Cholecystokinin

20. Acidosis
21. Anterior pituitary
22. Thyroxin
23. An excess of STH
24. Edema
25. Oxytocin
27. Testosterone
28. Cortex
29. Glycogenolysis
31. Pituitary
32. Testosterone
33. Sympathetic

CHAPTER 20

1. Seminiferous tubule, epididymis, vas deferens, urethra
3. Fertilized egg
8. Seminiferous tubules
11. Graafian follicle
14. Alkaline

15. Interstitial cells
16. Identical
17. Fallopian tubes
20. Exchange
21. Fallopian tubes
22. Hysterectomy
24. Fallopian tube

300

25. Vertebral column
27. Ectoderm
28. 14
32. LH
36. Amnion

37. Uterus
40. Seminiferous tubules
44. Cryptorchidism
45. Urethra
49. Vagina

CHAPTER 21

3. By both males and females
4. Not all
5. Not all
7. Will not
9. Do not always result
10. In males and females
11. May not have

13. Could possibly
14. Could have been
15. Homozygous
16. Gene
17. May be heterozygous or homozygous
23. Not all
29. Daughter's sons

RESULTS AND QUESTIONS FOR CHAPTER 1

EXERCISE 1-A. ORGANIZATION OF THE BODY AS A WHOLE
Part 1. Cavities of the Body

In the blanks provided, indicate the specific body cavity (or cavities) in which each of the following is located (dorsal and ventral are not answers):

1. Stomach. _____
2. Spinal cord. _____
3. Urinary bladder. _____
4. Uterus. _____
5. Fallopian tubes. _____
6. Large intestine. _____
7. Prostate gland. _____
8. Tongue. _____
9. Pancreas. _____
10. Aortic arch. _____

11. Brain. _____
12. Lungs. _____
13. Heart. _____
14. Kidneys. _____
15. Teeth. _____
16. Ovaries. _____
17. Appendix. _____
18. Small intestine. _____
19. Adrenal glands. _____
20. Spleen. _____

Part 2. Regions of the Body

1. Through what region of the body would a surgeon make an incision to perform an appendectomy? _____

2. Through what region of the body would an incision be made to perform surgery on the right kidney? _____

3. What is the name given to several tissues grouped into one structure performing one or more general functions? _____

4. Which organ system has the function of conducting air? _____

5. Which organ system eliminates body wastes? _____

6. Which organ system synthesizes hormones? _____

7. To which organ system(s) do sweat glands belong? _____

8. Of which organ system are leukocytes a part? _____

9. Of which organ system are lymph nodes a part? _____

10. Of which organ system is gastric juice a secretion? _____

EXERCISE 1-B. ANATOMIC TERMINOLOGY

1. Select the best answer for each blank. Use each term only once.

    _____ a. Two terms used for the back side of the body.
    _____

    _____ b. Term meaning farther away from a point of reference, such as the trunk.

    _____ c. Toward the midline of the body.

    _____ d. Layer of a membrane lining the walls of a cavity.

    _____ e. Layer of a membrane covering the organs within a cavity.

    _____ f. Toward the tail end of the body.

    _____ g. Sole of the foot.

    _____ h. Away from the center of the body; toward the outside of the body.

    _____ i. Term describing the location of a structure located in the middle of another structure, such as the arm.

    _____ j. Two terms used for the front side of the body.
    _____

    _____ k. Palm of the hand.

    _____ l. Term describing the location of the little toe with respect to the big toe.

1. anterior
2. caudal
3. cranial
4. distal
5. dorsal
6. dorsum
7. inferior
8. lateral
9. medial
10. median
11. parietal
12. peripheral
13. plantar
14. posterior
15. proximal
16. superior
17. ventral
18. visceral
19. volar

2. In anatomic position:

    a. Are the thumbs medial or lateral? _____

    b. Are the palms of the hands ventral or dorsal? _____

    c. Is the body in a supine or in a vertical position? _____

3. What is the advantage of having a standard anatomic position? _____

_____

Name _____

RESULTS AND QUESTIONS FOR CHAPTER 2

EXERCISE 2-A. STRUCTURE OF THE MICROSCOPE

1. What is the function of stage clips? _____
2. What is the function of the iris diaphragm? _____
3. Why should the coarse adjustment knob never be used to focus downward when high power is used? _____
4. What word refers to objectives or lenses that focus at the same position? _____
5. The magnification obtained with the microscope is the product of the magnification indicated on the ocular (usually 10X) times that on the objective (10X for low power). Determine the magnification obtained with the low power objective.

   _____

6. What magnification is obtained with the high power objective? _____
7. If the magnification of the ocular (eyepiece) is 15X and that of the objective is 20X, what is the total magnification obtained? _____
8. If the dimensions of a cell are 0.2 mm by 0.5 mm, what are the dimensions of this cell in microns? _____
9. The diameter of the low power field in a microscope (using the 10X objective and 10X ocular) is 1.5 mm. Express this diameter in microns. _____
10. Size of cells may be calculated from the formula

$$\frac{\text{Diameter of field}}{\text{No. of cells visible}} = \text{Size of cell}$$

    If ten cells are visible across the width of the microscope field (diameter 0.6 mm), and four are visible down the length of the microscope field, what are the dimensions of one cell in millimeters? _____
11. What are the dimensions of the same cell, in microns? _____
12. What is the area of the same cell, in square microns? _____

EXERCISE 2-C. ORIENTATION OF IMAGES
VIEWED THROUGH THE COMPOUND MICROSCOPE

1. Draw the letter p as it would appear through the microscope. _____
2. In Part 1, 4. or in Part 2, 5., in which directions did you move the slide to center the letter?

   _____

EXERCISE 2-D. THREAD SLIDE

1. In this exercise, which gave the best results, the low or the high power objective? _____
2. Relate this exercise to the procedure necessary for observing the parts of a cell.

   _____
   _____

303

RESULTS AND QUESTIONS FOR CHAPTER 3

EXERCISE 3-A. STRUCTURES AND FUNCTIONS OF CELLS

Part 1. Structures of a Cell Observed with a Light Microscope Compared with those Observed with an Electron Microscope

1. Give the primary function of each of the following structures:

    a. Vacuole. _____

    b. Nucleus. _____

    c. Chromosomes. _____

    d. Centrioles. _____

    e. Mitochondria. _____

    f. Nucleolus. _____

    g. Inclusions. _____

    h. Endoplasmic reticulum. _____

    i. Ribosomes. _____

    j. Cytoplasmic membrane. _____

    k. Lysosomes. _____

    l. Pinocytic vacuole. _____

    m. Golgi apparatus. _____

2. Which of these structures can only be observed with an electron microscope? (Write in the letter preceding the structure.) _____

Part 2. Observation of an Ameba

1. Briefly describe the movement of the ameba. _____

2. To what cells in the human body is the ameba comparable? _____

3. What properties of protoplasm were you able to discern as a result of your observations of the ameba? _____

EXERCISE 3-B. MITOSIS

1. What is the significance of mitosis? _____

2. In the spaces provided, indicate the phase of mitosis described in each of the following statements:

    a. Nuclear membrane present; two centrioles in a single centrosphere; chromosomes not visible. _____

   b. Chromatids completely separate into individual chromosomes and begin moving to opposite poles. _____

   c. The cleavage furrow has just made its appearance. _____

   d. The chromosomes are oriented along the equator. _____

   e. Centrioles begin moving to opposite poles. _____

   f. Nuclear membrane disappears; distinct chromosomes first observed. _____

3. Where does mitosis occur in the human body? _____

4. What cells in the human body do not undergo mitosis? _____

EXERCISE 3-C. EPITHELIAL TISSUE

1. Give two locations of simple squamous epithelial tissue. _____
_____

2. What is the main function of simple squamous epithelium? _____

3. Where is simple columnar epithelial tissue located? _____
_____

4. Where is ciliated columnar epithelial tissue located? _____
_____

5. Compare simple columnar epithelial tissue with ciliated columnar tissue using functions as a basis for differentiation. _____
_____
_____

6. What is the main function of cuboidal epithelium? _____

7. Give a location of stratified squamous epithelium that is moist. _____

8. Give a location of stratified squamous epithelium that is dry. _____

EXERCISE 3-D. CONNECTIVE TISSUE
Part 1. Areolar (Loose) Connective Tissue

1. Where is areolar connective tissue located? _____

2. What is the function of collagenous fibers? _____

3. What is the function of elastic fibers? _____

4. Give two functions of areolar connective tissue. _____
_____

Part 2. Adipose Tissue

1. List three functions of adipose tissue. _____
_____

2. What is the matrix of adipose tissue? _____

Name _____

Part 3. Hyaline Cartilage

1. List four locations of hyaline cartilage. _____
_____

2. What is the function of hyaline cartilage? _____
_____

3. How does hyaline cartilage differ from fibrous and elastic cartilage? _____
_____

Part 4. Osseous (Bony) Tissue

1. What is the function of the haversian canal? _____
2. What is the function of a canaliculus? _____
3. By what cells is the bony matrix deposited? _____
4. The preceding cells are located in depressions called _____

Part 5. Blood

1. What is the major function of erythrocytes? _____
2. What is the major function of leukocytes? _____
3. What is the major function of thrombocytes? _____
4. Where are erythrocytes manufactured in adults? _____
5. Where are erythrocytes produced before birth? _____
6. Where are leukocytes produced? _____
7. What kind of blood cell is anucleate? _____
8. In a normal human, what is the rarest kind of leukocyte? _____
9. In a normal human, what is the most common kind of leukocyte? _____

EXERCISE 3-E. MUSCLE TISSUE

1. Where is skeletal muscle tissue located in the body? _____
2. Why is skeletal muscle tissue also called voluntary muscle? _____
_____

3. Why is visceral muscle tissue also called smooth muscle? _____
4. Where is visceral muscle tissue located? _____
5. What does cardiac muscle tissue have in common with skeletal muscle? _____
_____

6. What does cardiac muscle tissue have in common with visceral muscle? _____
_____

7. Give an identifying characteristic of cardiac muscle tissue. _____
_____

EXERCISE 3-F. NERVE TISSUE

1. What is the function of myelin? _____

2. What is the function of the neurilemma? _____

3. In what parts of the nervous system is myelin found? _____

4. What general subdivision of the nervous system lacks a neurilemma? _____
_____

EXERCISE 3-G. SKIN

1. Where, within the skin, is melanin located? _____

2. What is the function of melanin? _____

3. What causes a suntan? _____

4. What is the function of the arrector pili muscle?

5. What region of the skin is made up of stratified squamous epithelium? _____
_____

6. What is the function of a sudoriferous gland? _____

7. What is the function of a sebaceous gland? _____

8. Is a hair alive or dead? _____ How is it nourished? _____
_____

9. What is the function of the stratum germinativum? _____
_____

RESULTS AND QUESTIONS FOR CHAPTER 4

EXERCISE 4-A. COMPOSITION AND STRUCTURE OF BONE

1. What is the scientific term for the shaft of a long bone? _____

2. From which part of a long bone were the slides of bone used in Exercise 3-D, Part 4, obtained? _____

3. What is the function of the organic material in bone? _____ _____

4. What is the function of the inorganic material in bone? _____ _____

5. Name the cells that build bone. _____

6. Where are the bone-building cells located in bone? _____

7. Describe the appearance of the bone soaked in acid. _____ _____

8. Describe the appearance of the bone subjected to intense heat. _____ _____

9. Name the most abundant inorganic salts in bone. _____

10. Define a "greenstick" fracture. _____

11. In what age group does a "greenstick" fracture occur most commonly? _____ Explain why: _____

12. What is the function of each of the following:
    a. Haversian canals _____
    b. Canaliculi _____
    c. Volkmann's canals _____
    d. Periosteal blood vessels _____
    e. Nutrient foramen _____

EXERCISE 4-B. THE SKELETON

1. Name the bones comprising the shoulder girdle. _____

2. Name the bones comprising the pelvic girdle. _____

3. Name the bones comprising the bony pelvis. _____

4. How does the female pelvis differ from the male pelvis? _____ _____ _____ _____

5. Define Colle's fracture. _____

6. What is a common cause of Colle's fracture? _____

7. Why is the clavicle particularly likely to fracture if a person falls on the shoulder?

_____

8. What is the common name of each of the following?
   a. Clavicle. _____   d. Phalanges. _____
   b. Scapula. _____   e. Femur. _____
   c. Os coxae. _____   f. Calcaneus. _____

9. How many carpals are there in the entire adult skeleton? _____

10. How many tarsals are there in the entire adult skeleton? _____

11. Define:
    a. Lordosis. _____
    b. Kyphosis. _____
    c. Scoliosis. _____

12. What is another name for the first cervical vertebra? _____

13. What is another name for the second cervical vertebra? _____

14. What is meant by a "slipped disc"? _____

15. What is the cause of spina bifida? _____

16. Name the bones making up each of the following structures:
    a. Nasal septum. _____
    b. Hard palate. _____
    c. Orbit. _____

    _____

17. List the bones possessing paranasal sinuses. _____

    _____

18. Into what do the paranasal sinuses drain? _____

19. List the five regions of the vertebral column and the distinguishing characteristics of each.

Region	No. of Vertebrae	Distinguishing Characteristics

20. What bones does the lambdoidal suture unite? _____

21. Name the bones forming the bony thorax. _____

22. What are wormian bones? _____

EXERCISE 4-C. THE FETAL SKELETON

1. Compare the fetal and adult skeletons by filling in the following table.

	Description of Bone in Fetal Skeleton
Frontal bone	
Sternum	
Patella	
Os coxae	
Spinous processes of vertebrae	
Carpals	
Proximal epiphysis of humerus	

2. What is a fontanel? _____

3. How many bones are there in the typical fetal skeleton? _____

4. What was the sex of the fetal skeleton examined? _____

5. What characteristics of the fetal skeleton enabled you to determine its sex? _____
_____

EXERCISE 4-D. JOINTS

1. Fill in the following table.

Name of Joint	Bones Comprising Joint	Types of Movement Possible at Joint
Hip joint		
Knee joint		
Elbow joint		
Wrist joint		
Interphalangeal joint		

2. How does the hip joint differ from the shoulder joint? Discuss both the structure of the joint and the range of movement. _____
_____
_____

3. What is the function of the synovial fluid? _____

4. What is a meniscus? _____

5. What is the function of a ligament? _____

6. What is the function of the patella? _____

7. What is a sesamoid bone? _____

8. Define the ligamenta flava. _____

9. What type of joint (classified as to structure **and** as to amount of movement possible) is found between

    a. the bodies of the vertebrae? _____

    b. the articular processes of the vertebrae? _____

    c. the os coxae bone and the sacrum? _____

RESULTS AND QUESTIONS FOR CHAPTER 5

EXERCISE 5-A. FILTRATION

1. a. Number of drops formed in first 10 seconds. _____

   b. Number of drops formed in a 10-second interval when fluid level is reduced by one-third.

   _____

   c. Number of drops in a 10-second interval when fluid level is reduced by two-thirds. _____

2. Give a brief explanation of the results obtained in no. 1. _____

   _____

   _____

3. What relationship (direct or indirect) was demonstrated between the weight (height) of the fluid

   column and the rate of filtration? _____

   _____

4. What substances passed through the filter paper? _____

   What substance did not pass through the filter paper? _____

5. What is the explanation for the results obtained in question 4? _____

   _____

6. Where in the human body does filtration occur? _____

EXERCISE 5-B. DIFFUSION

Part 1. Diffusion of a Liquid into a Gas

1. How long did it take for the first person to detect the odor of the ether? _____

2. How much time elapsed before the ether was detected in the

   a. first row. _____   d. fourth row. _____

   b. second row. _____   e. fifth row. _____

   c. third row. _____

3. What percentage of students detected the odor? _____

4. Did all of the students detect the odor? _____ If not, give a possible explanation for this fact.

   _____

5. If the diffusion of the ether did not follow a predictable pattern, what factors were present in

   the environment to cause deviations? _____

   _____

6. Give an example of diffusion of a liquid into a gas in the human body. _____

   _____

Part 2. Diffusion of a Solid in a Liquid

1. Give a brief explanation as to what happened in this demonstration. _____

    _____

2. Where in the human body does diffusion of a solid through a liquid medium occur? _____

    _____

Part 3. Diffusion of a Solid in Agar

1. The molecules of which substance diffused more rapidly? _____

2. What relationship (direct or indirect) was there between the molecular weight of the substance

    and the rate of diffusion? _____

3. What part of the cell can the agar be considered to represent? _____

4. Where in the body does diffusion of this kind take place? _____

EXERCISE 5-C. DIALYSIS

1. Which substances passed through the membrane? _____

2. Which substances did not pass through the membrane? _____

    Explain your results. _____

3. From your observations, which type of compound is dialyzable, crystalloids or colloids?

    _____

4. In which direction, in terms of concentration of particles, does dialysis occur? _____

    _____

5. Based on the results of this experiment, which components of blood would you expect to
    remain in the blood vessels and which could move out of the capillaries to form tissue fluid?

    _____

EXERCISE 5-D. PLASMOLYSIS

1. Was the water concentration greater inside or outside the cell when the leaf was first placed in

    the salt solution? _____

2. Did water move into or out of the cell? _____ Why? _____

    _____

3. What occupied the space between the plasma membrane and the cell wall of the plasmolyzed

    cell? _____

4. Which is the differentially permeable membrane in *Elodea*—the cell wall or the plasma
    membrane?

    _____

5. When the salt solution was replaced with distilled water, was there any indication of reversal of

    the previous results? _____

6. Explain the results indicated in question 5. _____

    _____

Name _____

7. What would have been the expected results in the experiment if the plasma membrane had been freely permeable to the salt as well as to the water? _____

_____

_____

EXERCISE 5-E. OSMOSIS

1. Give a complete explanation for the results observed in the experiment. _____

_____

_____

2. What effect would increased strength of the solution in the osmometer have on the final height of the column in the osmometer? _____

_____

EXERCISE 5-F. HEMOLYSIS AND CRENATION

1. What happened to the erythrocytes placed in 0.9% NaCl? _____
2. Describe the appearance of the erythrocytes placed in distilled water. _____

_____

3. Give the technical name for what occurred in no. 2. _____
4. Describe the appearance of the erythrocytes placed in 3% NaCl. _____
5. Give the technical name for what occurred in no. 4. _____
6. In what kind of solution were the erythrocytes in nos. 1, 2, and 4 (hypotonic, hypertonic, or isotonic)?

   a. 0.9% NaCl _____

   b. Distilled water _____

   c. 3% NaCl _____

7. Explain why you would expect crenation to occur in a 10% glucose solution. _____

_____

RESULTS AND QUESTIONS FOR CHAPTER 6

EXERCISE 6-A. GROSS ANATOMY OF THE MAJOR SUPERFICIAL HUMAN MUSCLES

1. Complete the following chart concerning muscle action. In the column headed Chief Antagonist, list a muscle that has an action antagonistic to the major action listed in the first column.

Muscle	Major Action	Chief Antagonist
Pectoralis major		
Biceps brachii		
Deltoid		
External intercostals		
Gluteus medius		
Gastrocnemius		
Triceps brachii		
Brachialis		
Quadriceps femoris		
Gluteus maximus		
Latissimus dorsi		
Rectus abdominis		

2. Contraction of which muscle will produce each of the following facial expressions?

    a. Smiling. _____

    b. Frowning. _____

    c. Pouting. _____

    d. Contempt and disdain. _____

3. Which muscle closes the eyes? _____

4. Which muscle opens the eyes? _____

5. Which muscle wrinkles the forehead to produce the expressions of fright, horror, and surprise?

    _____

6. Which muscle is called the trumpeter's muscle? _____

7. Which muscle is called the muscle of kissing? _____

8. Contraction of which muscle will pull down the corners of the lips? _____

9. Name the muscles of mastication. _____

_____

10. Contraction of which muscle flexes the head laterally? _____

11. Contraction of which muscle would raise the head from a position of lateral flexion back to the vertical position? _____

12. Name the lateral abdominal wall muscles in order, from the outside in. _____

_____

13. What is the difference between a tendon and a ligament? _____

_____

14. Define the term "retroperitoneal." _____

15. What is the linea alba? _____

16. Define the term "aponeurosis." _____

_____

17. Sometimes hard objects that cannot be chewed are found in bacon. What are these hard objects?

_____

18. Name two muscles making up the calf of the leg. _____

_____

19. What two muscles insert on the calcaneus by way of the tendon of Achilles? _____

_____

RESULTS AND QUESTIONS FOR CHAPTER 7

EXERCISE 7-A. FARADIC CURRENT

1. Did you feel a shock on either make or break with the voltage dial on 0? _____

   Explain: _____

2. Record the liminal stimulus for:

   make _____

   break _____

3. With faradic current, which is stronger, the make or break shocks? _____

4. Was a shock felt during the time the key was depressed between the make and the break? ___

5. Was a shock felt in steps 8 through 10? _____ Explain: _____

   _____

6. Does the faradic current flow while the key is held in a depressed position? _____

7. Describe in detail how it would be possible to short-circuit the break. _____

   _____

   _____

EXERCISE 7-B. TETANIZING STIMULATION

1. Fill in the following table using your results from Exercise 7-A and Exercise 7-B. Place the voltage range and the voltage dial setting in parentheses after the volts.

		Liminal Stimulus (volts)
Single Induction Faradic Shocks		
	Make	
	Break	
Tetanizing		

2. What conclusion can you draw concerning the relative intensity of the make single-induction shock, the break single-induction shock, and the tetanizing stimuli?

   _____

   _____

3. Why is tetanic stimulation stronger? _____

4. Are the shocks felt the entire time the key is on MULT? _____

EXERCISE 7-C. USE OF THE KYMOGRAPH AND INK RECORDING APPARATUS

1. At drum speed 6, an event was recorded on 10 cm of kymograph paper. What was the duration of this event?

Answer: _____

2. At drum speed 2, an event was recorded on 10 cm of kymograph paper. What was the duration of this event?

Answer: _____

3. At drum speed 3, the duration of an event was 15 seconds. How many centimeters did the drum move during the event?

Answer: _____

EXERCISE 7-D. THE SIGNAL MAGNET

1. Fasten your kymograph records from this experiment in the spaces provided below.

   a. Drum speed 6, 1-second intervals.

   b. Drum speed 2, 1-second intervals.

   c. Drum speed 11, 1-second intervals.

Name _____

2. Using the record obtained with drum speed 6, measure and record the length of each 1-second interval. (Record the value on the record as well as here.) _____
   a. What is the average value? _____
   b. What is the range in values? _____
   c. Discuss the cause of any deviation from the expected value (1 cm). _____
   _____
   _____

3. Is the signal magnet more useful as a timing device at fast drum speeds (e.g., 2), at intermediate speeds (e.g., 6), or at slow speeds (e.g., 11)? _____
   Explain: _____

4. Discuss the advantages and disadvantages of the signal magnet as a timing device.
   _____
   _____

5. Discuss the advantages and disadvantages of the signal magnet as a device for the indication of the precise time of application of a stimulus.
   _____

EXERCISE 7-E. THE TUNING FORK

1. Fasten your kymograph records from this experiment in the spaces provided below.
   a. Drum speed 6.

   b. Drum speed 4.

   c. Drum speed 2.

   d. Drum speed 1.

2. At which drum speed(s) could the tuning fork be used as a timing device? Note: It is essential to have the crests separated in order to count them.

    _____

3. Can the tuning fork be used to time events recorded on a slow drum? _____

4. Can the tuning fork be used to indicate the time of application of a stimulus? _____

    Explain: _____

5. How accurate is the tuning fork as a timing device? _____

6. Which can be used to measure short intervals of time more accurately, the tuning fork or the

    signal magnet? _____

7. Which is easier to use in measuring longer intervals of time? _____

8. Which can be used to indicate the time of application of a stimulus? _____

9. Which requires a rapidly moving drum? _____

EXERCISE 7-F. USE OF THE PHYSIOGRAPH

Part 1. Use of a Recording Channel and the Photoelectric Pulse Pickup

1. Fasten the record of your pulse at paper speed 0.5 cm/sec in the space below.

Name _____

2. It is possible to make the determination of time by two different methods. You may use either the second markers at the bottom of your record or the known time it takes the paper to travel between two dark-green lines. If using the former method, note that 1 second mark is missing every 60 seconds. The latter method is usually easier to use at paper speeds of 0.5 cm/sec. To determine the time elapsed between two dark-green vertical lines, measure the distance (in

centimeters) between two such lines. _____

Divide this distance by the paper speed (0.5 cm/sec). _____

Your answer (5 seconds) is the time it takes the paper to move between two dark-green vertical lines at paper speed 0.5 cm/sec.

Using that method, mark the 5-, 15-, 30-, and 60-second intervals on your record. To mark 60 seconds accurately, you should observe that there are 6 seconds between the last dark-green line on one page and the first dark-green line on the next page of recording paper. (Verify this either by counting the second marks or by measuring the distance in centimeters and dividing by the paper speed.)

3. Determine the number of heartbeats during each of the time intervals.

	No. of heartbeats in interval		No. of heartbeats per minute
5 Seconds	_____	× 12 =	_____
15 Seconds	_____	× 4 =	_____
30 Seconds	_____	× 2 =	_____
60 Seconds	_____	=	_____

4. What might be a possible explanation of variation in the number of heartbeats per minute in no. 3? _____

5. Which duration of determination of heart rate do you think is most accurate? _____

_____

6. Fasten the record of your pulse recorded at paper speed 5 cm/sec in the space below.

7. Calculate the duration of one heartbeat. Using a ruler, measure the length in centimeters of one heartbeat, from the beginning of the beat to the beginning of the next beat. _____

   Divide this distance by the paper speed (5 cm/sec) to obtain the duration of one heartbeat in seconds.

   _____

8. Determine the heart rate per minute, by setting up a proportion.

$$\frac{1 \text{ Heartbeat}}{\text{Duration (in seconds from no. 7)}} = \frac{n \text{ Heartbeats}}{60 \text{ Seconds}}$$

   Heart rate per minute _____

9. Compare the answer obtained here for heart rate per minute with that obtained in question 3 for heart rate per 60 seconds. _____

   _____

   Which do you feel is more accurate? _____ Why? _____

Part 2. Use of the Physiograph Stimulator

1. Insert the record here from Part 2, step 5. Label the 1-second time marks and the mark produced by the event marker, the single stimulus, and the continuous stimulus.

2. Mark and label on the record intervals of 5, 10, and 30 seconds.

3. Fill in the following chart with your results from Exercise 7-F, Part 2.

	Threshold stimulus (volts)
Single shocks, duration 7 milliseconds	
Single shocks, duration 2 milliseconds	
Continuous shocks, frequency 50/second, duration 7 milliseconds	

4. Why was the threshold stimulus higher when the duration was 2 milliseconds as compared with 7? _____

RESULTS AND QUESTIONS FOR CHAPTER 8

EXERCISE 8-A. STRENGTH OF STIMULUS AND HEIGHT OF CONTRACTION
Questions for Experiments with the Kymograph

1. Paste the kymograph record showing the make and break contractions in the space below. Label the make and break contractions.

2. Define the make threshold. _____

   What was your experimental value? _____

3. Define the break threshold. _____

   What was your experimental value? _____

4. Was the height of contraction greater on make or on break? _____

5. Was the current flowing between make and break when the key was depressed? _____

6. Did the muscle contract during the time the key was depressed between the make and the

   break contractions? _____

Questions for Both the Kymograph and Physiograph Experiments

8. Paste your fully labeled record of strength of stimulus and height of contraction in the space below. Label the voltage and the subliminal, liminal, submaximal, and maximal (and supramaximal, if evident) contractions.

9. Record the voltage at each contraction and the magnified height of contraction in the following table of results.

Voltage	Magnified Height of Contraction (mm)

10. Plot the results of this experiment on the grid on the next page, using the magnified height in mm on the Y axis (vertical axis) and the voltage on the X axis (horizontal axis).

11. Define irritability. _____

12. Define the all-or-none law. _____

_____

13. Did all muscle fibers in the muscle have the same degree of irritability? _____

14. What caused the increase in height of contraction with increasing strength of stimulus? _____

_____

15. Does each muscle fiber follow the all-or-none law or does the muscle as a whole? _____

_____

16. Was there any advantage to stimulating the muscle with a current stronger than maximal?

_____ Any disadvantage? _____

_____

Name _____

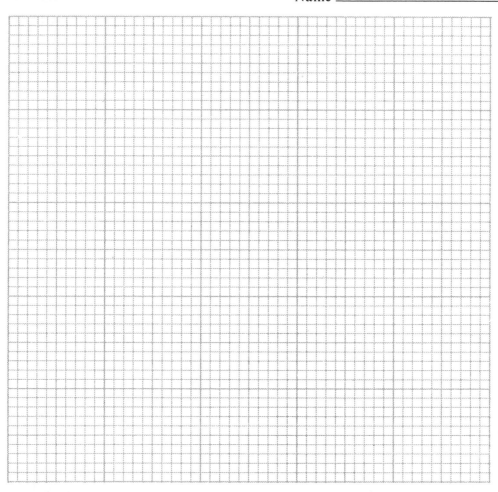

EXERCISE 8-B. GENESIS OF TETANUS

1. Define muscle tetanus. _____
   _____

2. Paste your record, fully labeled, in the space below. Label single twitches, incomplete tetanus, complete tetanus, and the frequency on each record.

3. Was the height of the tetanic contraction greater or less than that obtained with the simple muscle twitches? _____ Explain: _____

_____

4. What accounts for the smooth curve in complete tetanus? _____

_____

5. Are most of the contractions in the human body simple twitches or tetanic contractions? _____

_____

EXERCISE 8-C. DURATION OF A SINGLE MUSCLE TWITCH

1. Paste the record of a single muscle twitch in the space below. Label the record fully as illustrated in Figures 8-7 and 8-8.

2. Fill in the following table of results by calculating the duration of each of the listed events. Divide the length of each period (in centimeters) by the paper speed. Then calculate the percent of time of the entire muscle twitch occupied by the latent period, the contraction period, and the relaxation period. To do this, substitute in the following equation:

$$\frac{\text{Duration of the latent period}}{\text{Duration of the entire muscle twitch}} \times 100 =$$

Repeat the calculation for each phase of the muscle twitch.

Stages in a Muscle Twitch	Length of Each Phase (cm)	Duration (sec)	% of Time of Entire Twitch
Latent period (a - b)			
Contraction (b - e)			
Relaxation (e - d)			
Entire muscle twitch (a - d)			100

Name _____

3. How do the values obtained in this experiment agree with the expected values for the duration of each event in a muscle twitch? _____

4. Define the latent period. _____

5. How would a decrease in the temperature of the muscle affect each of the following?

    a. Duration of the latent period. _____

    b. Height of contraction. _____

    c. Duration of the relaxation period. _____

EXERCISE 8-D. MUSCLE FATIGUE

1. Fasten your record from muscle fatigue in the space below. Label treppe, contracture, fatigue, rest period, and recovery (if any) from fatigue.

2. List the possible causes of muscle fatigue. _____

    _____

3. Fatigue inhibits the complete relaxation of a muscle. Did you see any evidence of such inhibition in this experiment? _____

4. Define contracture. _____

5. Is the pH of a fatigued muscle likely to be more acid or more alkaline than usual? _____

    Explain: _____

    _____

EXERCISE 8-E. PHYSIOLOGY OF HUMAN MUSCLE

1. Record the size of the arm below:

	Size (inches)
With forearm extended	
With forearm flexed	

2. What caused the above changes in size? _____

   _____

3. Fasten your ergograph record below. Label each portion of the record.

4. Calculate the time required to cause fatigue by dividing the length of the record by the paper speed. Record all calculations in the following table. Fill in the results in the table.

	Time (sec)	Initial Force of Contraction (cm)
Time required for initial fatigue		
Time required for fatigue after a 30 second rest		
Time required for initial fatigue of partner		
Time required for fatigue of partner after a 30 second rest		
Time required for fatigue with sphygmomanometer		
Time required for fatigue of partner with sphygmomanometer		

Name _____

5. What caused the difference in time needed for fatigue in each part of the experiment? _____

_____

_____

6. Describe the chemical steps that occur during muscle contraction. _____

_____

_____

_____

7. Describe the chemical steps that occur during recovery from fatigue. _____

_____

_____

8. Assume the subject's hands were placed in ice water immediately preceding the rapid flexion and extension of the fingers. What effect would you expect this to have on the length of time necessary for inducing muscle fatigue? _____

9. Define an isometric contraction. _____

Give one example of where this type of contraction occurs in the body. _____

_____

10. Define an isotonic contraction. _____

Give one example of where this type of contraction occurs in the body. _____

_____

11. In which of the above is work performed? _____

RESULTS AND QUESTIONS FOR CHAPTER 9

EXERCISE 9-A. ANATOMY OF THE HUMAN DIGESTIVE SYSTEM

1. What is the dental formula for the deciduous set of teeth? _____

2. What is the dental formula for the permanent set of teeth? _____

3. What is another name for the cuspids? _____

4. What is another name for the premolars? _____

5. List the major functions of saliva. _____
_____

6. What is the function of the cecum? _____

7. Trace the path of food through the digestive tract to the point of absorption into the bloodstream. _____
_____

8. In which layer of the tooth are the nerves and blood vessels located? _____

EXERCISE 9-B. DISSECTION OF THE DIGESTIVE SYSTEM OF THE FETAL PIG

1. Name the most abundant tissue in the tongue. _____

2. Compare the dental formula for the deciduous teeth of the pig and human.

_____   _____
          Pig   Human

3. Name the bones that comprise the hard palate. _____
_____

4. What is the posterior extension of the soft palate called in humans? _____

5. Does the pig have this structure? _____

6. What is the function of the Eustachian tubes? _____
_____

7. What is the function of the common bile duct? _____
_____

8. How many lobes are in the human liver? _____

9. How many lobes are in the pig liver? _____

10. What is the function of the gall bladder? _____

11. Name the sphincter surrounding the opening of the common bile duct. _____

12. Name the sphincter between the small and large intestine. _____

13. List the functions of the large intestine. _____
_____

14. Name the microscopic fingerlike projections present in the lining of the small intestine.
_____

15. What is the function of the structures in question 14? _____

_____

16. Name the blood vessel that transports absorbed materials from the digestive tract to the liver. _____

17. Name the three regions of the small intestine. _____

18. To which curvature of the stomach is the greater omentum attached? _____

EXERCISE 9-C. ACTION OF SALIVARY AMYLASE

1. Complete the following table. In the column headed "Explanation," explain the changes in color of Lugol's solution and the appearance of Benedict's test.

Tube No.	Contents	Initial Lugol's Color	Final Lugol's Color	Achromic Time	Results of Benedict's Test	Explanation
1						
2						

2. Did you see any evidence of the formation of dextrins as an intermediate product? _____ What was your evidence? _____

_____

3. What is the purpose of performing Benedict's test after tube 1 becomes achromic? _____

_____

4. Write the equation for the action of salivary amylase on starch. _____

_____

5. Based on your observations in this experiment, list two ways in which it was proven that digestion of starch occurred. _____

_____

_____

6. What other digestive organ synthesizes amylase? _____

EXERCISE 9-D. PROTEIN DIGESTION

1. Complete the following table.

Tube No.	Contents of Tube	pH	Digestion (+ or −)	Explanation of Results
1				
2				
3				
4				
5				

Name _____

2. Which organ synthesizes pepsin? _____

3. Write the equation for the action of pepsin on protein. _____
    _____

4. What is the approximate percent of HCl in gastric juice? _____

5. What is the average pH of the stomach? (Assume this is the optimum pH for pepsin in discussing this experiment.) _____

6. List the functions of HCl in gastric juice. _____
    _____
    _____

7. What was the function of HCl in this experiment? _____

8. To which class of chemical compound does fibrin belong? _____

9. Why was 40 °C used for the temperature of the water bath in this experiment rather than 100 °C? _____

EXERCISE 9-E. EFFECT OF RENNIN ON MILK

1. How long did it take for the milk to curdle in step 3? _____

2. Write the equation for the action of rennin. _____
    _____

3. What is the main constituent of the solid curd? _____

4. Name the substances present in the whey. _____

5. What results were obtained with Benedict's test on whey? _____
    Explain: _____

6. Name the digestive organ that synthesizes rennin. _____

7. Would rennin be effective in the adult stomach, if present? _____
    Explain: _____

8. How is rennin used commercially? _____

EXERCISE 9-F. PANCREATIC DIGESTION OF FAT

1. Complete the following table.

Tube No.	Temp. of Water Bath (°C)	Change in pH (color)	Explanation of Results
1			
2			

2. Name the enzymes present in pancreatin. _____
    _____

3. Which enzyme was active in this experiment? _____

4. Write the equation for the action of the enzyme in question 3. _____
_____

5. What was the substrate of the enzyme in this experiment? _____
6. What color is litmus in alkaline solution? _____
7. What color is litmus in acid solution? _____
8. What was the color of the freshly prepared litmus milk? _____
9. What caused the change in color of the litmus milk in this experiment? _____
_____

EXERCISE 9-G. BILE

1. What color was the bile sample? _____
2. To what is this color due? _____
3. What results were obtained in Gmelin's test for bile? _____
_____

4. Where are bile pigments produced in the body? _____
5. Name the two common bile pigments. _____
6. Of what value are the bile pigments? _____
7. Did the particles of sulfur fall through the distilled water? _____
   Explain your answer: _____
8. Did the particles of sulfur fall through the diluted bile? _____
   Bile salts decrease the surface tension of the water in which they are dissolved. Use this fact to explain the behavior of the sulfur in the beaker containing dilute bile. _____
_____
_____

9. How does emulsification of fat by bile salts aid in the digestion of fat by lipase? _____
_____

10. Name the two common bile salts. _____
11. List the major functions of bile salts. _____
_____
_____

RESULTS AND QUESTIONS FOR CHAPTER 10

EXERCISE 10-A. BASAL METABOLIC RATE

1. Record the following personal data:

   Height _____ Weight _____ Age _____ Sex _____

2. As determined by the Dubois Body Surface Chart, record your BSA. _____

3. Record your heat loss per square meter of body surface area, using Table 10-1. _____

4. Calculate your basal metabolic rate.

   a. Calories/minute/meter² body surface area _____ × BSA _____ = Calories/minute _____

   b. Calories/minute _____ × 60 = Calories/hour _____

   c. Calories/hour _____ × 24 = Calories/day _____

5. The calculated standard metabolic rate may not correspond with your actual basal metabolic rate as determined with the respirometer (or some other method). Explain why this is true.

   _____

6. What is a Calorie? _____

   _____

7. Which would you expect to be greater in a young child, caloric intake or expenditure? _____ Explain: _____

   _____

8. Which of the two in question 7 would you expect to be greater in an adult of constant weight? _____ Explain: _____

   _____

9. Using the BMR calculated in question 4, solve the following problems:

   a. Assume you are typing an assignment (e.g., a term paper) and that this activity increases your BMR by 51%. Determine the number of calories you would consume in this activity for 20 minutes. Show all calculations.

      Answer _____

   b. Assume you are running up the stairs of a twenty story building, and that this activity increases your BMR by 780%. If it took you 3 minutes to reach the top of the building, how many calories would you consume for the activity? Show all calculations.

      Answer _____

EXERCISE 10-B. DIURNAL VARIATIONS IN BODY TEMPERATURE

Part 2. Body Temperature Variations During a 24-Hour Period

1. What was your basal temperature? _____

Temperature Readings Taken at 4-Hour Intervals

	AM 4 - 8	AM 8 - 12	PM 12 - 4	PM 4 - 8	PM 8 - 12	AM 12 - 4	AM 4 - 8	♀	♂
Personal Data									
1									
2									
3									
4									
5									
6									
7									
8									
9									
10									
11									
12									
13									
14									
15									
16									
17									
18									
19									
20									
21									
22									
23									
24									
25									
26									
27									
28									
29									
30									
31									
32									
TOTALS									
AVERAGES									

2. Record the seven temperature readings you took during a period of 24 hours on the first line of the table on the following page. If you took your temperature at 7 AM, this would be recorded under the 4-8 AM range, an 11 AM reading would be recorded under the 8-12 AM range, etc.

3. Record the temperature readings obtained by each member of the class in the remaining spaces in the table. Make certain that the temperatures are recorded in the appropriate time range. Add each column and determine the average. (Check in the spaces provided whether the subject was male or female.)

4. Plot your personal temperature data and the class averages on the grid on page 339 in accordance with the instructions given under Procedure, steps 4 and 5.

5. If variations in body temperature were observed, were they cyclic? _____

Name _____

Time

6. If the variations were cyclic, how would you explain this fact? _____
_____
_____

7. If some observations did not fit the cyclic pattern, how can you account for them? _____
_____

8. In general, at what time interval are temperatures lowest for the class? _____
Highest? _____ Explain these results: _____
_____
_____
_____

EXERCISE 10-C. EFFECT OF EXERCISE ON TEMPERATURE

1. Record the data obtained, in accordance with steps 2 through 5 under Procedure, in the table on page 340. To obtain the percentages required for the table, use the following equations, showing all calculations (use temperature obtained before exercise as the "normal" temperature):

$$\% \text{ Increase} = \frac{\text{T after exercise} - \text{normal T}}{\text{Normal T}} \times 100 = \underline{\hspace{3cm}}$$

$$\% \text{ Decrease} = \frac{\text{Normal T} - \text{T after exercise}}{\text{Normal T}} \times 100 = \underline{\hspace{3cm}}$$

Body Condition	Subject's Temperature	% Increase or Decrease
Before exercise "normal temperature"		
After mild exercise		
After severe exercise		
Ten minutes after severe exercise		

2. What caused the changes that occurred in body temperature upon exercise? _____

    _____

    Compare your results with those of four other class members. _____

    _____

3. Upon waiting 10 minutes after severe exercise, did your temperature return to normal? _____

    If it did, explain why. If it did not, explain why it didn't. _____

    _____

4. On the basis of your results in this series of experiments on body temperature, comment on the

    figure 98.6 °F as the "normal" oral body temperature. _____

    _____

EXERCISE 10-D. MAPPING OF SWEAT GLANDS

1. Record the data obtained in the experiment in the following table:

Body State	Number of Active Sweat Glands per Square Inch		
	Forehead	Neck	Arm
At rest			
Mild exercise			
Severe exercise			

2. Explain how the colored dots were transferred to the bond paper. _____

    _____

3. Explain any differences observed in the number of active sweat glands as a result of the three

    experimental conditions (rest, mild exercise, and severe exercise). _____

    _____

    _____

4. Why was it necessary to use bond paper rather than filter paper in this experiment? _____

    _____

RESULTS AND QUESTIONS FOR CHAPTER 11

EXERCISE 11-A. ANATOMY OF THE HUMAN RESPIRATORY SYSTEM

1. Name the bones in the skull that possess paranasal sinuses. _____
_____

2. Into which part of the respiratory tract do these sinuses open? _____

3. What is the function of the paranasal sinuses? _____
_____

4. Name the specific cartilage(s) in the larynx
   a. that serves as a lid for the larynx.   _____
   b. to which the vocal folds are attached.   _____
   c. shaped like a signet ring.   _____
   d. shaped like a shield.   _____
   e. that forms the Adam's apple.   _____

5. What are the functions of the larynx? _____
_____

6. What is the name for the opening between the vocal folds? _____

7. Describe the location of the trachea with respect to the esophagus. _____
_____

8. Trace the path of air from a point outside the nose to the point of exchange of gases with the pulmonary capillaries. _____
_____
_____

9. Why was it impossible to swallow while depressing the larynx? _____
_____

10. Describe the events that occur during the swallowing process. _____
_____
_____
_____

EXERCISE 11-B. DISSECTION OF THE RESPIRATORY SYSTEM OF THE FETAL PIG

1. What is the common name for the trachea? _____

2. What is the function of the cartilage in the wall of the trachea? _____
_____

3. Are the rings of cartilage in the trachea incomplete dorsally or ventrally? _____

4. What is the common name for the larynx? _____

342

5. What is the function of the thymus gland? _____
    _____

6. What is the function of the thyroid gland? _____
    _____

7. Name three serous membranes. _____

8. What is the name given to the space in between the lungs? _____

9. Name five structures located in this space. _____
    _____

10. What is the function of the phrenic nerve? _____

11. Compare the number of lobes in the lungs of the pig with the number present in human
    lungs. _____

12. What is the function of the esophagus? _____

13. Does the trachea divide into two bronchi dorsal or ventral to the heart? _____

EXERCISE 11-C. CHEST MEASUREMENTS DURING RESPIRATION

1. Record the dimensions of your chest in the following table.

	Quiet Breathing		Forced Breathing	
	Inspiration	Expiration	Inspiration	Expiration
Antero-posterior Diameter (in cm)				
Lateral Diameter (in cm)				
Circumference (in inches)				

2. Plot the dimensions of the chest recorded in question 1 on the grid on page 343, using four
    different colors. Place a dot representing the backbone in the center of the lowest horizontal
    line of the grid, as indicated below. This dot should be the point common to all four plots of the
    chest. Label each curve (quiet inspiration, quiet expiration, forced inspiration, forced
    expiration).

3. The thorax should be at its maximum dimensions in forced inspiration, smallest in forced
    expiration. Do your results agree with the theoretical results? _____

    Explain: _____
    _____

4. Name the muscles that contract during quiet inspiration. _____
    _____

5. Name the additional muscles that contract during forced inspiration. _____
    _____

6. Name the muscles used in forced expiration. _____

7. Which dimension of the thorax is increased by contraction of the diaphragm? _____
    _____

Name _____

8. To which structure in the human respiratory system does each of the following structures in the lung demonstration model (bottle thorax) correspond?

    a. Balloons _____ c. Glass Y tube _____

    b. Rubber sheeting _____ d. Bell jar _____

9. Explain why the balloons expand when the rubber sheeting is lowered. _____

    _____

EXERCISE 11-D. RESPIRATORY VOLUMES

1. Record your respiratory volumes (in milliliters) obtained with the spirometer in the following data chart. Compare your results with the average value (theoretical average) expected for each respiratory volume.

Respiratory Volumes (ml)	*1*	*2*	*3*	*Average*	*Theoretical Average*
Vital capacity (VC)					
Tidal volume (TV)					
Expiratory reserve volume (ERV)					
Inspiratory reserve volume (IRV) (directly measured)					

2. Compare your measured IRV with that calculated from the formula:

   IRV = VC – (TV + ERV) _____

3. Calculate the total amount of air inhaled (in liters) in one day:

   a. Respiratory rate per minute (step 10 of Procedure) _____

   b. Average tidal air (in milliliters) _____

   c. Average tidal air (in liters) _____

   d. Minute volume _____

   e. Amount inhaled per hour _____

   f. Amount inhaled per day _____

4. What is the predicted vital capacity for your sex, age, and height? (See Appendix 3, Sections B and C, for predicted vital capacity.)

   Age _____ Sex _____ Height (inches) _____ Height (cm) _____

   a. Predicted vital capacity _____

   b. Actual vital capacity _____

5. Discuss possible causes of any difference between the predicted and actual vital capacity noted in question 4. _____

6. Why would you expect males to have a larger vital capacity than females at a given age and height? _____

7. Fasten your record from the respirometer below. Label it according to the sample record (Fig. 11-12). Indicate on the record where you made your calculations.

Name _____

8. To calculate vital capacity with the respirometer, subtract the bottom reading from the top reading on your record for each of the three determinations of vital capacity and record the highest as your VC. On the sample record (Fig. 11-12), the three values for vital capacity are 3955, 4105, and 4005. Therefore, 4105 would be recorded as the vital capacity for the sample record. Fill in the following chart with your results for vital capacity.

Expiration	Beginning Volume (ml)	Ending Volume (ml)	Vital Capacity
First			
Second			
Third			

Using the largest value as your vital capacity, how do your results obtained with the respirometer compare with those obtained with the spirometer. (See Exercise 11-D, question 1, in Results and Questions for Chapter 11.) _____

Which do you think is more accurate? _____ Why? _____

_____

9. Tidal volume is the amount of air moved in and out of the lungs during quiet breathing. To calculate TV, look at the first five breaths in Figure 11-12, marked A, B, C, D, and E. Mark these five breaths in a similar fashion on your record. Then mark the beginning and end of each of these expirations (the pen moves downward during expiration). Record your answer in milliliters (the space between the horizontal lines is equal to 50 ml). In this example in Figure 11-12, breath A = 325 ml, B = 515 ml, C = 425 ml, D = 430 ml, and E = 675 ml. The average tidal volume thus is 474 ml in this example.

Calculate the tidal volume.

Breath A _____   Average tidal volume _____

B _____

C _____

D _____

E _____

How does your tidal volume compare with normal values? _____

10. Inspiratory reserve volume is the amount of air that can be forcibly inhaled into the lungs after a normal quiet inspiration. To calculate this volume, examine the portion of the same record labeled IRV. Mark the end of the forced inspiration (number 2). Mark the end of the normal inspiration of the previous breath (number 1). Subtract these two values to obtain the IRV. In the sample record, 5830 – 3010 = 2820 ml for the IRV.

End of forced inspiration (number 2) _____

End of normal inspiration (number 1) _____

Inspiratory Reserve Volume _____

11. Expiratory reserve volume is the amount of air that can be forcibly exhaled from the lungs above tidal volume after a normal quiet inspiration. To calculate this value, examine the portion of the sample record labeled ERV. Mark the end of the forced expiration (number 3). Mark the end of the previous normal expiration (number 4). Calculate the difference between the normal expiration and the forced expiration to obtain the ERV. In this example, 3565 – 2500 = 1065 ml for the ERV.

End of normal expiration (number 4) _____

End of forced expiration (number 3) _____

Expiratory Reserve Volume _____

12. Was there any change evident in the tidal volumes from the beginning to the end of your record? _____ If there was, what is a possible reason? _____

_____

13. Inspiratory capacity (IC) is the maximal volume of air that can be inspired from the resting end-expiratory position. It can be calculated by use of the following formula:

IC = IRV + TV

IRV _____

TV _____

IC _____

14. Combined vital capacity (CVC) is obtained by the addition of the separately recorded inspiratory capacity and expiratory reserve volume.

CVC = IC + ERV

IC _____ ERV _____ CVC _____

Your measured vital capacity was (question 8) _____

The combined vital capacity is often larger than the actual vital capacity. This may be due to the fact that patients with some kind of respiratory obstruction (particularly an obstruction resulting from bronchial asthma and pulmonary emphysema) are unable to move their thoracic cage from fullest inspiration to maximal expiration in a single maneuver.

15. What conclusion can you draw from a comparison of your combined and measured vital capacity? _____

_____

EXERCISE 11-E. RESPIRATORY MOVEMENTS

1. Paste the record of three normal breaths below. Label inspiration and expiration. Draw a horizontal baseline beneath the record. See Figure 11-15 if you used the physiograph. The pen falls during inspiration using the Marey tambour.

Name _____

2. Calculate the duration of both inspiration and expiration. Show all calculations in the space below. Measure the distance along the baseline in centimeters for both inspiration and expiration. Divide the length (in cm) of inspiration and of expiration by the paper speed.

Paper speed _____ Length of inspiration _____ Length of expiration _____

Duration of inspiration _____

Duration of expiration _____

Total duration of one breath _____

3. Calculate the breathing rate per minute by substituting in the following equation:

$$\frac{1 \text{ Breath}}{\text{Duration 1 breath (from Q. 2)}} = \frac{X \text{ Breaths}}{60 \text{ Seconds}}$$

Rate of breathing per minute _____

4. Separate the parts of your pneumograph record. Paste each part in the appropriate space. Next to each record discuss in detail what that record illustrates.

   a. Hyperventilation

   b. Reading aloud

    c.   Mental calculations

    d.   Sipping water

5.   Does the hyperventilation record show a period of apnea before the rate and depth of breathing returned to normal? _____

EXERCISE 11-F. EFFECT OF CARBON DIOXIDE ON THE RESPIRATORY CENTER

1.   What is the importance of the glossopharyngeal reflex (deglutition apnea)? _____

    _____

    _____

2.   Explain how hyperventilation causes an increase in the pH of the blood. _____

    _____

    _____

Name _____

3. Record all data and a short explanation of your results in the following table.

Respiratory Activity	Time of Breath Holding	Explanation of Results
After quiet inspiration		
After water sipping		
After hyperventilation		
After exercise		

4. Why might a person have no desire to breathe after a period of hyperventilation? _____

_____

EXERCISE 11-G. TEMPERATURE AND COMPOSITION OF EXHALED AIR

1. What was the temperature of the inhaled air (room temperature)? _____

2. What was the temperature of the exhaled air? _____

3. Explain what caused the difference between the temperature of the inhaled and the exhaled air.

_____

4. What collected on the surface of the glass plate? _____

5. What is the origin of this material? _____

6. Explain the formation of the precipitate in step 5 of Procedure. _____

_____

7. What functions of the respiratory tract are demonstrated in this experiment? _____

_____

RESULTS AND QUESTIONS FOR CHAPTER 12

EXERCISE 12-A. DETERMINATION OF ABO AND Rh BLOOD TYPES

1. Record the results of the entire class in the following table.

Blood Group	Number of Individuals	Percent	Theoretical Percent
O			45
A			41
B			10
AB			4
Total			100

Blood Group	Number of Individuals	Percent	Theoretical Percent
Rh+			85
Rh−			15
Total			100

2. Explain any differences in the percentages obtained in your class and the theoretical percentages. _____

_____

3. What was your ABO blood type? _____ Rh blood type? _____

4. Which agglutinins are contained in your blood plasma? _____

5. Which agglutinogens are contained in your blood cells? _____

6. List two possible reasons why the antisera should be placed on the slide before the blood.

   a. _____

   b. _____

7. The anti-D antisera must contain the Rh antibodies. Since these do not occur normally, can you suggest a source of the antibodies? _____

_____

8. The a and b antibodies, if present, would interfere with the determination of Rh blood type. How are they removed from the antiserum?

_____

EXERCISE 12-B. DETERMINATION OF HEMOGLOBIN CONTENT OF BLOOD

1. Results of determination of hemoglobin:

    a. Tallquist scale:

        (1) Grams of hemoglobin   _____

        (2) Percent hemoglobin   _____

        (3) Range (suggestive anemia, actual anemia, or normal)

                                                     _____

    b. Spencer Hb-meter:

        (1) Grams of hemoglobin   _____

        (2) Percent hemoglobin   _____

2. What value in grams is taken as 100% on both the Tallquist scale and the Spencer hemoglobinometer? _____

3. Why is it important not to use the first drop of blood? _____

4. Why is it important not to squeeze the finger? _____

5. Discuss sources of error in the use of the Tallquist scale. _____

6. Which method of determining hemoglobin used in this experiment is more accurate? _____

7. What is the normal hemoglobin value (in g/100 ml blood):

    For women? _____ For men? _____

8. Define anemia: _____

9. What was the class average hemoglobin value:

    For men? _____ For women? _____

10. What causes this characteristic difference in hemoglobin value between the sexes? _____

11. What is the function of hemoglobin? _____

12. Where is hemoglobin produced in the human body? _____

Name _____

EXERCISE 12-C. COAGULATION TIME AND BLEEDING TIME

1. Record your results in the following data chart.

Test	Time
Coagulation time—slide	
Coagulation time—capillary tube	
Bleeding time	

2. Were your results within the normal range? _____

3. Why was coagulation time longer than bleeding time? _____
_____

4. Name two diseases or conditions in which the coagulation time is lengthened. _____
_____

5. List four functions performed by blood plasma. _____
_____
_____

6. In the following table, indicate where each substance is found and the function each performs in the coagulation of blood.

Substance	Where Found in Blood	Function
Fibrinogen		
Prothrombin		
Thromboplastin (thrombokinase)		
Calcium		

7. How can the blood clotting time be shortened? _____
_____

8. What is the normal range for a RBC count? _____

9. What is the normal range for a WBC count? _____

10. What is the life span of a typical RBC? _____

11. Where are RBCs destroyed? _____

12. Where are RBCs produced? _____

13. What do the following changes in a blood count indicate:

    a. A white blood cell count above 15,000/mm^3 _____
    _____

    b. A red blood cell count below 4,000,000/mm^3 _____

c. A decrease in a normal white blood cell count _____

_____

d. An increase in a normal red blood cell count _____

EXERCISE 12-D. PREPARATION OF BLOOD SMEAR STAINED WITH WRIGHT'S STAIN

1. Draw and identify three types of leukocytes.

2. Describe the method for making a differential count. _____

_____

3. Under what conditions would a differential count prove useful? _____

_____

EXERCISE 12-E. HEMATOCRIT AND THE COMPOSITION OF PLASMA

1. Determine the hematocrit of the sample:

    a. Total volume of blood in tube _____

    b. Height of packed RBCs _____

    c. Hematocrit _____

2. Define hematocrit. _____

3. What was the origin of the calcium oxalate visible at the bottom of the tube? _____

_____

4. What is the average hematocrit for men? _____ For women? _____

5. What condition is indicated if the hematocrit is low? _____

6. Name two conditions that can cause a high hematocrit. _____

_____

7. Estimate the percentage of WBCs:

    a. Depth of layer of WBCs _____

    b. Total volume of blood in tube _____

    c. Percentage of WBCs (a/b × 100) _____

8. Why is the zone of WBCs lighter in color and in weight than the zone of RBCs?

_____

9. What results were obtained with Millon's test? _____

10. Name the plasma proteins. _____

11. What results were obtained with Benedict's solution? _____

12. Name the sugar responsible for the result in no. 11. _____

13. How much of this sugar should be present in 100 ml of blood? _____

14. What should be the color of plasma? _____

RESULTS AND QUESTIONS FOR CHAPTER 13

EXERCISE 13-A. STRUCTURE OF AN ARTERY, A VEIN, AND A LYMPH VESSEL VALVE

1. What is the function of each of the following in the wall of an artery?

    a. Endothelium _____

    b. Elastic connective tissue _____

    c. Vasa vasorum _____

2. Which type of vessels contains valves? _____

3. Explain the cause of the difference in shape of the interior of the artery and the vein. _____
    _____

4. Which contains proportionally more muscle, a large or a small artery?
    _____

5. Briefly describe, in the table below, the distinguishing characteristics of the following vessels:

Vessel	Structure	Function
Artery		
Capillary		
Vein		

EXERCISE 13-B. GROSS ANATOMY OF THE HUMAN CIRCULATORY SYSTEM

1. List the major organ(s) supplied by each of the following arteries:

    a. Brachial. _____

    b. Internal mammary. _____

    c. Celiac. _____

    d. Inferior mesenteric. _____

    e. Lumbar. _____

    f. Internal iliac. _____

    g. Anterior tibial. _____

    h. Inferior phrenic. _____

    i. Renal. _____

    j. Hepatic. _____

2. Trace the path of a molecule of glucose from the small intestine to the right arm and name all

    blood vessels and chambers of the heart passed through. _____
    _____
    _____
    _____

3. Trace the path of a drop of blood from the left fingers to the dorsum of the foot, following the same directions as for No. 2. _____

_____

_____

4. Describe the functions of blood as they pertain to each of the following organ systems:

System	Functional Relationship of Blood
Respiratory	
Digestive	
Excretory	
Endocrine	

5. How do the following organ systems aid the circulatory system?

a. Skeletal system. _____

b. Muscular system. _____

c. Nervous system. _____

6. Blood that flows away from the heart is always carried by blood vessels called _____ .

Is this blood always oxygenated? _____

Explain: _____

_____

7. Blood that flows toward the heart is carried by blood vessels called _____ .

Is this blood always oxygenated? _____

Explain: _____

_____

8. What functions do the capillaries perform in the circulation of blood? _____

_____

9. Explain why the heart is considered a double pump. _____

_____

10. What is the function of the portal system? _____

_____

EXERCISE 13-C. DISSECTION OF THE SHEEP HEART

1. Describe the location of the parietal layer of the pericardium. _____

_____

2. Describe the location of the visceral layer of the pericardium. _____

_____

Name _____

3. Name the major tissue in the myocardium. _____

4. What is the function of the myocardium? _____

5. What is the function of the pulmonary artery? _____

6. What is the function of the blood vessels in the anterior longitudinal sulcus? _____ _____

7. Which ventricle has thicker walls? _____

8. Which chamber makes up the apex of the heart? _____

9. How many pouches are present in the pulmonary semilunar valve? _____

10. Are chordae tendineae attached to these semilunar valve pouches? _____

11. Does the semilunar valve open during systole or diastole of the right ventricle? _____ _____

12. Is there a valve visible at the entrance of the superior vena cava into the heart? _____ _____

13. What is the function of the coronary sinus? _____

14. What is the function of the chordae tendineae? _____

15. What causes the tricuspid valve to open? _____

16. What causes the tricuspid valve to close? _____

17. What is the function of the pulmonary valves? _____

18. Are chordae tendineae attached to the bicuspid valve? _____

19. Is a moderator band visible in the interior of the left ventricle? _____ _____

20. How many pouches are visible in the aortic semilunar valve? _____

21. Name the three blood vessels branching from the aortic arch in humans. _____ _____

22. What is the internal layer of the artery wall called? _____

23. Name the tissue forming the lining of this internal layer. _____

24. Name the tissue found in largest amounts in the tunica media of the aorta. _____ _____

25. Based on your observations of the sheep heart, what is the easiest way to distinguish between an artery and a vein?

_____

26. What is the function of the ductus arteriosus? _____ _____ _____

EXERCISE 13-D. DISSECTION OF THE CIRCULATORY SYSTEM OF THE FETAL PIG

1. To what structures was the pericardium attached? _____
    _____

2. Name the branches of the celiac artery. _____

3. Name the remnant of the ductus arteriosus after birth. _____

4. How do the branches of the aortic arch in the human and in the fetal pig or cat compare?
    _____

5. Is there a common iliac artery in the pig? _____

6. Describe the base of the aorta in the fetal pig. _____
    _____

7. What is the special importance of the hemiazygos or azygos vein in the human? _____
    _____

8. What type of blood (oxygenated or deoxygenated) is located in each of the following in the adult pig?

    a. Pulmonary artery. _____   d. Renal artery.   _____
    b. Pulmonary vein.   _____   e. Heptatic vein. _____
    c. Aorta.   _____

9. Which type of blood (oxygenated, deoxygenated, or mixed) is located in each of the following in the fetal pig? (Study the coloring carefully in the model of the human fetal circulation.)

    a. Aorta.   _____   f. Pulmonary artery.   _____

    b. Ductus arteriosus. _____   g. Superior vena cava. _____

    c. Ductus venosus.   _____   h. Umbilical artery.   _____

    d. Inferior vena cava. _____   i. Umbilical vein.   _____

    e. Internal iliac artery. _____

10. Trace the path of a drop of blood from the ankle of the human fetus to the right side of the fetal brain; name all blood vessels and chambers of the heart passed through. _____
    _____
    _____
    _____

11. Trace the path of a drop of blood from the fetal brachial artery to the stomach. _____
    _____
    _____

12. List several causes of a "blue baby." _____
    _____
    _____

13. From which blood vessels do the umbilical arteries arise? _____

14. What is the function of the umbilical arteries? _____
    _____

RESULTS AND QUESTIONS FOR CHAPTER 14

EXERCISE 14-A. OBSERVATION OF THE FROG HEART CYCLE

1. Rate of contraction of the parts of the frog heart:

    a. Rate of atria. _____

    b. Rate of ventricle. _____

2. Should the rate of contraction of the parts of the frog heart agree? _____ Explain: _____
    _____

3. List the parts of the frog heart in the order of their contraction. _____
    _____

4. To what structures was the pericardium attached? _____

5. Was any moisture present between the two layers of the pericardium? _____

6. Compare the size of the heart before and after slitting the pericardium. _____
    _____

7. List the functions of the pericardium observed in this experiment. _____
    _____

8. What is meant by systole? _____

9. What is meant by diastole? _____

10. Compare the structure of the frog heart with that of the human heart. _____
    _____

EXERCISE 14-B. EXTRASYSTOLE

1. Paste the kymograph or physiograph record showing extrasystoles, completely labeled, in the space below. Label absolute refractory period, relative refractory period, extrasystole, compensatory pause, systole, and diastole. Indicate on the record where the heart was stimulated during systole and where it was stimulated during diastole.

2. What is meant by the absolute refractory period of the heart? _____

_____

3. When does the absolute refractory period occur in the cardiac cycle? _____

4. What results were obtained when the heart was stimulated during systole? _____

_____ Explain these results: _____

_____

5. What results were obtained when the heart was stimulated during diastole? _____

_____ Explain these results: _____

_____

_____

6. During which phase of the cardiac cycle (early or late diastole) was the greatest height of extrasystole obtained? _____ Explain: _____

_____

7. Define the compensatory pause. _____

8. Can the heart be stimulated to produce a tetanic contraction? _____

Explain: _____

Of what possible advantage to circulation is this fact? _____

_____

EXERCISE 14-C. PHASES OF THE CARDIAC CYCLE

1. Attach your recording of the phases of the cardiac cycle below. Paper speed _____

2. Draw a baseline across the record. Label atrial systole and diastole, ventricular systole and diastole. Place letters at each important point in the tracing, as illustrated in the discussion. If the contraction of the sinus venosus is visible, label it.

3. Determine the duration of each phase of the cardiac cycle by drawing vertical lines from the appropriate points of the contraction to the baseline.

4. Calculate and record the duration of each event in the cardiac cycle in hundredths of a second by substituting in the following formula:

$$\text{Duration of event} = \frac{\text{Length of event (cm)}}{\text{Paper speed (cm/sec)}}$$

5. Record your calculations in the following table.

Heart Condition	Letters Used	Distance	Duration	Total
a. Atrial systole				
b. Atrial diastole				a + b = _____
c. Ventricular systole				
d. Ventricular diastole				c + d = _____

6. What was the total length of time of the cardiac cycle (one heartbeat)? _____

7. Using the answers obtained in questions 5 and 6, calculate the percent of time:

   a. the atria work. _____

   b. the atria rest. _____

   c. the ventricle works. _____

   d. the ventricle rests. _____

8. Compare the values obtained in this experiment on the frog heart, as shown in question 5, with the average values for humans. _____

9. What is the significance of the long period of time required for atrial diastole? _____

_____

EXERCISE 14-D. EFFECT OF TEMPERATURE ON HEART RATE

1. If the Alternate Procedure was used, attach your physiograph or kymograph records below. Count the heart rate for at least 15 seconds on each record and convert to rate per minute.

2. Record the rate of the heartbeat at each temperature in the data chart. Calculate the Q_{10} as directed in the discussion.

Temperature	Rate/Minute	Q_{10}	Force of Beat

3. Using the records on heart rates you obtained from the physiograph, determine at which temperature the beat was most forceful. (Determine the force of the heartbeat by measuring the height of the contractions in millimeters on the record. Draw a baseline connecting the bottom of each heartbeat. Measure from there to the top of a typical beat at each temperature.)

4. At which temperature was the heartbeat more forceful? _____

5. Why does an increase in temperature, within limits, cause an increase in the rate of physiological processes? _____
    _____

6. Which would bring about a larger decrease in the rate of ventricle contraction, applying a cold probe to the sinus venosus or to the ventricle directly? _____
    _____ Explain your answer. _____
    _____

EXERCISE 14-E. HEART BLOCK

1. Record your results from the experiment on heart block in the following table.

	Atria	Ventricle
Rate before experiment		
Rate during gradual tightening		
Rate during ventricular arrest		
Rate after thread cut		

2. How did the pressure cause production of heart block in this experiment? _____
    _____
    _____

3. What causes the production of heart block in humans? _____
    _____

4. What are the symptoms of heart block in humans? _____
    _____

5. As the thread was tightened, was there any change in the rate of the beat of the atria? _____
    Should there have been any change? _____ Explain: _____
    _____

6. As the thread was tightened, was there any change in the rate of beat of the ventricle? _____
    _____ Explain: _____
    _____

7. Did the beating of the ventricle (after arrest) have any relationship to that of the atria?
    _____ Explain: _____
    _____

8. Trace the path of an impulse over the conducting system in the human heart. _____
   _____
   _____

EXERCISE 14-F. AUTOMATICITY OF THE HEART

1. Record your results in the following table.

Parts of the Heart	Heart Rate/Minute
Entire heart before removal	
Entire heart after removal	
Separated sinus venosus	
Combined atria-ventricle	
Separated atria	
Separated ventricle	
Apex	

Step 7 brackets Separated sinus venosus and Combined atria-ventricle.
Step 8 brackets Separated atria and Separated ventricle.

2. Was the rate of beat of the entire heart the same before and after removal from the body? _____ Explain any difference observed: _____
   _____

3. Define automaticity. _____
   _____

4. How was automaticity demonstrated in this experiment? _____
   _____

5. In this experiment, which parts of the heart were demonstrated to possess automaticity?
   _____

6. Arrange the parts of the heart in order of decreasing irritability and automaticity. _____
   _____

7. Name the pacemaker of the human heart. _____

8. Name the pacemaker of the frog heart. _____

9. Is the heart dependent on nerves for contraction? _____
   What is the function of the nervous supply to the heart? _____
   _____

RESULTS AND QUESTIONS FOR CHAPTER 15

EXERCISE 15-A. MICROCIRCULATION IN THE FISH OR FROG

1. Fill in the following table, comparing the three types of blood vessels based on your observations.

	Arteries	*Veins*	*Capillaries*
Rate of Movement			
Pulsations			
Diameter			

2. Of what advantage to the body is the slow rate of blood flow through the capillaries?

   _____

3. What determines the rate of flow of blood in the different types of blood vessels?

   _____

EXERCISE 15-B. HEART SOUNDS AND PULSE RATE

1. Describe the heart sounds with the heart at rest. _____

2. What is the cause of the first heart sound? _____

3. What caused the second heart sound? _____

4. Which sound may be called the systolic sound? _____

5. Describe the change in sounds after exercise. _____

   _____

6. What causes the increase in force of the sounds? _____

   _____

7. Define apical pulse. _____

8. Define radial pulse. _____

9. What is pulse deficit? _____

   What causes this condition? _____

10. Define pulse. _____

11. What is the normal pulse rate of women? _____ Of men? _____

12. Record your heart rate in the following table. (Include your labeled record if the physiograph was used.)

Body Position and State	*Heart Rate*
Reclining	
Sitting	
Standing	
During exercise	
First minute after exercise	
Second minute after exercise	

13. What was the average pulse rate for women in the class (use the figures obtained in step 6b, sitting at rest)? _____

14. What was the average pulse rate for men in the class? _____

15. What is the effect of physical training on pulse rate? _____

_____

16. Summarize the effect of body position on the heart rate. _____

_____

17. What was the effect of exercise on heart rate? _____

EXERCISE 15-C. BLOOD PRESSURE

1. Record all measurements of blood pressure. (Include your labeled physiograph record if you used the Alternate Procedure.)

Time	Systolic Pressure	Diastolic Pressure	Pulse Pressure	Pulse Rate
Before exercise				
Determination 1				
Determination 2				
Determination 3				
During exercise				
Minute 1				
Minute 2				
After exercise				
Immediately				
Minute 2				
Minute 4				
Minute 6				

Name _____

2. The sounds heard through the stethoscope or recorded by the physiograph in this experiment were not heart sounds. What caused the production of the sounds? _____

_____

3. Define each of the following:

   a. Hypertension. _____

   b. Hypotension. _____

4. What are the usually accepted limits of normal blood pressure for your age and sex? _____ If your values were outside these limits, discuss possible causes. _____

_____

5. What does each of the following indicate:

   a. Systolic pressure. _____

   b. Diastolic pressure. _____

6. The following commonly occur during and immediately following exercise. Discuss the causes of each.

   a. Increase in systolic pressure. _____

   _____

   b. Increase in heart rate. _____

   _____

7. How rapidly did the circulatory and respiratory systems return to normal after exercise?

_____

8. How would the trained athlete differ from the untrained individual with respect to the time of return to normal (recovery time)? _____

EXERCISE 15-D. ELECTROCARDIOGRAPHY

1. Label the P wave, QRS complex, and T wave on the records obtained on leads 1, 2, and 3. Separate all records and paste each section below.

   a. Normal ECG—Lead 1:

b. Normal ECG—Lead 2:

c. Normal ECG—Lead 3:

d. Clenching fist:

Name _____

e.   Lifting left leg:

f.   Lifting left arm:

g.   After exercise:

2. Calculate the rate of your heartbeat on lead 1. Use the initial normal lead 1 record. Determine the exact time between the beginning of two P waves by counting the number of small squares and multiplying by 0.04 seconds. This is the duration of one heartbeat. Divide the duration of one heartbeat into 60 to determine the heart rate per minute.

Duration of one heartbeat. _____

Heart rate per minute.   _____

3. Compare the duration of one heartbeat with the theoretical value. _____
_____

4. Measure the P-R interval on the normal lead 1 record. The P-R interval starts with the beginning of the P wave and ends with the beginning of the Q wave, if one is visible (use the R wave if there is no visible Q wave). Label the heartbeat used for this calculation. Count the number of small squares between the beginning of the P wave and the beginning of the Q wave (if visible) or the beginning of the R wave and multiply by 0.04.

P-R interval. _____

5. Compare the P-R interval obtained in this experiment with the theoretical results. _____
_____

6. In which disease condition may the P-R interval be lengthened? _____

7. In which lead (1, 2, or 3) was there the greatest amplitude of the QRS complex? _____ In which was there the least? _____

8. Determine the heart rate after exercise.

Duration of one heartbeat. _____

Heart rate per minute.   _____

9. What effect did clenching the fist have on the ECG? _____

10. Compare the effect of lifting the left arm and the left leg on lead 1 on the ECG. What is the cause of this difference? _____
_____

11. Explain, based on your results, why it is important to have the subject lying still and relaxed while an ECG is being made. _____
_____

12. What is the cause of the elapsed time between the P wave and the spread of the wave of excitation over the ventricles? _____
_____

13. What disease is indicated if the P wave is absent? _____

Name _____

EXERCISE 15-E. ELECTROCARDIOGRAPHY WITH THE PHYSIOGRAPH

1. Fasten the record obtained in this experiment at paper speed 2.5 cm/sec below. Label the ECG and the respiratory record. Label P, QRS, and T waves on the ECG.

2. Calculate the duration of one heartbeat by measuring the distance between the beginning of two P waves in centimeters. Label on the record which beat was used. Divide the distance by the paper speed (2.5 cm/sec) to obtain the duration in seconds of one beat.

Length of one beat in cm _____

Duration of one beat _____

3. Calculate the heart rate per minute. Divide the duration of one heartbeat into 60 to determine the heart rate per minute.

Heart rate per minute _____

4. Determine in a similar way the respiratory rate per minute.

Length of one breath in cm _____

Duration of one breath _____

Respiratory rate per minute _____

5. Determine the heart rate for a period of 10 seconds. Since the paper speed is 2.5 cm/sec, 25 cm of paper represents 10 seconds (see Figure 15-11). Mark off 25 cm on the record (ten sections between dark-green lines). Count the number of QRS waves in this 25 cm. Multiply your answer by 6 to obtain the heart rate per minute.

Number of beats in 10 seconds _____ Heart rate per minute _____

6. Do the answers obtained in questions 3 and 5 agree? _____

What do you think is the most likely explanation for any difference in answers? _____

_____

7. What causes the occurrence of each of the following?

a. P wave _____

b. QRS complex _____

c. T wave _____

8. Examine carefully your recording of heart action. Is the rate uniform throughout the record?

_____ Can you correlate any variation in the rate with inspiration or expiration? _____

9. Compare the duration of one heartbeat with the theoretical rate for humans. _____

_____

10. Fasten the record obtained at paper speed 10 cm/sec below.

11. Calculate the P-R interval. This interval starts with the beginning of a P wave and ends with the beginning of a Q wave if one is visible (use the R wave if no Q wave is visible). Measure the distance in centimeters as accurately as possible. Divide by the paper speed. (Show which section of the record you used.)

   Distance between P and Q. _____ Paper speed. _____ P-R interval. _____

12. Compare the P-R interval obtained in this experiment with the theoretical results. _____

   _____

13. What is the cause of the elapsed period of time between the P wave and the QRS complex?

   _____

   _____

14. In which disease condition may the P-R interval be lengthened? _____

RESULTS AND QUESTIONS FOR CHAPTER 16

EXERCISE 16-A. ANATOMY OF THE NERVOUS SYSTEM

Part 1. Structure of a Nerve

1. How is it possible to distinguish between an axon and a dendrite in the slide of the cross section of a nerve?
   _____

2. Define each of the following:

   a. Nerve. _____

   b. Tract. _____

   c. Ganglion. _____

   d. Vasa nervorum. _____

   e. Neuron. _____

3. What is the function of the neurilemma? _____
   _____

4. What is the function of the myelin sheath? _____
   _____

Part 2. The Spinal Cord

1. What is the function of each of the following?

   a. Dorsal horn. _____

   b. Lateral horn. _____

   c. Ventral horn. _____

   d. White matter. _____

   e. Dorsal root ganglion. _____

   f. Dorsal root. _____

   g. Ventral root. _____

2. Figure 16-A is an outline of a cross section through the spinal cord. Complete the diagram by drawing the roots and the beginning of the spinal nerve. Add to the diagram a simple reflex arc and label its components.

Figure 16-A.   Cross section of spinal cord.

3. What is the function of each of the following tracts and where does each cross over?

Tracts	Site of Crossing Over	Function
Posterior columns		
Lateral spinothalamic tract		
Spinocerebellar tract		
Lateral corticospinal tract		

4. How many pairs of spinal nerves emerge from the cord? _____

5. What is the cauda equina? _____

6. Name the major plexuses of spinal nerves and list which spinal nerves form each plexus.

_____

_____

7. Classify the neuron whose cell body was visible in the dorsal root ganglion as to structure _____ and function. _____

8. Classify the neuron whose cell body was located in the ventral horn as to structure _____ and function. _____

9. Where does the spinal cord terminate? _____

Part 3. Gross Structure of the Brain

1. What is the function of each of the following?
   a. Cerebellum. _____
   b. Hypothalamus. _____
   c. Thalamus. _____
   d. Pons. _____
   e. Superior colliculi. _____

2. Name the lobes of the cerebral cortex. _____

3. Name the three parts of the forebrain. _____

4. Which cranial nerves emerge from the medulla? _____

5. Name one example of commissural fibers seen in the sagittal section of the brain.

_____

6. Name the three layers of the meninges that surround the brain and the cord.

_____

EXERCISES 16-B AND C. DISSECTION OF THE SHEEP AND/OR THE PIG BRAIN

1. Where is cerebrospinal fluid manufactured? _____

2. Trace the path of cerebrospinal fluid through the brain. _____

_____

_____

Name _____

3. What is the advantage of having convolutions in the cortex? _____
_____

4. Describe the composition of white matter in the cord. _____
_____

5. Of what is gray matter composed? _____
_____

6. What is the function of cerebrospinal fluid? _____

7. Where is a spinal tap usually made? _____

8. What is the cause of hydrocephalus? _____

9. Compare the structure of the dura mater of the brain with that of the cord.
_____

EXERCISE 16-D. REFLEX ACTION IN THE NORMAL, SPINAL (SINGLE-PITHED), AND DOUBLE-PITHED FROG

1. Record all results in the chart below.

Reflex Activity	Normal Frog	Spinal (Single-Pithed) Frog	Double-Pithed Frog
a. Position of head and legs			
b. Rate of respiration			
c. Righting from back			
d. Elevation of head			
e. Swimming			
f. Withdrawal from pinch			
g. Withdrawal from hot water			
h. Corneal reflex			
i. Response to noise			

2. Which reflexes of those tested require the presence of the brain? _____
_____

3. Which reflexes of those tested require only the presence of the spinal cord? _____
_____

4. What evidence do you have that reflexes are purposeful? _____
_____

5. What structures must be present for most protective reflexes to occur? _____

_____

6. List one example, demonstrated in this exercise, of a flexor reflex. _____

_____

7. What is the function of flexor reflexes? _____

_____

8. Define a synapse. _____

9. How do nerve impulses cross a synapse? _____

_____

10. What is the function of cholinesterase? _____

_____

EXERCISE 16-E. DEMONSTRATION OF INDIVIDUAL HUMAN REFLEXES

1. Fill in the following chart concerning the reflexes demonstrated in this exercise.

Name of Reflex	Results Obtained	Nerve		Muscle Involved	Function of Reflex
		Afferent	Efferent		
Knee jerk					
Ankle jerk					
Corneal reflex					
Photopupil reflex					
Accommodation reflex					
Convergence reflex					

2. What effect did clenching the hands or adding a column of figures have on the extent of the knee jerk? _____

EXERCISE 16-F. REACTION TIME

1. Tape your kymograph records for sight, sound, and touch below. Label each record.

Name _____

2. Calculate the duration of your reaction time in seconds by measuring the length of each in centimeters and dividing by the drum speed (in centimeters per second). Record your results in the table below.

	1	2	3	4	Average
Sight					
Sound					
Touch					

3. Compare your results with the theoretical results. _____

_____

4. Why were there differences in the reaction times to the three types of stimulation?

_____

5. Did practice have any effect on the reaction time? _____

6. What might be some sources of error in this experiment? _____

_____

_____

RESULTS AND QUESTIONS FOR CHAPTER 17

EXERCISE 17-A. GROSS ANATOMY OF THE EYE

1. Indicate, in the blanks provided, whether the following structures are part of the sclera, choroid, or retina.

   a. Rods and cones. _____   c. Cornea. _____

   b. Iris. _____   d. Ciliary body. _____

2. Identify the structures having the following functions (a structure may be used more than once since it may have several functions):

   a. Protects and gives form and shape to the eyeball. _____

   b. An outer, transparent structure that refracts light and thus aids in focusing light rays. _____

   c. Essential in accommodation of the eye. The contraction of its muscle fibers results in change of shape of the lens. _____

   d. Contains many blood vessels to provide for the nourishment of the retina. _____

   e. Provides place of attachment of extrinsic eye muscles. _____

   f. Contains a pigment that prevents internal reflection of light rays. _____

   g. Contraction results in dilation of the pupil. _____

   h. Contraction results in constriction of the pupil. _____

   i. Contains the light receptors. _____

3. Give the primary function of each of the following:

   a. Rods. _____

   b. Cones. _____

   c. Fovea centralis. _____

   d. Vitreous humor. _____

4. What is the location of the aqueous humor? _____
   _____

5. Which humor is more gelatinous? _____

6. Which one of the three eye coats is completely anterior? _____

7. At what point is the retina attached dorsally? _____

8. Which cranial nerves supply the extrinsic eye muscles? _____

9. Describe the location of the optic nerve. _____
   _____

10. Name the intrinsic eye muscles: _____

11. Name the extrinsic eye muscles and, after each, give its function.

        <u>Muscle</u>   <u>Function</u>

_____   _____

_____   _____

_____   _____

_____   _____

_____   _____

_____   _____

EXERCISE 17-C. ACCOMMODATION

1. When you opened your eyes with your fingers in front of them, which was in focus, your fingers or some distant object? _____

2. Did the pin appear to be double or single when you looked at a distant object (see step 5 under Procedure) in the back of the room? _____

3. Where in the eye was the focus of the distant object in the preceding question? _____

4. Where in the eye was the focus of the pin? _____

5. When you accommodated for it, where was the focus of the pin? _____

6. Make two diagrams to account for the appearance of the pin in steps 5 and 6 of Procedure.

EXERCISE 17-D. MEASURING THE NEAR POINT OF ACCOMMODATION

1. Record the near point for each eye in centimeters.   Right eye _____ Left eye _____

2. Record the age group from Table 17-1 to which your near point corresponds.

                                       Right eye _____ Left eye _____

3. Did the near point of each of your eyes fall within an age range that is compatible with your present age? _____

   Discuss your answer. _____

_____

4. Were you right-eyed or left-eyed? _____

5. List three changes that take place in the eyes during accommodation.

_____

_____

_____

Name _____

6. What property of the lens is essential for accommodation? _____

7. The property indicated in question 6 is lost, to some extent, in what condition?

_____

8. How would myopia affect the near point? _____

9. How would hyperopia affect the near point? _____

EXERCISE 17-E. SNELLEN CHART TEST FOR VISUAL ACUITY

1. Record your data for visual acuity in the following table.

Eyes	Snellen (d/D) (without glasses)	Snellen (d/D) (with glasses)	Illiterate "E" Chart
Right eye			
Left eye			
Both eyes			

2. What type of lens would be used to correct a nearsighted eye? _____

3. What lens would be used to correct a farsighted eye? _____

4. What lens could be used to make an emmetrope nearsighted? _____

5. What lens could be used to make an emmetrope farsighted? _____

6. If you wear corrective lenses, does your prescription completely correct the abnormality? _____ Explain: _____

7. What does a visual acuity of 20/15 indicate? _____

8. What does a visual acuity of 20/40 indicate? _____

9. Explain the cause of presbyopia and tell how it is corrected. _____

EXERCISE 17-F. TEST FOR ASTIGMATISM

1. In the spaces provided, indicate if astigmatism was detected and whether it was the vertical or horizontal type.

Right eye: _____

Left eye: _____

2. What causes astigmatism? _____

3. How is the condition corrected? _____

EXERCISE 17-G. THE BLIND SPOT

1. What is the blind spot? _____

_____

2. Why is this spot blind? _____

3. Draw three diagrams below that show the precise points of focus on the retina of the cross and circle from steps 2, 3, and 4.

4. In the preceding, what was the point of focus of the circle when it was not visible?

_____

5. Why are we unable to observe the blind spot when we see with both eyes at the same time?

_____

EXERCISE 17-H. COLOR BLINDNESS

1. How many errors were made in this test? _____

2. Were you color-blind? _____ List any of your relatives who are also color-blind. _____

_____

3. Explain why color blindness occurs more frequently in males than in females. _____

_____

EXERCISE 17-I. ANATOMY OF THE EAR

Give the function of each of the following structures:

1. Tympanic membrane. _____
2. Ear ossicles. _____
3. Eustachian tube. _____
4. Semicircular canals. _____
5. Cochlear nerve. _____
6. Vestibular nerve. _____
7. Organ of Corti. _____
8. Endolymph. _____
9. Fenestra ovalis. _____
10. Fenestra rotunda. _____

EXERCISE 17-J. BONE CONDUCTION OF SOUND WAVES

1. Compare the intensity of the sound heard with:
   a. both ears open. _____

Name _____

   b.   one ear covered. _____

   c.   both ears covered. _____

2.   How was the sound received when both ears were covered? _____

   _____

3.   Describe and discuss the results obtained in the Rinné test for middle-ear deafness.

   _____

4.   How has the principle involved in the Rinné test for middle-ear deafness been used in some

   hearing aids? _____

5.   Which is superior, air or bone conduction? _____

EXERCISE 17-K. LOCALIZATION OF SOUNDS

1.   Results (indicate the precise location of the sound and the subject's localization of the sound):

Actual Location of Sound	Subject's Localization of Sound
In front of the head	_____
Above the head	_____
Behind the head	_____
On either side of the head	_____

2.   Explain why it was not possible to localize the source of the sound each time. _____

   _____

   _____

EXERCISE 17-L. LOCALIZATION OF TOUCH SENSATION

Part 1

Fill in the following table with the results obtained from the localization experiment. Record the number of millimeters by which the subject missed the precise point of stimulation.

Point of Stimulation	Trial 1 (mm)	Trial 2 (mm)	Trial 3 (mm)	Average (mm)
Palm of hand				
Back of hand				
Fingertip				
Back				
Ventral forearm				
Ventral upper arm				

Part 2

1. Complete the following table with the results obtained while using the esthesiometer.

Point of Stimulation	Trial 1 (mm)	Trial 2 (mm)	Trial 3 (mm)	Average (mm)
Ventral thumb				
Palm of hand				
Back of hand				
Ventral forearm				
Ventral upper arm				
Back				
Tip of tongue				

2. In Part 1, was there a general pattern to the distribution of the ability to localize the precise point of stimulation? _____ Explain: _____

_____

3. In Part 2, why was there a difference in ability to feel the points of the esthesiometer as two points in different parts of the body? _____

_____

4. Give a general conclusion concerning the distribution of touch receptors. _____

_____

EXERCISE 17-M. CUTANEOUS SENSATIONS

1. Record the sites of the receptors on the grid below:

Touch "T"	Cold "C"	Heat "H"	Pain "P"

2. Tabulate the total number of each type of receptor that was mapped in the skin area and record in the space provided below:

   Touch. _____ Cold. _____ Heat. _____ Pain. _____

3. What results did you obtain from stimulating a touch receptor site with a cold nail? _____

   Explain your results: _____

4. Are different kinds of receptors located at the same sites? _____

5. How do your results compare with the theoretical distribution of cutaneous receptors?

_____

6. What is meant by punctiform distribution of cutaneous receptors? _____

_____

7. Identify the cutaneous receptors localized in this experiment by their scientific names.

_____

_____

EXERCISE 17-N. PRESSURE SENSATION

1. In the spaces provided, record the total number of sheets of paper through which the bristle (hair) could be detected.

   a. Fingertips. _____   d. Elbow. _____

   b. Knuckle. _____   e. Chin. _____

   c. Palm of hand. _____   f. Nose. _____

2. What area of your body was most sensitive to pressure? _____

3. Which part of your body was least sensitive to pressure? _____

EXERCISE 17-O. RECEPTOR ADAPTATION

Part 1. Touch Stimulation

1. Record, in seconds, the length of time the coin was felt on the ventral surface of the forearm.

_____

2. When two coins were added to the first coin, did the touch sensation return? _____

3. If the sensation did return, record, in seconds, the length of time it lasted (with the three coins).

_____

4. Briefly explain your results. _____

_____

_____

Part 2. Temperature Stimulation

1. Describe your sensations for each of the exercises involving water stimuli:

   a. Warm water (first one index finger, then the other). _____

   _____

   b. One index finger in warm water, other in ice water. _____

   _____

   c. One finger in warm water, one in ice water, then both in cold tap water. _____

   _____

   _____

388

2. Explain any observed differences in the preceding. _____

_____

_____

Part 3. Chemical Stimulation

1. Record, in seconds, the time required for the odor to disappear. _____

2. Did you observe any difference in the intensity of the odor with the newly opened nostril? _____ Describe the sensation. _____

_____

3. Based on your results in all three parts, what are your conclusions concerning receptor adaptation? _____

_____

4. Is it advantageous for receptors to adapt? _____ Explain: _____

_____

5. Pain receptors show limited adaptation. Why is this advantageous? _____

_____

EXERCISE 17-P. REFERRED PAIN

1. Exactly where did you feel the referred pain? _____

2. Using the following information, give an explanation for the referred pain you felt: the ulnar nerve, supplying the ring and little fingers and the inner side of the hand, passes over the elbow joint.

_____

_____

EXERCISE 17-Q. LOCATION OF TASTE BUDS

1. Indicate on the diagram below where each of the four solutions could be tasted most readily on the tongue.

2. Name the nerves for taste. _____
3. Which nerve carries messages of touch from the tongue? _____
4. Which nerve is necessary for movement of the tongue? _____

RESULTS AND QUESTIONS FOR CHAPTER 18

EXERCISE 18-A. ANATOMY OF THE HUMAN URINARY SYSTEM

1. What is the function of each of the following?
    a. Glomerulus. _____
    b. Uriniferous tubule. _____
    c. Renal pelvis. _____
    d. Ureter. _____
2. What is the function of the adipose tissue that surrounds the kidney? _____
3. Into which blood vessel does the renal vein empty? _____
4. What is the name given to the portion of the renal cortex located between the pyramids?

    _____
5. What is the name given to the layer of the kidney that contains the pyramids? _____
6. What is the name given to the apex of a pyramid? _____
7. List the functions of a kidney. _____

    _____
8. What is the usual blood pressure in the glomerulus? _____
9. What is the advantage of this high blood pressure in the glomerulus? _____

    _____
10. In which body cavity is each of the following organs located?
    a. Kidney. _____   c. Ureter. _____
    b. Urinary bladder. _____
11. What is the trigone of the bladder? _____
12. Which subdivision of the autonomic nervous system prevents elimination of urine? _____

EXERCISE 18-B. DISSECTION OF THE URINARY SYSTEM OF THE FETAL PIG

1. Trace the path of urine from its site of formation to the outside of the body. _____

    _____

    _____
2. Define the term "retroperitoneal." _____
3. Which parts of the nephron are located in the cortex? _____
4. Which parts of the nephron are located in the medulla? _____
5. Name the structure located in the renal sinus. _____
6. Trace the path of blood from the renal artery to the glomerulus. _____

    _____
7. Trace the path of blood from the glomerulus to the renal vein. _____

    _____

8. Compare the internal structure of the pig kidney with that of the human kidney. _____
_____

9. Compare the location of the adrenal glands in the pig with those in man. _____
_____

EXERCISE 18-C. URINALYSIS

Part 1. Analysis of a Urine Specimen

1. Specific gravity:

    a. Temperature of urine specimen. _____
    b. _____ −15 °C
    c. Difference. _____
    d. Temperature correction factor (round off to nearest whole number):

    $$\frac{\text{Difference}}{3} = _____$$

    e. Uncorrected specific gravity (step 2 of Procedure). _____
    f. Temperature correction factor (d) (add to thousandths place if urine temperature is above 15 °C, subtract if temperature is below 15 °C). + _____
    g. Corrected specific gravity. _____

2. What is the normal specific gravity range of urine? _____

3. If the result you obtained was outside the normal specific gravity range, suggest a possible reason. _____
_____

4. Name two conditions of the body that result in an increase in the specific gravity of urine.
_____

5. Name two conditions of the body that result in a decrease in the specific gravity of urine.
_____

6. What is the function of the antidiuretic hormone (ADH)? _____
_____

7. What relationship is usually found between the volume of urine voided and specific gravity (direct or indirect)? _____
_____

8. What was the color of your urine specimen? _____

9. Name the pigment responsible for the normal color of urine. _____

10. As the volume of urine voided increases, what usually happens to the color of the urine? _____
_____

11. Describe the degree of transparency of the urine specimen. _____
_____

12. If your specimen was cloudy, what results were obtained when a drop of nitric acid was added to it? _____

Name _____

13. What conclusion concerning the origin of the cloudiness of urine (question 12) can be drawn?

_____

14. Explain why all urine specimens become cloudy on long standing at room temperature.

_____

_____

15. What was the pH of the urine specimen? _____

16. What is the average pH of urine? _____ What is the normal range of pH for urine? ____

_____

17. Name the compound usually considered responsible for the acidity of urine. _____

_____

18. Would you expect the following to result in an increase or a decrease in the pH of urine? (Check the appropriate space.) Explain each answer.

	pH Increased	pH Decreased	Explanation
Eating a large amount of protein			
Starvation			
Diabetes mellitus			
Vegetarian diet			
Renal tract infection			

19. Fill in the following chart concerning the urine tests.

Protein and Glucose Tests	Purpose of Test	Results	Explanation of Results
Benedict's			
Clinitest			
Clinistix			
Hay's			
Ketostix			
Bili-Labstix			

392

20. How could you determine if the sugar resulting in a positive Benedict's test in the urine of a lactating woman was lactose or glucose? _____

_____

21. Name the disease that is the most probable cause of a high amount of sugar in the urine.

_____

22. What is the most likely explanation for the appearance of a trace of sugar in the urine?

_____

23. Which term is used for the presence of each of the following in urine?

   a. Pus. _____

   b. Protein. _____

   c. Glucose. _____

   d. Ketone bodies. _____

24. Name a disease in which you would expect Ketostix to be positive. _____

_____

25. Compare the composition of the blood in the glomerulus, the glomerular filtrate, and urine by filling in the following chart. Place + in the blank if the substance is normally present, – if it is usually absent.

	Blood	Glomerular Filtrate	Urine
Water			
Protein			
Glucose			
Sodium chloride			
Ketone bodies			
Erythrocytes			

Part 2. Analysis of Urine Specimens for Unknowns

In the table below, place a + sign to indicate the presence of the substance (positive) and a – sign to indicate the absence of the substance (negative). In the space provided, write the name of the test(s) that helped you obtain your results.

Tube No.	Glucose	Protein	Tests Used
1			
2			
3			

Name _____

EXERCISE 18-D. MICROSCOPIC EXAMINATION OF SEDIMENT OBTAINED FROM URINE

1. What disorders might be indicated by the presence of blood in the urine? _____
   _____

2. Draw and identify different types of substances in the urine sediment.

Name _____

RESULTS AND QUESTIONS FOR CHAPTER 19

EXERCISE 19-A. ENDOCRINE GLANDS

1. Define an endocrine gland. _____
2. Which endocrine glands are considered mixed glands? _____
3. Which endocrine gland is embedded in the dorsal surface of the thyroid gland? _____

_____

4. Fill in the following chart concerning function of hormones.

Function	Hormone
Regulates absorption of glucose into cell	
Regulates BMR	
Regulates thyroid gland	
Stimulates spermatogenesis	
Regulates calcium balance	
Regulates reabsorption of water in kidney	
Stimulates contraction of pregnant uterus	
Stimulates ovulation	
Regulates mental development	
Regulates sodium and potassium balance	
Increases heart rate and blood pressure	

5. The table on the following page contains a list of symptoms resulting from endocrine disorders. In the spaces provided, write the name of the specific part of the gland (whenever possible), the name of the hormone involved, and the disease and place a check mark under hyposecretion or hypersecretion.

6. A ductless gland has been found to secrete a substance that influences growth and development as well as metabolic rate. How would you determine whether the active ingredient in the

   secretion was a hormone? _____

   _____

7. How would you determine if more than one hormone was involved in the substance in question

   6? _____

   _____

Symptoms of Endocrine Dysfunction	Gland (or Part of Gland)	Hormone	Name of Disease	Hyposecretion	Hypersecretion
Failure of physical, sexual, and mental development					
Muscle spasms due to increased irritability of nerves and muscles					
Precocious sexual development					
Continued growth of bones in children					
Shock, convulsions, marked decrease in blood sugar					
Copious excretion of urine					
Loss of vigor, falling hair, puffy skin, lowered BMR					
Development of secondary sexual characteristics of male in adult female					
Obesity, sexual infantilism, often subnormal intelligence	both anterior and posterior pituitary	all hormones	Frolich's syndrome		
Coma, marked increase in blood sugar					
Demineralization of bones, with spontaneous fractures					
Bulging eyeballs, goiter, loss of weight, nervousness, rapid pulse					
Lower jaw, hands, and feet become larger in adults					

Name _____

8. On the basis of your study of the endocrine system, which gland was most likely to be producing the secretion in question 6? _____

_____

9. Name three symptoms of Cushing's disease. _____

_____

10. Name three symptoms of Addison's disease. _____

_____

11. Name three hormones produced by the ovary. _____

_____

12. Which endocrine gland produces vasopressin? _____

13. Which gland is called the master gland? _____

14. What is the function of the pineal gland? _____

_____

15. Which hormone is sometimes called an emergency hormone? _____

16. Which two glands are called glands of childhood? _____

17. What is the common name of the somatotropic hormone? _____

EXERCISE 19-B. EFFECTS OF INSULIN ON A FISH

1. Briefly describe what happened to the blood glucose level of the fish as a result of diffusion of insulin into the bloodstream. _____

_____

2. Explain what happened to cause the fish to return to normal when it was placed in the glucose solution. _____

3. What is the purpose of a glucose-tolerance test? _____

4. What is insulin shock? _____

5. What first aid treatment is recommended for a person in insulin shock? _____

_____

6. How may a diabetic avoid insulin shock? _____

RESULTS AND QUESTIONS FOR CHAPTER 20

EXERCISE 20-A. THE HUMAN MALE REPRODUCTIVE SYSTEM

1. Was there any evidence of spermatogenesis in the wall of the epididymis? _____ Should there be? _____

2. What is the function of each of the following?

    a. Epididymis. _____

    b. Vas deferens. _____

    c. Prostate gland. _____

    d. Cowper's gland. _____

    e. Urethra. _____

    f. Seminal vesicle. _____

    g. Seminiferous tubules. _____

    h. Interstitial cells. _____

3. Define cryptorchidism. _____

    What is the significance of this condition? _____

4. Trace the path of sperm from the site of production to the outside. _____

5. Name the three male accessory reproductive glands. _____

6. Define semen. _____

7. What is the spermatic cord? _____

8. How many sperm are required to fertilize one ovum? _____

9. Why would enlargement of the prostate gland interfere with the passage of urine? _____

10. List three defects that might cause sterility. _____

11. What structure in the male is homologous to the labia majora? _____

EXERCISE 20-B. THE HUMAN FEMALE REPRODUCTIVE SYSTEM

1. Describe the location of each of the following:

    a. Broad ligament. _____

    b. Round ligament. _____

    c. Ovarian ligament. _____

2. What is the endometrium? _____

3. Trace the path of the egg from the site of production to the outside. _____

4. What type of muscle is located in the wall of the uterus? _____

Name the muscular layer. _____

5. What is meant by salpingitis? _____

6. Would pregnancy be possible in case of a bilateral salpingectomy? _____

Explain: _____

Would menstruation be possible in this case? _____ Explain: _____

_____

7. Define the hymen. _____

8. Name the two parts of the uterus. _____

9. Name the hormone produced by the ovarian follicle. _____

Name those produced by the corpus luteum. _____

10. What is a retroverted uterus? _____

11. How many mature Graafian follicles are produced by the ovary at one time? _____

12. What is the mons pubis? _____

13. Define the perineum. _____

What is the obstetrical perineum? _____

14. What is the function of Bartholin's glands? _____

15. What is the name of the erectile tissue located near the anterior junction of the labia minora?

_____

16. What is an oophorectomy? _____

EXERCISE 20-C. THE ENDOMETRIAL (MENSTRUAL) CYCLE

1. What is the name of the hormone secreted by the Graafian follicle? _____

2. What is the function of this hormone? _____

3. In which phase (see diagram in Procedure) is this hormone active? _____

4. What is the name of the hormone that stimulates the growth of the follicle? _____

5. Which gland produces the hormone in question 4? _____

6. Which gland produces the luteinizing hormone? _____

7. In which phase of the menstrual cycle is this hormone active? _____

8. What is the function of the luteinizing hormone? _____

9. Name the hormones secreted by the corpus luteum. _____

10. On which day of a 40-day menstrual cycle does ovulation usually occur? _____

11. On which day of a 28-day menstrual cycle does ovulation usually occur? _____

12. How long does an ovum survive if it is not fertilized? _____

13. Lack of which hormone causes the endometrium to break down? _____

14. Failure of the fertilized ovum to become embedded in the endometrium results in cessation of

the secretion of _____; this in turn results in the disintegration of the endometrium, a

process called _____ or _____

Name _____

15. Fill in the following chart concerning the hormones in the menstrual cycle.

Hormone	Gland Secreting Hormone	Stimulus for Production of Hormone	Function of Hormone in Menstrual Cycle
FSH			
Estrogen			
LH			
Progesterone			

EXERCISE 20-D. THE PLACENTA

1. Name the two human fetal membranes. _____

2. Define the decidua basalis. _____

3. What is the origin of the placenta? _____

4. What is the function of the placenta? _____

   _____

5. What are the major components of the afterbirth? _____

6. What is the function of the chorion? _____

7. What is the function of the amnion? _____

EXERCISE 20-E. DISSECTION OF THE REPRODUCTIVE SYSTEM OF THE FETAL PIG

1. List any differences noted between the reproductive organs of the human and of the fetal pig.

   _____

   _____

2. What is the function of the urogenital sinus in the female pig? _____

   _____

3. Compare the place of development of the fetus in the human with that in the pig. _____

   _____

4. Trace the path of sperm from the site of production to the outside in the pig. _____

   _____

EXERCISE 20-F. EMBRYOLOGY

1. Compare the blastula stage in the starfish with that in humans. _____

   _____

2. Compare the gastrula stage in the starfish with that in humans. _____

   _____

3. When does implantation of the fertilized egg occur? _____

4. What is the vernix caseosa? _____

5. What is the average duration of pregnancy? _____

6. Name the three germ layers in the developing embryo and two structures produced from each layer.

Germ Layers	Structures Produced

RESULTS AND QUESTIONS FOR CHAPTER 21

EXERCISE 21-B. GENETICS PROBLEMS

In solving the following problems, show all symbols used and designate their meaning, give genotypes of the parents, and show all work (e.g., Punnet squares). Write answers in the spaces provided.

1. How many different types of gametes can be produced by an individual of genotype aaBbCcDdEe?

   _____

2. The gene for brown hair is dominant over that for blond hair. If two people heterozygous for brown hair married, what types of hair color would you expect to find in their offspring? List the proportions of each type.

   _____

3. Curly hair shows a lack of dominance over straight hair. The heterozygote possesses wavy hair. If a person with curly hair marries a person with straight hair, what hair types would you expect to find among their offspring?

   _____

4. A mother is blood type O, her child also type O. She claims a man of type AB is the father.

   Could he be? _____ Explain: _____

   _____

5. A man of blood type A marries a woman of blood type O. Their first four children are all of blood type A.

   a. Can you be certain whether the man is homozygous or heterozygous? _____

   b. Which is more likely? _____

   c. If the fifth child has blood type O, will that settle the question? _____

      Explain: _____

6. A trait is always transmitted directly from a father to all his sons and from these to all their

   sons. It is likely that the gene for this trait is on which chromosome? _____

7. In humans the gene for farsightedness is usually inherited as a dominant. A man and a woman (both heterozygous for farsightedness) marry. What fraction of their children would be expected to be farsighted?

   _____

8. The gene for astigmatism is inherited as a dominant. Two people heterozygous for astigmatism marry. What is the probability that their first child will be a girl with astigmatism?

   _____

9. What is the probability of a husband and wife having three girls in a row?

_____

10. Two brown-eye parents have a blue-eyed child. What is the probability that their next child will be brown-eyed?

_____

11. Two normal parents are each heterozygous for a recessive gene for feeblemindedness.

   a. What is the probability that they will have four normal children in a row?

_____

   b. If this family had one feebleminded child, what is the probability that the next child would be normal?

_____

12. In humans the gene for ability to taste phenylthiocarbamide (PTC) is dominant over that for inability to taste PTC. The gene for brown eyes is dominant over that for blue eyes. What proportion of the offspring of two parents, each heterozygous for both traits, would be brown-eyed nontasters?

_____

13. Red-green color blindness is due to a sex-linked recessive gene. Two normal parents (the mother blue-eyed, the father heterozygous for brown eyes) produce a color-blind son.

   a. What proportion of all sons born would be expected to be blue-eyed and color-blind?

_____

   b. What proportion of their daughters would you expect to be color-blind?

_____

   c. What is the probability that two sons in a row in this family will be blue-eyed and color-blind?

_____

   d. What is the probability that two children in a row will be blue-eyed and color-blind?

_____

Name _____

14. A woman carrying the genes for both color blindness and hemophilia (she inherited both these traits from her father) marries a man who is color-blind but not hemophilic.

    a. What is the probability that the first child will be either a color-blind boy or a color-blind girl?

_____

    b. What proportion of the sons would be expected to be both color-blind and hemophilic?

_____

15. In each of the following situations, state whether it is possible or impossible for these parents to have produced the child and give the reason for your answer.

Mother	Father	Child	Possible or Impossible?	Reason
a. AB, M, Rh–	A, MN, Rh–	B, M, Rh+		
b. A	A	O		

16. In humans, normal pigmentation is due to a dominant gene, albinism to its recessive allele. These are not sex-linked. A normal man marries an albino woman. Their first child is an albino. Use this information to solve the following problems:

    a. What is the genotype of the mother?

_____

    b. What is the genotype of the child?

_____

    c. What is the probability of these parents having two albino children in a row?

_____

EXERCISE 21-C. VARIABILITY IN MAN

1. Write your genotype for ability or inability to taste PTC. _____
2. Write your genotype for pigmented or nonpigmented iris. _____
3. What is your genotype for middigital hair? _____
4. What is your genotype for ear lobes? _____
5. What is your genotype for bent little finger? _____
6. Write the genotypes for your blood types (ABO and Rh). _____
7. Write the genotype for your singing voice. _____

406

8. What is your genotype for double-jointed thumbs? _____

9. What is your genotype for the long palmar muscle? _____

10. What is your genotype for hair color? _____

11. In the preceding (questions 1-10), which genotypes are you certain are correct? _____
_____

12. In the cases where there is a possibility you are either homozygous or heterozygous, how could you determine your exact genotype? _____
_____

Student Survey

A Laboratory Manual and Study Guide for Anatomy and Physiology, Fourth Edition
by Kenneth G. Neal and Barbara H. Kalbus

Students, send us your ideas!

The authors and the publisher want to know how well this book served you and what can be done to improve it for those who will use it in the future. By completing and returning this questionnaire, you can help us develop better textbooks. We value your opinion and want to hear your comments. Thank you.

Your name (optional) _____ School _____

Your mailing address _____

City _____ State _____ ZIP _____

Instructor's name (optional) _____ Course title _____

1. How does this manual compare with other manuals you have used? (Check one)

   ☐ Better than any other   ☐ Better than most

   ☐ About the same as the rest   ☐ Not as good as most

2. Circle those chapters you especially liked:

   Chapters: 1 2 3 4 5 6 7 8 9 10 11 12 13 14 15 16 17 18 19 20 21

   Comments:

3. Circle those chapters you think could be improved:

   Chapters: 1 2 3 4 5 6 7 8 9 10 11 12 13 14 15 16 17 18 19 20 21

   Comments:

4. Please give us your impressions of the manual. (Check your rating below)

	Excellent	Good	Average	Poor
Logical organization	( )	( )	( )	( )
Readability of text material	( )	( )	( )	( )
General layout and design	( )	( )	( )	( )
Match with instructor's course organization	( )	( )	( )	( )
Illustrations that clarify the manual	( )	( )	( )	( )
Up-to-date treatment of subject	( )	( )	( )	( )
Explanation of difficult concepts	( )	( )	( )	( )
Selection of topics in the manual	( )	( )	( )	( )
Instructions for dissection	( )	( )	( )	( )

OVER, PLEASE

5. Please list any chapters that your instructor did not assign. _____

_____

6. What additional topics did your instructor discuss that were not covered in the manual? _____

_____

7. Did you buy this book new or used?   ☐ New   ☐ Used

   Do you plan to keep the book or sell it?   ☐ Keep it   ☐ Sell it

   Do you think your instructor should continue to assign this book?   ☐ Yes   ☐ No

8. After taking the course, are you interested in taking more courses in this field? ☐ Yes ☐ No

   Are you a major in biology?   ☐ Yes   ☐ No

9. GENERAL COMMENTS:

May we quote you in our advertising?   ☐ Yes   ☐ No

To mail, remove this page and mail to: Mary L. Paulson
                                                Burgess Publishing Company
                                                7108 Ohms Lane
                                                Minneapolis, MN 55435

THANK YOU!